Cherishing Antiquity

Harvard-Yenching Institute Monograph Series 89

Cherishing Antiquity

The Cultural Construction of an Ancient Chinese Kingdom

Olivia Milburn

Published by the Harvard University Asia Center
Distributed by Harvard University Press
Cambridge (Massachusetts) and London 2013

Printed in the United States of America

The Harvard-Yenching Institute, founded in 1928, is an independent foundation dedicated to the advancement of higher education in the humanities and social sciences in Asia. Headquartered on the campus of Harvard University, the Institute provides fellowships for advanced research, training, and graduate studies at Harvard by competitively selected faculty and graduate students from Asia. The Institute also supports a range of academic activities at its fifty partner universities and research institutes across Asia. At Harvard, the Institute promotes East Asian studies through annual contributions to the Harvard-Yenching Library and publication of the *Harvard Journal of Asiatic Studies* and the Harvard-Yenching Institute Monograph Series.

Library of Congress Cataloging-in-Publication Data

Milburn, Olivia.
Cherishing antiquity : the cultural construction of an ancient Chinese kingdom / Olivia Milburn.
pages cm. — (Harvard-Yenching Institute monograph series ; 89)
Includes bibliographical references and index.
Summary: "Describes the commemoration within Chinese literature and culture of the ancient southern kingdom of Wu, which collapsed in 473 BCE. This book, through an analysis of the history of Wu as recorded in ancient Chinese texts and then of its literary legacy, illuminates the remarkable cultural endurance of this powerful but short-lived kingdom"—Provided by publisher.
ISBN 978-0-674-72668-0 (hardcover : alk. paper) 1. China—History—Spring and Autumn period, 722–481 B.C. 2. China—History—Spring and Autumn period, 722–481 B.C.—Historiography. I. Title.
DS747.15.M55 2013
931'.03—dc23

2013007730

Index by Olivia Milburn

Printed on acid-free paper

Last figure below indicates year of this printing

22 21 20 19 18 17 16 15 14 13

Contents

Figures and Tables

Following part 1

Figures

Tables

Acknowledgments

In a colophon attached to one of his landscape paintings, the late Qing Hanlin academician and imperial tutor Weng Tonghe 翁同龢 (1830–1904, *jinshi* 1856) states that he was hoping to achieve a work of art in which the mountains soared like leaping dragons, and yet all that he had managed was a group of "inky pigs" (*mozhu* 墨猪). It is now my turn to unleash an inky pig upon the public.

The initial research for this book began when I received a grant from the National Central Library, Taipei, Taiwan in 2003. A subsequent research trip to Suzhou in 2004 was funded by the Sino-British Fellowship Trust, and as the project neared completion, the final stages were supported by the Research Settlement Fund for new Faculty of Seoul National University. For their assistance during my research, I would like to thank the staff of the National Central Library, Taipei; the library of the National Palace Museum, Taipei; Suzhou Library; Shanghai Library; Cambridge University Library; the library of the School of Oriental and African Studies, University of London; the library of Seoul National University and the Kyujanggak Archives. Material for chapter 1 first appeared in an article entitled "The Sage in the South: Confucian Traditions from Wu and Yue," in the *Bulletin of the Museum of Far Eastern Antiquities* 78 (2006). Material for chapter 5 concerning the burial of King Helü of Wu first appeared in "The Tomb at Tiger Hill: The History of a Wu Royal Tomb of the Spring and Autumn Period (771–475 BC)" in *Acta Orientalia* 66 (2005), while the introduction to the discussion concerning tower construction in chapter 6 is derived from an article entitled "The Towers of Yue," in *Acta Orientalia* 71 (2010). The section on Xi Shi is based on an article entitled "The Silent Beauty: Changing Portrayals of Xi Shi in Imperial Era Literature," published by *Asia Major* 26.1 (2013). The quotations from the *Yuejue shu* scattered throughout the book are derived from my earlier translation, *The Glory of Yue: An Annotated Translation of the Yuejue Shu*, published by Brill in 2010. In each case I am very grateful to the relevant authorities for giving me permission to reprint my work. Every effort has been made to contact the copyright owner for figures 1 and 2 (images derived from Umehara Sueji 梅原末治, *Shōkō kokyō shūei* 紹興古鏡聚英) but without success. I can only apologize if the rights of the owner have been infringed.

Three anonymous readers for the Harvard University Asia Center provided many helpful comments and suggested revisions, thus sparing me from some egregious errors. At an earlier stage, various friends took time off from their own research to answer inquiries and read the manuscript. I would particularly like to thank Yan Zinan (School of Oriental and African Studies) and Luke Hambleton (Beishida) for their many helpful comments, especially given that they had so much else to do. Further assistance and encouragement came from Desmond Cheung, Craig Clunas, Peter Ditmanson, Kaspars Eihmanis, Bernhard Fuehrer, Thomas and Maya Hjørnet, Marc Howe, Huang Lanyin, Jo Jungeun, Kim Bokyong, Kim Jinsoo, Lee Hyunjeong, Andrew Lo, Shih Ching-fei, Tan Tianyuan, Wang Tao, Marcus White, and Zhang Honglin. Having dedicated my first book to Kangta, I feel that I should continue the trend. Therefore I dedicate this book to Hu Ge and Yuan Hong.

—O.M.

Introduction

The title of this book, *Cherishing Antiquity*, is a translation of the Chinese term: *huaigu* 懷古. In principle, *huaigu* could encompass the act of remembering any historical occurrence or individual, but in practice it has often been applied to contemplation of the cultural significance of places where events of historic importance happened. In literary terms, *huaigu* is a genre that describes the emotions of a visitor to a famous historical site now in ruins. It is at once a form of travel writing and a type of historical literature. As *huaigu* is related to travel writing, it can be distinguished from historical genres by its predication upon a personal visit by the writer to the site in question. On the other hand, *huaigu* is distinct from other kinds of travel writing in its use of images and vocabulary derived from ancient historical records to evoke an often highly detailed representation of the past glories of the site in question, and in its conventional presentation of a poignant contrast between the magnificence that had once been and the present desolation meeting the eyes of the traveler-author. The writer plays on the tension between the transience of human endeavor and the continuity of the natural world; the destruction of great palaces and famous monuments, and the survival of weed and bramble-covered ruins; the disappearance of important historical figures; and the visibility of such melancholy remnants as tombs and stone steles.

The focus of this book is on the cultural construction, in particular through *huaigu* writings, of the ancient kingdom of Wu. This state, situated in what is now southern Jiangsu Province, had its capital located at the city of Suzhou. The kingdom of Wu has a recorded history in ancient Chinese texts of almost exactly one century, beginning with the reign of King Shoumeng of Wu 吳王壽夢 (r. 585–561 BCE) who first opened up diplomatic relations with the states of the Zhou confederacy, and ending with its conquest by enemy forces in the reign of King Shoumeng's great-grandson in 473 BCE. However, given that all texts about the history and culture of the kingdom of Wu were written after its sudden and precipitate collapse, they reflect not the wealth and might of its kings when they were at the height of their powers, but the bewilderment of later observers attempting to understand how such an important country could simply implode in the face of an enemy invasion. In this first phase of the development of the cultural legacy of Wu, there was little room for nostalgia or regret at the rise and fall of this immensely powerful and bellicose southern kingdom, but there was certainly great bafflement and a search for some kind of explanation for how such a thing could be possible. In its numerous military campaigns against its neighbors, the Wu army had seemed almost invincible. The destruction of the kingdom at the beginning of the Warring States era resulted in a major shift in the balance of power in the region, with lasting consequences for the history of China as a whole.

During the imperial era, a new phase began in the cultural construction of the ancient kingdom of Wu. The impression given in ancient Chinese texts is that the kingdom sprang out of nowhere, and that its kings and princes through a combination of ruthless use of military force and subtle diplomacy forced their way into the counsels of the Zhou confederacy during the late Spring and Autumn period, only to vanish in a sea of blood and flame when their country was conquered by the kingdom of Yue. These dramatic and romantic events seem to have had a considerable hold over the imaginations of members of the literati elite in imperial era China, and to have been the subject of ongoing commemoration within popular traditions in the lands of Wu. Throughout the imperial era, tourists were attracted to sites supposedly linked to the royal house of Wu, and a considerable body of *huaigu* literature was written on the subject. In addition, a number of commemorative monuments were constructed, some in the form of temples and shrines, others in the shape of secular pavilions, stone inscriptions, and so on, which served to remember individuals and events from the history of Wu. These monuments, in turn, also attracted their own visitors, who wrote of their feelings at seeing this evidence of the remembrance of the ancient kingdom of Wu, at first centuries, and then millennia after its collapse.

This book consists of two parts. The first concerns the history of the royal family of Wu during the century of its recorded existence.

Given that virtually no written records survive of any Wu person except for members of the royal family, it is at present impossible to write a history of this kingdom that does not focus almost exclusively on members of the ruling house. However, there are a number of problems with understanding the history of Wu through its royal family. The first is that different ancient historical texts ascribe different relationships even to some of the best-recorded kings and princes of Wu. Given that the most basic facts about these individuals seem to be disputed, it is very difficult to understand interaction between various members of the family. Likewise, nothing is known about the law or practices of inheritance in the kingdom of Wu in the late Spring and Autumn period (771–475 BCE); this means that it is extremely difficult to interpret the complex and highly contentious issues of succession that occurred at this time. In the circumstances it would be impossible to write a conventional history of the kingdom of Wu. Instead, chapter 1 concentrates on the representation in early Chinese texts of by far the most famous prince of the royal house: Jizha of Wu 吳王子季札 (dates unknown). The youngest of the sons of King Shoumeng of Wu, the first historically recorded monarch of the kingdom, the prince seems to have received an exceptionally fine education, which combined with a pleasing manner, made him the ideal candidate to represent his king on a number of important diplomatic missions. Prince Jizha is the first, and the best known, of the diplomats sent by the kingdom of Wu to the states of the Zhou confederacy; his first mission was undertaken just a few decades after the earliest known mention of the kingdom of Wu in Chinese records. His deep respect for the customs and culture of the Zhou states, his ingratiating manners, and considerable intelligence made a great impression on his contemporaries, as a result of which he became not only the best-recorded member of his generation in the Wu royal family but also the only prince whose biography was extensively documented in ancient Chinese texts. Given that Prince Jizha never succeeded to the throne of Wu (unlike three of his older brothers), it was his diplomatic success that ensured his lasting fame.

Chapter 2 focuses on the reigns of the last two kings of Wu. King Helü of Wu 吳王闔閭 (r. 514–496 BCE) came to the throne after arranging for the assassination of his predecessor, King Liao 吳王僚 (r. 526–515 BCE). In the wake of King Liao's murder, King

Helü consolidated his grip on power by forcing a number of his relatives into exile, and in some cases he is thought to have sent assassins after them as well. With his authority within the kingdom unchallenged, King Helü turned his army against one of his long-standing enemies, the kingdom of Chu. With a series of stunning victories, the Wu armies marched on the capital of Chu and sacked it, forcing the king into panic-stricken flight and eventually leading to a full-scale evacuation of the city to a new site. More than any other campaign, it was the victorious campaign against Chu, which culminated in the fall of their capital, that defined the military might of Wu and caused their neighbors such anxiety. Where the urbane and educated Prince Jizha represented the civilized diplomatic face of the kingdom of Wu, King Helü represented its barbarity and the brute force of its people. However, in the end he overreached himself. Invading the kingdom of Yue during a period of national mourning, King Helü met the newly enthroned King Goujian of Yue 越王勾踐 (r. 496–465 BCE) in battle. King Helü was wounded and died on the retreat, thus bringing to a sudden end a career that had otherwise gone from one success to another. The death of the penultimate king of Wu set in train a sequence of events that would eventually end in the destruction of his kingdom.

Coming to the throne unexpectedly—following first the demise of his older brother, Crown Prince Zhonglei 吳太子終纍, and then the death of his father of wounds received in battle—the early years of the reign of King Fuchai 吳王夫差 (r. 495–473 BCE) were overshadowed by the need to avenge King Helü's untimely death. In the third year of his reign, King Fuchai of Wu invaded Yue and forced King Goujian into an ignominious surrender at Kuaijishan 會稽山. The kingdom of Yue became in effect a protectorate of Wu, and King Goujian spent a number of years in exile before he was finally allowed to return to his home. In the years that followed the terrible defeat inflicted on Yue, the Wu army went from strength to strength, defeating numerous enemies, most notably the state of Qi in a famous engagement at the battle of Ailing 艾陵. This was then followed by what should have been the final triumph for King Fuchai of Wu, when he participated in the covenant at Huangchi 黄池, an occasion intended to confirm his status as the most powerful ruler of the day, second only to the Zhou king in authority. As it transpired,

Huangchi was in fact the beginning of the end. King Goujian of Yue took advantage of the king of Wu's absence from his kingdom to launch an invasion in the first stage of his long-matured plan for revenge. After a series of devastating campaigns, the Wu capital fell to the enemy, and King Fuchai of Wu was captured alive. He committed suicide, unwilling to survive the loss of his kingdom.

Chapter 3 is concerned mainly with archaeological evidence concerning the history of the royal house of Wu and their cultural legacy. In the last couple of centuries, a number of inscribed bronzes have been discovered or excavated with inscriptions indicating that they were made for members of the Wu royal house. These vessels and weapons pose particular problems of interpretation, given that in many cases they record different names for members of the Wu ruling house from those found in ancient historical texts, and they also add a number of new members to the family tree. In this chapter I propose a new methodology for understanding the texts found on these excavated bronzes that focuses on the evidence these vessel texts provide of social and linguistic change within the ancient kingdom of Wu. This chapter also considers the portrayal of key events from Wu history on Eastern Han (25–220) dynasty bronze mirrors made in the Jiangsu-Zhejiang region. These exceptionally high-quality objects, often signed by their makers, represent the flowering of a local artistic tradition concerned with depicting the fall of the kingdom of Wu. Although many aspects of this tradition remain obscure, this would seem to be both a response to contemporary political changes as well as a representation of ongoing interest in the Jiangnan region about the most famous events in its history.

The second part of this book consists of three case studies, each concerned with the posthumous commemoration of a member of the Wu royal family and the literary legacy of this remembrance. Chapter 4 describes the imperial era deification of Prince Jizha of Wu. The prince was commemorated in a wide range of monuments in and around the presumed site of his fief at Piling 毗陵 (in what is now Changzhou, in Jiangsu Province): these included his tomb and its commemorative stele, incorporating an inscription said to have been composed by and perhaps even written in the calligraphy of Confucius himself; as well as a series of shrines and temples in the immediate vicinity. Some of these temples are of considerable interest, not least because of their association with individuals claiming descent from the prince. Although the imperial era deification of this prince was confined to the locale in which he had lived, where he was worshipped as a god of examination success, this worship was an extremely important function in an area that, from at least the Song dynasty onwards, was highly education-oriented.

Chapter 5 describes the remembrance of King Helü of Wu. Surprisingly for such a great monarch, whose reign represented an apogée for the power and authority of the kingdom of Wu, commemorative monuments dedicated to King Helü are few and far between, and he never seems to have been the subject of worship at a temple or shrine. Instead, interest in the penultimate king of Wu was focused on the site of his tomb at Tiger Hill, just northwest of his capital, now the city of Suzhou. The earliest recorded visitors to his grave did not come to muse there upon his great military triumphs and the suddenness of his death, but rather to rob the tomb; and the landscape of the tomb-site is, to the present day, defined by what is said to be the flooded access-pit dug by order of the First Emperor of Qin 秦始皇 (r. 221–210 BCE) in the hope of stealing the treasures buried deep within. King Helü's grave at Tiger Hill became a major tourist attraction from at least the Tang dynasty (618–907) onwards, and the commemorative pavilions and calligraphic inscriptions found there, together with the poetry and prose written by visitors throughout the imperial era, vividly attest to the many generations of visitors drawn to this site by the wish to remember the penultimate king of Wu. However, rival attractions to the drowned tomb quickly sprang up. Tiger Hill also became the site of a major Buddhist monastery founded early in the Age of Disunion (220–589), the location of the tombs and shrines dedicated to many other later local worthies and famous individuals, and an important focus for literati activity in the Jiangnan region. The ways in which the presence of King Helü's tomb at Tiger Hill complemented and rivaled these alternative attractions is the subject of this second case study.

Given the terrible circumstances in which the kingdom of Wu fell, and the long-standing enmity between King Fuchai and his conqueror, King Goujian, it is hardly surprising that every building and monument attributed to the last king of Wu went up in flames at the time of the Yue conquest. Chapter 6 describes the two sites most strongly associated with the tragic and romantic figure of the last king of Wu, of which one—Lingyanshan 靈巖山 or Numinous Cliff Mountain, the site of his summer palace—has no surviving ancient remains, and the other—Gusu Tower, a monument erected to commemorate King Fuchai's military victories and built at least in part with timbers presented by the conquered kingdom of Yue—is so comprehensively lost that not even its original location is known. In spite of this, both Numinous Cliff and Gusu Tower were the subject of much literature in the imperial era, and they offered writers and poets the opportunity to describe the luxurious and sybaritic life of the last king of Wu, which was of necessity almost devoid of any considerations of the contemporary appearance of the scene of his triumphs. In these works the possibilities of the *huaigu* genre may be said to be pushed to their greatest limits, as scant historical sources were mined for any information that might bring accounts of these imaginary pleasure domes to life, given that their desolate and weed-covered ruins existed only as literary conventions.

The history of Wu was largely written by people far removed in time, place, and cultural background from the inhabitants of this ancient southern kingdom. There is considerable reason to doubt that even some of the most basic facts about the history and civilization of Wu were correctly recorded in the texts of the Central States during the Warring States (475–221 BCE) and early imperial eras. However, these records were crucial for understanding the way that later generations interpreted events in the kingdom of Wu at the end of the Spring and Autumn period, and they determine the way that its kings and princes were portrayed in the literati tradition. When commemorative monuments were constructed at sites associated with these men, what was being remembered was the individual as described in ancient Chinese texts, though this was occasionally mediated by popular traditions and later interpretations of events. When composing *huaigu* literature about sites associated with the ruling house of Wu, the writings of classical antiquity did not form a dead hand lying on the creativity of later imperial era poets, but rather, served as a source of inspiration, a way of understanding the scene before their eyes. In an age before archaeology, early imperial descriptions of the architecture of Wu were of particular importance given that many exceptionally beautiful and historically significant buildings had left no above-ground remains at all. Visiting these sites was an important cultural experience, given their association with the most romantic figures of the ancient past, men whose cunning and intelligence, bravery and wit changed the course of history.

The development of *huaigu* literature and popular perceptions of the last kings of Wu, not to mention tourism to the city Suzhou throughout the imperial era, were closely intertwined. Sites associated with the royal family of Wu fulfilled every expectation of literati travelers. They were exotic thanks to their location in southern Jiangsu Province, in lands that had in antiquity stood beyond the borders of the Zhou confederacy in a kingdom inhabited by tattooed men armed with sharp swords, who lurked among lush primeval forests threaded with silver rivers. At the same time, by the imperial period, the lands of the former kingdom of Wu were located safely within the Chinese cultural sphere, having joined the empire at the time of unification. Possessing a reputation for being sinicized that long predated any such political settlement, their diplomats were noted for their courtesy and education, and their princes were admired by Confucius himself. For much of the imperial era the former capital of the kingdom of Wu, Suzhou, was numbered one of the richest, most cultured, most glamorous and exciting cities in the empire, a place that was a pleasure to visit and a sorrow to leave. For members of the literati and the ruling elite, two overlapping but nevertheless distinct groups, Suzhou and the surrounding region represented the gratification of every sensual delight, and this can be seen in the literature written about it. Given the power that descriptions of the wealth and might of the ancient kingdom of Wu had over the imaginations of ancient Chinese authors, it is hardly surprising that this should also be reflected in the works of later writers. Though the solitude and desolation that culminates the descriptions of ancient ruins in many works of *huaigu* literature was no doubt hard to come by at most important Wu sites in the imperial era, any such lack could easily be remedied by the romantic imagination. Thus the kingdom of Wu lived on, embalmed within its literary legacy.

The People of Wu

By the time the kingdom of Wu entered Chinese records in the late Spring and Autumn period it was noted for the high degree of sinicization and the close links maintained by its royal family and ruling elite with the states of the Zhou confederacy; however the inhabitants of this kingdom were not part of the Hua-Xia ethnicity but instead formed the northernmost branch of the Bai Yue 百越 peoples. The kingdom of Wu was crucially placed to dominate cultural and commercial exchange between the Bai Yue and the Central States of the Zhou confederacy.[1] In ancient Chinese texts, the kingdom of Wu was almost always known simply as Wu 吳. However from inscriptions on bronzes it is known that the kings of Wu claimed to be the rulers of Gongwu 攻敔, also known as Gouwu 勾吳. A number of theories have been advanced to explain the meaning of the term *Gouwu*. The earliest is that this is a transliteration of a dialect word of unknown meaning, which is based on the commentary by Yan Shigu 顏師古 (581–645) on the "Dili zhi" 地理志 (Treatise on geography) chapter of the *Hanshu* 漢書 (History of the Han dynasty).[2] A large number of dialect words from Wu (particularly place names) survive as transliterated terms, but in the vast majority of cases the original meaning is not known. Serious problems are caused by the lack of a standard method in early Chinese texts to transliterate words from the ancient language of the kingdom of Wu, or indeed from any other foreign language.[3] A second theory is that it is a place name, based on the evidence of the *Zhengyi* 正義 (Correct meanings) commentary by Zhang Shoujie 張守節 (fl. 737) on the *Shiji* 史記 (Records of the Grand Historian) chapter on the hereditary house of Wu.[4] A third theory is that Gouwu is a contraction of the names of two ancient states, either Gou and Wu or Gan 干 and Wu.[5] There is evidence in a number of ancient texts that the kings of Wu used a double title of this kind: for example the *Zhanguo ce* 戰國策 (Records of the Warring

1. Xie Chen, *Gouwu shi xinkao*, p. 61; Li Xueqin and Wang Linchang, "Yue wenhua zai Zhongguo wenmingshi zhong de diwei," p. 8.

2. *Hanshu* 8B.1667, n. 2. The importance of this theory is that it makes Gongwu/Gouwu (whatever it meant) the name that the indigenous people of the region used to designate themselves, as opposed to any term used by the people of the Central States to describe them.

3. Zhou Chenghe and You Rujie, "Gu Yueyu diming chutan," p. 61. The authors consider in particular detail the problems posed by such characters as *gou* 勾, *jiu* 鳩, *gu* 姑, *yu* 于, *wu* 烏, *yu* 餘, *wu* 無 and *fu* 夫, since these were commonly used for transliterating ancient Wu and Yue words.

4. *Shiji* 31.1445, n. 1.

5. Yin Weiren, "Gouwu, Gouhua yuwen zhi guo," pp. 123–24.

States) uses the latter in a discussion of the amazing qualities of southern swords: "As for the swords of Wu-Gan, if you test them on flesh they cut apart oxen and horses; if you test them on metal they cleave bowls and basins; if you place them on a pillar and strike, they will chop it into three pieces; if you position them on a stone and hit, they will crush them into hundreds of bits" 夫吳干之劍, 肉試則斷牛馬; 金試則截盤匜; 薄之柱上而擊之, 則折爲三; 質之石上而擊之, 則碎爲百.[6] Today, most scholars ascribe to the theory that the term Gouwu should be understood as the name of the ancient people of this region of China. This word is also regarded as related, if not identical, to the word Gusu 姑蘇—the oldest known designation for the region around the city of Suzhou, as well as the name of the mountain that was the heartland of the kingdom. (This mountain was once the site of the Gusu Tower, one of the major prestige projects undertaken to proclaim the power and wealth of the kings of Wu.) The confusion between these terms is certainly something that has caused problems for centuries; in the Song (960–1279) dynasty Zhu Changwen 朱長文 (1041–1100) noted in the *Wujun tujing xuji* 吳郡圖經續記 (Supplement to the Illustrated Gazetteer of Wu Commandery) that Gusu Mountain was also sometimes known by the alternative names of Guxu 姑胥 and Guyu 姑餘.[7] Be that as it may, when the name of the ancient capital of the kingdom of Wu was changed during the Sui dynasty (in 589) the *su* 蘇 of Suzhou was chosen to honor the ancient name of Gusu. At all stages of the development of Wu regional culture, the ancient history of the Gouwu people remained an important source of pride, inspiration, and identity. Although at the time of the unification of China the history of the kingdom of Wu became part of Chinese history, it is clear that throughout the imperial era the people of Suzhou and the surrounding region remained deeply committed to a sense of an individual, special Wu iden-

---

6. *Zhanguo ce*, p. 1002 (Zhao ce 趙策 2: "Zhao Huiwen wang sanshi nian" 趙惠文王三十年). A number of bronzes record the monarchs of Wu as having a double title as the kings of Wu and Gan. Rong, *Shang Zhou yiqi tongkao*, p. 45. The conquest of Gan (written either 干 or Han 邗) is not recorded in any historical text, but is mentioned in the *Guanzi*, p. 974 ("Xiaowen" 小問). The importance of this double title is discussed in Shang, "Wuguo ducheng de bianqian ji Helü jiandu Suzhou de yuanyou," p. 11.

7. Zhu Changwen, *Wujun tujing xuji*, p. 41.

tity, which could not be swamped by the arrival of waves of immigrants from China proper, nor attenuated by the passage of time.

In the era prior to the unification of China, the kingdom of Wu was located at the southernmost edge of the Chinese world. However, from the Warring States era onwards, writers based in the Central States began to produce accounts of the landscape, history, and culture of this southern kingdom. These records stressed the enormous natural wealth of the region: not only was this a land without famine, with vast natural resources, but it was a place with an unimaginable abundance of new and strange flora and fauna. By the Han dynasty (206 BCE–220 CE) Chinese writers were attempting to chronicle that abundance: the primeval forests where dozens of species of trees unknown in other parts of China grew, the enormous variety of plants, the strange birds and animals of the region. The amazing experiences waiting for ancient Chinese visitors to the south were catalogued in such works as the "Wudu fu" 吳都賦 (Rhapsody of the Wu capital) by Zuo Si 左思 (ca. 250–ca. 305). The rhapsody, a genre noted for its use of listing, was ideally suited for conveying the overwhelming foreignness and wealth of Wu, and this rhapsody in particular was crucial for maintaining the exotic reputation of the region in the early imperial era:

> The land unfurls in rolling hills,
> The plants grow tall and wide.
> Walking through the wilderness, it seems like a park,
> Even when encountering a forest, it seems like a garden.
> Exotic flowers bloom from every tree and shrub,[8]
> They are magnificent in summer, evergreen in winter.
> Local histories describe these things,
> They are envied by the Central States.
> 地勢坱圠, 卉木䖸蔓.
> 遭藪爲圃, 值林爲苑.
> 異荂蓲蘛, 夏曄冬蒨.
> 方志所辨, 中州所羨.[9]

8. In the section translated here, the exotic effect is heightened by the use of a local dialect word *fu* 荂, meaning flower, which is identified as such (it also means a variety of camellia) in the Guo Pu 郭璞 (276–324) commentary on the Erya 爾雅 dictionary. *Erya*, p. 296 ("Shicao" 釋草).

9. *Wenxuan*, p. 66. An alternative translation is given in Knechtges, *Wen xuan or Selections of Refined Literature, vol. 1*, p. 385.

The first serious ethnographical studies of non-Chinese peoples were produced in the Han dynasty. This is obviously unfortunate for the Gouwu people, whose independent kingdom had vanished some four hundred years too early to be properly recorded, and whose territories had subsequently been assimilated into a series of more or less unsympathetic regimes. As a result, in the absence of any proper discussion of Wu culture and the degree to which it was alien from that of the Zhou confederacy (a realm of enquiry that was impossible to pursue until modern archaeological discoveries provided a significant body of data), ancient Chinese records concentrated almost exclusively on superficial signs of difference. In particular, virtually every pre-Han and Han dynasty text commented on the fact that the inhabitants of the kingdom of Wu were tattooed. No doubt in the cultural context of the times this added greatly to the perception that the south was a strange and exotic place, a land of mystery and danger. Tattooing was known to the people of the Central States, but there it was used as a means of punishment; minor criminals were tattooed, and the marks on their skin were a sign of their shameful past.[10] This connection between tattooing and criminality would cause considerable misunderstanding and distress when the states of the north came into contact with the peoples of Wu and Yue, for whom it was a culturally (rather than legally) significant act. The repugnance that was felt in the Central States for the practice of tattooing can be seen in the fact that it was banned even as a punishment in 167 BCE and that southern people who were conquered by or surrendered to the Han were required to give up this cultural practice.[11]

The significance of tattooing to the people of Wu is not well understood, for to the people of the north whose written records provide the vast majority of descriptions of this southern people, they were barbarians whose alien practices were hardly worthy of detailed comment. As a result, virtually nothing is known of the methods used, or the kind of designs favored within Wu society. It is entirely possible that the tattoos had significant distinguishing elements, understood within these communities, which were simply

---

10. *Baihutong*, p. 439 ("Wuxing" 五刑); Hulsewé, *Remnants of Ch'in Law*, p. 15.
11. Hulsewé, *Remnants of Han Law*, p. 125.

ignored by those unfamiliar with and hostile to this cultural practice.[12] In recent times a number of ancient bronze figures that represent Bai Yue peoples have been excavated, and the patterns on their cheeks and bodies are thought to depict tattooed designs.[13] However, in spite of the comment that Wu cultural practices clearly occasioned in the people of the Zhou confederacy, there are but few references to people from the south experiencing any prejudice because of this. In fact, the only story concerned with discrimination against any of the Bai Yue peoples on the grounds of their alien customs describes a confrontation in the kingdom of Chu between a courtier and an ambassador from the kingdom of Yue. This story from the *Hanshi waizhuan* 韓詩外傳 (Mr. Han's outer traditions of the *Book of songs*) thus provides a unique account of the kind of prejudice faced by the peoples of the ancient south:

> King Goujian of Yue sent Lian Ji to present people to the king of Chu, and one of the king [of Chu's] envoys said: "Yue is a barbarian country. I ask leave to make fun of their ambassador." The king [of Chu] said: "The king of Yue is a wise man, and his ambassador is also a clever man, you should think carefully before doing this." The envoy went out to see Lian Ji, and said: "If you wear an official hat, then you can have audience [with our king] according to the rules of ritual propriety. If you do not put on a hat, then you cannot see him." Lian Ji said: "Yue was separately enfeoffed by the Zhou royal house, but we have not been included among the Central States, and live between river and sea, with salt-water and fresh-water turtles, eels, and fish as our companions. It is only after tattooing our bodies and cutting our hair that we have been able to live there. Now I come to this great kingdom, and you say if I put an official hat on then I can have audience, and if I do not put a hat on then I cannot. If this is the case, when you send an ambassador to Yue, then he will also have to be

---

12. One of the few references to the technique of tattooing used in the south is found in a commentary to the Nan Man 南蠻 (Southern Man barbarian) chapter of the *Hou Hanshu* 86.2834, n. 1, which states that these people "cut lines in their flesh and then coloured them with red and green [pigments]" 刻其肌以丹青涅也. Wang Wenqing, "Zailun Wu Yue tongzu," gives an interesting discussion of the importance of northern prejudice towards southern culture as a shaping force for the surviving documentation on this subject.

13. Liang Baiquan, *Wu Yue wenhua*, pp. 54–56, figs. 64, 67, 69, 70; Peters, "Tattooed Faces and Stilt Houses," p. 16.

> tattooed by cutting his skin and [rubbing in] ink, and have his hair cut, and only after that will he be allowed to have audience according to our customs. How would that be?"
> 越王勾踐使廉稽獻民於荆王, 荆王使者曰: "越, 夷狄之國也, 臣請欺其使者." 荆王曰: "越王, 賢人也. 其使者亦賢, 子其慎之!" 使者出, 見廉稽曰: "冠, 則得以俗見. 不冠, 不得見." 廉稽曰: "夫越, 亦周室之列封也, 不得處於大國, 而處江海之陂, 與魭鱣魚鱉爲伍, 文身翦髮, 而後處焉. 今來至上國, 必曰: '冠, 得俗見. 不冠, 不得見.' 如此, 則上國使適越, 亦將劓墨文身翦髮, 而後得以俗見, 可乎?"[14]

In the early imperial era, the lands of the Yangtze River delta region were perceived as exceptionally rich, just as southern people were believed to be fearsomely dangerous. This reputation was not unjustified, for the talents of these southern people had been honed by countless generations of tribal warfare, and many luckless migrants and soldiers from the north died at their hands. Tales of southern prowess in warfare were so prevalent that even long after the lands of Wu had been absorbed into the great southern kingdom of Chu, fighters from this region were feared across the rest of China. This early reputation for fearless bellicosity is perhaps surprising, given that after the fall of the Han the male inhabitants of this region came to be conventionally portrayed as effeminate and indolent, too luxury-loving to be any good at fighting. In spite or perhaps because of this reputation—a stereotype that has continued largely unchallenged to the present day—the martial prowess of the ancient Gouwu people was a source of considerable pride to imperial era inhabitants of the region.

From at least the Qin dynasty onwards significant numbers of migrants began to arrive in Gouwu territory from northern China. Some came as soldiers in the military campaigns to subdue the south, a small handful were administrators sent to govern the region. More importantly, there were countless ordinary people who fled the north to escape warfare, drought, famine, persecution, and lack of opportunity, and who created the present landscape of Jiangsu. These men cut down the great forests, drained the swamps, and extended the polder and canal system originally developed by the Gouwu people,

---

14. *Hanshi waizhuan*, p. 271 (8.1). The significance of this story in early representations of tattooing in Chinese literature is discussed in Reed, "Early Chinese Tattoo," pp. 6–7.

thus harnessing the natural resources of the region and developing its potential. These migrants were crucial for the development of the region and its successful integration into the Chinese cultural sphere. Thanks to the history of this region, framed by romantic images of wealth, the strangeness and bellicosity of its original inhabitants, and the impact of subsequent immigration, perceptions of the Jiangnan region in traditional Chinese culture were founded upon an interesting dichotomy: Jiangnan was at once an exotic border region and an entirely safe and stable place to visit. It enjoyed both a rich cultural legacy (thanks to the residual remnants of Wu civilization and the ongoing commemoration of the triumphs and tragedies of this ancient kingdom throughout the imperial era), as well as an unassailable position within traditional Chinese culture from having become part of China proper at the time of the unification in 221 BCE. Representations of the Jiangnan region were profoundly influenced by this dual vision; the literature that describes this part of China plays at once on a sense of the comfortably familiar and of the dangerously exotic.

PART ONE

The Kingdom of Wu

1

The Royal House of Wu

The history of Wu, as it is recorded in ancient Chinese historical texts, is the history of its royal family. This is in large measure due to the paucity of sources; the vast majority of the individuals from the kingdom of Wu whose names and histories are recorded in ancient Chinese texts were members of the ruling house, and all were members of the ruling elite. Though no doubt much interesting research remains to be done on the people of Wu, it will have to wait for further archaeological discoveries and cannot be written solely on the basis of the textual record. As a result of this situation, in order to understand the history of the kingdom of Wu, it is necessary to understand the interrelationships between the various different members of the family, and the legal and social consequences of these relationships. Unfortunately, just as the history of the non-elite population of Wu remains beyond our understanding, much of the history of the ruling house is also impossible to comprehend. Partly this is because the family tree of the Wu ruling house in the short century of its recorded existence is not particularly well-documented, and because such relationships as are described are often contradicted in other texts of similar venerability; and partly it is because our knowledge of Wu custom and practice, especially in the crucial field of inheritance, is patchy to nonexistent. I have already addressed some of the manifold problems of understanding the family tree of the Wu ruling house in an earlier publication.[1] Here I intend to expand upon that analysis, and in chapter 3 to introduce a new source of evidence: the inscribed bronzes which record that they were made by and for members of the Wu royal family.

---

1. Milburn, "Kingship and Inheritance in the State of Wu."

The Early History of the Kingdom of Wu

All the textual evidence concerning the history of the kingdom of Wu comes from a very short period of time—just over a century long—beginning with the reign of King Shoumeng of Wu and ending with the conquest of Wu and the death of King Fuchai in 473 BCE. During this brief period of florescence, Wu inserted itself among the states of the Zhou confederacy and played a major role in the affairs of the Central States. This was made possible by the kingdom's military might, and was rendered more or less acceptable by the Wu royal family's claim to be members of the Ji 姬 clan, and hence blood relatives not only of the kings of Zhou, but also of many if not all of the *zhuhou* 諸侯 (rulers of Zhou confederacy states). The degree to which the claims of the Wu kings were genuinely accepted by their peers is not clear, but many Warring States era and early imperial texts do make reference to the Wu royal family as members of the Ji clan.[2] The state of Wu was said in many ancient texts to have been founded by Wu Taibo 吳太伯, the uncle of King Wen of Zhou 周文王 (r. 1056–1050 BCE), who gave up his claims to his father's noble title to allow first his younger brother and then his nephew to succeed him and eventually to found the Zhou dynasty. Having decided to yield his inheritance to younger and more able members of the family, Wu Taibo and his younger brother Zhongyong 仲雍 then left their homeland and travelled to the margins of the Chinese world, bringing civilization to the barbarians of the south.[3] Many early references to the state of Wu that was founded by the uncles of King Wen of Zhou suggest that it was in fact situated in what is now Shaanxi Province, rather than in the Jiangnan region. There are numerous surviving accounts of a powerful state named Wu or Yu 虞 in ancient Chinese

---

2. *Chunqiu Zuozhuan*, p. 1677 (Ai 13), henceforward *Zuozhuan*; *Lunyu*, p. 74 ("Shuer" 述而 7.31).

3. Occasionally the Japanese claimed descent from Wu Taibo. "The Japanese live in the ocean to the southeast, and they completely tattoo their faces and pattern their bodies, and they claim to be descended from Wu Taibo. They love to swim and catch fish, and they pattern their bodies in order to frighten the denizens of the water. When they die they have an inner coffin but not an outer vault and they pile up earth to make a tomb" 倭人在帶方東南大海中, 悉黥面文身, 自謂太伯之後. 好沉没取魚, 文身以厭水禽. 死有棺無槨, 封土爲冢. *Jinshu* 97.2535.

texts, which was located in the vicinity of present-day Long County 隴縣 on the border between Gansu and Shaanxi provinces.[4] This state was eventually conquered by Jin in 654 BCE. The earliest text to associate Wu Taibo with the Spring and Autumn period kingdom of Wu in the south is the *Shiji* and Sima Qian's 司馬遷 (ca. 145 or 135–86 BCE) sources of information on the early history of this kingdom are not known.[5] Most early references to Wu Taibo, rather than providing concrete geographical information about the location of his state, concentrate instead on his principled behavior in giving up his claim to the title to allow his brilliant nephew to succeed: a prime example of the Confucian virtue of *rang* 讓 (yielding one's position to a better man).[6] Many admiring statements were made in ancient Chinese texts concerning this generous behavior; the following example is derived from the *Lunyu* 論語 (Analects of Confucius): "The Master said: 'Taibo could be described as [possessing] an exceptionally fine moral sense!'" 子曰: "泰伯, 其可謂至德也已矣![7] Wu Taibo is supposed to have left no heir, and hence in the end it was the descendants of his younger brother, Zhongyong, who founded the royal house of Wu.

There are only three known king-lists for the kingdom of Wu recording the rulers between Zhongyong and the first historically

4. *Guanzi*, p. 425 ("Xiaokuang" 小匡). An exhaustive discussion of the evidence found in ancient texts on the existence and history of this northwestern state is given in Wei Juxian, "Taibo zhi feng zai Xiwu."

5. The discovery of the "Yi Hou Ze *gui*" 宜侯夨簋 in Tomb 1 at Yandunshan 煙墩山, Dantu County 丹徒縣, Jiangsu Province is the only bronze inscription found to date that has been interpreted as providing evidence to support Sima Qian's assertion that Wu Taibo was enfeoffed in the Jiangnan region. Since it was first discovered in the 1950s, this extremely problematic inscription, which contains numerous illegible characters and many others whose reading is controversial, has provoked much debate. Guo, "Ze gui ming kaoshi"; and Chen Mengjia, "Xi Zhou tongqi duandai" give transcriptions and interpretations that favor a link with Jiangsu. For alternative interpretations see Li Xueqin, "Yi Hou Ze gui de ren yu di"; and Huang Shengzhang, "Tongqi mingwen Yi, Yu, Ze de diwang ji qi yu Wuguo de guanxi."

6. Zhang Yachu, "Wushi xinzheng," p. 31.

7. *Lunyu*, p. 78 ("Taibo" 泰伯 8.1). The admiration of Confucius and early Confucian philosophers for the supposed founder of the Wu royal house is discussed in Wang Suijin, *Wu Yue wenhua shihua*, p. 10.

documented monarch, King Shoumeng. The earliest of these lists is found in the *Shiji* and the sources used to compile it are completely unknown. This account records twenty-five rulers of the kingdom of Wu in total, and suggests that the state practiced father-to-son succession until this system was disrupted in the generation of King Shoumeng's sons. The *Wu Yue chunqiu* 吳越春秋 (Spring and Autumn Annals of the kingdoms of Wu and Yue) includes a very similar king-list, giving identical names and family relationships for the early rulers of Wu. The *Wu Yue chunqiu*, however, records twenty-six rulers of the kingdom of Wu, since Xiongsui 熊遂 from the *Shiji* list is split into two separate individuals: Xiong 熊 and Sui 遂 (see table 1). The final important king-list to be produced for the Wu ruling house is that found in the appendix to the *Wudi ji* 吳地記 (Records of the lands of Wu), a Tang dynasty gazetteer compiled by Lu Guangwei 陸廣微 (fl. ninth century). Although the text states that the list should incorporate the names of twenty-five rulers of the kingdom of Wu, in fact only twenty-one names are given. Although some are the same as those found in the much earlier *Shiji* and *Wu Yue chunqiu* lists, many names are either completely different or given in a different order of succession. Although most editions of the text do not include further information, the recension produced by Zhang Haipeng 張海鵬 (fl. 1804–33), a Qing dynasty (1644–1912) bibliophile, also describes the family relationship between the various rulers listed. Unlike the two earlier accounts that suggest the Wu royal house practiced father-to-son inheritance, the *Wudi ji* records a much more complex pattern of inheritance in the pre-Shoumeng era, suggesting that the fraternal succession seen in the kingdom of Wu's recorded history is not the aberration that some imperial-era scholars might have suggested.

The history of Wu really begins in the reign of Shoumeng, who according to ancient Chinese texts was the first ruler of Wu to declare himself king. The events of King Shoumeng's reign are extremely poorly recorded in early Chinese texts, and there are only three particularly important incidents that are described in any detail. The first incident was the king's generous welcome to a refugee from Chu, Shengong Wuchen 申公巫臣, who repaid him by taking charge of the Wu army and training the soldiers in chariot warfare and battle-tactics, branches of military science in which they had

Table 1. The king-lists of Wu. (In this table the recorded relationship of each individual to the previous ruler is given in brackets after his name).

	Shiji king-list for the kingdom of Wu	*Wu Yue chunqiu* king-list for the kingdom of Wu	*Wudi ji* king-list for the kingdom of Wu
1.	Taibo 太伯	Taibo 太伯	Taibo 泰伯
2.	Zhongyong 仲雍 (younger brother)	Zhongyong 仲雍 (younger brother)	Zhongyong 仲雍 (younger brother)
3.	Jijian 季簡 (son)	Jijian 季簡 (son)	—
4.	Shuda 叔達 (son)	Shuda 叔達 (son)	—
5.	Zhouzhang 周章 (son)	Zhouzhang 周章 (son)	Zhouyao 周繇
6.	Xiongsui 熊遂 (son)	Xiong 熊 (son) Sui 遂 (son)	Xiongsui 熊遂 (son)
7.	Kexiang 柯相 (son)	Kexiang 柯相 (son)	Zaozhen 早軫 (son)
8.	Qiangjiuyi 彊鳩夷 (son)	Qiangjiuyi 彊鳩夷 (son)	Kuanwu 款吾 (son)
9.	Yuqiaoyiwu 餘橋疑吾 (son)	Yuqiaoyiwu 餘喬疑吾 (son)	Yichu 夷處 (older brother)
10.	Kelu 柯盧 (son)	Kelu 柯盧 (son)	Biyu 壁羽 (nephew)
11.	Zhouyao 周繇 (son)	Zhouyao 周繇 (son)	Qiyuan 齊元 (son)
12.	Quyu 屈羽 (son)	Quyu 屈羽 (son)	Kelu 柯盧 (son)
13.	Yiwu 夷吾 (son)	Yiwu 夷吾 (son)	Kezhuan 柯轉 (younger brother)
14.	Qinchu 禽處 (son)	Qinchu 禽處 (son)	Jiaoyi 嬌夷 (son)
15.	Zhuan 轉 (son)	Zhuan 轉 (son)	Jiuyi 鳩夷 (nephew)
16.	Pogao 頗高 (son)	Pogao 頗高 (son)	Jiesi 界嗣 (son)
17.	Jubei 句卑 (son)	Jubi 句畢 (son)	—
18.	Quqi 去齊 (son)	Quqi 去齊 (son)	Zhiji 知濟 (son)
19.	Shoumeng 壽夢 (son)	Shoumeng 壽夢 (son)	—
20.	Zhufan 諸樊 (son)	Zhufan 諸樊 (son)	Zhufan 諸樊 (son)
21.	Yuji 餘祭 (younger brother)	Yuji 餘祭 (younger brother)	Yuji 餘濟 (younger brother)
22.	Yumei 餘眛 (younger brother)	Yumei 餘眛 (younger brother)	Yumei 餘眛 (younger brother)
23.	Liao 僚 (son)	Liao 僚 (son)	Liao 僚 (son)
24.	Helu 闔廬 (first cousin)	Helü 闔閭 (first cousin)	Guang 光 (first cousin)
25.	Fuchai 夫差 (son)	Fuchai 夫差 (son)	Fuchai 夫差 (son)

previously not been well versed. This allowed Wu to conduct a series of highly successful campaigns against Chu 楚, Chao 巢, and Xu 徐, culminating in their attacks against the states of Tan 郯 and Zhoulai 州來 in 584 BCE. As noted in the *Zuozhuan* 左傳 (Zuo's Tradition): "Wu took over all the Man and the Yi peoples who had previously surrendered to Chu, and from this point on they began to be important.

Wu opened up contact with the Upper States (Zhou confederacy)." 蠻夷屬於楚者, 吳盡取之, 是以始大. 通吳於上國.[8]

The second major incident in the reign of King Shoumeng to have come to the attention of chroniclers based in the Central States was the attendance of Wu at the interstate meeting held at Zhongli 鐘離 in 576 BCE, the first time the kingdom of Wu was recorded as having participated in such an event. On this occasion, representatives from the states of Lu, Qi, Song, Wei, Zheng, and Zhu met with "Wu"–whether this was King Shoumeng himself or a government official (other participating states sent ministers) is not clear. This meeting was followed by an invitation to participate in a further conference in Jize 雞澤 in 570 BCE, which King Shoumeng for unspecified reasons did not attend. Thus, King Shoumeng's first and last confirmed appearance on the international stage was at the major meeting held in 563 BCE with the rulers and representatives of many important states in the Zhou confederacy. On this occasion, the king of Wu met with Lord Xiang of Lu 魯襄公 (r. 572–542 BCE), Lord Dao of Jin 晉悼公 (r. 573–558 BCE), Lord Ping of Song 宋平公 (r. 575–532 BCE), Lord Xian of Wei 衛獻公 (r. 576–544 BCE), Lord Cheng of Cao 曹成公 (r. 577–555 BCE), and Lord Xiao of Qi 杞孝公 (r. 566–550 BCE) together with the rulers of Ju 莒, Zhu 邾, Teng 滕, Xue 薛, Xiaozhu 小邾, and a representative of the state of Qi. The terms in which this meeting is described in the *Chunqiu* 春秋 (Spring and Autumn Annals) caused subsequent imperial era commentators much trouble, for this text states that these illustrious individuals "met Wu at Zu" (*hui Wu yu Zu* 會吳于柤), an extremely unusual circumlocution that was also used in the context of the previous meeting at Zhongli.[9] This has traditionally been interpreted as meaning that these other states wished to enlist the kingdom of Wu (which was already at that time a growing power in the south) in their struggles against the kingdom of Chu.[10]

On the death of King Shoumeng, he was succeeded by three of his sons in turn: Kings Zhufan 吳王諸樊 (r. 560–548 BCE), Yuji 吳王餘祭 (r. 547–544 BCE), and Yumei of Wu 吳王餘昧 (r. 543–527 BCE).

8. *Zuozhuan*, p. 835 (Cheng 7).
9. *Chunqiu*, p. 973 (Xiang 10).
10. Cui, *Cuishi Chunqiu jingjie* 9.12b.

According to the *Zuozhuan*, King Shoumeng's death was attended by exceptional obsequies; although nothing explicit is said about the reasons for this, the mourning was apparently of a sufficiently unusual character to be mentioned in ancient Chinese accounts. This is one of the first records to suggest that the ruling house of Wu were already successfully asserting their claim to be descended from a senior branch of the Ji clan:

> In the autumn, the Unratified Monarch of Wu, Shoumeng, died, and an official mourning ceremony was held [by Duke Xiang of Lu] at the temple of [King Wen of] Zhou, as was ritually correct. When mourning a feudal lord, if he was a member of a different clan the ceremony should be held outside [the city walls], if a member of the same clan then at the ancestral temple, if of the same branch of the family then at the shrine [of their common] ancestor, and if of the same family then at the paternal shrine. Therefore [the duke of] Lu mourned for all members of the Ji clan at the ancestral temple, but he mourned the ruling houses of Xing, Fan, Jiang, Mao, Zha, and Ji at the temple to the Duke of Zhou.
> 秋, 吳子壽夢卒, 臨於周廟, 禮也. 凡諸侯之喪, 異姓臨於外, 同姓於宗廟, 同宗於祖廟, 同族於禰廟. 是故魯為諸姬, 臨於周廟; 為邢, 凡, 蔣, 茅, 胙, 祭, 臨於周公之廟.[11]

The death of King Shoumeng in the seventh lunar month of 561 BCE placed his family in a considerable quandary. Although King Shoumeng was initially succeeded by his oldest son, King Zhufan, when the new monarch completed the prescribed term of mourning for his father, he apparently wished to abdicate in favor of his youngest brother Prince Jizha.[12] However, the prince categorically refused

---

11. *Zuozhuan*, p. 996 (Xiang 13).

12. The dates of the prince's birth and death have not been recorded, but he made his first appearance in the *Zuozhuan* in 559 BCE, when the prescribed period of mourning for his father, King Shoumeng of Wu, had been completed. The final mention of the prince in this text was in 485 BCE, some seventy-four years later, when Prince Jizha presided over the negotiations which eventually led to the successful conclusion of a peace treaty, whereby an invading army from the kingdom of Chu agreed to withdraw from the state of Chen. Ibid., p. 1007 (Xiang 14); p. 1656 (Ai 10). According to this chronology, it is entirely possible that the prince lived into his late eighties or early nineties, assuming that he was not a small child at the time of his father's death. Some scholars have doubted the life-span accorded to the prince in the *Zuozhuan*, and suggest that Prince Jizha of Wu was not the

this offer, citing both a historical precedent and a moral obligation. Prince Jizha based his refusal to accept the throne on a belief in the efficacy of ritual. Once his older brother had been formally installed as the new king of Wu it was inappropriate to attempt to remove him, even though the new monarch himself wished to give up the throne. To remove a ritually sanctioned ruler would smack of usurpation, and in the eyes of the prince that would be an immoral thing to do. King Zhufan's expressed intentions suggest a wish to yield his official position to a better man, a virtuous act also attributed to his ancestors, Taibo and Zhongyong.[13] However, he was forestalled by Prince Jizha's insistence that he be allowed to preserve his integrity, as the prince made clear in the following speech recorded in the *Zuozhuan*:

> On the death of Lord Xuan of Cao (r. 594–578 BCE), the lords of the confederacy and the people of Cao disapproved of the [new] lord of Cao, and wanted to establish Zizang.[14] Zizang left Cao, so they could not make him [become the new earl], in order to establish the position of the lord of Cao. A gentleman would say: "He was able to preserve his moral integrity." You are the rightful heir, who would dare to rebel against you? It is against my principles to have the kingdom. Even though I lack ability, I wish to follow Zizang's example, so as not to lose my integrity.
> 曹宣公之卒也, 諸侯與曹人不義曹君, 將立子臧. 子臧去之, 遂弗爲也, 以成曹君. 君子曰: "能守節." 君義嗣也, 誰敢奸君? 有國非吾節也. 札雖不才, 願附於子臧, 以無失節.[15]

In order to make absolutely clear his determination never to become the king of Wu, Prince Jizha is said to have left home and taken

---

same person as Master Ji of Yanling, in which case the dates of the prince's birth and death must be entirely speculative. Although it may seem unlikely that a member of the Wu royal family in the late Bronze Age should succeed in living into his nineties, such a length of life is not unheard of among his near contemporaries. Zhang Weixiang, *Piling mingren yinianlu*, 1.1a.

13. Qian Mu, "Lun Chunqiu shidai ren de daode jingshen," p. 67.

14. When Lord Xuan of Cao died, he left two commoner brothers, Fuchu 負芻 and Xinshi 欣時, in addition to his own son. Fuchu killed Lord Xuan's son and heir, and established himself as the new ruler, Lord Cheng of Cao 曹成公 (r. 577–555 BCE). Xinshi, here called by his style name Zizang 子藏, refused to rebel against his brother's authority as described by Prince Jizha. *Zuozhuan*, p. 867 (Cheng 13), p. 873 (Cheng 15).

15. Ibid., pp. 1007–8 (Xiang 14).

to ploughing the fields. It would seem that this final detail was included to highlight the prince's firm refusal to undertake the usual duties of his rank. It also serves to emphasize the degree to which he had turned his back on a life of privilege. This story of the prince's giving up his rights to succession in order to preserve his moral principles is known in several versions from texts dating up until the end of the Han dynasty.[16] Over time, the number of occasions that the prince refused the throne seems to have increased: from the Han dynasty onwards, it became common to suggest that Prince Jizha first declined the throne during the reign of his father. The earliest account of this multiple renunciation can be found in the "Wu Taibo shijia" 吳太伯世家 (Hereditary House of Wu) chapter in the *Shiji*.[17] It was also subsequently recorded in other works, including the *Wu Yue chunqiu*, which in addition to describing Prince Jizha's refusal to accept the throne from his oldest brother also records his words when he objected to being installed as Crown Prince by his father: "[Prince] Jizha was wise, and [King] Shoumeng wanted to establish him [as Crown Prince] but Jizha refused, saying: 'Ritual is bound by ancient regulations, so surely you cannot set aside the principles of former kings for the sake of the personal affection between a father and son?' " 季札賢, 壽夢欲立之, 季札讓, 曰: "禮有舊制, 奈何廢前王之禮, 而行父子之私乎?[18] Once again, the prince is said to have expressed doubts concerning the morality of allowing personal affection—or indeed any other consideration—to interfere with the ritual principles established by the ancestors.

The Rule of King Zhufan and His Brothers

The first year of King Zhufan's reign saw the newly enthroned monarch take advantage of the death of King Gong of Chu 楚共王 (r. 590–560 BCE) to invade that kingdom. Countries often availed themselves of opportunities offered by an enemy's period of national mourning (in the hopes that a new and inexperienced enemy monarch would be

---

16. The same story is also found in the *Shiji* 31.1449–50; *Hanshu* 28B.1667; *Shuoyuan*, pp. 344–45 ("Zhigong" 至公).

17. *Shiji*, 31.1449.

18. *Wu Yue chunqiu*, p. 19 ("Wuwang Shoumeng zhuan" 吳王壽夢傳).

unable to deal effectively with the invasion). In this case the invaders had miscalculated: the battle of Yongpu 庸浦 ended with their army being defeated by Chu and Prince Dang of Wu 吳王子黨 being captured by the enemy.

This defeat, which took place in the autumn of 560 BCE, resulted in a massive interstate meeting being held the following year at Xiang 向 in the state of Jin, attended by representatives of fifteen states, to discuss how to deal with the increasing threat posed by Chu. In the autumn of the same year, 559 BCE, the Chu army invaded Wu under the command of General Zinang 子囊. Thanks to his arrogance and unwillingness to take the threat posed by the Wu army seriously, the kingdom of Chu suffered defeat in the battle of Gaozhou 皋舟, and Prince Yigu of Chu 楚王子宜穀 was taken prisoner. General Zinang died on the retreat—according to the *Lüshi chunqiu* 呂氏春秋 (Spring and Autumn Annals of Lü Buwei) he committed suicide by falling on his sword to demonstrate his loyalty to Chu.[19] No further conflict between the two countries was reported until 549 BCE, when Chu launched an unsuccessful invasion of the kingdom of Wu. In the winter of the following year, King Zhufan of Wu attacked Chu in return. During a truly disastrous assault on the gates of the city of Chao 巢, the king of Wu was shot dead by a sniper lying in ambush behind a low wall.

It is striking that nothing is recorded of the reign of King Zhufan of Wu, other than his campaigns against Chu. But records about his younger brother and heir, King Yuji, are even scarcer: the king seems to have been involved in neither diplomacy nor armed conflict with the powerful southern kingdom of Chu. Thus, nothing is recorded at all about Yuji's short reign, other than the circumstances of his murder (the king was stabbed to death by a Yue prisoner of war).[20] The

---

19. *Lüshi chunqiu*, pp. 1255–56 ("Gaoyi" 高義).

20. *Zuozhuan*, p. 1157 (Xiang 29). The same story is also found in the *Chunqiu shiyu* 春秋事語 (Tales of the Spring and Autumn Period) text excavated from Tomb 3 at Mawangdui 馬王堆. Mawangdui, *Mawangdui Hanmu boshu*, p. 18 ("Wu fa Yue zhang" 吳伐越章). The *Chunqiu Gongyang zhuan*, p. 265 (Xiang 29), henceforward *Gongyang zhuan*, contains a comment suggesting that King Yuji's death was his own fault, though it focuses criticism on his idiocy in approaching a prisoner of war without proper precautions, rather than recognizing the assassin as a Yue person

Wu Yue chunqiu is the only ancient text to describe any other events from the biography of King Yuji, but these are derived from a conflation of his life with that of his younger brother, King Yumei.[21]

The rule of King Yumei, the last of King Shoumeng's sons to sit on the throne of Wu, seems to have been marked not only by growing conflict with Chu, but also by military victories indicative of a competent and well-trained army. The problems with Chu first seem to have come to a head in the autumn of 538 BCE, when King Ling of Chu 楚靈王 (r. 540–529 BCE) led an invading army into Wu, together with his coalition partners Marquis Ling of Cai 蔡靈侯 (r. 542–530 BCE), Marquis Ai of Chen 陳哀侯 (r. 568–530 BCE), Baron Dao of Xu 許悼男 (r. 546–523 BCE), the rulers of the lesser states of Dun 頓, Hu 胡, and Shen 沈, and the Huai Yi 淮夷 people. According to the *Zuozhuan*, the Heir Apparent of Song and the earl of Zheng both originally intended to take part in this campaign, but they made their excuses and went home, leaving ministerial-level officials to represent them. The stated aim of this invasion was to kill Qing Feng 慶封, a refugee from Qi who had been taken in and given office by King Yuji. Though the Chu army and their allies were successful, they paid a price that winter when Wu attacked the Chu cities of Ji 棘, Yue 櫟, and Ma 麻.[22] Relations worsened the following year, when Chu captured Prince Jueyou of Wu 吳王子蹶由, the king's younger brother, with the intention of executing him and using his blood to anoint their wardrums. Only a wholesome fear of the likely reaction of the king of Wu to the news of his brother's ignominious end prevented this, and the prince was allowed to return home. No further military campaigns are reported, either by or against the kingdom of Wu, until 529 BCE, when Wu destroyed Zhoulai, formerly an independent state and later a Chu protectorate. When this was reported to King Ling of Chu, Prime Minister Ziqi 子旗 asked permission to launch a campaign against Wu. The Chu king responded: "I have not yet succored my people, nor have I sacrificed to the ghosts and spirits. I have made no defensive

---

and hence intrinsically inimicable to Wu. This line is discussed in Wu Enpei, *Gouwu wenhua de xianzai chanshi*, p. 173.

21. *Zuozhuan*, p. 1157 (Xiang 29); *Wu Yue chunqiu*, p. 20 ("Wuwang Shoumeng zhuan").

22. *Chunqiu*, p. 1245 (Zhao 4); *Zuozhuan*, p. 1255 (Zhao 4).

preparations, nor have I settled the country. Should I use the people's strength in this way I will be defeated, which is only just. For Zhoulai to belong to Wu is the same as if it belonged to Chu. You have only to wait [and we will recapture these lands]." 吾未撫民人, 未事鬼神. 未脩守備, 未定國家. 而用民力, 敗不可悔. 州來在吳, 猶在楚也.[23]

The reign of King Yumei is almost entirely overshadowed by one event that occurred towards the beginning of his rule and that came to be seen as a defining moment in the interaction between the kingdom of Wu and the states of the Zhou confederacy: this was the 544 BCE embassy to the state of Lu led by the king's younger brother, Prince Jizha. (This was followed in 542 BCE by Qu Huyong's 屈狐庸 embassy to the state of Jin, an event undocumented in the *Zuozhuan* other than the report of a speech made by Viscount Wen of Zhao 趙文子 concerning his appreciation of the exceptional abilities and moral character of Prince Jizha). Unlike his father, King Yumei seems to have trusted his diplomacy entirely to ambassadors; in fact, the only time he ever attempted to meet one of his peers was in the autumn of 529 BCE. A meeting was scheduled to be held that year between the king of Wu and the marquis of Jin at Liang 良 (in what is now Pei County 邳縣, Jiangsu Province) but due to unfavorable travel conditions King Yumei could not reach the chosen site and the meeting had to be abandoned.[24] King Yumei's failure to take an active role on the international stage allowed his younger brother, Prince Jizha, to become by far the most famous member of his generation of the Wu royal house, a man much appreciated in the Central States for his great respect for Zhou traditional culture.

Prince Jizha's Embassies

Prince Jizha of Wu was one of the great travellers of ancient China; his peregrinations are comparable in range to those of the Honorable Chonger of Jin 晉公子重耳, the future Lord Wen 晉文公

23. Ibid., p. 1361 (Zhao 13). The *Zuozhuan*, p. 1445 (Zhao 23), records a further campaign in which Wu attacked Zhoulai in the eighth year of the reign of King Liao (519 BCE), indicating that at some point in the interim Chu had indeed recaptured this much fought-over city.

24. Ibid., p. 1353 (Zhao 13).

(r. 636–628 BCE), who was perhaps the greatest of all ancient Chinese travellers.[25] However, in contrast to Lord Wen of Jin—who was constantly on the move to avoid assassins sent by his relatives, and who suffered great privations during his many years in exile—Prince Jizha traveled in style, as an occasional roving ambassador for the state of Wu. For at least thirty years, the prince made his journeys across the Zhou confederacy at the behest of a succession of Wu kings, making friends among powerful noble families. On these occasions he was an honored guest of the courts of the Central States; he met many of the most important ministers and aristocrats of the day; and he gained a considerable reputation as a wise and highly cultured man.

The 544 BCE embassy to Lu appears to have been the first occasion on which Wu attempted to open diplomatic relations with the states of the Zhou confederacy to the north. The brief reference given in the *Chunqiu* is the subject of a much longer story in the *Zuozhuan* that describes the prince's visits to the states of Lu, Qi, Zheng, Wei, and Jin. While in Lu, Prince Jizha listened to the songs of various states of the Zhou confederacy, and during his travels he met many of the leading ministers of the day: this enabled the prince to make a series of predictions about the destiny of nations and the fate of individuals. This story is of particular importance, because it describes the performance of the songs found in the *Shijing* 詩經 (Book of songs). This is the only description of an aesthetic judgment of a cultural event to survive from the pre-unification period.

According to the *Zuozhuan*, when Prince Jizha of Wu arrived in the state of Lu, in present day Shandong Province, he visited Shusun Muzi 叔孫穆子, a junior member of the ruling family who also held ministerial office. The prince took the opportunity to ask if he might hear the music of Zhou. In the concert that followed, the musicians played through, as far as can be ascertained, every part of the *Shijing* in the order found in the present text. It has been calculated that, playing at a moderate rate, it would take between ten and fifteen

25. The two most important accounts found in ancient texts of the future Lord Wen of Jin's travels are those in the *Zuozhuan*, pp. 405–11 (Xi 23); and *Guoyu*, pp. 337–65 ("Jinyu" 晉語 4).

hours to perform the whole of the *Shijing*: this has led some scholars to consider the story apocryphal.[26] It is, however, possible that either only a selection was played from each section, or that just part of each song was performed. The musicians began with the folk songs from the various states of the Zhou confederacy found in the "Guofeng" 國風 (Airs of the states), then proceeded to play through the "Xiaoya" 小雅 (Minor elegant songs) and the "Daya" 大雅 (Major elegant songs), before finishing with the "Song" 頌 (Hymns of praise). After each section was performed, the prince made suitable comments on the historical and cultural associations of the songs he had just heard, thus demonstrating his great wisdom and profound knowledge of Central States civilization. When the prince listened to the "Guofeng" section, as songs from various states in the Zhou confederacy were performed, his comments made it clear that he saw the artistic development of each state in the light of its relationship with the Zhou royal house.[27] The occasion ended with a display of traditional Zhou dancing. After the "Shaoxiao" 韶簫 (Shao pipes) dance—supposedly handed down from the sage-king Shun—was performed, Prince Jizha demanded that the performance should be stopped, on the grounds that he had no right to see any more. This famous critique of the traditional music and dance of the Zhou dynasty is so important that it deserves to be quoted in full:

> [Prince Jizha of Wu] requested that the music of Zhou be performed. [Shusun Muzi] ordered the musicians to sing the Zhounan and Shaonan [odes] for him. He said: "How beautiful! They have begun to found [the Zhou state] but it is still not yet complete. Nevertheless [in these songs] there is earnest exertion without any resentment." They sang [the odes of] Bei, Yong, and Wei for him, and he said: "How beautiful! How profound! [In these songs] there is concern but no distress. I have heard that the virtue of Kangshu and Lord Wu of Wei was like this, so these must be the airs of Wei!" They sang [the odes of] the Royal Domain for him, and he said: "How beautiful! They are thoughtful but not frightened, this must be [the music] from when Zhou moved to the east!" They sang [the odes of] Zheng for him, and he said: "How beautiful! However [this music] is already

26. DeWoskin, *A Song for One or Two*, p. 22.
27. Schaberg, *A Patterned Past*, p. 89.

overrefined and the people will not be able to endure this; surely [Zheng] will be the first to be destroyed!" They sang [the odes of] Qi for him, and he said: "How beautiful! How impressive! These are indeed great airs! They represent the eastern seas, so they must [reflect the character of] the Great Lord [of Qi]! This state still cannot be encompassed." They sang [the odes of] Bin for him, and he said: "How beautiful! How great! They are joyful without being excessive, they must be [the music] from when the Duke of Zhou moved to the east!" They sang [the odes of] Qin for him, and he said: "This is what is called a grand sound. That which can become grand will become great; and [Qin's] greatness is derived from their occupation of the site of the former Zhou [capital]." They sang [the odes of] Wei for him, and he said: "How beautiful! How harmonious! They are grand and yet delicate, as well as being deceptively easy. If they are assisted by virtue, [this state] will certainly produce an enlightened ruler." They sang [the odes of] Tang for him, and he said: "Their meaning is indeed profound! This must have come from the descendants of the Taotang lineage! Otherwise, how could their concern reach so far? Who other than the scion of a virtuous [line] is capable of this?" They sang [the odes of] Chen for him, and he said: "This state has no ruler, how can they continue for long?" From [the odes of] Kuai onwards he made no comment. They sang the "Lesser elegant songs" for him, and he said: "How beautiful! Their thoughts are loyal; and resentment is not expressed here, but surely [this music expresses] a decline in the virtue of Zhou? But there are still some [worthy] descendants of the former kings." They sang the "Greater elegant songs" for him, and he said: "How impressive! How resplendent! [These melodies] are contorted and yet their structure is straight; this must be the virtue of King Wen!" They sang the "Hymns" for him, and he said: "How perfect! They are straight but not rigid, flexible but not crooked, close but not intruding, distant but not alienating, moving but not licentious, repetitious but not boring, sad but not tragic, joyful but not inane, useful but not exhausting, extensive but not ostentatious, generous but not wasteful, accepting but not greedy, settled but not fixed; and [they] pervade [the realm] without becoming debased. The five notes [of the "Hymns"] are harmonious, the eight airs are finely balanced, the intervals are ordered and the parts are defined. This reflects the most flourishing virtue." He watched the dances "Ivory Pipes" and "Southern Flutes" and said: "How beautiful! And yet there is still a sense of regret [expressed in these dances]." He watched the dance "Great Wu" and said: "How beautiful! It is because Zhou was flourishing that it is like this!" He

> watched them dance "Shaohu" and said: "[This reflects] the magnanimity of the sage, but still there is a flaw in his virtue, the difficulties [experienced by] the sage." He watched the dance "Great Xia" and said: "How beautiful! [It reflects] labor without any assumption of power. Who other than Yu would be capable of this?" He watched the dance "Shao Pipes" and said: "This is the most perfect virtue. It is great! You could compare it to Heaven which shelters all [who live beneath it] or Earth that supports all [who walk upon it]. Even the most flourishing virtue can add nothing to this. Let the exhibition stop. If there is any further music, I shall not presume to ask [to hear it]."
> 請觀於周樂. 使工爲之歌周南召南, 曰: "美哉! 始基之矣, 猶未也, 然勤而不怨矣." 爲之歌邶, 鄘, 衛, 曰: "美哉! 淵乎! 憂而不困者也. 吾聞衛康叔武公之德如是, 是其衛風乎!" 爲之歌王, 曰: "美哉! 思而不懼, 其周之東乎!" 爲之歌鄭, 曰: "美哉! 其細已甚, 民弗堪也, 是其先亡乎!" 爲之歌齊, 曰: "美哉! 泱泱乎! 大風也哉! 表東海者, 其大公乎! 國未可量也." 爲之歌豳, 曰: "美哉! 蕩乎! 樂而不淫, 其周公之東乎!" 爲之歌秦, 曰: "此之謂夏聲, 夫能夏, 則大, 大之至乎其周之舊也." 爲之歌魏, 曰: "美哉! 渢渢乎! 大而婉, 險而易, 行以德輔, 此則明主也." 爲之歌唐, 曰: "思深哉! 其有陶唐氏之遺民乎! 不然, 何憂之遠也, 非令德之後, 誰能若是?" 爲之歌陳, 曰: "國無主, 其能久乎!" 自鄶以下, 無譏焉. 爲之歌小雅, 曰: "美哉! 思而不貳, 怨而不言，其周德之衰乎? 猶有先王之遺民焉." 爲之歌大雅, 曰: "廣哉! 熙熙乎! 曲而有直體, 其文王之德乎!" 爲之歌頌, 曰: "至矣哉! 直而不倨, 曲而不屈, 邇而不偪, 遠而不攜, 遷而不淫, 復而不厭, 哀而不愁, 樂而不荒, 用而不匱, 廣而不宣, 施而不費, 取而不貪, 處而不底, 行而不流. 五聲和, 八風平, 節有度, 守有序, 盛德之所同也." 見舞象箾南籥者, 曰: "美哉! 猶有憾." 見舞大武者, 曰: "美哉! 周之盛也, 其若此乎!" 見舞韶濩者, 曰: "聖人之弘也, 而猶有慚德, 聖人之難也." 見舞大夏者, 曰: "美哉! 勤而不德, 非禹其誰能脩之." 見舞韶箾者, 曰: 德至矣哉! 大矣, 如天之無不幬也, 如地之無不載也, 雖甚盛德, 其蔑以加於此矣. 觀止矣. 若有他樂, 吾不敢請已.[28]

This description of Prince Jizha listening to the traditional music of Zhou and of the states that made up the Zhou confederacy was to prove not only the earliest, but also one of the most important descriptions of an aesthetic judgment found in Chinese literature. At the end of the nineteenth century, the Jesuit missionary Albert Tschepe described the reaction of Chinese scholars to this famous piece, thus indicating the enduring popularity of this judgment

28. *Zuozhuan*, pp. 1161–65 (Xiang 29). The relationship between dance and music in the *Shijing* is considered in C. H. Wang, *From Ritual to Allegory*, pp. 34–35.

among the literati of his day: "C'est un des morceaux les plus célèbres de la haute litérature; tous les étudiantes disent le savoir par cœur; elle est d'une saveur si pure, si deliceuse, que tout vrai lettré en la récitant oublie de respirer, et laisse la salive couler de sa bouche entre'ouverte."[29] (This is one of the most famous passages in classical literature; all students are supposed to know it by heart, it has a flavor so pure, so delicious, that every true scholar forgets to breathe when reciting it, and lets the saliva roll out of his half-open mouth.) Over the years, this passage from the *Zuozhuan* was to prove of great importance in establishing the enduring legend of Prince Jizha of Wu. The prince was a scion of a southern state, an area which at that time was regarded at best as an exotic land of opportunity, and at worst as the home of barbarians.[30] The prince is portrayed in this section of the *Zuozhuan* as a cultured man, able to distinguish the finest nuances of meaning contained within the greatest music known to the Zhou. The acceptance of the prince as a man of exceptional education and sensibility by the custodians of Zhou culture (above and beyond his status as a member of a major branch of the Zhou royal family) was to form an important element in Prince Jizha's legend.

After leaving the state of Lu, Prince Jizha of Wu travelled to Qi (also in today's Shandong Province), and then on to Zheng and Wei (both in present day Henan Province), and to Jin (Shanxi Province). At every stage in his travels, he met the most senior ministers of the state. In Zheng the prince met the famous minister Zichan 子產, a junior member of the ruling house, and presented him with a white silk sash, while in Jin he met Zhao Wenzi, Han Xuanzi 韓宣子, and Wei Xianzi 魏獻子. These last three were all great ministers whose descendants would one day partition the state of Jin among themselves. At each stage of his travels, the prince advised and admonished the senior ministers that he met, predicting the rise of individuals or clans and prophesying the ruin of states. The respect accorded to the prince's pronouncements by everyone that he met is

29. Tschepe, *Histoire du Royaume de Ou*, p. 42.

30. The area covered by Wu and Yue continued to be seen as an area of economic opportunity long after the unification of China. Xiao Fan, "Qin Han shiqi Zhongguo dui nanfang de jingying," pp. 17–46.

evident from the following vignette, where his remonstrance produced a lasting reformation:

> On his way from Wei to Jin, [the prince] was going to spend the night in Qì (a city in Wei, the fief of Sun Wenzi 孫文子, a junior member of the Wei ruling family), when he heard the sound of bells there, and said: "How strange! I have heard it said that to be eloquent but without virtue is sure to lead one to execution. [Sun Wenzi] has offended against his ruler, and that is why he is here. [It seems that] this has not been enough of a fright, how can he be playing music? His position here is like that of the swallow that builds its nest on a tent. How is it possible to play music when the lord's [body] is lying in its coffin?" Then he left. [Sun] Wenzi heard about it and for the rest of his life he never so much as listened to a lute.
> 自衛如晉, 將宿於戚, 聞鍾聲焉, 曰: "異哉! 吾聞之也, 辯而不德, 必加於戮. 夫子獲罪於君以在此. 懼猶不足, 而又何樂? 夫子之在此也, 猶燕之巢於幕上. 君又在殯, 而可以樂乎?" 遂去之. 文子聞之, 終身不聽琴瑟.[31]

The feudal lord of Qì, Sun Wenzi, had been instrumental in forcing Lord Xian of Wei 衛獻公 (r. 576–559, and 546–544 BCE) into exile in Qi, and establishing his younger brother Qiu 秋 as Lord Shang of Wei 衛殤公 (r. 558–547 BCE). It was Lord Shang who had enfeoffed Sun Wenzi with the lands of Qì. When Lord Xian returned after twelve years in exile, he was backed by the military might of Jin. Although the other conspirators were executed, Sun Wenzi survived: perhaps due to the timely death of Lord Xian, who (as described in the passage quoted above) was lying in his coffin at the time of Prince Jizha's visit, but had not yet been buried. The prince's comments showed that he believed it inappropriate for one who had so narrowly escaped punishment to draw further attention to himself by playing music, presumably in celebration of his enemy's demise. (Sun Wenzi clearly agreed that he could ill-afford to attract attention in this way because he completely stopped listening to lute music.) This kind of story stresses the intellectual and moral authority of the prince, who was able to ascertain the minute signs of decadence at work within the state, from just the sound of a bell. This story is related to that of the prince listening to music in Lu, where he was able to discern clues about the rise and fall of states from their music. Prince Jizha's

---

31. *Zuozhuan*, pp. 1166–67 (Xiang 29).

were to be victorious he would have to go to war immediately, to avoid disaster. Such was his success that: "in one fell swoop Zigong brought civil war to Qi, destroyed Wu, advanced Jin, and strengthened Yue." 子貢一出, 亂齊, 破吳, 興晉, 彊越.[70]

At the beginning of this story, Confucius directs his disciple Zigong to save the state of Lu from attack, on the grounds that Lu is his home state and the site of his parents' graves. Zigong then proceeds to set out on a round of visits to kings and other rulers, sowing discord wherever he goes. At every step, Zigong is aided by his clever rhetoric and knowledge of the deepest hopes and fears of these powerful men. The story might be seen as one of unparalleled success, for the state of Lu is saved through Zigong's efforts. Alternatively, it could be seen as indicative of the growing barbarism of the age, because the safety of Lu is guaranteed only by embroiling half a dozen other states in conflict, thus causing untold suffering to their people. Although this story concerns Confucius and one of his most important disciples, it cannot be called "Confucian." This point is stressed when the "Chen Cheng Heng" chapter is described in the "Pianxu" 篇叙 (Concluding remarks) chapter of the *Yuejue shu*, which states that this text is the product of a time of decadence and decay, in which the proper order has been overturned and people act with great cruelty and barbarity to others: "When sons plot against their fathers, when subjects kill their rulers, this is something that Heaven and Earth will not bear. Evil is then indeed deep dyed, and therefore [the book] finishes with the "Chen Huan" chapter." 子謀父, 臣殺主, 天地所不容載. 惡之甚深, 故終於陳恒也.[71]

---

70. Ibid., p. 105 ("Pianxu"). This sentence seems to have been practically proverbial. In the "Chen Cheng Heng" chapter this phrase is given slightly differently: *Zigong yi chu, cun Lu, luan Qi, qiang Jin, ba Yue* 子貢一出, 存魯, 亂齊, 彊晉, 霸越 (In one fell swoop Zigong saved Lu, brought civil war to Qi, destroyed Wu, strengthened Jin, and made Yue hegemon). Ibid., p. 55. Zigong's success was commemorated in monuments such as the shrine to his memory erected beside Jiexihu 介西湖 in Zhejiang, recorded in the "Zigong shi Yue ci ji" 子貢使越祠記 (A record of the shrine dedicated to Zigong's embassy to Yue) by Zhang Shifei 章士斐, which is quoted in Jiao Hong, *Zhejiang tongzhi* 262.50b–52b.

71. *Yuejue shu*, p. 106 ("Pianxu").

The Death of Wu Zixu

In the wake of the conquest of Yue by Wu, King Fuchai of Wu became alienated from one of his most senior advisors, Wu Zixu. The outcome of the battle of Ailing, which Wu Zixu had so resolutely opposed, seems to have convinced King Fuchai that he was now a prisoner of his preconceived ideas. Likewise, the great success of Prime Minister Pi who had consistently promoted a campaign against Qi, ensured that the king would place enormous trust in his competence. The whole situation was made much worse by Wu Zixu's remarkable tactlessness, which seems on occasion to have verged on deliberate provocation. For example, Wu Zixu is said to have realized that his position at the Wu court was becoming increasingly parlous, so he sent his son to safety at the Qi court. The breathtaking insensitivity of such a move, which was guaranteed to enrage the king, and most likely convince him that Wu Zixu was a traitor, seems to have been part and parcel of his general arrogance and lack of concern for how his actions would be perceived by others. Given that Wu Zixu's exceptionally tiresome character seems to have prompted him to irritate King Fuchai at every possible opportunity, it is hardly surprising that, in the end, he could be saved neither by his privileged status as a key player in the events that brought King Helü to the throne nor by his long and distinguished service at the Wu court.

Ancient historical texts give different reasons for Wu Zixu's death; however, all versions agree that he was ordered to commit suicide by King Fuchai of Wu, who had become deeply frustrated and angered by his intransigence. The *Zuozhuan* links these events specifically to the outcome of the battle of Ailing. As described above, Wu Zixu was profoundly opposed to King Fuchai's plans to attack Qi and attempted to persuade the king of the necessity of destroying Yue instead.[72] In the wake of the battle of Ailing, Wu Zixu was sent as an envoy to Qi, and he took this opportunity to entrust his son to the

72. The role played by Wu Zixu's own tiresome character in his tragic falling-out with King Fuchai of Wu is rarely mentioned in traditional Chinese scholarship. An exception is Yao Nai, *Xibaoxuan quanji* Wen 文 1.3a. The position of a remonstrator was, however, generally agreed to be potentially extremely dangerous. Liu Zehua and Wang Liansheng, "Xian Qin shidai de jianyi lilun yu junzhu zhanzhi zhuyi."

protection of the Bao family, changing his surname to Wangsun 王孫. King Fuchai of Wu is said to have been so deeply enraged by such commerce with the enemy that he ordered Wu Zixu to commit suicide.[73] Wu Zixu's actions on this occasion—which by any standards might be said to smack of treason—seem to have been overlooked in many subsequent accounts of these events, particularly those that focus on his reputation as an outstandingly loyal minister. The *Zuozhuan* records that when King Fuchai had finally had enough, he sent the sword Zhulou 屬鏤 to Wu Zixu with orders to commit suicide. Wu Zixu's final words were traditionally regarded as good advice for the king of Wu, though in the circumstances it is hardly surprising that King Fuchai interpreted them as a curse: "Plant my tomb with catalpa trees, for catalpas can be used to make coffins. Wu will be destroyed! Within three years [Wu] will begin to become weak. What has waxed must then wane; this is the Way of Heaven." 樹吾墓檟, 檟可材也. 吳其亡乎! 三年, 其始弱矣, 盈必毀, 天之道也.[74]

With the passage of time, accounts of the death of Wu Zixu and the treatment of his corpse became more brutal, and, in these accounts, his last words more violent. According to the *Shiji* biography, Wu Zixu was ordered to commit suicide by the king after he had been slandered by his political enemies (following his resolute determination to remonstrate in favor of an attack on Yue). In this account, Wu Zixu uses his final words to warn King Fuchai of the coming attack by the kingdom of Yue, and announces his plan to "see" the arrival of the enemy army with his own eyes: "Then [Wu Zixu] told his major-domo: 'You must plant catalpa trees above my tomb, that they can be used to make coffins; and you must pull out my eyes and hang them above the eastern gate of Wu, that I can see the entry of the Yue invaders when they destroy Wu.' Then he cut his throat and died. The king of Wu was furious when he heard about this and had Zixu's body put into a leather sack and thrown into the

---

73. According to the *Yuejue shu*, pp. 37–38 ("Qingdi"), King Fuchai of Wu had already been convinced prior to the battle of Ailing that Wu Zixu was no longer loyal to him, thanks to the machinations of Feng Tong.

74. *Zuozhuan*, p. 1664 (Ai 11). *Jia* 檟 later became one of the Chinese names for the camellia. However, the *Shuowen jiezi*, p. 242 ("Mubu" 木部) glosses *jia* as *qiu* 楸 (catalpa).

river." 乃告其舍人曰: "必樹吾墓上以梓, 令可以爲器; 而抉吾眼縣吳東門之上, 以觀越寇之入滅吳也." 乃自剄死. 吳王聞之大怒, 乃取子胥尸盛以鴟夷革, 浮之江中.[75]

From both these accounts, it is clear that King Fuchai of Wu understood that Wu Zixu had crowned all his previous irritating actions with one final affront—cursing the kingdom with his dying breath. This explains the king's rage, and his determination to destroy Wu Zixu's body rather than allow it to be buried. Exactly the same motivations can be seen in the way that King Fuchai dealt with an earlier remonstrance, from an individual named Gongsun Sheng 公孫聖, which the king also interpreted as a curse upon himself and his kingdom. In this little-known story, King Fuchai of Wu is said to have been spending the night at Gusu Tower when he had a long, complex, and strange dream. When the king demanded that Prime Minister Pi interpret his dream for him, the Prime Minister explained each phase in the most flattering and auspicious terms, with particular reference to the forthcoming campaign against the kingdom of Qi. When a specialist dream-diviner, Gongsun Sheng, was called in, he announced that each phase of the dream presaged the terrible destruction of the kingdom of Wu at the hands of King Goujian, and the miserable death of the king himself. (What is a particularly remarkable feature of this divination account is that both interpretations of the king's dream were in fact correct; it is just that Prime Minister Pi's prognostication concerned the short term and those of Gongsun Sheng the longer-term destiny of the kingdom.) Faced with the appalling second analysis of his dream, King Fuchai ordered that Gongsun Sheng be beaten to death. Gongsun Sheng demanded that his body not be buried, but rather that it should be exposed upon a mountainside, so that he could become an echo: "The king of Wu ordered someone to expose him [Gongsun Sheng] on Qinyuhang Mountain, [with the words]: 'May tigers and wolves eat your flesh, may the wildfires roast your bones, so that when the east wind arrives it can stir your ashes. How will you ever be able to speak again?' Prime Minister Pi came forward and bowed twice. Then he said: 'These inauspicious words have been exorcised, the liar is dead, let us

---

75. *Shiji* 66.2180.

now pour a libation, for the time has arrived when you can set out [for Qi] with your army.'" 吳王使人提於秦餘杭之山: "虎狼食其肉, 野火燒其骨, 東風至, 飛揚汝灰. 汝更能爲聲哉!"太宰嚭前再拜. 曰: "逆言已滅, 讒諛已亡, 因酌行觴, 時可以行矣."[76]

Just as with the much more famous example of Wu Zixu, King Fuchai of Wu was determined to destroy the corpse of the man that he believed had cursed his kingdom. In the description of Wu Zixu's suicide found in the "Dexu" 德序 (Narratives of virtue) chapter of the *Yuejue shu*, a grandee of the kingdom of Wu, Feng Tong 逢同, was sent to preside over Wu Zixu's death, and on seeing him the old minister knew exactly why he had come. This Eastern Han dynasty account is significant for its incorporation of supernatural elements, which reflect the importance of Wu Zixu in the imperial era as a major southern water deity: the god in charge of the Hangzhou tidal bore. Although the *Shiji* records that Wu Zixu's body was collected from the river and that a shrine was erected to his memory, the *Yuejue shu* account is the earliest surviving text to invest Wu Zixu's spirit with any special powers:

> Angrily [Wu Zixu] said: "His majesty does not care for supportive and helpful ministers, but he does trust the words of those pigs! This is why my life will be cut short! Hang my head somewhere high, that I may see the Yue army enter Wu and his majesty captured alive! Throw my body into a deep river, that this may be an end on it!" The king of Wu heard about this, and he thought [his last words] were intended as a curse, as a result of which he was even angrier with Wu Zixu. The king of Wu ordered someone to throw [his body] into the mouth of the great river.
>
> Some brave knights collected [the body], at which it made a noise.
> It emitted a shout of rage into the air, with the energy of a stampeding horse.
> Terrifying everything in its path, the homing spirit [returned to] the ocean.
> Wandering between [river and ocean], its cry is always to be heard.

---

76. *Yuejue shu*, p. 75 ("Ji Wuwang zhanmeng"). A number of other later versions of this story are known; see for example Yan Zhitui, *Huanyuan ji*, pp. 141–42. The same story is quoted verbatim in the important early Buddhist text, the *Fayuan zhulin* 法苑珠林 (The Forest of Pearls in the Garden of the Dharma), compiled by a monk named Daoshi 道世 in 668. Daoshi, *Fayuan zhulin*, p. 490.

洩言曰:"王不親輔弼之臣而親眾豕之言, 是吾命短也. 高置吾頭, 必見越人入吳也, 我王親爲禽哉! 捐我深江, 則亦已矣!" 胥死之後, 吳王聞, 以爲妖言, 甚咎子胥. 王使人捐於大江口.

勇士執之, 乃有遺響.
發憤馳騰, 氣若奔馬.
威凌萬物, 歸神大海.
彷彿之間, 音兆常在.[77]

Wu Zixu's role in Chinese traditional culture has been much studied but is a topic that has still not been exhausted. There have been discussions of his role as a paragon of loyalty, as a water deity in command of the Hangzhou tidal bore, as a key personage portrayed on the pictorial mirrors that formed a major part of the metal-working tradition in the Suzhou and Shaoxing regions in early imperial China, and as the subject of an important local cult.[78] Likewise, there has been interesting research on his historical significance as the single best recorded individual of the Spring and Autumn period, and as the focus of many important literary works, of which perhaps the single best-known is the *Wu Zixu bianwen* 伍子胥變文 (Wu Zixu transformation text) discovered at Dunhuang.[79] Hence, the death of Wu Zixu was merely the beginning of a legend, which quickly grew to such proportions that it dominates discussion of events that occurred in the kingdoms of Wu and Yue in the last years of the Spring and Autumn period. This has caused a serious distortion of the historical record, in that the major conflicts that took place at the heart of the government of the kingdom of Wu in the wake of such important events as the conquest of Yue and the defeat of Qi at the battle of

77. *Yuejue shu*, p. 102 ("Dexu").

78. Wu Zixu was often represented in tomb art, identified as a loyal minister. Such representations apparently drew their power from the fact that he died a violent and unjust death. Thompson, "Confucian Paragon or Popular Deity?" p. 21. For the association of the Duanwu 端午 festival with Wu Zixu; see Lu Kanru, "Wuyue wuri"; Ouyang Feiyun, "Duanwu wuri kao." The development of the cult of Wu Zixu is discussed in Johnson, "Epic and History in Early China"; Rudolph, "The *Shih Chi* Biography of Wu Tzu-hsü."

79. Wang Zhongmin et al., *Dunhuang bianwen ji*, pp. 1–28. The *Wu Zixu bianwen* has been translated at least twice into English; Waley, *Ballads and Stories from Tun-huang*, pp. 25–52; Mair, *Popular Narratives from Tun-huang*, pp. 123–65.

Ailing, are reduced to a squabble between Prime Minister Pi and Wu Zixu. Likewise, the dominance of Wu Zixu in the records ensures that in some texts he is presented as the chief mourner of King Helü of Wu and as the architect of the campaign to punish King Goujian. This results in a serious denigration of the role of King Fuchai of Wu in these events, to the point where the king may be perceived as simply a puppet in the hands of his manipulative ministers. This does great disservice to one of the most interesting rulers of the Spring and Autumn period—a man who endured exceptional vicissitudes during his lifetime, and whose actions, at the beginning of the Warring States era, were vital in determining the direction of Chinese history (not only in the ancient south, but also in the Central States as a whole).

Much of what occurred in the final stages of the conflict between Wu and Yue seems to depend upon the characters of the main protagonists involved. A less subtle and intelligent man than King Goujian of Yue would have been executed in the wake of his surrender at Kuaiji, or would have aroused suspicion at some point during his long and patient battle to rebuild his kingdom and rearm for the long war of conquest against Wu. Had Wu launched a preemptive attack on Yue, that state would not have been able to withstand it. Much of King Fuchai's historical importance also rests on his character: he was a man of some magnanimity, in that he settled for humiliating King Goujian rather than demanding his death, and he put up for years with the constant fighting between Wu Zixu and Prime Minister Pi. We can only speculate how differently events would have turned out if Wu Zixu had been conciliating and persuasive in his dealings with King Fuchai, rather than displaying an obnoxious and pig-headed obstinacy.

Prime Minister Pi, whether motivated by bribery or feelings of humanity, achieved a peace treaty with Yue of a kind reminiscent of an earlier and less brutal age. In the "Qingdi" 請糴 (Asking for food aid) chapter of the *Yuejue shu*, there is an account of a lengthy exchange between Wu Zixu and Prime Minister Pi, which supposedly occurred at court in the presence of King Fuchai of Wu. The topic under debate was whether or not Wu should send food aid to Yue (then in the grip of a terrible famine). This discussion is interesting, for although the arguments advanced by Wu Zixu against sending food aid (and in favor of completely destroying the kingdom of Yue) are similar to those recorded elsewhere, the position taken by Prime Minister Pi in this debate is unique and worthy of more attention than it has received to date:

> The king of Wu said: "I forced Yue to surrender, I took over their altars of soil and grain, Goujian became my vassal and attended to the royal stables for me, walking in front of my horses. Every feudal lord has heard of this. Now Yue is in the grip of famine, and I will give them grain; I know that Goujian will certainly not dare [to turn against me]." Shen Xu (i.e., Wu Zixu) said: "[The king of] Yue was innocent, and your majesty brought disaster upon him. Now not only have you not killed him, you are listening to what he says; this is going against [the will of] Heaven. Loyal remonstrators have been alienated, while flatterers have become your friends. Now when a fox catches a pheasant, the fox pretends to be weak and the pheasant believes him.[80] If even beasts and insects can deceive in order to achieve their ends, how much worse are human beings?" . . . Prime Minister Pi, who had been standing to one side, then replied: "Was not King Wu the vassal of Zhou? He led the feudal lords to kill his lord. Even though he was victorious, how can this be called just?" Shen Xu said: "King Wu did this and still established a good reputation." Prime Minister Pi said: "[A vassal] may murder his ruler and thus become famous, but most people would not care to do such a thing."
> 吳王曰: "我卑服越, 有其社稷. 句踐既服爲臣, 爲我駕舍, 卻行馬前, 諸侯莫不聞知. 今以越之饑, 吾與之食, 我知句踐必不敢." 申胥曰: "越無罪, 吾君王急之, 不遂絶其命, 又聽其言, 此天之所反也. 忠諫者逆, 而諛諫者反親. 今狐雉之戲也, 狐體卑而雉懼之. 夫獸虫尚以詐相就，而況於人乎?" . . . 太宰嚭從旁對曰: "武王非紂臣耶? 率諸侯以殺其君. 雖勝, 可謂義乎?" 申胥曰: "武王則已成名矣." 太宰嚭曰: "親僇主成名, 弗忍行."[81]

The terms in which the debate is framed (one side seeing a constant, harsh, and brutal struggle in which no quarter can be shown

80. It is possible that the text is corrupt here, or it may be that the analogy was never properly thought out. The *Wu Yue chunqiu*, p. 149 ("Goujian yinmou waizhuan" 勾踐陰謀外傳) completes the thought: *gu hu de qi zhi er zhi bi si* 故虎得其志而雉必死 (In the end the fox achieves his ambition and the pheasant is dead).

81. *Yuejue shu*, p. 36 ("Qingdi").

to a defeated enemy, and the other side carefully weighing moral obligation) reflects not just the different personalities of the two protagonists, but also the changing political climate of the age. Prime Minister Pi cannot conceive of circumstances in which an intelligent and moral man would choose to betray his ruler and turn his back on his moral obligations, and in this he harks back to the core values of the Zhou confederacy, which were then already under threat from the growing militarization and brutality of the times. Wu Zixu, on the other hand, can imagine no situation in which an intelligent man would not take ruthless advantage of any opportunities offered, and hence he may be said to represent the trends of thought that would bring such violence to ancient China in the Warring States era. This account, unique among references to the conflict between Wu Zixu and Prime Minister Pi, records their ideological differences and thus elevates their disagreement from one merely between an obstinate and disagreeable, though loyal, minister and an unctuous and corrupt Prime Minister. Here for once both parties are allowed to hold reasonable points of view.

The Beauty Xi Shi

Xi Shi 西施, the beauty from Yue who was King Fuchai's favorite, is accorded a major role in the downfall of Wu in Chinese popular culture. However, her name is hardly recorded at all in the ancient Chinese texts that are the main source of information for the biography of the last king of Wu. The earliest surviving reference to her is thought to be given in the *Mozi* 墨子, where she is described as a woman of outstanding beauty who suffered a terrible fate, though this does not mention any association with either the kingdom of Wu or Yue:

> As for the five weapons, the sharpest are the first to be broken. As for the five blades, the most finely ground are the first to be worn out. The sweetest wells quickly run dry; the highest-quality timber is soon felled. The most numinous turtles are the first to be put to the fire; the most sacred snakes are the first to be sacrificed. Bi Gan was cut to pieces because he was so upright; Meng Ben was killed because he was so brave, Xi Shi was drowned because she was so beautiful; and Wu Qi was torn apart because he was so successful.

今有五錐, 此其銛, 銛者必先挫. 有五刀, 此其錯, 錯者必先靡. 是以甘井近竭, 招木近伐. 靈龜近灼, 神蛇近暴. 是故比干之殪, 其抗也, 孟賁之殺, 其勇也, 西施之沈, 其美也, 吳起之裂, 其事也.[82]

The first text to give any details of Xi Shi's life is the "Jidi zhuan" chapter of the *Yuejue shu*, and the "Jiushu" 九術 (Nine Methods) chapter from the same text. The former records that she came from Zhuluoshan 苧蘿山 (Kudzu vine mountain); modern archaeology has confirmed that this place (now known as Xishishan 西施山) was indeed the location of a major Yue settlement at that time.[83] She is said to have been trained at the Meirengong 美人宮 (Palace for beautiful women), for King Goujian apparently originally feared that she was too rustic to appeal to the refined tastes of King Fuchai of Wu.[84] As described in the "Jiushu" chapter, she and her companion, Zheng Dan 鄭旦—a figure largely neglected in later popular traditions concerning these events—then travelled to Wu, where her job was to seduce the king into neglecting his duties. Much the same story is given in the *Wu Yue chunqiu*, though this text adds the detail that Xi Shi and Zheng Dan's studies lasted for three years before they were adjudged ready to appeal to the king.[85] Xi Shi is presented in these Eastern Han dynasty texts as a silent witness to history, and is accorded neither a personality nor a point of view; what is important is *who* she is. Xi Shi is so beautiful that King Fuchai will love her and favor her; at the same time, she is a loyal subject of King Goujian of Yue, so that the king of Wu cannot invade Yue without causing her great distress.

Later imperial era accounts added a few details to Xi Shi's biography. Of these, the most important is that rather than dying at the time of Wu's fall, Xi Shi instead ran away with one of King Goujian's most important advisors, Fan Li, to live a long and happy life roaming around Lake Tai. This version seems to have been derived from an Eastern Han dynasty tradition; however, the earliest extant reference to this tale is found in a Tang dynasty gazetteer, the *Wudi ji*.[86] These events were later amplified to form a narrative structure that frames

82. *Mozi*, pp. 4–5 ("Qinshi" 親士).
83. Zhou Yuebao and Luo Haidi, *Shaoxing wenwu*, pp. 3–4.
84. *Yuejue shu*, p. 59 ("Jidi zhuan").
85. Ibid., p. 84 ("Jiushu"); *Wu Yue chunqiu*, p. 147 ("Goujian yinmou waizhuan").
86. Lu Guangwei, *Wudi ji*, p. 47.

Xi Shi's experiences in Wu and gives them meaning. She and Fan Li met and fell in love, but they set aside their hopes of marriage and a life together out of motives of loyalty and patriotism. Xi Shi then travelled to Wu, where King Fuchai fell madly in love with her and gratified her every whim. Then, after the fall of Wu, the couple met again and went off together. This interpretation provides Xi Shi not only with honorable reasons for her acceptance of a sexual relationship with the king of Wu, but also elevates her status from the completely passive figure recorded in early accounts of these events to a woman capable of great self-sacrifice, who endures enormous unhappiness for the sake of her king and her country. In this version of events, Xi Shi is rewarded for all her travails: both in the happy ending finally granted to her and Fan Li (in direct contradiction with the older traditions that both lovers suffered miserable deaths), and in her lasting position as one of the great beauties of ancient China and the heroine of one of the most famous love stories in traditional Chinese culture.

As a result of his association with the legendary beauty Xi Shi, King Fuchai of Wu is conventionally portrayed as a highly romantic figure. Regardless of the intrusion of the character of Fan Li, the last king of Wu is described as a great lover, determined to make his beloved Xi Shi happy. This perception endures to the present day and informs many interpretations of both historical events and excavated artifacts. For example, in 1995, the Shanghai Museum purchased a bronze ewer from a dealer in Hong Kong. The inscription on this vessel, now known as the "Wuwang Fuchai *he*" 吳王夫差盉, reads: "King Fuchai of the [Gou]wu smelted metal to make this vessel for his woman. Auspicious. 敔王夫差吳金鑄女子之器, 吉.[87]

It is natural that this object has been interpreted as a gift of love from King Fuchai of Wu to Xi Shi, particularly as no name is mentioned for the woman, making it highly unlikely that it was made for an individual of high status. The fact that King Fuchai became so besotted with Xi Shi provided a highly conventional explanation for the downfall of his kingdom, which could thus be attributed to personal moral failings on the part of the last king, without having to seek complex geopolitical and social explanations for Wu's sudden

87. Chen Peifen, *Xia Shang Zhou qingtongqi yanjiu*, p. 194.

and catastrophic collapse. But the king's attachment for Xi Shi also created a legendary love affair with great appeal to the literati imagination. Without this romantic tale, the cultural legacy of the ancient kingdom of Wu would be much poorer.

The Covenant at Huangchi

In the wake of his victory at the battle of Ailing, King Fuchai of Wu clearly hoped to make his influence felt across the Central States. This was the motivation behind his participation in the covenant at Huangchi, through which he hoped to establish himself not only as the monarch of the preeminent military power of the age, but also as the accepted representative of the most ancient branch of the Zhou royal house (as a descendant of an uncle of the founder of the dynasty). Had this latter claim achieved general acceptance, King Fuchai of Wu would have been in a position to assert moral authority over his peers as well, because he would then have ranked second only to the Zhou king in the hierarchy of the ruling Ji clan. However, King Fuchai's claims were hotly disputed, particularly by the marquis of Jin, who claimed the hereditary role of *mengzhu* 盟主 (Head of covenants) for the states of the Zhou confederacy, and who was himself descended from a younger brother of King Cheng of Zhou 周成王 (r. 1042–1006 BCE).[88]

The covenant at Huangchi in 482 BCE represents the apogée of Wu's power in the late Spring and Autumn period and is the most famous of the multistate covenants held under the auspices of King Fuchai of Wu. The Wu monarch had participated in a series of more or less successful covenants in previous years, involving a number of states of the Zhou confederacy. Earlier, in the spring of 487 BCE, the forces of Wu attacked the state of Lu. The duke of Lu, unable to resist militarily, agreed to a covenant with the invaders, and after this agreement was reached, the invaders went home. This is the first recorded covenant between the states of Wu and Lu, and seems to have been entirely typical of late Spring and Autumn era covenants, in

88. Wang Guowei, *Yin-Zhou zhidu lun*, p. 11; Gao Shiqi, *Zuozhuan jishi benmo*, p. 351; Rosen, "Changing Conceptions of the hegemon in Pre-Chin China," pp. 105–106.

that one party was under duress.[89] Four years later, in 483 BCE, the king of Wu again attempted to force the duke of Lu to make a covenant between their two states at Tuogao 橐皋. According to the *Zuozhuan*, the duke of Lu was unwilling to renew his covenant with the king of Wu, and sent Zigong to explain matters to Wu: "A covenant is the way in which you affirm your good faith, therefore you use your heart to determine it, you use jade and silk to honor it, you use words to make it binding, and you use the bright spirits to preserve it. My lord believes that it is enough to make a covenant, for it cannot be changed. If it can be changed, then what would be the advantage, even if you covenanted daily? Now you say: 'We must warm our relationship,' but if it can be warmed, then it can also cool." 盟, 所以周信也, 故心以制之, 玉帛以奉之, 言以結之, 明神以要之. 寡君以爲苟有盟焉, 弗可改也已. 若猶可改, 日盟何益? 今吾子曰: "必尋盟,"若可尋也, 亦可寒也.[90]

In this case, no covenant was made. The failure of this covenant in Lu was followed by a tense encounter between the king of Wu and the marquis of Wei at Yun 鄖. This was actually a multistate covenant, involving Marquis Chu of Wei 衛出公 (r. 492–481, 476–456 BCE), Duke Ai of Lu 魯哀公 (r. 494–468 BCE), and a representative from the state of Song named Huang Yuan 皇瑗. There were clearly significant underlying tensions at this meeting that are not explained in any surviving text, for although the duke of Lu agreed to participate in the covenant with Wei and Song, he refused to do so with Wu. The *Zuozhuan* again suggests that there was some element of coercion involved, for Wu forces at one point held the marquis of Wei hostage. The account in the *Zuozhuan* then goes on to describe the reaction of the marquis of Wei to his meeting with people from the southern state of Wu after his return to his own state. This account is particularly interesting because it stressed the foreignness of the Wu people, at a time when King Fuchai was attempting to assert their close links with the states of the Zhou confederacy and their blood-ties to the Zhou royal family: "The marquis of Wei went home, and

89. *Zuozhuan*, pp. 1647–50 (Ai 8). The use of force to create covenants is considered in Liu, *Origins of Chinese Law*, pp. 159–63; Zhou Bokan, "Chunqiu huimeng yu bazhu zhengzhi de jichu," pp. 47–48.

90. *Zuozhuan*, p. 1671 (Ai 12).

he imitated the barbarian [Wu] speech. Zizhi (a grandson of Lord Ling of Wei) was then still young, and he said: 'Our lord will not escape [from disaster], and he will die among the barbarians! He was held captive by them, but still enjoyed their way of speaking; he will certainly follow them.'" 衛侯歸, 效夷言. 子之尚幼, 曰: "君必不免, 其死於夷乎! 執焉而又說其言, 從之固矣."[91]

The following year, King Fuchai was the key protagonist at a meeting at Huangchi that was attended by a number of heads of state (including Duke Ai of Lu, Marquis Ding of Jin 晋定公 [r. 511–475 BCE], and Lord Ping of Dan 單平公). This last was a grandee from the Royal Domain of the Zhou kings, who attended this meeting as the representative of King Jing of Zhou 周敬王 (r. 519–476 BCE). There are numerous ancient Chinese texts that mention this meeting, and make it clear that at the time Wu was regarded as an exceptionally powerful state. This is evident even though all surviving references to the events at Huangchi postdate the collapse of the kingdom of Wu and the death of King Fuchai—and hence might be supposed to reflect the king's terrible fall. The account of these events given in the *Huainanzi* 淮南子 is typical, in that it stresses the military might that the king of Wu possessed and the fear that he induced in his neighbors. King Fuchai of Wu was able to command enormous resources, and although some ancient Chinese texts were clearly written with the benefit of hindsight, references of this kind no doubt reflect the reaction in the Central States to the early part of his rule, when it must have seemed that the Wu military machine was well-nigh unstoppable: "King Fuchai of Wu had two thousand *li* of territory; he commanded seven hundred thousand troops; to the south he fought with Yue and pinned them down at Kuaiji [Mountain]; to the north he did battle with Qi and crushed them at Ailing; to the west he met with the lord of Jin and captured him at Huangchi." 吳王夫差地方二千里, 帶甲七十萬, 南與越戰, 棲之會稽, 北與齊戰, 破之艾陵, 西遇晉公, 禽之黃池.[92]

---

91. *Zuozhuan*, p. 1672 (Ai 12). According to Du Yu's 杜預 (222–85) commentary on the *Zuozhuan*, Marquis Chu of Wei died in Yue. Du Yu, *Chunqiu jingzhuan jijie*, p. 1786, n. 16.

92. *Huainanzi*, p. 1097 ("Binglue xun" 兵略訓).

The events at Huangchi were of particular significance for King Fuchai of Wu, because he intended to use the occasion to assert his authority, not just over those members of the Zhou confederacy whose armies he had already defeated in battle, but over the whole of the Central States. The account of the covenant at Huangchi given in the *Shiji* chapter on the hereditary house of Wu suggests that King Fuchai's aim in participating in this meeting was to preserve the security of the Zhou royal house (*quan Zhoushi* 全周室), but this is a unique interpretation of these events and it is not supported by other ancient texts.[93] There were two particularly problematic issues discussed at this conference: the identity of the Wu royal family and the status of the Wu kings as hegemons. King Fuchai of Wu wished to be recognized both as the head of the most senior branch of the Ji royal house and also as a direct linear descendant of Zhongyong (the younger brother of Wu Taibo, the founder of the kingdom of Wu, and the uncle of King Wen of Zhou). Opinion among modern scholars remains divided as to whether the Wu royal family members were, in fact, members of the Ji clan; there may well have been an ethnic division between the royal family and its subjects, the Gouwu people. However, regardless of the facts, King Fuchai intended to use the meeting at Huangchi to publicize his new-found status as the head of the most senior branch of the Ji clan.

The second issue of particular importance that was discussed at Huangchi was the relative status of the ruling house of Jin, represented by Marquis Ding of Jin, and the kings of Wu. From the time of Chonger, Lord Wen of Jin, the marquises of Jin had held the title of *mengzhu* as a hereditary perquisite, and this position enabled them to assert considerable influence over other states in the Zhou confederacy. Lord Wen of Jin also held the title of Ba 霸 or "Hegemon," an extraordinary title granted to particularly important members of the aristocracy by the Zhou king in reward for exceptional service to the crown. Although later marquises of Jin did not hold the title hegemon, possession of the hereditary office, Head of Covenants, did ensure that they had an exceptionally important position within the

93. *Shiji* 31.1473.

aristocratic hierarchy of the Central States.[94] At the meeting at Huangchi, King Fuchai of Wu was determined to assert his superiority over the marquis of Jin, though accounts vary as to whether he was successful or not.[95] There is evidence that King Fuchai of Wu prepared extremely carefully for the meeting at Huangchi. In the 1920s a pair of bronze vessels, the "Wuganwang *hu*" 禺邗王壺, were discovered in Hui County 輝縣, Hunan Province, with inscriptions stating that they were made on the occasion of the meeting at Huangchi. These bronzes are, to date, the only objects discovered that can clearly be related to the events at Huangchi, and hence they form a particularly important resource. The inscriptions on the vessels read: "The king of Wugan (i.e., Wu) was at Huangchi, and on behalf of Zhao Meng [I] accepted a present of bronze from the king, and used it to make these sacrificial vessels." 禺 [吳] 邗王于黄池, 爲趙孟介邗王之惕金, 以爲祠器.[96] The individual named in this inscription, Zhao Meng, has been identified as Zhao Yang 趙鞅, whose participation in the covenant at Huangchi was mentioned in both the *Zuozhuan* and *Guoyu*.[97] Zhao Yang represented the Jin side at the covenant meeting, and when the argument between the two states was at its worst, he offered to fight a duel with Sima Yin 司馬寅 to decide the issue of precedence.

Unlike all other extant accounts of these events, the *Yuejue shu* suggests that Huangchi in 482 BCE was not just the site of a covenant between the major states of the Zhou confederacy, but also the occa-

---

94. Tong Shuye, *Chunqiu shi*, pp. 164–81; Yoshimoto Michimasa, "Shunjū Shinha kō."

95. The *Zuozhuan*, p. 1677 (Ai 13), says that Jin in the end was able to retain their position at the most important branch of the Ji ruling house. The *Guoyu*, p. 615 ("Wuyu"), and the *Gongyang zhuan*, p. 351 (Ai 13), both state that it was Wu that was victorious in this debate and that ultimately presided over the covenant. Rao Hengjiu, in his study of the covenant at Huangchi, suggests that the "Wuyu" chapter of the *Guoyu* represents a more reliable account of these events than the *Zuozhuan*. Rao Hengjiu, "Wu Jin Huangchi zhengmeng shishi kaobian," pp. 127–28.

96. Dong Chuping and Jin Yongping, *Wu Yue wenhua zhi*, p. 84; Dong Chuping, *Wu Yue Xu Shu jinwen jishi*, pp. 76–78. Slightly different transcriptions of this vessel text have been made by Chinese scholars, but they all agree that the name of the person who made the vessel does not appear in the inscription. Wen Yiduo, "Yuhanwang hu ba," pp. 609–10; Yang Shuda, *Jiweiju jinwen shuo*, p. 192.

97. *Zuozhuan*, p. 1677 (Ai 13); *Guoyu*, p. 612 ("Wuyu").

sion of a battle that Wu lost.[98] According to the "Ji Wuwang zhanmeng" 記吳王占夢 (Record of the divination of the king of Wu's dream) chapter, the armies of Jin and Wu fought a terrible battle at this time. Although there is no explicit reference to Huangchi in this text, it is nevertheless evident that this is where the battle between Jin and Wu occurred, given that it is said to have taken place in the immediate aftermath of Wu's great victory at Ailing: "[King Fuchai of Wu] stationed his troops [in Qi] for three months without removing them, and then they marched on to attack Jin. Jin knew that their weapons were used up, and their armor was worn out, and that their supplies of grain and other food had all been exhausted; so [Jin] raised an army and attacked [Wu] and inflicted a terrible defeat on the Wu army. They crossed the river, which ran red with blood and was full of floating bodies, too many to be counted." 師兵三月不去, 過伐晉. 晉知其兵革之罷倦, 糧食盡索, 興師擊之, 大敗吳師. 涉江, 流血浮尸者, 不可勝數.[99]

In the light of subsequent events, the covenant at Huangchi has taken on a significance that its participants could not have anticipated. When King Fuchai of Wu travelled northwards to attend this meeting, he was expecting that this great occasion would set the seal on his position as the most powerful ruler in the Chinese world. In fact, the covenant at Huangchi, instead of marking the start of a glorious new phase in the history of the kingdom of Wu, turned out to be the beginning of the end. Before the covenant had even begun, just after King Fuchai had arrived, the news came that King Goujian of Yue had invaded Wu, defeated their armies in a series of battles, and captured the Crown Prince alive. By any standards, this was disastrous news, and according to the *Zuozhuan*, King Fuchai reacted to it with explosive anger: "On Dinghai day, [the Yue army] entered Wu.

---

98. The *Guoyu*, p. 608 ("Wuyu"), account suggests that there was some use of military might at the covenant at Huangchi, but attributes this to the kingdom of Wu. The different versions of events given in various ancient Chinese texts are considered in Zhang Yiren, *Guoyu Zuozhuan lunji*, p. 75.

99. *Yuejue shu*, p. 75 ("Ji Wuwang zhanmeng"). This account clearly links the victory of the king of Wu's army at Ailing with the subsequent events at Huangchi; however, such a connection has been rejected by some scholars. Liang Yusheng, *Shiji zhiyi*, p. 842.

The people of Wu reported their defeat to the king. The king was so enraged by the news that he personally slit the throats of seven men in his tent." 丁亥, 入吳. 吳人告敗于王. 王惡其聞也, 自剄七人於幕下.[100]

It is now extremely difficult to get any accurate impression of the meeting at Huangchi, because of the historical events that overshadow it. In texts such as the *Zuozhuan* and *Shiji*, references to the covenant are intercut with accounts of the invasion, giving the events at Huangchi a significance that was not obvious to the participants at the time. This is particularly true, given that the king of Wu was presumably not anxious to blaze his domestic troubles abroad, and so it is not clear if the other parties to the Huangchi covenant even knew about the invasion of Wu or the capture of the Crown Prince. Likewise, although King Fuchai was clearly aware that his army had been defeated, it is not known how many details he was given about these events. Evidently the king did not believe that the defeat was serious enough to warrant calling off his participation in the covenant and returning home to deal with the crisis. Because of the way historical texts present the events of 482 BCE, King Fuchai subsequently gained a reputation as an ineffectual monarch, who fussed about issues of precedent while his people were dying.

The Death of King Fuchai of Wu

From a historical perspective, the reign of King Fuchai of Wu can be considered as an arc. After the shock of his father's death in the wake of the battle of Zuili, King Fuchai returned to Wu to build up his armies. He subsequently attacked Yue and won a great victory at the battle of Fujiao (which ended with the surrender of King Goujian of Yue). From there King Fuchai went from strength to strength, to the point where he could almost be seen as suffering from hubris. His victories against other powerful states such as Qi, his diplomatic triumphs, his forcing of many feudal lords to recognize him as the most senior member of the Ji clan after the Zhou king: all these things served to make King Fuchai probably the single most important man in the Chinese world at that time. Had he died before the

100. *Zuozhuan*, p. 1677 (Ai 13).

summer of 482 BCE, he would doubtless have been regarded as the very greatest of all the kings of Wu. However, during the course of his ascent, he had made crucial mistakes. He had failed to fully integrate the lands of Yue into his kingdom: as a result, the Yue people were not assimilated into Wu and King Goujian of Yue retained much of his power. In the end, King Fuchai of Wu was defeated in battle, captured alive by the forces of Yue, and died by his own hand.

Accounts of the death of King Fuchai of Wu are found in many ancient texts. The suicide of the last king of Wu, after his country was conquered and his life ruined, was an enormously dramatic event, and the many texts that incorporated references to this story made full use of its possibilities. Given that the dominant tradition in Chinese historical writing was to extract a moral lesson from events, the death of King Fuchai of Wu is often presented as a parable. The precise nature of his failings vary from text to text; for some writers, his greatest crime was his extravagance, for he exhausted the resources of his people on numerous grandiose building projects, a subject that will be discussed in more detail in a later chapter. For others, it was the king's failure to appreciate the loyal advice of Wu Zixu, and his determination to employ the corrupt Prime Minister Pi in the teeth of all remonstrances on the subject. Alternatively, King Fuchai of Wu was blamed by some for launching protracted campaigns against the Central States and for ignoring the danger posed by Yue. However, whatever the precise nature of the failures ascribed to King Fuchai, his capture and ignominious death were always presented as a just punishment. In fact, it appears that the death of the last king of Wu came after a series of campaigns in which his army had been defeated time and again, which culminated in the siege and fall of his capital. The trauma of these long drawn-out campaigns of attrition is minimized in many ancient texts, which usually simply give the years of the successive invasions, or which so telescope history that the collapse of Wu seems to follow immediately after the covenant at Huangchi.

All accounts of the collapse of the kingdom of Wu and the death of its last monarch agree on two points: that King Fuchai was captured alive by the Yue army after his capital was taken and that he subsequently committed suicide. The earliest account of the death of King Fuchai, one of the simplest, is found in the *Zuozhuan*: "In the winter, in the eleventh month, on Dingmao day, Yue destroyed Wu. They [the Yue conquerers] asked permission to send the king of Wu to live in east of Yong, but he refused and said: 'I am old, how can I serve a ruler?' He then hanged himself. The people of Yue took the body home." 冬, 十一月, 丁卯, 越滅吳. 請使吳王居甬東, 辭曰: "孤老矣, 焉能事君?" 乃縊. 越人以歸.[101]

In the *Zuozhuan*, and indeed in a number of other later accounts of these events, King Fuchai is said to have been given the option of going into exile. Yong has been identified as the ancient name for the township of Dinghai 定海, the largest settlement on the Zhoushan 周山 archipelago in Zhejiang Province. The reason given for King Fuchai's suicide (in this text and in a number of other early versions of the story) was his refusal to accept the loss of his kingdom and the degradation in his status. King Fuchai had ruled for twenty-three years when he was captured by the Yue army; he may have believed himself unable to endure even a fraction of the humiliation that he had earlier meted out to King Goujian. (Also, King Goujian had himself only been on the throne for three years when he surrendered to the Wu army at Kuaiji, and was thus presumably a much younger man.) The *Zuozhuan* account is interesting, for it makes clear that it was King Fuchai's own decision to commit suicide and that he was in no way forced to do so by his captors. The magnanimity displayed by the Yue side in this account mirrors that of King Fuchai following the earlier Yue surrender at Kuaiji: that is, neither ruler wished to take the life of the enemy monarch. This makes the position articulated by Prime Minister Pi (quoted above) concerning the moral obligations of the king of Yue vis-à-vis King Fuchai seem entirely reasonable. In the long run, Wu Zixu's advocacy of brutal decisiveness would have saved the king of Wu's life, but it would also definitely have marked a downward trend in the conduct of relations between Wu and Yue, which at this time were apparently still managed on a comparatively civilized plane.

The account of the capture and death of King Fuchai of Wu given in the *Guoyu* is related to that found in the *Zuozhuan*, but is significantly more detailed. The "Wuyu" chapter of the *Guoyu* includes a

101. *Zuozhuan*, 1719 (Ai 22).

short discussion between King Goujian of Yue and King Fuchai of Wu concerning the possibility of exile for the latter. The *Guoyu* account is particularly significant in terms of the later developments of this story because it contains the first account of King Fuchai's last words, which speak of his shame at not having realized the wisdom of Wu Zixu's loyal remonstrance:

> [King Goujian of Yue] then sent someone to tell the king of Wu: "Heaven has given Wu to Yue and I do not dare to refuse it. Since no man lives forever, there is no need for your majesty to die! People are but lodgers on the earth; who knows for how long? I will send your majesty to live east of Yongju, together with three hundred men and [three hundred] women, so that your majesty may be comfortable and live out your years." [King] Fuchai refused: "Heaven has sent down disaster on the kingdom of Wu, as was only a matter of time. However instead of [punishing] me alone, [Heaven] has destroyed the ancestral temples and the altars of soil and grain. Yue now already has the people and the lands of Wu, [so] how can I face the world!" When Fuchai was about to die, he sent someone to report to [Wu] Zixu: "If the dead have no awareness then it is all over, but if they are aware then how can I bear to see you?" Then he killed himself.
> 因使人告于吳王曰: "天以吳賜越, 孤不敢不受. 以民生之不長, 王其無死! 民生于地上, 寓也; 其與幾何? 寡人其達王于甬句東, 夫婦三百, 唯王所安, 以沒王年." 夫差辭曰: "天既降禍于吳國, 不在前後. 當孤之身, 實失宗廟社稷. 凡吳土地人民, 越既有之矣, 孤何以視于天下!" 夫差將死, 使人説于子胥曰: "使死者無知, 則已矣, 若其有知, 君何面目以見員也!" 遂自殺.[102]

This passage from the *Guoyu* provides a reflection of the dominant discourse in Warring States era and Han dynasty discussions of King Goujian's surrender at Kuaiji. When King Fuchai refused to incorporate the lands of Yue into his own kingdom and preserved the life of King Goujian, he signed his own death warrant. These events are never presented in early Chinese texts as an example of the virtue of *ren* 仁 or kindness, and King Fuchai is never praised for his magnanimity and generosity in saving the life of King Goujian of Yue and eventually allowing the king to return to his kingdom to administer it as a protectorate of Wu. Instead, by failing to destroy

---

102. *Guoyu*, pp. 627–28 ("Wuyu").

Yue and sparing its king, King Fuchai of Wu is frequently said to have disobeyed the will of Heaven. Heaven intended Yue to be destroyed; the signs were all there, but King Fuchai did not read them. By his actions, King Fuchai not only protected his greatest enemy but also ensured that the fate he had prevented from falling on Yue would rebound upon his own people. To the authors of many early Chinese texts this was perhaps King Fuchai's greatest failing: his disobedience to the will of Heaven destroyed not just himself but the whole kingdom of Wu.

The *Guoyu* version of events also gives an added poignancy to the death of King Fuchai by having him realize, too late, the importance of Wu Zixu's advice. In the traditional portrayal of King Fuchai of Wu found in early Chinese texts, a crucial part of the characterization is that he is seen flanked by his two most important ministers, the corrupt and venal Prime Minister Pi, and the loyal and outspoken Wu Zixu. The *Guoyu* intensifies the moral lesson provided by the circumstances of King Fuchai's death by having him realize at the very last moment that Wu Zixu was right. The same theme is found in the *Shiji* account of the last king of Wu's death, which is apparently an amalgam of the *Zuozhuan* and *Guoyu* versions. In the *Shiji*, King Goujian of Yue offers to allow King Fuchai to go into exile, but he refuses for two reasons: because he could not learn to serve another monarch in his old age, and because he regretted his treatment of Wu Zixu.[103] The only major variation introduced in the *Shiji* account is that King Fuchai of Wu is said to have committed suicide by cutting his own throat. This detail gives a "southern flavor" to the account, for there are numerous stories in ancient Chinese texts of southern sword craft, and many important historical figures from the pre-unification southern kingdoms of Wu and Yue are said to have killed themselves in this way. These individuals famously include not only Wu Zixu himself, but also later Grandee Zhong 大夫種 from the kingdom of Yue.[104] The introduction of this detail into the *Shiji* account seems to be intended to bring the death of King Fuchai into

103. *Shiji* 31.1475.

104. The *Wu Yue chunqiu*, p. 176 ("Goujian fa Wu waizhuan" 勾踐伐吳外傳), states that Grandee Zhong died by cutting his throat with the sword Zhulou just like Wu Zixu.

line with the portrayal of the suicide of these other key figures in the history of the conflict between the kingdoms of Wu and Yue.

The *Yuejue shu* contains several different accounts of the death of King Fuchai of Wu that are worth considering in some detail, for they contain important variations on the tale of his suicide following his capture by the Yue army. Of particular interest is the fact that all versions of this tale that are found in the *Yuejue shu* suggest that King Fuchai of Wu was effectively forced to commit suicide, and that he did so in order to avoid execution by the victorious Yue army. One account is found in the "Qingdi" chapter, a text very closely related to the "Wuyu" chapter of the *Guoyu*.[105] This story gives a detailed account of the pressure exerted on King Fuchai following his capture to ensure that he would commit suicide:

> [Wu] instigated battle [five times] and lost five times, and the king of Yue could not bear [the carnage] any longer, and wanted to leave them in peace.[106] Fan Li said: "How is it possible that what your majesty has planned for in the palace you are prepared to lose on the battlefield? We have been plotting this for seven years, and now you want to give it up. Your majesty cannot leave them in peace, for then Wu will soon conquer us [instead]." The king of Yue said: "I agree." After a siege of three months, Wu collapsed. Prime Minister Pi then ran away, and the king of Wu led his officials and advisors to break

---

105. Zhou Shengchun, "*Yuejue shu* chengshu niandai ji zuozhe xintan," p. 126, suggests that the "Qingdi" chapter dates to the late Warring States era. Dating of the "Wuyu" is an extremely vexed question. Zhang Jun, "*Guoyu* chengbian xinzheng," p. 80, suggests that this chapter was compiled after the Chu conquest of Yue in ca. 330 BCE, and that the two chapters of the "Yueyu" were produced subsequently in the same context. Although most modern scholars have followed the lead of Wei Juxian 衛聚賢 (1898–1989) in regarding the "Wuyu" as the earliest of the *Guoyu* chapters dealing with these ancient southern kingdoms (dated to 431–384 BCE), followed by "Yueyu shang" (after 384 BCE) and "Yueyu xia" (after 314 BCE), this has been contradicted by Li Xueqin 李學勤, who regards the "Yueyu xia" as an early Warring States era text, written within a very few years of the conquest of Wu in 473 BCE. Li Xueqin, "Fan Li sixiang yu boshu *Huangdi shu*," pp. 98–99. This position is also supported by Rao Hengjiu, "*Guoyu* 'Yueyu xia' zuoshi xianyi." At present, the only consensus seems to be that all the chapters of the *Guoyu* were written during the Warring States era and hence predate the *Shiji*.

106. The character *fu* 父 (father, or elder) has been translated as *fan* 反 (to be defeated) in accordance with the commentary by Zhang Zongxiang, *Yuejue shu jiaozhu* 5.6a.

through [the forces surrounding them]. Yue went in pursuit, and when they reached [Qin]yuhang Mountains, they captured Fuchai alive and killed Prime Minister Pi. The king of Yue told Fan Li to kill the king of Wu, but Li said: "I do not dare to kill a ruler." The king said: "Castrate him." Fan Li said: "I would not dare to castrate a ruler." The king of Yue then spoke to the king of Wu himself: "Once upon a time Heaven gave Yue to Wu, but you did not take it.[107] You killed Shen Xu, even though he was innocent. You promoted a host of flatterers and toadies, and killed loyal and trustworthy knights. These are your three great mistakes, which have brought you to destruction. Do you understand this?" The king of Wu said: "I do." The king of Yue then gave him a sword with which to kill himself. A few days later the king of Wu committed suicide. The king of Yue buried him at the mountains of Beiyou.

謝戰者五父. 越王不忍, 而欲許之. 范蠡曰: "君王圖之廊廟, 失之中野, 可乎? 謀之七年, 須臾棄之. 王勿許, 吳易兼也." 越王曰: "諾." 居軍三月, 吳自罷. 太宰嚭遂亡, 吳王率其有祿與賢良遯而去. 越追之, 至餘杭山, 禽夫差, 殺太宰嚭. 越王謂范蠡: "殺吳王." 蠡曰: "臣不敢殺主." 王曰: "刑之." 范蠡曰: "臣不敢刑主." 越王親謂吳王曰: "昔者上蒼以越賜吳, 吳不受也. 夫申胥無罪, 殺之. 進讒諛容身之徒, 殺忠信之士. 大過者三, 以至滅亡, 子知之乎?" 吳王曰: "知之." 越王與之劍, 使自圖之. 吳王乃旬日而自殺也. 越王葬於卑猶之山.[108]

This passage is related to the traditional discourse on these events, in that the collapse of the kingdom of Wu and the capture of King Fuchai are described as part of the vengeance meted out by Heaven, in retribution for Wu's failure to destroy Yue. It is striking that, in many accounts of the prolonged conflict between Wu and Yue, neither side particularly wished to inflict suffering on the other, and yet this sensitivity is always portrayed as a weakness rather than a sign of kindness or humanity. This account of the death of King Fuchai is also interesting because it includes two protagonists: King Goujian of Yue himself, and Fan Li. In this version, King Goujian demands King Fuchai's death, and his majesty's suicide apparently saves him from a much worse fate at the hands of his enemies. In another chapter of the

---

107. In the parallel passage in the *Guoyu*, p. 627 ("Wuyu"), this is the only reason mentioned for King Fuchai's defeat. King Goujian reproaches him for having failed to conquer Yue fully when he had the chance, arguing that this turned Wu's luck.

108. *Yuejue shu*, p. 39 ("Qingdi").

Yuejue shu—the "Jice kao" 紀策考 (Stratagems for the age), which includes a lengthy account of the endgame of the protracted conflict between Wu and Yue—the blame for King Fuchai's death is placed solely on Fan Li. This version of the story, which focuses particularly on the figure of Wu Zixu, describes how King Fuchai's failure to appreciate the loyal advice of his ministers brought about his downfall and death: "Fuchai was arrogant and extravagant and he abandoned the siege of Yue. When Zixu remonstrated, he was executed. Prime Minister Pi flattered him [the king] and in the end he destroyed Wu. When Fuchai was in dire straits, he asked permission to be degraded to the status of a commoner, but Fan Li would not agree to this, and so he died at the Five Lakes." 雖夫差驕奢, 釋越之圍. 子胥諫而誅. 宰嚭諛心, 卒以亡吳. 夫差窮困, 請爲匹夫. 范蠡不許, 滅於五湖.[109]

This version of events places the entire burden of responsibility for the death of King Fuchai upon Fan Li. Although it is true that the king of Wu was guilty of many mistakes, he was nevertheless prepared to accept the humiliation of abject surrender, just as King Goujian of Yue had been willing to do so some two decades earlier. It was Fan Li who forced the final tragedy by refusing to accept King Fuchai's terms of surrender. Just as in some accounts of events in Wu, King Fuchai's role is downplayed in favor of Wu Zixu; in this story, Fan Li completely overshadows King Goujian of Yue.

The third and final account of the death of King Fuchai of Wu given in the *Yuejue shu* is found in the chapter entitled "Ji Wuwang zhanmeng," and this version is highly distinctive for a number of reasons. First, as mentioned above, this chapter is one of the few to suggest that what occurred at Huangchi was not a covenant, but a battle between Wu and Jin. However, in this chapter the events at Huangchi in 482 BCE, when Wu and Jin fought a battle, are conflated with those of 473 BCE, when the Yue army approached the capital city of Wu, in the final days of Wu's existence as an independent kingdom. This account records how the remnants of the Wu army turned towards the Qinyuhang Mountains, where they ate their last meal and drank from water holes that they had dug in the ground. It was at this point that King Fuchai remembered that these mountains were the place where

109. Ibid., p. 44 ("Jice kao").

he had ordered his men to dump the body of Gongsun Sheng—the man he had earlier tortured to death for an inauspicious dream prognostication. It was while the king of Wu was musing on the accuracy of Gongsun Sheng's prophecy that the Yue army, led by King Goujian himself, turned up and captured him. This capture is followed by an enumeration of the king of Wu's faults, apparently as part of the process of *sui* 誶 (reading out a list of crimes committed by a person who has been ordered to commit suicide).[110] In ancient China, this was customarily part of the humiliation suffered by a disgraced individual, and this process is described here as prelude to the king's suicide:

> Fan Li enumerated the king of Wu's [mistakes]: "Your majesty made five mistakes; do you know what they are? You killed your loyal vassals Wu Zixu and Gongsun Sheng. Xu was farsighted, loyal and trustworthy, but you killed him and threw [his body] into the river. Sheng spoke out and told you the truth, but you executed him and that achieved nothing. Were they not two major mistakes? [The people of] Qi had committed no crime [against you], and yet you repeatedly attacked them.[111] You made sure that the ghosts and spirits were not fed with blood, and that the altars of soil and grain were destroyed or overgrown; that fathers and sons were separated, and that brothers were forced apart. Was that not your third major mistake? Even though King Goujian of Yue lives on the eastern edge of the world, he was still crowned as a king. He had done nothing to you, but your majesty still insisted on making him cut grass to feed horses, like a slave. Was that not your fourth major mistake? Prime Minister Pi flattered and fawned over you while backstabbing everyone else. He has destroyed the royal house, yet you listened to him and employed him. Was that not your fifth major mistake?" The king of Wu said: "Today my fate is in your hands." . . . The king of Yue told the king of Wu: "There is no-one in the world that can live for a thousand years, death comes to us all." Fan Li held a drum with his left hand, and seized the drumstick with his right hand and struck it. He chanted:
>
> "Heaven above is equally blue,
> Whether you live or whether you die.
> Is it necessary for our soldiers

110. Liu, *Origins of Chinese Law*, p. 219.

111. The character *kong* 空 (empty) in this line may indicate a missing character. Liu Jianguo, *Xinyi Yuejue shu*, p. 244, suggests inserting the character *fan* 反 (instead) at this point.

> To break your neck?
> To crack your bones?
> Is this not the worst option of all?"
>
> The king of Wu said: "I accept my fate. Cover my two eyes with a three-inch strip of silk. If there is consciousness after death, I would be ashamed to see Wu Zixu and Gongsun Sheng. Even if there is no consciousness [after death], I am still humiliated before the living." The king of Yue cut his seal-cord and used it to cover his eyes.[112] Then [the king of Wu] fell on his sword and died.
> 范蠡數吳王曰: "王有過者五, 寧知之乎? 殺忠臣伍子胥, 公孫聖. 胥爲人先知, 忠信, 中斷之入江; 聖正言直諫, 身死無功. 此非大過者二乎? 夫齊無罪, 空復伐之, 使鬼神不血食, 社稷廢蕪, 父子離散, 兄弟異居. 此非大過者三乎? 夫越王句踐, 雖東僻, 亦得繫於天皇之位, 無罪, 而王恒使其芻莖秩馬, 比於奴虜. 此非大過者四乎? 太宰嚭讒諛佞諂, 斷絶王世, 聽而用之. 此非大過者五乎?" 越王謂吳王曰: "世無千歲之人, 死一耳." 范蠡左手持鼓, 右手操枹而鼓之, 曰: "上天蒼蒼, 若存若亡. 何須軍士, 斷子之頸, 挫子之骸, 不亦繆乎?" 吳王曰: "聞命矣. 以三寸之帛, 幎吾兩目, 使死者有知, 吾慚見伍子胥、公孫聖. 以爲無知, 吾恥生."越王則解綬以幎其目, 遂伏劍而死.[113]

This account follows the tradition established in other chapters of the *Yuejue shu*—that is, that the main protagonists on the Yue side during these events were King Goujian himself and his advisor Fan Li. Again, as with the other *Yuejue shu* accounts, this version makes it clear that King Fuchai of Wu was, in fact, forced to commit suicide. Because this is not something mentioned within the mainstream textual tradition of historical and philosophical works found in the Central States, it may represent a local story handed down within the Wu-Yue region. This last version of the death of King Fuchai of Wu also makes literal the motif of blindness that appears in texts from

---

112. There is no evidence that the kings of Yue used seals in the late Spring and Autumn, early Warring States era. Where seals have been excavated from ancient southern sites, such as from the tomb of Zhao Mo, the king of Nanyue 南越王趙眜 (r. 137–122 BCE), they belonged to members of an ethnic Chinese family ruling a Bai Yue kingdom. Mai Yinghao and Wang Wenjian, *Lingnan zhi guang*, pp. 22, 27. The curious detail that King Fuchai of Wu covered his eyes, or according to some records his face, before he killed himself is mentioned in a number of Han dynasty texts, as can be seen for example in the *Shuoyuan*, p. 231 ("Zhengjian" 正諫).

113. *Yuejue shu*, pp. 75–76 ("Ji Wuwang zhanmeng").

the "Wuyu" onwards.[114] Here, the last words of King Fuchai stress his inability to face the shade of Wu Zixu; the king's blindness to his minister's merits during his lifetime is mirrored by the king's insistence on covering his face before he died. It is not entirely clear why King Goujian of Yue was so determined that King Fuchai should commit suicide, particularly since the king of Yue apparently had no objection to enduring the odium of ordering Fan Li to execute his defeated enemy. However, this may follow contemporary norms. Studies of attitudes to violent death among the ruling elite of the Spring and Autumn of the Zhou confederacy suggest that members of the aristocracy showed considerable unwillingness to spill the blood of their peers: in such situations a captured nobleman would be put under great pressure to commit suicide. The reason for this unwillingness is not entirely clear, and is largely unelucidated by ancient texts, though it is thought to derive from a belief in vengeful ghosts; certainly it was considered unlucky to have such blood on one's hands.[115] Nevertheless, it is far from clear that such attitudes would also have pertained in the kingdom of Yue, particularly given that, at this time, contact with the states of the Zhou confederacy was still fairly minimal and there is little concrete historical evidence of cultural assimilation.

The *Wu Yue chunqiu* and the *Yuejue shu* both refer to the final disposal of King Fuchai of Wu's body after his suicide. According to the *Wu Yue chunqiu* King Fuchai was buried by the victorious forces of Yue, and this account, though brief, states specifically that the last king of Wu was interred according to the rites (*Yuewang nai zang Wuwang yi li* 越王乃葬吳王以禮).[116] This reference to the performance of proper rituals at the burial has been cited by scholars who argue that the kings of Wu participated in the mainstream culture of the states of the Zhou confederacy, even though the funeral was actually carried out by the Yue army.[117] The tomb of King Fuchai of Wu is mentioned in the "Ji Wudi zhuan" (記吳地傳 Record of the lands of Wu) chapter of the *Yuejue shu*. This extremely brief account has been much

114. Durrant, *The Cloudy Mirror*, p. 95.
115. Li Zongtong, "Chunqiu shidai shehui de biandong," p. 301.
116. *Wu Yue chunqiu*, p. 96 ("Fuchai neizhuan" 夫差內傳).
117. Xiao Menglong, "Dui Wuguo lishi wenhua de xin tansuo," p. 22.

discussed in the wake of the discovery of the tomb of King Yunchang of Yue, which was apparently created by a technique similar to that used for King Fuchai's tomb (that is, earth was piled up on top of a wooden structure containing the king's body): "The tomb of Fuchai [is located at] Beiyouwei, west of Yougao [neighborhood]. Each of the king of Yue's spearmen brought a basketful of earth to bury him. "夫差冢, 在猶亭西卑猶位. 越王候干戈人一累土以葬之.[118]

In spite of these apparently detailed directions, the tomb of the last king of Wu has never been found. In 1986, some two hundred and four jades (out of a total of 402 objects) were excavated at Yanshan 嚴山 outside Suzhou and scholars have argued that this represents an offering pit of objects associated with the tomb of King Fuchai of Wu. These jades are of exceptionally high quality; some have been described as heirlooms of the royal house, for they are Neolithic objects associated with the ancient Liangzhu 良渚 culture. Also, the discovery of this cache has frequently been cited by scholars as verification of the *Wu Yue chunqiu*'s description of the burial of King Fuchai of Wu, suggesting that he was indeed interred by his enemies with every sign of respect and care.[119] However, in the absence of further discoveries, this cache of jades remains an isolated and mysterious memento of the collapse of the kingdom of Wu and the suicide of the last king.

In many ways, the decline and fall of the kingdom of Wu during the reign of King Fuchai has posed enormous problems of interpretation for subsequent historians and scholars. How could such a wealthy and powerful kingdom crumble to nothing within such

---

118. *Yuejue shu*, p. 15 ("Ji Wudi"). A detailed description of the construction of the tomb of King Yunchang of Yue can be found in Zhejiangsheng, "Zhejiang Shaoxing Yinshan damu fajue jianbao"; Lin Huadong and Liang Zhiming, "Yuewang Yunchang lingmu kao." This translation follows the *Suoyin* commentary to the *Shiji*, in interpreting Yougao as the name of a neighborhood, and Beiyouwei as the name of a place. *Shiji* 31.1475, n. 2 and 3.

119. Qian Gonglin, "Guanyu Wuxian Lingyanshan Chunqiu yuqi jiaozang xingzhi de zai renshi," pp. 13–17. An alternative explanation is that these precious objects were buried here for safety at the time of the final attack by Yue. Yin Zhiqiang and Ding Bangdiao, *Dongzhou Wu Chu yuqi*, pp. 46–47. The role of the Liangzhu jades discovered in this cache is considered in Yao Qinde and Gong Jinyuan, *Wuguo wangshi yuqi*, p. 9.

a short space of time? The brilliant strategy of King Goujian of Yue, and his determination to crush Wu in revenge for the humiliation he had suffered after his own defeat at Kuaiji was certainly one factor, but it does not serve to completely explain the catastrophic collapse suffered by Wu in the last years of the Spring and Autumn period. This has led to the development of many explanations which purport to account for this disaster, and which usually concentrate on King Fuchai's failure to listen to the wise if unpalatable advice of Wu Zixu, on the king's immoderate trust in the corrupt Prime Minister Pi, and also on his personal extravagance and arrogance. These factors are discussed in the "Feigong" 非攻 (Against attacks) chapter of the *Mozi*, where there is an attempt to explain King Fuchai's terrible fate as the result of that monarch's failure to understand and appreciate his people, in spite of his famous military successes. Thus, the last king of Wu's loss of his kingdom is presented as entirely the outcome of his own personal shortcomings:

> When it comes to Fuchai, to the north he attacked Qi, and stationed himself above the Wen River, and did battle at Ailing, where he inflicted a terrible defeat on the people of Qi and captured Taishan; to the east he attacked Yue, crossing the three rivers and the five lakes, and besieged Kuaiji. Every kingdom inhabited by the nine eastern barbarian people submitted to his authority. However when he turned homewards he did not succor the orphans [of these campaigns], nor did he house his veterans; but instead, believing himself to be invincible, he gloated over his success, praised his own cleverness and neglected the instruction [of his people]. Then he built the tower at Gusu, which was not finished for seven years. Because of this, he was alienated from the people of Wu. King Goujian of Yue observed that the ruler and subjects in Wu were not in harmony, and so he gathered together his people to take revenge on his enemy, entering the northern outer city wall, penetrating into the citadel, surrounding the royal palace, and thus destroying the kingdom of Wu.
> 至夫差之身, 北而攻齊, 舍於汶上, 戰於艾陵, 大敗齊人而葆之大山; 東而攻越, 濟三江五湖, 而葆之會稽. 九夷之國莫不賓服. 於是退不能賞孤, 施舍群萌. 自恃其力, 伐其功, 譽其智, 怠於教. 遂築姑蘇之臺, 七年不成. 及若此, 則吳有離罷之心. 越王句踐視吳上下不相得, 收其眾以復其讎, 入北郭, 徙大内, 圍王宮而吳國以亡.[120]

120. *Mozi*, pp. 136–38 ("Feigong zhong" 非攻中).

The different reasons given for the sudden destruction of the mighty kingdom of Wu and for the suicide of its last king no doubt reflect the confusion felt in the wake of a massive political upheaval. Just as the states of the Zhou confederacy had begun to familiarize themselves with this new southern power, Wu disappeared forever. Just as Wu's rise under the aegis of King Shoumeng had been meteoric, its fall under his great-grandson was similarly swift. In the absence of further information, explanations were sought in the personalities and actions of key individuals at the Wu court, not least those of King Fuchai himself. This means that the victor of the battles of Fujiao and Ailing, the conqueror of Yue, and the successful diplomat of the covenant at Huangchi, is reduced to being portrayed as a weak and deluded man, unable to sustain the burdens of kingship. The fall of Wu thus defines King Fuchai's reputation, overshadowing all that went before.

3

Reflections on the Royal House of Wu

During the century of its recorded history, the kingdom of Wu underwent enormous changes, which posed great challenges for successive Wu monarchs, for their administrations, and for Wu society as a whole. Though the nature of these transformations is often documented in ancient Chinese texts, their impact on traditional Wu culture is still not well understood. During this time, the kingdom of Wu was suddenly exposed to a wide range of foreign civilizations and this profoundly influenced Wu society. First, the kings of Wu were determined to be recognized by their peers among the lords of the Zhou confederacy as the first among equals, and this prompted numerous diplomatic missions to other states, as well as more interaction between the Wu kings and members of the confederacy ruling elites. Secondly, not only did the kingdom of Wu regularly invade other countries, it also conquered considerable stretches of territory inhabited by people of a different ethnicity and culture. Something of the extent of these conquests can be gauged by the decision of King Goujian to return considerable parcels of Wu territory to their original rulers, in the wake of his military victories. This suggests that the king of Yue was unsure of his ability to hold these lands and that he perhaps hoped to forestall the internal and external conflicts inherent in governing a multicultural kingdom. There can be no doubt that Wu's wars of conquest not only brought wealth to the state, but also provided both the ruling class and ordinary people with considerable exposure to the culture of the states of the Zhou confederacy (as well as the kingdom of Chu and the kingdom of Yue). A third factor that influenced Wu was the arrival of refugees. The Spring and Autumn period was an era of intractable conflict among the states of the Zhou confederacy, and the cycles of violence unleashed by wars and civil conflicts periodically set off waves of refugees seeking shelter anywhere that they could. Though only the most famous of these fugitives are documented in the history of the kingdom of Wu—such as those who went on to marry into the royal house or to hold high civil and military office—it is likely that this only represents the tip of the iceberg. These refugees were the forerunners of those who, from at least the time of the Han dynasty, would flee south from conflicts and natural disasters. These refugees no doubt made a considerable contribution to the development of Wu and left their mark on its history. However, the impact of these events is only hinted at in the surviving accounts of the lives of members of the Wu ruling elite.

The Wu Royal House in Ancient Chinese Texts

The *Zuozhuan*, which provides the earliest and in many ways the fullest account of the Wu royal family, almost entirely ignores the early history of that family: for this account simply mentions the tradition that they were descended from the virtuous and noble Taibo and Zhongyong, and describes only those members of the Wu ruling house that came to the attention of the chroniclers of the history of the Zhou confederacy. The accounts found in the *Zuozhuan* can therefore be grouped into two categories: some members of the Wu royal house are described in some detail and the precise nature of their relationship is clearly stated; but others are merely mentioned by name and their connection to the ruling house is not made clear. In some instances, later commentaries on the *Zuozhuan* have attempted to assign a specific relationship to individuals in this latter class: in this respect Du Yu's *Chunqiu jingzhuan jijie* 春秋經傳集解 (Collected explanations on the Spring and Autumn Annals classic and [Zuo's] tradition) is particularly important. The account of the Wu family tree given in the *Zuozhuan* itself, however, may be described as the classic tradition. Later texts either elaborate on or criticize the *Zuozhuan*, but this does not detract from its importance as the most detailed account that we have on the subject of Wu's royal family. It is the *Zuozhuan* that is the focus of all modern research on Wu inscribed bronzes, as scholars attempt to fit problematic nomenclature into the received tradition. The dominance of the textual tradition in scholarship in this field has been much criticized, but in this instance it appears unavoidable. The record provided by the *Zuozhuan* gives a conceptual framework and chronology into which inscribed Wu bronzes can be fitted; the paucity of bronzes of this type and the brevity of their inscriptions ensures that any attempt to make them stand on their own would merely result in fragmentation and confusion.

According to the *Zuozhuan*, King Shoumeng was the first ruler of Wu to declare himself king, which suggests a sudden change in the balance of power, or perhaps an unexpected accretion of authority in the region thanks to an exceptionally capable and charismatic leader. (This stands in direct contradiction to the evidence of numerous inscribed bronzes recording the names of earlier kings of Wu.) He was succeeded by three of his sons (Zhufan, Yuji, and Yumei) in turn.[1] On the death of King Yumei of Wu, Yumei was succeeded by his son, King Liao. King Liao was subsequently murdered by his first cousin, the oldest son of King Zhufan, who crowned himself King Helü of Wu. King Helü's highly eventful reign saw his younger brother, King Fugai, temporarily usurping the throne during the monarch's absence on campaign in 506 BCE, but this interlude only lasted a couple of months. King Helü had two sons: the eldest—Crown Prince Zhonglei—died young. As a result, it was the younger son who, as King Fuchai of Wu, ascended the throne on his father's death. King Fuchai's own son and heir, Crown Prince You 吳太子友, was captured alive by the forces of Yue during the 482 BCE invasion of Wu, and his eventual fate is not recorded.

In the *Zuozhuan* account, the family relationships of the seven kings of Wu are clearly delineated. Seven members of the Wu royal house are mentioned by name, without any family relationship being recorded. Three of these individuals can be fitted into the Wu royal family tree thanks to the researches of Du Yu, who apparently had access to ancient traditions or additional texts that described their identity. For example, the *Zuozhuan* describes how two princes of the kingdom of Wu, Zhuyong and Yanyu, were forced into exile in the wake of the assassination of King Liao. Du Yu's commentary

1. Two other sons, Princes Jizha and Jueyou, never sat on the throne. Prince Jueyou of Wu is mentioned only once in the *Zuozhuan*, p. 1271 (Zhao 5), when he was captured on campaign by the Chu army in 537 BCE, during the reign of his older brother King Yumei.

identifies them as King Liao's younger brothers by the same mother.[2] Likewise, Zishan—a senior member of the Wu army who participated in the attack on Chu that led to the capture of the capital, and who subsequently took up residence in the palace of the Prime Minister there—is identified as a prince of Wu, the son of an unnamed king.[3] Four members of the Wu royal house are mentioned by name in the *Zuozhuan*, though their identity is not explained in any surviving ancient text or commentary. In the same campaign that saw Crown Prince You captured by the Yue army, Prince Di of Wu 吳王子地 and two Royal Grandsons (Miyong 王孫彌庸 and Shouyuyao 王孫壽於姚) were also involved. However, Prince Di was the only one to escape capture.[4] The precise relationship of these individuals to the Wu royal house is not known. Likewise, a Prince Gucao of Wu 吳王子姑曹 was considered at one time as a possible hostage, to be sent to Lu to guarantee an alliance between these two countries.[5] Such mysterious individuals were temporarily important enough for their names to be recorded in Chinese historical texts, before their names vanished forever. These examples remind us that much remains unknown about even the most senior members of the ruling elite in Wu—and given that we do not know the identity of these people, interpreting their role in the rise and fall of the kingdom of Wu is effectively impossible.

Among Han dynasty accounts of the family tree of the Wu royal house, the only text to record a significant variant is the *Wu Yue chunqiu*, which adds a new name—that of Crown Prince Bo 吳太子波—to the line, and states that King Fuchai of Wu was not the son of King Helü, but rather his grandson. This identification is based upon a corrupt passage in the "Helü neizhuan" 闔閭內傳 (Inner tradition of King Helü) chapter, which describes Crown Prince Bo (clearly the same individual as the Crown Prince Zhonglei mentioned in other texts) and his ill-fated marriage to the daughter of the ruler of Qi; and mentions the prince's subsequent death and the appointment of Fuchai as the new heir to the throne:

---

2. Du Yu, *Chunqiu jingzhuan jijie*, p. 1552, n. 2 (Zhao 27).
3. Ibid., p. 1633, n. 25 (Ding 4).
4. *Zuozhuan*, p. 1676 (Ai 13).
5. Ibid., p. 1650 (Ai 8).

> [King Helü] again planned to attack Qi, and the ruler of Qi sent his daughter as a hostage to Wu, and the king of Wu made Crown Prince Bo marry the girl from Qi. She was young and suffered homesickness for Qi, and day and night she cried and became sick from this. Helü then built the north gate [to the city], which was called "Looking Towards Qi Gate" and he allowed the girl to go and visit it. She never stopped feeling homesick, and her sickness got worse day by day until in the end she was dying. She said: "It may perhaps be that the dead have consciousness, and so you must bury me on the peak of Yushan, so that I can look towards the state of Qi." Helü was deeply upset by this and did exactly as she had requested, thus she was buried on the peak of Yushan. At this time, the Crown Prince also got sick and died. Helü intended to select one of the princes to be established [as heir apparent], but he had not yet reached a fixed decision. Bo's Crown Prince (?) Fuchai day and night spoke with Wu [Zi]xu, saying: "His majesty wants to establish a Crown Prince and who is more suitable than myself? I am looking to you for a plan [to support my candidacy]."
> 復謀伐齊, 齊子使女爲質於吳, 吳王因爲太子波聘齊女. 女少思齊, 日夜號泣, 因乃爲病. 闔閭乃起北門, 名曰望齊門, 令女往遊其上. 女思不止, 病日益甚, 乃至殂落. 女曰: "令死者有知, 必葬我於虞山之巔, 以望齊國." 闔閭傷之, 正如其言, 乃葬虞山之巔. 是時太子亦病而死, 闔閭謀擇諸公子可立者, 未有定計. 波太子夫差日夜告於伍胥曰: "王欲立太子, 非我而誰當立? 此計在君耳."[6]

It would seem that the text is corrupt at a crucial point where the precise nature of the blood relationship between Crown Prince Bo and Prince Fuchai is about to be clarified. The conventional interpretation, as given by Zhou Shengchun 周生春 in his interlinear commentary on the text, is that the phrase Bo Taizi 波太子 should be read as Taizi Bo 太子波 (Crown Prince Bo) and that at least one character is missing from in front of the name of Fuchai. For scholars who believe that the kingdom of Wu practiced primogeniture, the missing character is *zi* 子 (son), in which case the phrase *Bo Taizi Fuchai riye gao yu Wu Xu* 波太子夫差日夜告於伍胥 should be translated as: "Crown Prince Bo's son, Fuchai, day and night spoke with Wu [Zi]xu." However, there is nothing intrinsically impossible in the missing character being *di* 弟 (younger brother), which fits with

6. *Wu Yue chunqiu*, pp. 65–66 ("Helü neizhuan").

another convention expressed in many other ancient historical texts: that King Fuchai of Wu was King Helü's younger son.

Up until the reign of King Helü, the royal family of Wu seems to have practiced fraternal succession. The precise nature of the succession practices in the ruling house of Wu remain unclear, since there is no detailed account in any surviving text of the principles that determined who succeeded to the throne. The texts that do record the changes in succession practice in the Wu royal house are all associated with the culture of the Zhou confederacy and were all written in the Warring States period or Han dynasty. Hence, there is every reason to be concerned that they do not correctly reflect Wu practices during the Spring and Autumn period. However, when King Helü usurped the throne, he found it expedient to kill or send into exile many male members of the Wu royal house. Either this significantly reduced the number of possible claimants to the throne, or the succession practices of the Wu ruling house were altered at this time, for on his own death, King Helü was succeeded by his son, who thus became the last monarch of Wu.

The Wu Royal House in Bronze Inscriptions

Over the course of the last century, thousands of Wu bronzes have been excavated across China, and of these, inscribed vessels form only a small fraction. However, these artifacts constitute a major resource for understanding this short-lived but important state—given that there are no surviving contemporary written documents from Wu, and that the earliest historical and philosophical texts to describe the kingdom were written many centuries after Wu had ceased to exist by authors far removed in both culture and place from this ancient southern kingdom. The vessels analyzed here are those where the inscription specifically states that the person for whom the bronze was made was a member of the Gouwu people (or in one case, where the name given is that of a known king of Wu). The earliest known inscribed Wu bronze was discovered in 1761, the most recent in 2003. In total, sixty-nine inscribed Wu bronzes are known. Bronzes of three main types have been discovered: ritual vessels (16), weapons (29), and bells (24). The vagaries of archaeological excavation naturally mean that we do not know how well these bronzes represent the types of bronzes manufactured in the kingdom of Wu prior to its collapse in 473 BCE; nor do we know whether disproportionate numbers of one particular type of vessel have been discovered. However, the inscribed bronzes discovered to date allow certain conclusions to be drawn: in particular, that the right to make an inscribed bronze was apparently a royal prerogative, that the nomenclature of the Wu kings seen on bronzes differs markedly from that known from transmitted texts, and that changes in this nomenclature seem to be linked to the development of standard formulaic inscriptions. However, the discovery of these inscribed bronzes has, if anything, only served to confuse the vexed issue of relationships within the Wu royal house.

As might be expected, and as has been seen in the analysis of bronzes from other Zhou confederacy states of the pre-unification period, individuals are mentioned on Wu bronzes whose names do not tally with those known from historical records.[7] In particular, the names given to persons identified as being monarchs of the kingdom of Wu bear little or no relationship to the names given in ancient Chinese historical texts. This suggests that there are serious problems with the three known king-lists for the Wu royal family. In spite of these obvious concerns, however, bronzes that have been excavated with inscriptions suggesting that they were made for other members of the Wu royal house have consistently been analyzed with respect to the names recorded in ancient Chinese texts. There is no reason to suppose that all the individuals mentioned in bronze inscriptions must necessarily be people who are also described in transmitted texts, but this has been the dominant trend in scholarly interpretations of these vessel inscriptions. One of the few instances of a Wu bronze where this type of argument has been persuasive is the "Luo'er *yi*" 羅兒匜. This vessel was excavated in 1988 from Tomb 3, Chengqiao zhen 程橋鎮, Liuhe County 六合縣, Jiangsu Province, at the site of what appears to be an extremely large Wu royal graveyard. This transcription follows the standard conventions in that □ indicates a character that is illegible in the original, [character] provides a modern scholar's alternative reading, and 【character】 gives a word

7. von Falkenhausen, *Chinese Society in the Age of Confucius*, pp. 89–90.

that is missing from the inscription that has been supplied by modern scholars: "Luo'er [two characters illegible], the maternal nephew of the king of Wu, the son of Guayi, Lord Jiaofa, selected the auspicious [metal] and made this *yi*-vessel for himself." 羅兒□□吳王之姓[甥]𠂤[教]伐公瓜 𨛭之子擇氒吉【金】自乍[作]盥鉈[匜].[8]

Jiaofa 教伐 was the title given to Qu Ziling 屈子靈, otherwise known as Shengong Wuchen, who, as mentioned above, sought asylum in Wu in the reign of King Shoumeng.[9] Qu Ziling's son, Huyong, is mentioned in several ancient Chinese texts as an important figure in the history of the kingdom of Wu. According to the *Wu Yue chunqiu*, Qu Huyong was appointed Prime Minister of Wu in the seventeenth year of the reign of King Shoumeng (569 BCE). Qu Huyong is also mentioned as an ambassador to the state of Jin during the reign of King Yumei of Wu in the *Zuozhuan*, and as a significant figure in the government of Wu, according to the *Guoyu*.[10] The identification of Guayi as Huyong is neat and persuasive, although the person who made this bronze is not himself mentioned in any ancient Chinese text. However, Dong Chuping 董楚平 suggests that this bronze does not derive from the kingdom of Wu but from the state of Luo, while He Linyi 何琳儀 suggests that the "Luo'er *yi*" was made by order of the son of a princess of Wu who had married into the ruling house of Xu.[11] (This is based upon He Linyi's reading of the character *yi* 𨛭 as identical with the character *ping* 坪, the character that appears in the inscription on the "Gongwu Zangsun *bianzhong*" 攻敔臧孫編鐘 as the name of the maker's father.) According to this theory, Zangsun would then be the personal name of the maker and Luo'er his style name.

The transmitted textual record serves as good preparation for one of the major problems confronting scholars interested in Wu inscribed bronzes: there is virtually no agreement about what any of

8. Xu Bohong, "Chengqiao sanhao Chunqiu mu chutu pan yi fu mingwen shizheng," p. 153.

9. *Zuozhuan*, pp. 834–35 (Cheng 7).

10. Ibid., p. 1189 (Xiang 31); *Wu Yue chunqiu*, p. 18 ("Wuwang Shoumeng zhuan"); *Guoyu*, p. 539 ("Chuyu shang" 楚語上).

11. Dong Chuping, *Wu Yue Xu Shu jinwen jishi*, p. 44; He Linyi, "Chengqiao sanhao mu panyi mingwen xinkao," p. 80.

the kings of Wu were called. The exception is King Fuchai, who seems to have been able to establish a standard nomenclature both within the transmitted textual record and on bronze inscriptions. In ancient Chinese historical texts, the kings of Wu appear with both single character and two-character names, and in some cases there seems to be considerable confusion about which characters should be used. Thus King Shoumeng of Wu is also named Cheng 乘.[12] King Zhufan is known by the alternative name Ye 謁.[13] King Liao of Wu is occasionally named Zhouyu 州于.[14] Though in ancient Chinese texts the penultimate king of Wu is always called Prince Guang before his accession to the throne and King Helü afterwards, the latter name is written in a number of different forms, including 闔廬 and 闔閭. However, as we now know from excavated inscribed bronzes, this distinction in nomenclature was not made during his lifetime and all the vessels made for him give his name as King Guang. The distinction between one character and two character names for the kings of Wu has traditionally been interpreted as evidence of the use of personal names and style names within Wu culture, though commentators have noted that the kings of Wu do not seem to have followed Zhou practice regarding name taboos.[15] However, recently scholars have pointed out that the one character names, familiar from many ancient historical texts, are in fact translations of the two character names (which apparently represent cut down versions of the name of the individual in the Wu language).[16] This would seem to be a significant breakthrough in our understanding of the nomenclature used for the kings of Wu and other members of the royal house. Originally, the kings of Wu seem to have used names consisting of many characters, which represented a transliteration from their own language. Subsequently they began to use single character names (a translation of the meaning of their Wu language name) in their interactions with the Central States and in documentation

---

12. *Zuozhuan*, p. 995 (Xiang 12); *Chunqiu Guliang zhuan*, p. 552 (Xiang 12), henceforward *Guliang zhuan*.

13. Ibid., p. 579 (Xiang 25); *Gongyang zhuan*, p. 261 (Xiang 25).

14. Du Yu, *Chunqiu jingzhuan jijie*, p. 1449, n. 17 (Zhao 20).

15. Wei Juxian, "Wu Yue minzu," p. 331.

16. Dong Chuping and Jin Yongping, *Wu Yue wenhua zhi*, pp. 95–96.

using the Chinese language. At the same time, they also seem to have developed the practice of using two character "cut down" versions of their Wu language names, which some of the kings of Wu seem to have preferred for use in such formal contexts as the manufacture of ritual bronzes.

The names of the Wu kings given in bronze inscriptions can hence be divided into two main groups. The first group is the complex names, consisting of up to half-a-dozen characters, which are in many cases entirely unrelated to any name appearing in historical texts. The second category is the simple names, consisting of one or two characters, which are the same as those known from historical texts. Although the name of the king mentioned on the "Qiegoushu *jian*" 䖝戗郚劍, a sword excavated in Shaoxing in 1997, is recognizable as "King Shoumeng of Wu," the nomenclature found in this inscription is nevertheless demonstrably distinct from later Wu practice: "[I], Qiegoushu, the son of King Gufa'nanshoumeng of the Gouwu, travelled to Yi and [one character missing]. [I] began by accepting the order to attack [one character missing], and took captives. Chu attacked Xu and I personally went to intercept them. I defeated the three armies, capturing horses and chariots, and launched attacks on the seven lords." 攻敔[敔]王姑發難壽夢之子䖝戗郚之義□，初命伐□，【有】隻[獲]. 型[荆]伐郐[徐]余寴[親]逆攻之. 敗三軍，隻[獲]【車】馬，攴七邦君.[17]

The term Gufa 姑發 also appears on a number of other bronzes as part of the names of members of the Wu royal house. It is not clear whether this represents a clan name, or if it was part of the personal name of a succession of monarchs. However, the usage of this term is important, because it points to the reigns of King Zhufan of Wu and his brothers as a time of great cultural change in Wu: this is supported by the nomenclature on bronzes made for King Zhufan's personal use, or for members of his family. There are four bronzes that record the name of King Zhufan, and the first, the "Gouwu Taizi Gufa *jian*" 工鳸王大子姑發劍 dates to the time when he was still the Crown Prince of Wu: "I, Gufazhufan, the Crown Prince of

17. Cao Jinyan, "Wuwang Shoumeng zhi zi jianming kaoshi," p. 14; Feng Puren, *Wu Yue wenhua*, p. 120.

the Gouwu, made this for my own use before setting out, in order to make use of it, in order to capture [the enemy] with it, that no one should dare to oppose me, I take my place on the north bank of the river, from where I can travel south and travel west." 工𢊁王大子姑发𦣞反自乍[作]元用, 才[在]行之先, 以用以蒦[獲], 莫敢卸[御]余. 余处江之阳, 至于南行西行.[18]

This particular sword was excavated in 1959, from a site in Caijiagang 蔡家崗, in Huainan County 淮南縣, Anhui Province. It came from a rich tomb containing more than one hundred bronzes. Two other swords have also been excavated with inscriptions recording that they were made for relatives of King Zhufan. The relative chronology of these two objects is not clear, but both must have been made after King Zhufan came to the throne in 560 BCE. The first of these two swords, the "Gouwu Jizi *jian*" 工𢊁季子劍, was excavated in 1985, at Yushe County 榆社縣 in Shanxi Province: "[I], Jizi Zheshang, the younger brother of King Gufazhufan of the Gouwu, received this auspicious metal, and used it to make a sword for my own personal use." 工𢊁王䏵[姑]發𦣞反之弟季子脌[者]扃[尚]受余氒[厥]吉金台[以]乍[作]其元用鐱[劍].[19]

Jin Hua 晋華, in his 1990 study of this particular inscription, provides a highly controversial interpretation, which must be incorrect, in light of the inscriptions found on other Wu bronzes. He argues that the term *Gufa* was the personal name of King Zhufan of Wu, and reads the character *zhu* 𦣞 as *zi* 訾 (to criticize), a phonetic loan for the character *ci* 疵 (to be ill). The character *fan* 反 he reads as *ye* 謁, which is glossed in the *Shuowen* dictionary as meaning "to make a request." Likewise the two characters *qi* 脌 and *shang* 扃, which Dong Chuping reads as a personal name, Jin Hua reads as the names of two sacrifices.[20] Thus, according to this interpretation, the inscription should be translated: "Gufa, King of the Gouwu, was ill and ordered his younger brother Jizi to perform the *qi* and the *shang* rituals. Afterwards he received auspicious metals [from me, and I said: 'Make] a

18. Ibid., p. 120; Xu Zhongshu, *Yin-Zhou jinwen jilu*, p. 875.

19. Jin Hua, "Shanxi Yushe chutu yijian Wuwang Gufa jian," p. 77; Dong Chuping, *Wu Yue Xu Shu jinwen jishi*, pp. 95–96.

20. Jin Hua, "Shanxi Yushe chutu yijian Wuwang Gufa jian," pp. 77–79.

sword for your own personal use.'" This interpretation is based on the theory that Wu monarchs performed rituals indistinguishable from those of the Zhou kings, and incorrectly asserts that Gufa is a personal name, although in all cases where *Gufa* is given in a Wu bronze vessel inscription, it comprises the first two characters of a longer appellation.

Another Wu bronze to use this kind of nomenclature is the "Caobei *jian*" 曹𩵦劍, a sword excavated in 1982 at Xiangfan County 襄樊縣 in Hubei Province. This sword inscription adds yet another previously unknown prince to the family tree of the Wu royal house: "Caobeixiangzhongfeiyuan, the son of King Gufafan of the Gouwu, made this for his own personal use." 攻盧王姑發𨚕之子曹𩵦象众飛員自乍[作]元用.[21]

The final bronze to mention the name of King Zhufan of Wu was also made for one of his sons, Prince Tong 王子通. The "Wuwang Zhufan zhi zi Tong *jian*" 吳王諸樊之子通劍 was excavated from a very rich Eastern Zhou dynasty tomb in Zhoujiazhuang 周家莊, Shandong Province, in 2003. This bronze provides a particularly interesting contrast with the "Caobei *jian*," since the nomenclature used suggests that some significant cultural change had occurred in the kingdom of Wu in the time between the manufacture of these two swords: "[I], Tong, the son of King Gufa Zhufan of the Gouwu, made this for my own personal use." 攻敔王姑發者反[諸樊]之子通自乍[作]元用.[22]

This is a transitional bronze, in that it preserves some signs of the older nomenclature in use in the Wu royal house when it mentions the term Gufa, but it also is clearly moving towards the form of characters used to designate King Zhufan in ancient Chinese historical texts. By the time of the reign of King Yumei of Wu, the transition is complete. Only one bronze has been excavated from this time: in 1984, a *mao* 矛 was discovered at Beishan 北山, Dantu County, Jiangsu Province in a tomb now frequently said to be that of King

21. Feng Puren, *Wu Yue wenhua*, p. 121.

22. Ren Xianghong and Zhang Qingfa, "Wuwang Zhufan zhi zi Tong jian ji xiangguan wenti tantao," p. 15.

Yumei of Wu himself. The inscription on this bronze reads: "Yumei made this for his own personal use." 余眜自乍[作]工其元用.[23]

From the reign of King Yumei of Wu onwards, the names of the Wu kings found in bronze vessel inscriptions are found in a form that is either identical to that used in ancient Chinese texts, or is clearly recognizable as similar. The exact significance of this change is not clear. This practice may represent cultural imperialism on the part of the Zhou confederacy, in that the Zhou succeeded in imposing its own terminology on the kings of the Gouwu people. Alternatively, it may be the result of increased contact between the Central States and the kings of Wu, so that the Wu people began to adopt shorter name forms. Or perhaps, as the Wu kings became increasingly powerful—launching wave after wave of attacks against their neighbors, and forcing the states of the Zhou confederacy to recognize their authority—the names of the kings of Wu came to be recorded with ever greater accuracy in Chinese historical texts. However, this change in nomenclature means that all Wu bronzes that contain the names of individuals referred to as kings (but where these rulers cannot be identified with individuals recorded in the transmitted texts) must refer to monarchs who reigned prior to King Shoumeng of Wu.

As with the nomenclature, inscriptions on Wu bronzes can be divided into two main groups: complex inscriptions and simple

---

23. Ye Wenxian, *Wuguo lishi yu Wu wenhua tanmi*, p. 76. The inscribed halberd blade was one of numerous inscribed bronzes that were discovered in this tomb, together with the "Shiji *fou*" 尸祭缶 (31 characters), "Shenliu *ding*" 甚六鼎 (47 characters), and "Shenliu *bianzhong*" 甚六編鐘 (a set of twelve bells, with an inscription 72 characters long in total, including repetitions). All these objects have conventionally come to be described as Wu bronzes, and have been published as such; see for example Yang Zhenghong and Xiao Menglong, *Zhenjiang chutu Wuguo qingtongqi*, pp. 134–36, 140–41, 144–46; Dantuxian ed., *Dantu xianzhi*, p. 765. The inscription on the "Shiji *fou*" is often claimed to contain the names of four kings of Wu; where this idea comes from is not at all clear given that not only does the inscription not name a single member of the Wu royal house, but also the maker is clearly identified as a grandson of the ruler of Xu 徐. Similarly the Shenliu bronzes have been identified as deriving from the kingdom of Shu 舒. Cao Jinyan, "Beishan tongqi xinkao."

inscriptions. Complex inscriptions feature detailed information such as the date of manufacture, the occasion on which a bronze was made, the name of the donor who commissioned the object, the ancestor to whom the bronze was to be dedicated, and a pious wish that the vessel would be used by many generations of descendants. This type of complex inscription is very closely related to the highly standardized forms seen in the vessels made in the Central States during the Zhou dynasty, though given how little is known about Wu culture it is not clear if they participated in the same assumptions about bronze making as the Zhou confederacy, or if the Wu simply felt that these inscriptions were appropriate for such objects. The "Wuwang Guang *jian*" 吳王光鑑, a pair of identical Wu bronze *jian* excavated from the tomb of the marquis of Cai at Shou County 壽縣, Anhui, in 1955, are good examples of vessels with complex inscriptions. They were made on the occasion of the wedding of a daughter of the Wu royal house to the marquis of Cai. These dowry vessels made by King Helü of Wu were clearly intended to demonstrate the high status of the bride to the Central States ruling family she was marrying into and hence are perhaps not entirely representative of contemporary Wu royal bronze manufacture:

> In the Fifth month, First Auspiciousness, the first Geng day of the Jishengba phase of the moon, King Guang of Wu selected his auspicious metal, copper, and tin, in order to make this ritual vessel, a sacrificial basin, for the younger Lady Ji, named Siyu. May she use it for feasting, and may she use it for filial sacrifices. May she have felicitous longevity without end. May the younger Lady Ji use it with respect. Later on may the grandsons of her grandsons never forget!
> 隹王五月既子白期吉日初庚, 吳王光擇其吉金, 玄銑白銑台[以]乍[作]弔[叔]姬寺吁宗䵼[彝]薦鑑. 用享用孝, 釁[眉]壽無疆往巳[矣]. 叔姬虔敬, 乃后孫" 勿忘.[24]

The other main group contains simple inscriptions, and within this group, such inscriptions can be found in two main types of bronzes. First, ritual bronzes feature inscriptions with variations on the for-

24. Xu Zhongshu, *Yin-Zhou jinwen jilu*, p. 470; Shirakawa, *Kimbun tsushaku* 40.589.

Table 2. Types of bronze inscriptions from the kingdom of Wu.

	Simple Inscriptions	Complex Inscriptions
Pre-Shoumeng	1	10
Shoumeng to Liao	5	5
King Helü of Wu	6	5
King Fuchai of Wu	16	1
Undatable	5	15
Total	33	36

mula: "X selected his auspicious metals and made this bronze vessel of type Y for himself" (X *xuanjue jijin zizuo* 擇厥吉金自作 Y). The second type of bronze, inscribed weapons, includes variations on the shorter formula: "X made this bronze weapon of type Y for his own personal use" (X *zizuo qi yuanyong* 自作其元用 Y). The vast majority of Wu bronzes use inscriptions of this simple type, which again is closely related to the rise in popularity of this type of dedication in the bronze vessel inscriptions of the Zhou confederacy during the Spring and Autumn period.[25]

The type of object being made does not seem to be a significant factor in the use of simple or complex inscriptions. However, when the chronology of these bronzes is considered, then a much more interesting development in the typology of Wu bronze vessel inscriptions can be seen. It is clear that over time, the use of complex inscriptions decreased, and simple inscriptions became more popular. This transition seems to have occurred at the same time that the nomenclature in use on Wu bronze vessels was changing. This again suggests that there was significant cultural change in Wu during the reigns of King Zhufan and his brothers.

To date, almost all inscribed Wu bronzes that have been discovered clearly indicate that they were made for members of the Wu royal house. Thirty-two bronzes state that they were made for a Wu king, seventeen for a Wu prince, one for the younger brother of a king of Wu, one for a nephew of the king, and four for grandsons of a king

25. Mattos, "Eastern Zhou Bronze Inscriptions," pp. 86–88.

Table 3. Identity of the makers of Wu bronzes.

	Ritual Vessels	Military Bronzes	Bronze Bells	Total
Kings	9	22	1	32
Princes	—	5	12	17
Royal Brothers	—	1	—	1
Royal Nephews	1	—	—	1
Grandsons	3	1	—	4
Total	13	29	13	55

of Wu. In other words, of the sixty-nine known inscribed Wu bronze vessels, fifty-five (79.8 percent) were certainly made for members of the Wu ruling house.

Fourteen inscribed Wu bronzes have been excavated that do not include information that allows them to be immediately associated with a member of the royal house. Three of these are ritual vessels and eleven are bells from related tombs at Chengqiao zhen. However, many researchers believe that these fourteen bronzes should also be understood as objects made for the use of members of the Wu ruling house. The first of the unidentified ritual bronzes is also derived from the 1988 excavations at Chengqiao zhen: the "Gouwu Dashu *pan*" 工䱷大叔盤, an inscribed vessel on which, unfortunately, the two characters of the name of the maker have proved illegible. The designation *Dashu* was an honorific term used in the states of the Zhou confederacy to designate a younger full brother of the ruler. It is therefore quite possible that the person concerned was the younger brother of a Wu king: "Dashu [two characters illegible] of the Gouwu had this *pan*-vessel manufactured for his own use while travelling." 工䱷大叔□□自乍[作]行盤.[26]

Xu Bohong 徐伯鴻 suggests that the two illegible characters should be read as Shouyue 壽越. Grandee Shouyue of Wu is recorded in the *Zuozhuan*, and if the royal house did follow the standard honorific usage of the Zhou kings then this individual would probably have been the younger brother of King Shoumeng of

26. Dong Chuping, *Wu Yue Xu Shu jinwen jishi*, pp. 40–41.

Wu.[27] Another reading of the two illegible characters is 吉石甬: a completely unknown individual.[28] The second ritual vessel with an ambiguous inscription is the "Gongwu Jisheng *yi*" 工虞季生匜. This bronze was discovered in 1985, by peasants digging a fishpond in Yutai County 盱眙縣, Jiangsu Province. The inscription reads: "Jisheng of the Gouwu made this *yi*–vessel for [use at] meetings and covenants." 工虞季生乍[作]其盥[盟]會盥[匜].[29]

The assumption, made by many scholars of inscribed Wu bronzes, has been that Jisheng is Prince Jizha of Wu. This may well be correct, and if so, this vessel was in fact yet another one made by a member of the Wu royal house. The same is true of the "Gongwu Zangsun *bianzhong*." This matched set of nine bells, plus two more related bells, were excavated from tombs at Chengqiao zhen. The inscription on each of the set of nine bells reads: "On Dinghai day, First Auspiciousness, First month, Zangsun, the son of Ping, and the maternal grandson of Second Son Zhongsui of the Gouwu selected this auspicious metal and made this harmonious bell for himself. May the sons of sons and the grandsons of grandsons always preserve this bronze." 隹王正月初吉丁亥, 攻敔中[仲]冬[終]𢧜之外孫, 坪之子, 戕[臧]孫擇氒[厥]吉金自乍[作]龢鐘子" 孫" 永保是從.[30]

Liu Xing 劉興, in his study of these bronzes, notes that the character 𢧜 is unique to this inscription, and suggests that it should be transcribed as *sui* 歲, which is being used as a phonetic loan for the character *lei* 纍.[31] The second son Zhongsui would therefore be Crown Prince Zhonglei of Wu, the son of King Helü of Wu, and older brother to King Fuchai, who died before he could come to the throne. These nine bells would then also be Wu royal bronzes, made by order of a great-grandson of King Helü of Wu, which would

27. Xu Bohong, "Chengqiao sanhao Chunqiu mu chutu pan yi fu mingwen shizheng," p. 153; *Zuozhuan*, p. 943 (Xiang 5).

28. Cao Jinyan, "Chengqiao xinchu tongqi kaoshi ji xiangguan wenti."

29. Qin Shizhi, "Yutaixian Wangzhuang chutu Chunqiu Wuguo tongyi"; Ye Wenxian, *Wuguo lishi yu Wu wenhua tanmi*, p. 171.

30. Xu Zhongshu, *Yin-Zhou jinwen jilu*, p. 449; Liu Xing, "Wu Zangsun zhong mingkao."

31. Ibid., p. 108.

mean that the related pair of bells from tombs M1 and M2, with the inscription: *Gongwu Zhong Zhong [one character illegible] zhi waisun* 攻敔仲終□之外孫 (the maternal grandson of Second Son Zhong [one character illegible] of the Gouwu), were also made for a descendant of the Wu royal house.

The remaining troublesome inscription is considerably more problematic. The "Wuwang *fu*" 吳王簠, originally known as the "Zhou Shusui *fu*" 周叔綏簠, was discovered in 1957 in the Haidian 海淀 district of Beijing. It did not form part of either a tomb or a cache, and was subsequently identified as a vessel from the Qing imperial collection that had gone missing. This vessel would have been understood from its form and decoration as a Chu bronze were it not for the inscription: "Shusun of the Yi clan, 'Completed Scholar' to the king of Wu, made this sacrificial *fu*-vessel." 吳王造士尹氏叔孫作旅簠.[32]

The scholars who have studied this bronze inscription regard the term "Completed Scholar" (Zaoshi 造士) as an official title. This title is known from a single text, the "Wangzhi" 王制 (Royal regulations) chapter of the *Liji*, which describes a system of education for men of exceptional ability.[33] However, as with the use of the honorific title Dashu mentioned above, it implies that the kingdom of Wu used exactly the same terminology as the states of the Zhou confederacy, an assertion that the evidence so far available does not support. An alternative transcription of these characters has been proposed by Ye Wenxian 葉文獻, who suggests they should be read Yushi 御士.[34] This too is an official title used during the Zhou dynasty and is recorded in both historical and ritual texts; all known holders of this office seem to have been members of the ruling houses of Zhou

---

32. The transcription of the inscription of this bronze is given according to the initial report of the discovery of this vessel. Beijingshi, "Haidianqu faxian Chunqiu shidai tongqi." The iconography of this bronze, which would have seen it identified as a Chu vessel were it not for the inscription, is discussed in Song Jian, "Wu wenhua huihuang de qingtongqi," p. 62.

33. *Liji*, p. 255 ("Wangzhi").

34. Ye Wenxian, *Wuguo lishi yu Wu wenhua tanmi*, p.175.

confederacy states.[35] It is therefore possible that this bronze should also be understood as a Wu royal vessel. The name of the maker has been transcribed in a number of different ways: 尹氏叔緐, 尹氏叔𡟰, 尹氏叔䋣, and 尹氏叔孫.[36] This must be a very late Spring and Autumn period or early Warring States era vessel, because the inscription names the king of Wu (Wuwang) rather than the king of the Gouwu (Gongwuwang/Gongyuwang). The term Wuwang is only seen in bronzes with inscriptions stating that they were made for King Guang or King Fuchai, and in the bronze *dings* made for the Royal Grandson Wuren 無壬/Wutu 無土, a set of three vessels that are believed to have been made after the fall of the kingdom of Wu.[37] If these attributions are correct, then all known inscribed Wu bronzes were made for members of the royal family, and the vast majority for the kings' own personal use. Though a lack of lengthy and detailed inscriptions means that at present these bronzes throw little light upon the problems of understanding the relationships between members of the Wu royal family, nevertheless they clearly demonstrate important changes taking place within the culture of the ruling elite during the time span also covered by ancient Chinese records.

The Wu Royal House in Modern Scholarship

In imperial era China, very few scholars turned their attention to attempting to resolve the contradictory accounts of the Wu royal family tree. An exception is the Song dynasty scholar Cheng Gongshuo 程公說, the author of the *Chunqiu fenji* 春秋分記 (Diverse records of the Spring and Autumn Annals). In this interesting but completely mad account of the family tree of the Wu kings, Cheng Gongshuo

---

35. *Liji*, p. 929 ("Ziyi" 緇衣); *Zuozhuan*, p. 1173 (Xiang 30), p. 1425 (Zhao 21).

36. Ye Wenxian, *Wuguo lishi yu Wu wenhua tanmi*, p. 175; Song Jian, "Wu wenhua huihuang de qingtongqi," p. 62; Xu Zhongshu, *Yin-Zhou jinwen jilu*, p. 357; Beijingshi, "Haidianqu faxian Chunqiu shidai tongqi," p. 72.

37. Dong Chuping, *Wu Yue Xu Shu jinwen jishi*, p. 79. The three identical Wuren/Wutu dings were excavated 1977 from a cache of Eastern Zhou bronzes at the Gaowang si 高王寺, Fengxiang County 鳳翔縣, Shaanxi Province. It has been suggested that this set was made at Houma for a member of the Wu royal house who escaped from the disaster of the fall of his kingdom to Yue in 473 BCE. So, *Eastern Zhou Ritual Bronzes*, p. 160.

turned his attention to the last five generations of the family, beginning with King Shoumeng. In this account, King Shoumeng is said to have had eight sons: Zhufan, Yuji, Yumei, Jizha, Liao, Jueyu, Zhuyong, and Yanyu. Seven of these men are said to have left no descendents, but Yumei is accorded two sons: Helü and Fugai. Of these, Fugai is said to have left no descendents but Helü is given three sons, here named as Zhonglei, Fuchai, and Zishan. Again the author seems to presuppose that only one out of each generation was able to marry and have children, hence King Fuchai is said to have had four sons, named You, Di, Gucao, and Qingji.[38] There is no point wasting much time in discussing this bizarre account of the history of the Wu ruling house, except to note that Cheng Gongshuo was clearly well aware of the tradition recorded in the *Gongyang zhuan* that King Liao of Wu was a younger commoner brother of Kings Zhufan, Yuji, and Yumei of Wu, and hence the author raises Princes Zhuyong and Yanyu into that generation of the ruling house. This family tree appears to be intended to account for those princes of Wu who are mentioned in the *Zuozhuan*, but whose precise relationship to the royal house is not recorded in any ancient Chinese text or early commentary. Cheng Gongshuo seems to have been motivated by a wish to tidy what remains a deeply confused situation.

When modern scholars have researched the Wu royal family tree, they have tended to combine the accounts given in ancient Chinese texts with information derived from selected bronze vessel inscriptions. Very few modern scholars have attempted a complete revision of the family tree; most have instead contented themselves with minor alterations, and with proposing associations between individuals named in bronze inscriptions and those recorded in ancient texts—though this analysis is based upon more or less flimsy linguistic evidence. One of the few scholars to have produced an extended discussion on the subject is Wu Enpei 吳恩培; his book entitled *Gouwu wenhua de xianzai chanshi* 勾吳文化的現在闡釋 (A modern evaluation of Gouwu culture) considers the lines of descent not just for the ruling house but also for other key members of the Wu elite, such as Wu Zixu (a member of a distinguished Chu ministerial family) and Sun Wu 孫

38. Cheng Gongshuo, *Chunqiu fenji* 16.23a.

武 (here identified as a member of the Tian 田 family of Qi, and hence a descendant of the ruling house of Chen 陳). Wu Enpei's account of the Wu royal family is significant, for having accepted the *Gongyang zhuan*'s suggestion that they practiced polygamy, and thus divided the listed offspring into noble and commoner, the author suggests that Kings Zhufan, Yuji, Yumei, and Prince Jizha represent King Shoumeng's noble sons, and that Princes Dang, Jueyou, Yanyu, and Zhuyong were his commoner sons.[39] What is striking about this account is that although he accepts the theoretical basis of the *Gongyang zhuan*'s revision of the Wu royal family tree, Wu Enpei is undecided about whether King Liao was King Shoumeng's commoner son or his noble grandson; and readers are left to make up their own minds.

A number of scholars working on comparisons between the records found in ancient historical texts and bronze vessel inscriptions have seized upon two of the major problems in understanding the Wu royal family tree: the precise identity of King Liao, and the theory that King Fuchai of Wu was not King Helü's son, but rather his grandson. Several bronze inscriptions have been brought into play to attempt to decide these issues once and for all. In the case of the first problem, the bronze inscription that is most frequently cited as contributory evidence is the "Bola *ge*" 伯剌戈, excavated in 1960 at Taowu township 陶吳鄉, Jiangning County 江寧縣. This bronze halberd-blade is now in the collection of the Nanjing Museum. To date three different transcriptions have been given for this inscription on this blade:

> Baicha, the grandson of King [one illegible character] ye, the son of Xiaozhong used this excellent metal to make this halberd for his own personal use.
> □野王之孫, 嚻中之子白茶, 用其良金, 自作其元戈.[40]

> Bosheng, the grandson of King Bimang, the son of Xiaozhong, used this excellent metal to make this halberd for his own personal use.
> 畢㭿王之孫, 嚻仲之子伯剩, 用其良金, 自作其元戈.[41]

---

39. Wu Enpei, *Gouwu wenhua de xianzai chanshi*, p. 206.

40. Shi Yongyun, "Jiangning Taowu chutu tongge mingwen shishi."

41. This transcription was published in 1985 by Zhou Xiaolu 周曉陸, in an article in *Nanjing bowuyuan jikan* 南京博物院集刊 (Journal of the Nanjing Museum) entitled "Wu Bosheng ge dukao" 吳伯剩戈讀考 (Research on reading [the inscrip-

> Bola, the grandson of King Xiye (Shoumeng), the son of Xiaozhong, used this excellent metal to make this halberd for his own personal use.
> 西野王之孫, 囂中(仲)之子白(伯)剌, 用其良金, 自乍(作)其元戈.[42]

The scholar who developed the third transcription, Wu Yuming 吳聿明, argues that the "Bola" for whom this bronze was made was King Liao of Wu, and hence, that the *Gongyang zhuan* is wrong. The doyen of Wu bronze studies, Dong Chuping, notes in his analysis of this inscription that Wu Yuming's transcription has much to recommend it. This is particularly true given that, in Dong Chuping's view, the suggestion is untenable that the first two characters should be read Bimang. Likewise, Dong Chuping does not accept the transcription of the second character of the maker's name as either *cha* or *sheng*. Though no name of a country or people is given in this inscription, this is definitely a southern bronze. However, in spite of the assertions made by Wu Yuming, it cannot be categorically ascertained that this bronze did indeed come from the kingdom of Wu—and even if such a contention were generally accepted, there remain problems with using this inscription to resolve problems of identifying individuals within the Wu family tree. In particular this inscription would seem to suggest (as indeed do other inscribed Wu bronzes, such as the "Gongwu Zangsun *bianzhong*" text quoted above and the example of Prince Jizha of Wu, where the character *ji* 季 suggests that he was the benjamin of the family) that the Wu royal house followed the practice of Zhou confederacy states in giving names indicative of each sibling's exact position in the family. This inscription implies that Bola was the oldest son of Xiaozhong, the second son of King Xiye. And yet all surviving ancient Chinese texts that state King Liao of Wu was King Shoumeng's grandson also say that Liao was the son of King Yumei of Wu (King Shoumeng's third son). If

---

tion on] Bosheng of Wu's halberd). I have not been able to locate a copy of this journal article, so the transcription is derived from Dong Chuping, *Wu Yue Xu Shu jinwen jishi*, p. 104. The maker of this inscribed bronze is here presumed to be Shoumeng himself, and Bimang is identified as Bizhen 畢軫, who according to the *Suoyin* commentary to the *Shiji* was indeed King Shoumeng of Wu's grandfather. *Shiji* 31.1448, n. 7.

42. Wu Yuming, "Bola ge kao."

that is the case then the "Bola *ge*" cannot have been made for King Liao of Wu.

The inscriptions on the "Peier *goudiao*" 配兒句鑃 have been used to add legitimacy to the theory that Crown Prince Bo of Wu was the father of King Fuchai, and also that the royal family of Wu discriminated between noble and commoner sons. This pair of bells were excavated 1977, from a site in Goutoushan 狗頭山, in Shaoxing 紹興, Zhejiang Province. The large bell bears an inscription fifty-six characters long; the small bell's inscription consists of twenty-six characters:

> [Two characters illegible] on Genwu day, [First] Auspiciousness, Peier, the *zhongzi* of King [three characters illegible] of Wu said: "I am experienced in warfare and military matters; I attack at the appointed moment without daring to question [my orders] or to be lax. I selected the [auspicious] metal: dark and shining, smooth and hard. I made this *goudiao* bell for myself in order to feast my guests and clients, and in order to make happy my fathers [i.e., father and paternal uncles]." May sons [and grandsons] use them, for the glorification of their ancestors."
> □□【初】吉庚午, 吳【王】□□□【之家】子配兒曰: 余孰[熟]戕于戎攻[敢][且]武; 余[卯][襲]【威】[期][期]不敢[詻]舍, 畢[擇]氒[厥]【吉】金鉉鏐鑪鋁, 自乍[作]鉤【鑃】余台[以]宴賓【客】, 台[以]樂余者[諸]父. 子【孫用】之, 先人之[訏][予].[43]

> Prince Peier, who is experienced in warfare and attacks at the appointed moment, selected the auspicious metal: dark and shining, smooth and hard, and made this *goudiao* bell for himself.
> 王子配兒孰戕于龔威[期]畢[擇]氒吉金鉉鑪鋁, 自乍[作]鉤鑃余.[44]

There are a number of problems with the inscription on the larger of these two bells. First, as noted above, only very late Spring and Autumn period bronzes used the term Wu, and earlier inscriptions use a two-character designation. This is not inconsistent with Prince Peier being identified as King Helü of Wu's son. It is extremely unfortunate that the beginning of this inscription is so badly damaged,

43. Two very closely related transcriptions of this inscription are given in Cao Jinyan, "Peier goudiao mingwen ba"; Sha Menghai, "Peier goudiao kaoshi."

44. This inscription is given in accordance with von Falkenhausen, *Suspended Music*, p. 100.

because what is likely to be the name of the king of Wu is illegible. This is where the first problem lies. All bronzes that were made for King Helü of Wu, or that give his name, record the name as a single character Guang, and yet there are still three characters illegible in this inscription. Even identifying Prince Peier as King Fuchai's son still leaves at least one illegible character unaccounted for. And yet Peier is specifically identified in the second bell inscription as the son of the king of Wu. The second major problem with this inscription comes with the interpretation of the expression *zhongzi* 冢子. Sha Menghai 沙孟海 in his study of the "Peier *goudiao*" suggested that *zhongzi* means the same thing as *dizi*: in other words Prince Peier was a noble son of a king of Wu, which would confirm the evidence of the *Gongyang zhuan*. Cao Jinyan 曹錦炎, on the other hand, suggests interpreting *zhongzi* as meaning *dazi* 大子, or Crown Prince. Neither of these interpretations is particularly convincing, given that there remains an inexplicable difference between the number of illegible characters in this inscription and the suggestions given by scholars for which characters could fill the gaps.

Though many inscribed Wu bronzes have been excavated, to date none of their inscriptions have served to elucidate the problems faced by scholars who are attempting to understand the relationships between members of the royal family. Some interesting conclusions can be drawn from these inscriptions (for example, regarding bronze production as a royal prerogative, and of evidence concerning the process of sinicization of the ruling elite), nevertheless the inscriptions are actually not helpful at all for one of the key areas in which they have been pressed into service—attempting to clarify the Wu royal family tree.

Eastern Han Pictorial Mirrors

During the Eastern Han dynasty a number of master craftsmen in the Jiangnan region began to produce high-quality bronze mirrors with representations of historical events on the back. These are among the earliest known Chinese bronze mirrors of this type and they illustrate events from the history of the ancient kingdoms of Wu and Yue, depicting key personages from the most famous conflict of the late Spring and Autumn period.[45] (Although mirrors with human figures were made in some abundance during the Eastern Han dynasty, these usually depict deities rather than historical individuals.) These mirrors are of considerable importance in the history of Chinese bronzes, for they are extremely early examples of low-relief portraiture in bronze. They are also significant because they represent the flowering of a major regional artistic tradition, produced as part of a renaissance in Jiangnan culture in the Eastern Han dynasty, which was also expressed through the compilation of a number of books on the history of this region (of which the most notable are the *Yuejue shu* and the *Wu Yue chunqiu*). The manufacture of these mirrors was a concrete expression of enduring interest in the glorious and bloody past of this region of China.

One of the most striking features of these mirrors is the way that they portray the inhabitants of the ancient kingdoms of Wu and Yue: that is, the inhabitants are depicted in standard contemporary Han dynasty costume, without the tattoos and short hair recorded in virtually every ancient text to mention these people. There is certainly no doubt that the representation of key figures from the history of Wu and Yue on mirrors is totally different from the descriptions given in texts such as the *Zhanguo ce*, which describes the—to Chinese eyes—extremely striking customs and regional dress of the people of the ancient south: "The people of Lin Yue cut their hair short and tattoo their bodies; they paint their arms and tie their clothes on the left. In the kingdom of Wu they blacken their teeth and scarify their faces, they wear hats made of fish skin, and

45. A rare example of an Eastern Han dynasty historical mirror made in the Jiangnan region and illustrating scenes not associated with the conflict between the kingdoms of Wu and Yue was excavated in 2004 from a contemporary tomb at Xingqiaozhen 星橋鎮, Yuhang County 餘杭縣 in Zhejiang Province. This particular mirror depicts four scenes from the romantic legend of Han Peng 韓朋 and his wife Zhenfu 貞夫, who suffered and died at the hands of the last king of Song. Wang Jiehua et al. eds., *Gu Yue yizhen yanjiu*, p. 90. Schwitzgebel, "Han Peng fu," discusses the development of literary representations of Han Peng and Zhenfu, with particular reference to their association with Jiangnan romantic figures such as King Fuchai and Xi Shi or Liang Shanbo 梁山伯 and Zhu Yingtai 祝英台.

stitch with an awl." 祝髮文身, 错臂左衽, 林越之民也. 黑齒雕題, 鯷冠秫縫, 大吳之國也.[46]

None of the Eastern Han dynasty mirrors that have been discovered to date depict the people of Wu and Yue in a realistic fashion. These highly artistic, beautifully made bronzes naturally lacked any reference to the actual appearance of the monarch and senior ministers of these two kingdoms in the late Spring and Autumn period. After all, these mirrors were produced approximately six hundred years after their deaths. However, it is striking that although virtually every pre-Han and Han dynasty text commented on the very strange appearance and alien ways of the inhabitants of the south (particularly in the case of the people of Yue), this was never reflected in their depiction on bronze mirrors. In fact, the depiction of the south on these ancient bronzes is comparable to the representation of historical events in other artistic mediums of the same date.[47] The style in which the southern kings and ministers were portrayed is closely related to that employed for other contemporary representations of the human figure, in particular low-relief stone carvings and murals. This failure to realistically represent the kings and ministers of these ancient southern kingdoms was most likely the result of education. That is, although scholars and educated persons with access to the records found in ancient historical texts would have been well aware of traditions concerning the dress and customs of the inhabitants of ancient southern kingdoms, it is not at all clear that, so many centuries after the event, artisans (even the masters of their craft who made these Eastern Han dynasty mirrors) would have known of these descriptions. In the circumstances it is entirely understandable that these craftsmen were unable to portray elite figures from Wu and Yue

46. *Zhanguo ce*, p. 967 (Zhao ce 2: "Wuling wang pingzhou xianju 武靈王平晝閒居"). In his commentary on this passage Zhu Zugeng 諸祖耿 notes that Lin Yue 林越 is normally understood as Ou Yue 甌越; *Zhanguo ce*, pp. 977–78, n. 45.

47. See for example the depiction of events from southern history in the carvings of the Wu Liang shrine, which features illustrations of the murder of King Liao of Wu and that of his son, Prince Qingji. Wu, *The Wu Liang Shrine*, pp. 233–327. This provides an extensive analysis of the relationship between artistic representation and ancient historical texts, demonstrating that just as is the case with Eastern Han dynasty mirrors, stone carvings also drew on a wide variety of sources to create their depiction and not all of these traditions are now known to us.

history accurately. Likewise, the artisans of the Eastern Han dynasty would never have had the opportunity to see contemporary three-dimensional representations of Wu and Yue people, either in the form of bronze sculpture or—in the case of one apparently unique example excavated in Guangzhou—in the form of wood.[48] These objects have only been recovered through archaeological excavations during the course of the twentieth century; when the Jiangnan master craftsmen were producing their mirrors they were still resting underground.

Mirrors depicting events from the history of the conflict between the states of Wu and Yue form a stylistically homogenous group, although it is known from the inscriptions that they were produced by at least a couple of different makers. At present, all published examples of these pictorial mirrors seem to have been produced in the two provinces of Jiangsu and Zhejiang—and many of the artifacts themselves were excavated in this region. This would suggest that these bronzes were produced for a local luxury market; people of wealth would have bought these mirrors as an expression of local pride. However, a couple of these mirrors are thought to have been exported to Japan in antiquity.[49] This suggests that the events of the late Spring and Autumn period, when Wu and Yue fought for dominance in the south, were no longer merely incidents in regional history but had become part of the broader history of China. When these exceptionally high-quality objects were exported, they then served both as beautiful depictions of Chinese history, and as advertisements for the advanced state of contemporary Chinese metal-working technology.

---

48. The Guangzhou wooden figure was excavated in 1982 from a Han dynasty tomb at Liuyuan gang 柳園崗, but it appears never to have been published. However, an excavation photograph is on display at the Guangzhou City Museum. In this context, the reference in the *Guoyu*, p. 659 ("Yueyu xia"), to the fact that after Fan Li left his service, King Goujian of Yue commissioned a statue of him in the finest bronze is extremely interesting.

49. To place this in context, works by the Han dynasty master mirror-maker Zhang 張 of Suzhou have been found in ancient tombs across southern China and even overseas, indicating a vast trading network. These fine mirrors have been excavated in Jiangsu, Zhejiang, Hubei, and Hunan Provinces and in Japan. Chou, *Circles of Reflection*, p. 9.

Mirror Manufacturing in Han Dynasty Jiangnan

In the Han dynasty, the area that had once formed the heartlands of Wu and Yue was one of the centers of the Chinese mirror-making industry. The people of this region had been renowned for generations as expert metal workers, though they have generally received a great deal more attention and recognition for their skills in making swords than for any other aspect of their craft. The excellence of southern swords was recognized early on, and numerous ancient texts made reference to the technical superiority and amazing quality of these weapons. Metalworking in the Jiangnan region was traditionally based in small workshops, unlike the massive official works developed in the Central States.[50] During the Eastern Han dynasty, many mirrors (not just from the Jiangnan region) were made to take advantage of a growing market for artistic bronzes, with either a master's signature, or with a place name attached to them. These types of mirrors are known as *xingshi jing* 姓氏鏡 (surname mirrors) and *shangfang jing* 尚方鏡 (place-name mirrors), respectively.[51] The long tradition in the Jiangnan region of producing bronzes in small local workshops, under the control of a single master, resulted in them being ideally situated to take advantage of the demand for high-quality signed pieces.

The earliest recorded mirror-making workshop in the Shaoxing region was founded in the year 140, by the Governor of the Commandery of Kuaiji, Ma Zhen 馬臻.[52] However, this was merely a rare expression of official interest rather than the creation of an industry. Both Shaoxing and Suzhou were famous centers of the mirror-making industry during the Han dynasty. Comparatively little is known of the resources available at Suzhou, but the mineral wealth that provided the raw materials for master craftsmen in the Shaoxing region is well recorded.[53] The locations of a number of southern mines are recorded in ancient texts; others have been discovered through recent archaeological excavations. A number of the mirrors

50. Wagner, *Iron and Steel in Ancient China*, p. 97.
51. He Tangkun, *Zhongguo gudai tongjing de jishu yanjiu*, p. 24.
52. Wei Zhonghua and Xu Bingruo, *Shaoxing*, p. 10.
53. Wang Shilun, *Zhejiang chutu tongjing*, p. 9.

have inscriptions indicating that they were made in Wu: that is in the city of Suzhou or its immediate environs. Some of these mirrors were excavated at Shaoxing, which led to them originally being erroneously designated as being made in that city.[54] A number of Eastern Han dynasty pictorial mirrors with historical scenes lack any indication of place of manufacture—such as, for example, all the mirrors made by the master craftsman Zou 騶—however, these mirrors seem to have been a regional specialty, and there are no surviving examples that record a place of manufacture outside the bounds of the ancient kingdoms of Wu and Yue.

Iconography of Eastern Han Dynasty Mirrors

A small number of mirrors, depicting events from the history of the conflict between Wu and Yue, are today found in museums and private collections around the world. Through comparison with the stories found in ancient texts, it is possible to gain some understanding of the way in which the master craftsmen of the south presented the Wu-Yue conflict pictorially to the wealthy members of the ruling elite who were the ultimate purchasers of these bronzes.[55] The craftsmen depicted major events in southern history in a medium that ensured that their visualization of these historical scenes would become known far beyond the confines of the region.[56] Mirrors with this kind of design have been recorded since the Song dynasty. In the *Xixi congyu* 西溪叢語 (Collected jottings of [Yao] Xixi), Yao Kuan 姚寬

54. Wang Zhongshu, "Wuxian, Shanyin he Wuchang."

55. Eugene Wang, "Mirror, Death and Rhetoric," provides an alternative study of the iconography of these mirrors and their relationship with the events described in ancient Chinese texts. This study, however, only discusses five examples of these pictorial mirrors.

56. In the *Lunheng*, p. 249 ("Shuxu"), the author Wang Chong noted that pictorial representations of the conflict between the kingdoms of Wu and Yue were crucial for later interpretations of these events. Although it is not clear what kind of representations he was talking about, it is quite possible that mirrors played an important part in disseminating legends about the history of the kingdoms of Wu and Yue.

(1105–1162)—a scholar with a considerable interest in ancient history, particularly of the Wu-Yue region—wrote of one of his purchases:

> Recently I have obtained an exceptionally fine mirror with a large central boss, and in the fields between the smaller bosses there are four important historical figures. One [field] has the epithet "the loyal vassal Wu Zixu" one has "the king of Wu" one has "the king of Yue" and one has "Fan Li." There are also two women who are identified as "two women from the Yue royal house." All this is written in small clerical script, and [the mirrors] seem to be extremely ancient. As Shen Cunzhong (1035–1091) says: "High quality mirrors are the most difficult to find."
> 近得一夾鏡, 大鼻, 叩之中虛. 有冠劍四人, 一題忠臣伍子胥, 一吳王, 一越王, 一范蠡. 又二婦人雲越王二女. 皆小隸字製作奇古. 沈存中云: "夾鏡最難得."[57]

This is the earliest surviving reference to a mirror with a design based on events from the history of the Jiangnan region. The ultimate fate of this bronze is not known. In the following section, various related examples are discussed, in an attempt to understand the iconography of this special group of Eastern Han dynasty mirrors.

The Shanghai Museum Mirrors

The collection of the Shanghai Museum contains two very fine examples of bronze mirrors illustrating scenes from the conflict between the states of Wu and Yue. The origins of both mirrors are unknown, but they are thought to have been unearthed in modern times in Shaoxing, and they have been dated to the Eastern Han dynasty. The smaller of these two mirrors (Shanghai A) has a diameter of 19.5 centimeters and weighs 840 grams; the larger (Shanghai B) has a diameter of 20.7 centimeters and weighs 980 grams. The design of the two mirrors is virtually identical. On each mirror, four scenes are grouped around a central boss. In the first scene on the mirror, Shanghai A, King Fuchai of Wu is shown seated in an enclosed area,

57. Yao Kuan, *Xixi zongyu* A.18b. Shen Cunzhong is better known as the polymath scientist and statesman Shen Kuo 沈括 (1031–95), a native of the city of Suzhou.

his left hand raised. He is identified by the words: *Wuwang* 吳王 (the king of Wu). Proceeding clockwise round the mirror, the next scene contains a striking image of King Fuchai's minister, Wu Zixu, at the moment that he cut his throat with the sword Zhulu. The depiction of Wu Zixu committing suicide is justifiably famous. This scene was included on almost all the mirrors whose ornamentation depicted the dramatic events that marked the history of the south in the last years of the Spring and Autumn period. The expression of pain and frenzy, the gritted teeth, combine to form a very powerful image. This dramatic depiction is identified by the words: *zhong chen Wu Zixu* 忠臣伍子胥 (the loyal minister Wu Zixu). The third scene shows King Goujian of Yue standing, identified by the words: *Yuewang* 越王 (the king of Yue). By his side there is a kneeling figure, conventionally identified as the minister, Fan Li. The last scene on the mirror shows two standing women, their hands hidden in their sleeves. These figures are not identified by inscription on the mirror Shanghai A.[58]

There remains considerable ambiguity about the events depicted, since not all the scenes are easily identifiable. The depiction of King Fuchai of Wu, in particular, is highly enigmatic. The king of Wu is shown seated in an enclosure, raising his hand, but this does not seem to fit closely with any description of the events of his life found in ancient historical texts. In *Circles of Reflection*, Ju-hsi Chou has suggested that this image of King Fuchai sitting alone represents this monarch "filled with immense pride at his victory" against the state of Yue.[59] Alternatively, Kong Xiangxing 孔祥星 and Liu Yiman 劉一曼 suggest that this scene should be interpreted as depicting the king of Wu overcome with guilt at his involvement in the death of Wu Zixu.[60] In the absence of any obvious iconographical indications to point to a specific event in the life of the last king of Wu, it is impossible to rule out any interpretation categorically, but of these two theories, the first would seem to be the most likely. References to these events in ancient texts agree that King Fuchai of Wu only

---

58. A rubbing of Shanghai A is published in Kong Xiangxing and Liu Yiman, *Zhongguo tongjing tudian*, p. 451.

59. Chou, *Circles of Reflection*, p. 48.

60. Kong Xiangxing and Liu Yiman, *Zhongguo gudai tongjing*, p. 97.

regretted the death of Wu Zixu right at the end of his own life, just before his suicide at Qinyuhang Mountain. This does not seem to be related to what is depicted on these mirrors.

The larger mirror in the collection of the Shanghai Museum, Shanghai B, is more technically accomplished—the detailing being much finer. This bronze reverses the order of the last two scenes in Shanghai A, depicting King Goujian and Fan Li, and the images of the two women. On the mirror, Shanghai B, there is an inscription next to the figures of the two women, but there is some disagreement on how these words should be read. Some scholars have read this phrase as a two-character inscription: *Yunü* 玉女 (Jade girl), a mythological figure often depicted on mirrors with the Queen Mother of the West.[61] My reading is that this inscription is a four character phrase: *wang nü er ren* 王女二人 (Two ladies of the royal house), which is also the interpretation favored by Wang Shilun 王士倫 in his study of mirrors excavated in Zhejiang Province.[62] It was not uncommon for mirrors depicting historical events to also contain scenes from Chinese mythology. However, it seems to have been an artistic convention to pair scenes, so that for example a depiction of the Queen Mother of the West would be placed opposite a representation of the King Father of the East. Alternatively, two scenes of human figures would be paired with two depictions of animals. It is therefore unlikely, though not impossible, that the maker intended to depict three historical and one mythological scene on the mirror. The Shanghai B mirror also has a long inscription that forms a border around the four historical scenes. This inscription runs:

> Mr. Bo of Wuxiang Village made this mirror; the barbarian tribes of the four directions have surrendered; greatly I congratulate the country and the people; the Hu-barbarians have been removed and destroyed, and the world is restored; wind and rain come in season and are temperate; the five grains ripen.[63] May you long preserve your

61. Kong Xiangxing and Liu Yiman, *Zhongguo tongjing tudian*, p. 452.

62. Wang Shilun, *Zhejiang chutu tongjing*, p. 12.

63. By comparison with other mirrors with similar inscriptions, one character is missing from this line, *xi* 息 (to be at peace). This phrase should read "and the people are at peace." Chen Peifen, *Shanghai bowuguan zang qingtong jing*, p. 30.

> two parents; may you gain strength from Heaven; may you pass it on to later generations; and may you have joy that does not end.
> 兮吳向里柏氏作竟(鏡), 四夷服, 多賀國人民, 胡虜殄威(滅), 天下復, 風雨時節, 五穀孰(熟), 長保二親, 得天力, 傳告後世, 樂無亟(極).[64]

This kind of inscription was extremely common on Eastern Han dynasty mirrors made in the Jiangnan region. Such auspicious words were thought to form an appropriate border decoration for bronze mirrors. This inscription rhymes: the rhyming words being *fu* 服 (to submit), *fu* 復 (to be restored), *shu* 孰 (to ripen), *li* 力 (strength), and *ji* 亟 (end). Depending on the size of the mirror, phrases from this blessing could be omitted to produce a better fit.[65] The words *feng yu shi ji, wu gu* [*deng*] *shu* 風雨時節, 五穀【登】熟 (wind and rain are timely and temperate, the five grains [flourish] and ripen) is a quotation from the *Huainanzi*, describing the golden age when China was under the sagely rule of the Yellow Emperor: "In antiquity, when the Yellow Emperor ruled the world . . . thus the sun and moon were bright, the stars did not lose their courses, wind and rain were timely and temperate, and the five grains flourished and ripened." 昔者黃帝治天下 . . . 於是日月精明, 星辰不失其行, 風雨時節, 五穀登熟.[66]

Both these mirrors are traditionally said to have been found in Shaoxing, which was once the site of the capital of King Goujian's kingdom. It is likely that, in the Eastern Han dynasty, there were people in Zhejiang who were very proud of their former ruling house and who would have purchased representations of the chief events of their glorious history. Unfortunately, the role that local pride played in the manufacture and purchase of these exceptionally high-quality mirrors is difficult to gauge, since knowledge of the cultural conditions of the Jiangsu region in the Eastern Han dynasty is patchy to nonexistent.

---

64. Shanghai bowuguan, *Shanghai bowuguan zang qingtongqi*, fig. 95; Shanghai bowuguan, *Shanghai bowuguan zang qingtongqi fuce*, p. 100.

65. This kind of inscription was not the prerogative of one particular maker. These auspicious words, with variants, can also be seen on the works of the master mirror-makers Wang 王, Long 龍, and Xiao 肖. Karlgren, *Early Chinese Mirror Inscriptions*, pp. 38–40.

66. *Huainanzi*, pp. 476–78 ("Lanming xun" 覽冥訓).

The Yamaguchi Collection Mirror

This mirror, which was probably produced by the same maker as Shanghai B, is of the type known as a *chema* 車馬 (chariot and horses) mirror. As with other Eastern Han dynasty pictorial mirrors, there are four scenes depicted on the back of the Yamaguchi mirror, arranged around a central boss. The distinguishing characteristic of *chema* mirrors was that two of the scenes depict a chariot pulled by a team of four horses. Other mirrors of this kind feature depictions of deities such as the ever-popular Queen Mother of the West, but on the Yamaguchi mirror, there is an illustration of the scene where Wu Zixu cut his throat with a sword; in the field opposite, King Fuchai is shown in a dramatic stance, while behind him an unidentified person rears back in horror, eyes wide. As on the Shanghai mirrors, Wu Zixu is identified by the words: *zhong chen Wu Zixu*, while King Fuchai is identified with the phrase: *Wuwang*. The Yamaguchi mirror, like Shanghai B, has an inscription around the edge, forming a border around the central pictorial area. Mr. Mo of Wushang Village is identified as the maker of the mirror, and it is highly probable that this mirror-maker was the same as the Mr. Bo of Wuxiang Village who made the Shanghai B mirror: "Mr. Mo of Wushang Village made this mirror; the barbarian tribes of the four directions have submitted; greatly I congratulate the country; the people are at peace; the foreign barbarians have been removed and destroyed; the world is restored; wind and rain is timely and temperate; the five grains ripen. May you long preserve your two parents and Heaven's strength." 吳尚里陌氏作竟[鏡], 四夷服, 多賀國家, 人民息, 胡虜殄威[滅], 天下復, 風雨時節, 五穀孰[熟], 長保二親, 天力.[67]

The scene on this mirror—which shows the king of Wu in a dramatic posture, while a second figure starts back in alarm—is most enigmatic. This does not obviously correspond with any event of King Fuchai's life (or indeed with the lives of any other king of Wu), at least as described in pre-Eastern Han dynasty texts. One of the few scholars to have considered this scene, Hayashi Minao 林巳奈夫, suggests that it represents an argument between Wu Zixu and King

67. Umehara Sueji, *Shōkō kokyō shūei*, fig. 49.

Fuchai.[68] My suggestion is that this scene depicts the divination of King Fuchai of Wu's dream, which was the occasion of a dramatic confrontation. This story occurs in both the *Yuejue shu* and the *Wu Yue chunqiu*. According to both these texts, King Fuchai had a dream that he believed to be prophetic and that Prime Minister Pi interpreted very favorably. When the dream was interpreted as inauspicious by Gongsun Sheng, King Fuchai had Gong beaten to death.[69] This scene would then depict the king of Wu's rage at Gongsun Sheng's unfavorable interpretation of his dream.[70] However, it is entirely possible that the master mirror-makers of the Jiangnan region were not dependent on the accounts found in surviving historical texts for the scenes that they depicted on their mirrors. They may well have been drawing upon oral traditions that were never transcribed, which would explain the difficulties of identifying scenes featuring King Fuchai.

The Kawai Collection Mirror

This interesting mirror lacks any inscription to place its manufacture in context. As with the Yamaguchi mirror, the provenance of this mirror is not known, but it is thought to have been made in the Jiangnan region during the Eastern Han dynasty. The Kawai Collection mirror depicts a highly ornate dragon and tiger in two of the four scenes arranged around the central boss. These beasts are depicted opposite each other. In the other two scenes, there is an extremely unusual juxtaposition of a historical event with a mythological scene. In one scene, the Queen Mother of the West is depicted seated on a raised dais. She is shown with two standing attendants. Beside her are the identifying words: *Xiwangmu* 西王母. Opposite her sits the figure of King Fuchai of Wu, elaborately dressed, and seated

---

68. Hayashi Minao, *Kandai no kamigami*, pp. 119–20.

69. *Yuejue shu*, pp. 74–75 ("Ji Wuwang zhanmeng"); *Wu Yue chunqiu*, pp. 78–80 ("Fuchai neizhuan").

70. This depiction seems to be related to that found on an Eastern Han dynasty tomb painting. In 1954, a tomb was excavated at Beizhai Village 北寨村, Yi'nan County 沂南縣, Shandong, which contained wall paintings of both King Fuchai of Wu and Wu Zixu. The depiction of the former seems close to that found on the Yamaguchi mirror. This tomb has been dated to the 150s. Thompson, "Confucian Paragon or Popular Deity?" p. 20.

on a dais. The king is identified by the inscription: *Wuwang*. He is accompanied by five attendants apparently carrying pikes or spears: four of them stand; one of them kneels. There is an inscription near these figures reading: *bo gong* 帛貢 (silk is presented).[71]

The presentation of silk scene on this artifact does not correspond closely to any story, now found in Han dynasty or earlier texts, describing the history of the kingdoms of Wu and Yue. However, King Fuchai of Wu reportedly received numerous gifts from King Goujian, and there are references to the king of Yue presenting silk to a number of other rulers of the late Spring and Autumn period. In the *Guoyu* the program of bribery instituted by King Goujian of Yue in the wake of his surrender at Kuaijishan with a view to gaining allies among the rulers of other states was described in detail: "The king said: 'To the south of the state of Yue there is Chu, to the west there is Jin and to the north there is Qi. Every spring and autumn, I humbly present skins and coins, jade and silk, men and women to them; and I have never yet dared to break off [this tribute] because I want to use [my good relationship with these states] in order to take revenge on Wu.'" 王曰: "越國南則楚, 西則晉, 北則齊. 春秋皮幣, 玉帛, 子女以賓服焉, 未嘗敢絶求以報吳."[72]

This passage was apparently written by someone with little awareness of the geography of pre-unification China, given that the kingdom of Chu in fact lay to the west of Yue, and Jin lay to the northwest. Although the depiction of the king of Wu on the Kawai mirror is not readily identifiable as a scene from the history of the Wu-Yue conflict, it is possible that it was intended to depict the presentation of tribute from King Goujian to King Fuchai.

The Nanjing Museum Mirror

This mirror is very close in appearance to those in the Shanghai Museum, and the mirror from the Yamaguchi collection. This mirror shows exactly the same scenes as the two in the Shanghai Museum,

71. Umehara Sueji, *Shōkō kokyō shūei*, fig. 56. The present whereabouts of this mirror are not known.

72. *Guoyu*, p. 620 ("Wuyu"). The same story is recorded in the *Wu Yue chunqiu*, p. 163 ("Goujian fa Wu waizhuan"), which also used the term *gong* 貢 (to pay tribute) in its description of what the king of Yue was doing.

clockwise in the following order. First there is the scene of King Fuchai of Wu sitting alone in an enclosure. This is followed by the depiction of Wu Zixu cutting his throat. Then there is the scene of King Goujian of Yue standing next to his kneeling minister, Fan Li. Finally, there is the scene depicting the two standing women. This mirror gives a different identification for these women. Here they are described in the accompanying inscription as: *Yuewang er nü* 越王二女 (Two women of the king of Yue). The Nanjing mirror was unearthed at Hanjiang County 邗江縣 in Jiangsu Province. The mirror measures 21 centimeters in diameter. As with several other mirrors of the same kind, depicting the important events of Spring and Autumn period history in the states of Wu and Yue, there is a border around the central pictorial field, which contains an inscription, including the maker's name. The inscription in the border runs:

> Mr. Zou made this mirror; the barbarian tribes of the four directions submit; greatly I congratulate the country; the people are at peace; the foreign barbarians have been removed and destroyed; the world is restored; the wind and rain is timely and temperate; the five grains ripen. May you long preserve your two parents, and gain strength from Heaven, may you pass it [your strength] on to later generations, and may you have joy that does not end.
> 鄒氏作竟[鏡], 四夷服, 多賀國人民息, 胡虜殄威[滅], 天下復, 風雨時節, 五穀熟, 長保二親, 得天力, 傳告後世, 樂無極.[73]

The wording of this auspicious inscription was clearly seen as being particularly appropriate for a mirror with scenes illustrating the great events of southern history on the back: hence this text was chosen by a number of different makers to ornament their works. Although the inscription was also used by other makers to ornament mirrors that did not feature depictions of events from the conflict between Wu and Yue, there are no known mirrors showing such historical figures as Wu Zixu and King Fuchai of Wu that have an alternative auspicious inscription.

---

73. Kong Xiangxing and Liu Yiman, *Zhongguo tongjing tudian*, p. 453.

The Lizhu Mirror

The master mirror-maker Zou is known to have made at least four mirrors depicting events in the conflict between the states of Wu and Yue. The whereabouts of the second are not known, but it left the country in 1949, and is now reported to be in a private collection outside China. (This mirror is known to scholars only through rubbings).[74] Little is known of the circumstances in which this second mirror was found, but it was thought to have been discovered at Lizhu 離渚, a village in Shaoxing County. It is slightly smaller than the Nanjing Museum mirror, measuring 20.5 centimeter in diameter, and shows exactly the same scenes in the same order. On both mirrors, the identifying wording by each figure is exactly the same, as is the inscription that forms the border.[75]

The British Museum Mirror

The third known mirror made by the master mirror-maker Zou is now in the British Museum. Again, four historical scenes are shown, in the same order (as in the previous examples of mirrors made by the same maker). On this mirror, all the figures except that of King Fuchai carry identifying inscriptions—as the loyal vassal Wu Zixu, the king of Yue, Fan Li, and the two women of the king of Yue—that are identical to the mirror in the Nanjing Museum collection. This mirror was chosen as a frontispiece by Umehara Sueji 梅原末治 for his book *Shōkō kokyō shūei* 紹興古鏡聚英 (Selected fine ancient mirrors from Shaoxing).[76] This mirror is identified as coming from the private collection of a Mrs. Sedgwick of London. In 1968, this mirror was given to the British Museum, where it is now on permanent display in the Chinese gallery.

Mirrors in Chinese Private Collections

Three of the mirrors made by the master Zou are well known—those in the collections of the Nanjing and the British Museum—and images of the Lizhu mirror have been extensively published.

74. Wang Jiehua et al. eds., *Gu Yue yizhen yanjiu*, pp. 89–90.
75. Wang Shilun, *Zhejiang chutu tongjing*, fig. 33.
76. Umehara Sueji, *Shōkō kokyō shūei*, p. 8.

The fourth mirror surfaced in 2011 in an important article in the journal *Shoucangjia* 收藏家 (Collectors), which described nine previously unknown mirrors of this type in private collections in China. The first of these is a newly discovered mirror by the master Zou, now in a private collection in Hangzhou; see figure 4. Featured in the same article was a mirror of almost identical design, now in a private collection in Shaoxing; but this mirror is attributed in the inscription around the edge to a maker named Zhou 周 (see figure 5). A further mirror (also said to derive from Shaoxing and again with identical scenes) is also depicted, though no information is given about the present whereabouts of this object. This mirror features an inscription around the edge, which is unfortunately unreadable in the published photograph; see figure 6. Zhang Honglin 張宏林 transcribes part of this inscription as: "*Shang you zhu wang bi bu yang* 上有諸王辟不羊 [祥]" (Above there are the kings who ward off ill fortune). This mirror has also been attributed to Master Zhou.

The author of the article also features two mirrors (depicting the four standard historical scenes) from his own private collection. These are of perhaps slightly lower quality than other examples, and neither of these are signed by their maker. See figures 7 and 8. Both these objects are said to have been discovered in the Shaoxing region. A further two mirrors from Zhang Honglin's collection feature two scenes from Wu history paired with two directional animals similar to the example in the Kawai Collection; the king of Wu is depicted sitting in an enclosure opposite the scene of Wu Zixu's suicide. In the other fields a dragon—the symbol of the east—is shown opposite a tiger—the symbol of the west. Again, neither of these two mirrors is signed and only one scene is identified with an inscription; that of the death of Wu Zixu; see figures 9 and 10. This article also mentions a further pair of mirrors in which different mythological figures appear. The first shows an unusual combination of deities, as well as living humans and animals. In one pair of scenes, the suicide of Wu Zixu is depicted in the field opposite a representation of the Queen Mother of the West, with a couple of feathered attendants (identified by the author as *yuren* 羽人) by her side. In the other pair of scenes, a horse (ridden by another of these winged creatures) is depicted opposite a *Bixie* mythological creature;

see figure 11.[77] In the case of the ninth mirror described in this article, which is now in a private collection in Shaoxing, the scene of the king of Wu sitting in his enclosure is paired with the depiction of Wu Zixu. In the opposite fields, one scene shows a single Bixie and the other shows a pair of these animals. This last mirror is identified in the inscription around the edge as the work of a master maker named Tian 田; see figure 12.[78] Most unusually, the feet of the three Bixie intrude into the border inscription, disrupting the auspicious message found there.

The Cleveland Museum Mirror

This very fine mirror has been dated to the late Eastern Han dynasty. It measures 19.5 centimeters in diameter and weighs 847 grams. The mirror was broken at some point in the past, repaired, and then coated with black paint to give it an even appearance and a fine finish. Two of the fields depict the Queen Mother of the West and her attendant the Jade Girl, which are arranged opposite the King Father of the East. On this mirror only the Queen Mother of the West is identified by an inscription. The other two fields have historical scenes: one depicts King Fuchai of Wu seated in a screened off enclosure. Opposite the king of Wu there is a highly unusual representation of King Goujian of Yue and his minister Fan Li. As was common to other representations of these two men on bronze mirrors, the king of Yue stands and Fan Li kneels at his side. However, in this example there is a small object on a stand in between them—which, as Ju-hsi Chou remarked in the catalog of the Cleveland Museum's collection of Chinese mirrors, looks remarkably like a pineapple; see figure 13.[79] This object was the gall that King Goujian reportedly kept beside his seat, and that he tasted to remind himself of the

77. Zhang Honglin is almost certainly incorrect in his attribution of these figures. Given that there are a trio of these winged creatures represented in attendance on the Queen Mother of the West, they almost certainly represent the three Blue Birds (*qingniao* 青鳥) described in the *Shanhaijing* 山海經 (Classic of mountains and seas) as responsible for feeding her. *Shanhaijing*, p. 358 ("Hainei beijing" 海內北經).

78. Zhang Honglin, "Yi shi wei jian de Wu Zixu huaxiang jing."

79. Chou, *Circles of Reflection*, p. 48.

bitterness of his defeat at Kuaiji. However, it would seem likely that this scene, being so similar to the common depiction of the king of Yue and his minister Fan Li, was that which was intended to be represented in all cases, even though other known examples of this scene do not actually show the gall. What is further remarkable about this mirror is that it is the only known example showing scenes from southern history that does not include a depiction of the suicide of Wu Zixu.

Eugene Wang, in his study of a selection of this group of Eastern Han dynasty mirrors, represents them as a warning from history; as a remonstrance in a flat, round, bronze form. He noted the way in which both scenes and individuals appear on these mirrors in contrasting pairs: the clever King Goujian who listened to the advice of his ministers is depicted opposite the foolish King Fuchai who did not. The king of Yue is portrayed working hard, in conversation with his ministers, whereas the king of Wu is either alone, quarrelling with someone, or reveling in luxurious living. The more interesting pairing is that of the two women from Yue with Wu Zixu. The women are shown in calm and demure poses, and Wu Zixu in a moment of frenzy. The women represent sex; Wu represents death. This juxtaposition was no doubt intended to remind viewers that women posed a great danger to national security: beautiful women could force loyal ministers to commit suicide and could bring the state to the brink of destruction. Eugene Wang associates this theme with political issues in Eastern Han dynasty China, in particular with the interference of women in the government.[80] It is certainly correct to say that during the Eastern Han dynasty the growing power of empresses, empress dowagers, and other maternal relatives of the emperor was a source of considerable concern, particularly among members of the ruling elite, who would have been the prospective purchasers for the exceptionally high-quality signed mirrors featuring scenes from southern history on the backs. However, though images of seventeen mirrors of this type have been published to date, none have been derived from archaeological excavations; and there remains considerable uncertainty about exactly when these mirrors

80. Eugene Wang, "Mirror, Death, and Rhetoric," pp. 515–16.

were produced. There is also no strong evidence that an interest in the rise and fall of ancient southern kingdoms was necessarily strongly correlated with a concern about women becoming involved in politics. It would seem more likely that the master mirror-makers of Jiangnan created these magnificent works in response to their own cultural heritage, rather than reflecting contemporary political problems in faraway Luoyang.

Zhang Honglin, in his study of examples of these mirrors found in Chinese private collections, suggests that they functioned in some kind of apotropaic manner. Unlike earlier scholars studying the iconography of these mirrors, Zhang Honglin has had access to a number of examples featuring mythological animals and deities, particularly the Bixie (whose name literally means warding off evil), which did not appear in earlier publications on the subject. The predominance of this theme in mirrors of his sample, and the examples of mirrors in Japanese collections featuring mythological scenes, led him to conclude that by the Eastern Han dynasty (when these mirrors were made) Wu Zixu had become an important deity within the Jiangnan region: hence depictions of this powerful figure accompanied by mythological creatures were intended to preserve the possessor from harm. It is unfortunate that Zhang Honglin does not seem to have been aware of the Cleveland Museum mirror, which features deities and historical figures from Wu and Yue, but crucially does not contain the figure of Wu Zixu himself.

One of the key problems for understanding these mirrors is that, to date, in spite of thousands of such objects being excavated from Eastern Han dynasty tombs, none of these historical mirrors has come from an archaeological site in a datable context. This means that any attempt to determine the cultural milieu in which they were produced is highly problematic. In his study of the dating of these objects, Wang Zhongshu 王仲殊 proposed a late Eastern Han dynasty date, perhaps even as late as the Jian'an 建安 reign era (196–219).[81] If this is correct, then the production of these mirrors should be understood in the context of the rise to power of the Sun family (the eventual founders of the Three Kingdoms era state of Wu) in the Jiangnan

81. Wang Zhongshu, "Qingyang wei Wujun jing gongkao," p. 642.

region. The Sun family famously claimed descent from Sun Wu, the military strategist who is said to have played an important role in King Helü's extremely successful campaigns, and to whom the *Sunzi bingfa* 孫子兵法 (Master Sun's arts of war) is attributed. If these mirrors were intended as a direct compliment to the Sun family it is hard to see why none of them would depict Sun Wu. On the other hand, if these mirrors are viewed as a more subtle reflection on contemporary political issues, then they might be seen as indicating both a rising interest in the history of the kingdom of Wu among the Jiangnan ruling elite (at a time when the single most powerful family in the region claimed a strong personal connection with these events), as well as a more practical concern about the fact that the Han empire was crumbling. Being faced with the prospect of growing autonomy and freedom from central control, this may have aroused great interest in the history of Wu and Yue, a time when the cities of Suzhou and Shaoxing were the capitals of these ancient southern kingdoms. The partition of the Han dynasty during the Three Kingdoms era would see the lands of Wu become independent for the first time in nearly seven hundred years. Contemplating this prospect, it is hardly surprising that the ruling elite might have found a special message in these mirrors: a warning from history and an encouragement for the future. In this reading of their meaning, the bronze mirrors of the Eastern Han represent a very special manifestation of the cherishing of antiquity in the region. They are a commemoration and representation of the ongoing cultural importance of the history of the kingdom of Wu, both for the Jiangnan region and for China as a whole.

Representing the Royal House of Wu

The names of very few individuals from the kingdom of Wu have been transmitted to the present day, either in ancient texts or in the inscriptions recorded on bronze vessels. For many of these people, little more than their name is known. Nevertheless, sufficient records do survive to be able to speak of certain striking characteristics manifest within the Wu royal family that deserve to receive more attention than has perhaps been the case so far. It is clear that Wu society in the late Spring and Autumn period was highly bellicose, and that this kingdom was regularly at war with its neighbors, both small and large. The historical significance of these campaigns (for example, the campaign against Chu during the reign of King Helü, which led to the sack of their capital, or the victory over Qi at the battle of Ailing in the reign of King Fuchai) has been much discussed. What has been less frequently mentioned is that the kings of Wu directed these triumphant campaigns personally. Although these monarchs could have called upon the services of such distinguished generals as Sun Wu and Wu Zixu, it is clear that, in fact, the kings took personal control of their armies. Every text that records the history of the kingdom of Wu mentions the military experiences of members of the Wu royal house and these clearly took their toll. For example, had King Zhufan of Wu not been in the front line, directing his army into battle at Chao, he would not have been shot by a hidden sniper; had King Helü not been determined to lead the attack against Yue he would not have received the wound from which he eventually died. Although command of the Wu army held its own risks for members of the royal family, it seems to have been necessary for them to prove their worth in this way, generation after generation. The importance of military competence for the kings and princes of Wu often seems to have been underestimated or ignored, perhaps because several non-royal generals became so famous in the history of this ancient southern kingdom.

Although extravagant claims have been made with regard to what is known about the civil administration of the kingdom of Wu, in fact very little can be determined. Studies of the administration of a wide variety of Spring and Autumn period states, from both within and without the Zhou confederacy, have demonstrated that the profile of individuals appointed to high office varied enormously from one state to the next (as well as displaying considerable differences over time).[82] Some states, most notably Jin after the usurpation of the marquisate by the Quwo 曲沃 lineage, excluded junior members of the ruling house from government, in favor of other aristocratic families and maternal relatives; however, others welcomed these princelings' participation. It has been suggested that the government of Wu

82. Blakeley, "Functional Disparities in the Socio-Political Traditions of Spring and Autumn Period China."

changed its composition significantly in the wake of the usurpation of the throne by King Helü: prior to this event, high office within the kingdom was normally held by members of the royal family; afterwards, with so many princes and royal grandsons having been forced into exile by the king, Helü had no choice but to recruit men from outside the royal family. To support this argument, the examples of General Sun Wu from Qi, together with Wu Zixu and Prime Minister Pi from Chu are frequently cited; and these men did indeed play a highly significant part in the administration, first under King Helü and later under his son, King Fuchai. These instances of such high-profile positions being awarded to foreigners might appear to be conclusive evidence of a significant change in government practice in the reigns of the last two kings of Wu—but in fact this is not the case. The examples of the Qu family in the reign of King Shoumeng, or that of Qing Feng from Qi (appointed to a senior government position by King Yuji), indicate that this was a long-standing practice in the kingdom of Wu, and suggests that foreigners were not excluded on principle from the highest offices in the kingdom.

Perhaps the most surprising characteristic accorded to the royal house of Wu is their reputation as an extremely affectionate family. This may seem paradoxical particularly in view of King Helü's role in the assassination of King Liao, and his subsequent famous persecution of numerous members of his immediate family. And yet this reputation was perhaps not unearned. This can be seen in the story of fraternal succession between the Kings Zhufan, Yuji, and Yumei, which is often explained as the result of their great love and respect for their younger brother Jizha. This impression of family affection is not belied by the records found on bronze vessel inscriptions such as the "Gouwu Jizi *jian*" quoted above. Comparatively good relations between members of the ruling house may also serve to explain the fact that King Helü's brother and cousins seem to have lived long lives in comfortable exile. Providing that they did not attempt to set foot within the borders of the kingdom of Wu, he seems to have regarded it as unnecessary to pursue them further. The quality of magnanimity (not a common characteristic among the rulers of states of the Zhou confederacy when dealing with troublesome relatives) was also displayed towards more serious enemies: how else to explain the survival of King Goujian of Yue after his surrender? Some members of the Wu government, most notably Wu Zixu, were in favor of executing the king; others such as Prime Minister Pi advocated accepting King Goujian's surrender and turning him into a vassal. (The prime minister's position was ever afterwards ascribed to his having accepted bribes from the kingdom of Yue.) Yet the final decision in this matter must have been made by King Fuchai of Wu, and the king chose to spare the life of his greatest enemy, not just on this occasion but every time that the growing threat posed by Yue was mentioned. Kindness and affection were not common characteristics among the rulers of the Spring and Autumn period, and in the case of King Fuchai, they eventually brought him and his kingdom terrible suffering and pain.

1. *Mirror with horses and chariots*. Yamaguchi collection. Image derived from Umehara Sueji, *Shōkō kokyō shūei*.

2. *Mirror with Wu Zixu, a deity, a dragon, and a tiger.* Kawai collection. Image derived from Umehara Sueji, *Shōkō kokyō shūei.*

3. *Mirror with figures from the story of Wu Zixu, the Loyal Minister.* Eastern Han dynasty. British Museum, Gift of Mrs. Walter Sedgwick. © Trustees of the British Museum.

4. *Mirror with figures from the story of Wu Zixu, by Master Zou.* Private Collection (1). From Zhang Honglin, "Yi shi wei jian." Image courtesy of Kong Zhen.

5. *Mirror with figures from the story of Wu Zixu, by Master Zhou*. Private Collection (2). From Zhang Honglin, "Yi shi wei jian." Image courtesy of Tang Qinbiao.

6. *Mirror with figures from the story of Wu Zixu, attributed to Master Zhou*. Private Collection (3). From Zhang Honglin, "Yi shi wei jian." Image courtesy of Zhang Honglin.

7. *Mirror with figures from the story of Wu Zixu.* Private Collection (4). From Zhang Honglin, "Yi shi wei jian." Image courtesy of Zhang Honglin.

8. *Mirror with figures from the story of Wu Zixu.* Private Collection (5). From Zhang Honglin, "Yi shi wei jian." Image courtesy of Zhang Honglin.

9. *Mirror with figures from the story of Wu Zixu, a dragon and a tiger.* Private Collection (6). From Zhang Honglin, "Yi shi wei jian." Image courtesy of Zhang Honglin.

10. *Mirror with figures from the story of Wu Zixu, a dragon and a tiger.* Private Collection (7). From Zhang Honglin, "Yi shi wei jian." Image courtesy of Zhang Honglin.

11. *Mirror with Wu Zixu, a deity, a dragon, and a tiger.* Private Collection (8). From Zhang Honglin, "Yi shi wei jian." Image courtesy of Kong Zhen.

12. *Mirror with Wu Zixu, a king, a Bixie, and another mythical animal.* Private Collection (9). From Zhang Honglin, "Yi shi wei jian." Image courtesy of Sun Haifang.

13. *Mirror with deities and kings, 2nd century.* China, Eastern Han dynasty (25–220). Bronze, 19.5 cm. The Cleveland Museum of Art, Gift of Drs. Thomas and Martha Carter in Honor of Sherman E. Lee 1995.331.

PART TWO

Case Studies

4

Commemorating Master Ji of Yanling

Land is shaped by climate and time. Landscape is man-made; it is land seen by mankind and reshaped by people's attitudes towards that environment and the emotions evoked by memory. Perceptions of landscape are refined by awareness of history and culture: the great men who walked through this landscape and the artists and writers who described it.[1] The physical geography and architecture of the province of Jiangsu have been documented more thoroughly, and over a longer period of time, than almost anywhere else in China. As a result of this documentation, the landscape of Jiangsu is embedded with many layers of meaning, which have been created by generations of scholars, artists, poets, and writers. The association of this storied landscape with the history and culture of the ancient kingdom of Wu profoundly affected the understanding of many who travelled to sites in this area. The earliest surviving account of the historical landscape of Wu is found in the "Ji Wudi zhuan" chapter of the *Yuejue shu*, a text compiled towards the beginning of the Eastern Han dynasty. This text described, among other things, the landscape of the kingdom and the famous buildings of its capital city; so great was the subsequent importance of the "Ji Wudi zhuan" chapter (and of the related chapter concerning the landscape of the kingdom of Yue) that these two texts came to be regarded as the most significant part of the *Yuejue shu*. As a result, the *Yuejue shu* is often described as an early forerunner of the gazetteer.[2] The "Ji Wudi zhuan" records two specific places associated with Prince Jizha of Wu, the location of his home, and the site of his grave:

---

1. This definition of land and landscape is drawn from Hunter, *Land into Landscape*, p. 53.

2. Lin Tianwei, *Fangzhixue yu difangshi yanjiu*, p. 15.

Piling was formerly known as Yanling, and Master Ji of Wu lived here.
毗陵，故爲延陵，吳季子所居.[3]

The Central Tomb at Shanghu (Upper Lake) in Piling is the grave of Master Ji of Yanling. It stands seventy *li* from town (29.05 km). Shanghu drains into Shangzhou (Upper Marsh). In antiquity, the tomb of Master Ji was known as the wastes of Yanling.
毗陵上湖中冢者，延陵季子冢也，去縣七十里. 上湖通上洲. 季子冢古名延陵.[4]

Throughout the imperial period, many detailed accounts were written of later developments in the lands that had once belonged to the kingdom of Wu. A number of these gazetteers describe the building or restoration of monuments to the memory of Prince Jizha of Wu. These local histories record the changing fortunes of the temples, memorials, and shrines dedicated to the prince. They describe the waxing and waning of his cult over the centuries, and the interplay of a number of social groups brought together by a common interest. National and local elites, scholars and officials, artists, poets, and local people all joined together to commemorate the prince and to pay tribute to his memory. Their financial patronage allowed for repairs, extensions, and, if necessary, the complete rebuilding of commemorative sites, while literary patronage through the writing of a poem or essay, or perhaps the editing of a temple gazetteer, allowed for a high prestige involvement in an important local site.[5] However, perhaps as a reflection of the prince's marginal status during his own lifetime, the monuments raised to Prince Jizha never managed to achieve the broad appeal (nor the number of visitors) of other sites in Jiangsu Province that were more strongly associated with the royal house of Wu, its rise to glory, and its ignominious collapse. Nor were commemorative structures apparently ever erected to Prince Jizha

3. *Yuejue shu*, p. 15 ("Ji Wudi zhuan"). The association between Piling and Prince Jizha of Wu is discussed exhaustively in Luo Wobai and Shi Hong, *Changzhou shihua*.

4. *Yuejue shu*, p. 15 ("Ji Wudi zhuan").

5. The significance of these two main types of patronage, often indulged in by the same people, is stressed in Katz, *Images of the Immortal*, p. 121.

outside the immediate confines of the territory of his fief, or the area of the ancient kingdom of Wu itself.

As with many other important historical figures from the ancient kingdom of Wu (including several of Prince Jizha's closest relatives) a number of memorials were built to commemorate the prince, and religious foundations were created to offer sacrifices to his memory. These monuments were visited by people from every social class, from the emperor downwards. However, by and large, there seems to have been very little interest in recording the precise dates of restorations or rebuildings. Accounts tend to stress the antiquity of the tradition handed down from earlier generations—rather than describing the successive ruin and abandonment, followed by rebuilding, of monuments commemorating the great figures of local history. As a result, it can be very hard to get a clear sense of the development and history of the monuments erected to commemorate Prince Jizha. However, enough has been recorded in gazettes and local histories to make it apparent that sites and temples associated with the prince underwent spectacular changes in their fortunes during the imperial period. Buildings erected to commemorate Prince Jizha of Wu fall into two main categories. There are those which were directly associated with him: that is, his grave and the nearby temple (*miao* 廟) with the stone stele erected outside. The tomb is still found at what is now Shen'gang 申港 in Jiangyin County 江陰縣, though the temple is long gone. In addition to these sites, there were a number of other temples and shrines, dedicated to Prince Jizha, that were built throughout the imperial period in towns of the Jiangnan region. These memorials were occasionally criticized for lacking any direct association with the memory of the prince, which is indicative of the strictly local nature of the cult of Prince Jizha of Wu. Indeed, the vast majority of these memorials seem to have been built within the borders of the area believed to have once formed Prince Jizha's fief.

Over the centuries, a number of members of the literati wrote poems or prose that recorded their visits to the sites of monuments dedicated to the famous Prince Jizha of Wu. These literary works were crucial for attracting visitors from further afield, and for establishing the reputation of monuments among the educated ruling elite, the group of visitors that left by far the best records of their travels. These visitors participated in (and helped sponsor) the cult of Prince Jizha, and this was crucial for the survival of the cult until modern times. To help place these structures in their proper historical and social context, the remaining chapters of this book will, where appropriate, include biographical information about the individuals mentioned in gazettes and local histories. This should give some sense of the type of people who became involved in the restoration and beautification of the monuments that commemorated members of the royal family of the ancient kingdom of Wu, and of the relationship of these individuals with other patrons of these shrines and temples.

The Tomb of Prince Jizha of Wu

There are very few accounts in Chinese imperial-era literature of visitors recording their travels to the tomb of Prince Jizha of Wu. After the Han dynasty reference in the "Ji Wudi zhuan" chapter of the *Yuejue shu*, the existence of the prince's tomb is not mentioned until the 813 CE Tang dynasty general gazetteer for the empire, the *Yuanhe junxian tuzhi* 元和郡縣圖志 (Illustrated gazetteer of commanderies and counties in the Yuanhe reign era, 806–820) by Li Jifu 李吉甫 (758–814, *jinshi* after 806)—at which point in history the grave was located within the boundaries of Jinling County 晉陵縣. The tomb is described in this text as being situated seventy *li* to the north of the county seat, to the west of Shenfu 申甫 (now Shen'gang).[6] Unlike some other major historical figures of the Spring and Autumn period, Prince Jizha of Wu is only said to possess a single tomb, and the traditional attribution of this site has not been disputed. As a result, gazetteers which describe the tomb of Prince Jizha focus their attention on changes in administrational boundaries and differences in nomenclature, rather than disputing the precise location of the grave or weighing the rival claims of different tomb sites. Since the tomb of the prince generally seems to have attracted very little attention

6. Li Jifu, *Yuanhe junxian tuzhi*, p. 658. Li Jifu, styled Hongxian 弘憲, was the son of Li Qiyun 李栖筠. During the Yongtai 永泰 (765) reign-period, Li Qiyun wrote a dozen poems about the Changzhou region, as recorded in Shi Nengzhi, *Xianchun Piling zhi*, p. 3574.

from imperial-era literati there are only a handful of references to this site in poetry. A rare example of verse on the subject of Prince Jizha's tomb is found in the work of the Southern Song dynasty poet Liu Zihuan 劉子寰 (*jinshi* 1217), who wrote a *jueju* verse entitled "Jizi mu shi" 季子墓詩 (A poem on the tomb of Master Ji):[7]

> Once, travelling to the shrine and temple, I sacrificed to the [princely] hermit,
> I have come to understand the pettiness of the conflicts between the [kingdoms of] Man and Chu.[8]
> Does not every successive generation of Wu [kings] have their own tombs?
> But ten thousand generations only care about the grave of Master Ji.
> 一上祠宮酹白雲, 始知蠻觸浪汾汾.
> 有吳何代無陵墓, 萬世惟知季子墳.[9]

This poem would seem to have been written on the occasion of the poet's visit to the prince's grave, and the verse thus falls into the *huaigu* genre—that is, it describes the poet's personal response to the sight of a historic, culturally important place. At this point in the Song dynasty, there were already apparently a number of commemorative buildings associated with the tomb. As was conventional in this genre of poetry, regret is implicitly expressed for the loss of so great a man as the prince, whose like will not be seen again. For the poet, there seems to have been no need to elaborate on Prince Jizha of Wu's significance in Chinese history or traditional culture. In spite of the prince's "foreign" origins (so consistently stressed in the ancient texts), by the

---

7. The poet Liu Zihuan was styled Qifu 圻父, and entitled Huangli Weng 篁塛翁. In the gazetteers that quote this poem, Liu is frequently described as a Yuan dynasty person, a confusion that seems to have arisen as a result of the date of his *jinshi* exams, since there was both a Song Emperor Ningzong (r. 1195–1224) and a Yuan Emperor Ningzong (r. 1332). In fact, Liu Zihuan passed his *jinshi* exam in the tenth year of the Jiading 嘉定 (1208–1224) reign period.

8. According to the *Zhuangzi* 莊子, the kingdom of the Man was located on the right horn of a snail, and the kingdom of the Chu on the left horn, and the two regularly fought each other with the loss of tens of thousands of lives. *Zhuangzi*, p. 891 ("Zeyang" 則陽). The Man and the Chu were regularly used as metaphors for the pointless violence of warfare and they are mentioned in many imperial era works of literature about the conflict between the kingdoms of Wu and Yue.

9. Quoted in Zhang Gun, *Jiangyin xian zhi* 8.17b.

Southern Song dynasty the prince had a fixed reputation within the Chinese world as a great Confucian gentleman. In this poem, the graves of the kings of Wu are ignored, for visitors are only interested in Prince Jizha of Wu. However, this is a poetic conceit, because with the exception of the tomb of King Helü, no other grave sites are known for the recorded kings of Wu—which would make the failure of subsequent generations to visit them an involuntary omission. In fact, as will be seen in the next chapter, King Helü's tomb at Tiger Hill was an extremely popular attraction for visitors and residents of the city of Suzhou; and this tomb was certainly not neglected at any point in its history.

A similar sensibility to that displayed by Li Zihuan informs the poem entitled the "Jizi ci" 季子祠 (The shrine of Master Ji), by Li Fengxiang 李鳳翔, which also seems to refer to the temple at the prince's mausoleum complex:

Putting up the oars at [Lord] Chunshen's harbor,
I have come to see Master Ji's shrine.
The rosy clouds part, illuminating the further bank,
The evening sun glitters on the funerary banners.
From the state altars, I look at the remains of the tomb,
Wind and lightning guard the broken stele.
Yanling was a land of bows and swords,
Their excellent reputation has been handed down to the present day.
放棹春申浦, 來瞻季子祠.
落霞明遠渚, 夕日閃靈旗.
社稷看遺冢, 風雷護斷碑.
延陵弓劍地, 芳躅至今垂.[10]

In this opening couplet of this *huaigu* poem Prince Jizha of Wu is paralleled with Lord Chunshen of Chu. In spite of his contemporary significance as one of the four great lords of the Warring States era, remarkably little is known about Lord Chunshen, and his biography is based upon just a handful of stories. For example, the *Shiji* biography of Lord Chunshen concentrates on two main events: the first being when Huang Xie 黃歇, the future Lord Chunshen, was the chosen companion of Crown Prince Wan of Chu 楚太子完, when

10. Quoted in Chen Yan'en and Li Zhaoluo, *Jiangyin xian zhi*, p. 2739.

the prince was sent as a hostage to the kingdom of Qin. During their time in exile, Huang Xie forged an extremely close friendship with the Crown Prince, and became closely acquainted with many of the leading political figures in Qin. This would stand Huang Xie in good stead in 263 BCE, when news reached Qin that the king of Chu was dying. Huang Xie then assisted Crown Prince Wan's escape from Qin and to return unannounced to Chu. These events—described in some detail in the *Shiji*—were not without danger for Huang Xie himself, who could easily have been executed by the irate king of Qin for aiding and abetting his hostage to escape. However, both the prince and the future Lord Chunshen returned safe and sound to Chu, and Crown Prince Wan succeeded to the throne as King Kaolie of Chu 楚考烈王 (r. 262–238 BCE), the antepenultimate monarch of the kingdom. One of the new king's first acts was to appoint Huang Xie as Prime Minister, and he was also given many other honors by his erstwhile companion in exile. The close relationship between Lord Chunshen of Chu and King Kaolie was never disrupted during their long lives. This was in spite of the scabrous gossip claiming that King Kaolie was not the father of the Crown Prince Han 太子悍, the future King You of Chu 楚幽王 (r. 237–228 BCE).[11] In the second famous story concerning Lord Chunshen, the mother of Crown Prince Han was said to have been his concubine before being presented to King Kaolie. According to gossip she was pregnant at the time, which would make Lord Chunshen the real father of King You of Chu.

Lord Chunshen was a figure of great importance in the early history of the city of Suzhou, for he was given the ruins of the former capital of the kingdom of Wu as his fief. Lord Chunshen and his son are said to have gone to great trouble to restore the glory of the former Wu capital, as can be seen from the prominence accorded to buildings constructed under his auspices in the "Ji Wudi zhuan." Among other projects, they are said to have restored the citadel, though Lord Chunshen's work was destroyed by fire early in the Qin dynasty.[12] Lord Chunshen seems to have been much admired as the

---

11. *Shiji* 78.2387–2399.

12. *Yuejue shu*, pp. 16–17 ("Ji Wudi zhuan"). The history of the citadel, and the uses the land was put to after it was razed to the ground by order of Ming Hongwu 明洪武 (r. 1368–1398), is described in Pan Junming, *Zicheng*.

man who had returned the city to a semblance of its pre-conquest beauty, and indeed in his concluding remarks at the end of the *Shiji* biography of Lord Chunshen, Sima Qian notes the magnificence of the buildings then still to be seen at the site of his former fief.[13] During the imperial era, the works attributed to Lord Chunshen would be much increased, and many further major monuments and projects were said to have been completed under his auspices, including some located a considerable distance away from those recorded as his work in the "Ji Wudi zhuan."[14] Lord Chunshen of Chu seems to have been remembered affectionately in Suzhou, and he was eventually worshipped there as the city god. Although his cult was suppressed as heterodox during the Tang dynasty, it subsequently recovered its popularity.[15] Perhaps surprisingly, in view of the strong association between Lord Chunshen and Suzhou, he is also often mentioned in works of literature about Prince Jizha of Wu's tomb. The link between Prince Jizha and Lord Chunshen seems to represent a strictly local tradition, for nothing of this kind is recorded in any ancient text; however, the two names frequently appear together in imperial-era poetry and prose concerning the region. For example, in the Yuan dynasty, the poet Chen Fu 陳孚 (fl. second half of the thirteenth century) wrote a lyrical description of the prince's tomb in his poem "Guo Piling" 過毗陵 (Travelling through Piling), which again links both Prince Jizha and Lord Chunshen with this locale:

> To the west of the city walls of Piling, the fishermen's lanterns shine red,
> From every house at night fragrant smoke burns in the empty blue sky.
> The reed flowers cluster thickly round the tomb of Master Ji;
> The maple leaves mass around the palace of Lord Chunshen.
> The cackling of fowl and the voices of men are heard for thirty *li*;
> Boats large and small are knocked together by the waves.
> A pair of purple mandarin ducks flies into the air together,
> The men at the helm brave the autumn floods.

---

13. *Shiji* 78.2399.

14. Chen Yan'en and Li Zhaoluo, *Jiangyin xian zhi*, p. 379.

15. Di Renjie was responsible for a major inquisition against heterodox cults in the Wu-Yue region following his appointment in 688 as the Pacification Commissioner (*Xunfushi* 巡撫使) of Jiangnan, during which hundreds of shrines were destroyed. McMullen, "The Real Judge Dee," 6–8.

毘陵城西漁火紅, 家家夜香燒碧空.
荻花離離季子塚, 楓葉索索春申宮.
雞聲人語三十里, 大船小船浪相倚.
鸂鶒一雙飛上天, 人在柁樓弄秋水.[16]

This poem emphasizes the enduring significance of the waters of Jiangsu in the life of the people who live alongside its rivers. In the late imperial era, a number of gazetteers would record that the canal that debouched into the Yangtze River at Shen'gang (the town where Prince Jizha was buried) was originally built by order of Lord Chunshen.[17] In a similar manner, in the second couplet above, the name of Prince Jizha of Wu is juxtaposed with that of Lord Chunshen of Chu—for both of these men were members of royal houses living in the same region of southern Jiangsu Province prior to the unification of China. In the poem, the ancient sites associated with these great men have reverted to nature and become overgrown with weeds and trees. Typically for *huaigu* writings about this site, the choice to pair the two men seems to be derived from their significance in the local history of the region rather than any similarities in their biographies. Within traditional Chinese culture, Prince Jizha was conventionally framed as a man of exceptional intelligence, sensitivity, and moral probity, while Lord Chunshen was usually blamed for his role in placing an imposter on the throne of Chu, and for passing off his own son as the legitimate heir. Here, however, both men are significant because they are famous former residents of the region, and because their association with this site ensured continued attention to the place.

The Temple to Prince Jizha

The most important, and the best documented, monument dedicated to Prince Jizha is the main temple that was built in conjunction with his tomb. The development of this temple during the course of its history is hard to trace, given that most writers who mentioned the edifice merely referred to its existence, often in terms that are extremely vague or difficult to interpret. Where further information

---

16. Quoted in Liu Guangsheng and Tang Haozheng, *Chongxiu Changzhou fu zhi* 16.100b.

17. Ibid., 2.55a.

is given, the great antiquity of the temple is stressed. In fact, the recorded history of the cult of Prince Jizha of Wu begins in the Tang dynasty, in 688 CE. This was the year that Di Renjie 狄仁傑 (630–700) was appointed Pacification Commissioner of Jiangnan by Empress Wu Zetian 武則天 (r. 684–704). Under his auspices, local cults across the south were suppressed and their temples and shrines were burnt to the ground. It is said that seven hundred (or alternatively one thousand seven hundred) religious buildings were destroyed at this time. Among the shrines and temples known to have been put to the torch were those dedicated to the memory of King Fugai of Wu.[18] Only four regional cults were spared from this destruction: cults dedicated to Prince Jizha, to Wu Taibo, to Wu Zixu (King Helü of Wu's wise minister), and to the memory of the mythical sage-king Yu. The early recorded history of the temple should therefore be understood in the context of this repression. During the Tang dynasty there was much official concern about the development of unsanctioned shrines and the conduct of unorthodox sacrifices. The people of the Jiangnan region were believed to be unusually superstitious and credulous—an attitude that had its roots in the period before the unification of China, when this region was governed by the kingdoms of Chu, Wu, and Yue (states whose religious life was completely different from the northern states of the Zhou confederacy).[19] It is not clear why the cult of Prince Jizha was spared during this period of Tang religious intolerance, but its inclusion in the list with the spared cults dedicated to Yu, Wu Taibo, and Wu Zixu is suggestive of the way his legend was seen during the Tang dynasty. Yu was one of the sage-kings of antiquity: the founder of the Xia dynasty, who was traditionally said to have saved the world from a terrible flood by diverting the waters. During this time of natural disaster,

---

18. This attempt to suppress the cult of King Fugai was unsuccessful because in the Song dynasty there were a number of temples dedicated to this monarch in the Jiangnan region. Hansen, *Changing Gods in Medieval China*, p. 194.

19. Derogatory comments on the credulousness of southerners can be found in a number of ancient texts, but was particularly strongly expressed in the *Lüshi chunqiu*, which took a very hard line against the manifestations of the southern shamanic religion. *Lüshi chunqiu*, p. 558 ("Yibao" 異寶).

even though he passed the gate to his own home a number of times, he is said to have been so devoted to duty, and to the greater good of the community, that he did not even enter his own house to see his family. When he died, Yu is said to have been buried at Kuaijishan, in what is now Zhejiang Province.[20] The second cult to be spared in the Tang dynasty persecutions was one dedicated to Wu Taibo, who recognized the brilliance of his own younger brother and thus virtuously withdrew into obscurity (an act that paved the way for the succession of King Wen of Zhou).[21] The object of devotion for the third cult was Wu Zixu, a loyal minister who at the risk of his own life continued to warn King Fuchai of Wu of the dangers posed by King Goujian of Yue. These cults—which were devoted to regional historical figures who were far more famous than Prince Jizha of Wu—seem to have been found over a much larger geographical area than the prince's cult, and seem to have been considerably more significant in the religious practices of the region. It would therefore seem likely that the cult of Prince Jizha was spared because of his association with Confucius, and his reputation as a wise southerner who fully appreciated the culture of the Zhou confederacy. At a time

---

20. Within Chinese mythology, Yu was described as the great-grandson of the Yellow Emperor, and it was claimed that the royal family of Yue was descended from him. According to the account of the Hereditary House of Yue given in the *Shiji*, 41.1739, King Goujian was descended from one of the Xia kings, Shaokang 少康. Shaokang enfeoffed one of his commoner sons in Yue in order that the sacrifices to their ancestor Yu should not be disrupted. Some of the legends in which Yu figured were strongly associated with the south, but by no means all of them. However, from the Warring States period onwards, Yu was increasingly envisaged as a southern deity, and particularly associated with Kuaijishan in Zhejiang Province. Zhang He, *Wu Yue wenhua*, p. 12.

21. The history of the main temple to Wu Taibo at Meili 梅里 (traditionally identified as the site of his fief in Wu) is described in detail in Ye Wenxian, *Wuguo lishi yu Wu wenhua tanmi*, pp. 37–39. This temple is believed to have been founded in the Eastern Han dynasty, though the present structure dates to the Ming. The deity is known to have received numerous enfeoffments in successive dynasties; for example Emperor Ming of the Jin dynasty 晋明帝 (r. 323–325) granted the title "Sanrang wang" 三讓王 (King of three yieldings), with the right to represent the Great Earl of Wu in royal robes. The cult of the Great Earl of Wu also received extensive imperial patronage in the Tang and Qing dynasties.

when regionalism was still strong, a figure such as Prince Jizha, whose posthumous reputation was built largely on his admiration and respect for Zhou culture, could play a significant role in encouraging integration of the state.

During the Northern Song dynasty, a local poet, Cao Que 曹確 (*jinshi* 1059), wrote a poem entitled "Jizi miao shi" 季子廟詩 (A poem on the temple of Master Ji), also sometimes known by the alternative title of "Ti Jizi mu" 題季子墓 (Written on the tomb of Master Ji). As with many other *huaigu* poems, the supposed neglect into which the temple has fallen is attributed to the fact that the cult of Prince Jizha had been entrusted to the local peasantry. Whether or not the temple was going through a period of ill fortune at the time, it is certainly the case that it was a standard trope in Chinese poetry on historical sites to bewail the lack of attention paid by later generations to places and people that were once of great significance. This, in turn, then highlights the sensitivity of the poet himself, the sole visitor of note (at least in this poetic conceit) to have made the effort to travel to this remote wilderness:

> The affairs of the kings of Wu are not recorded in the human realm,
> Yet Master Ji's temple still survives standing above the Yangtze River.
> Rain falling through the green brambles lashes against the ruined walls,
> Wind whistling through the white elms at times disturbs the broken eaves.
> Everywhere the tombs of nobles are buried in spring grass,
> The sacrifices of chicken and wine are each year entrusted to rustics and old men.
> Getting down from my horse, I look around once and think of ancient virtue,
> Ephemeral fame should be seen as being as empty as the evening clouds.
> 人間不記吳王事, 江上今存季子宮.
> 壞壁亂飄青蘇雨, 破簷時蕩白榆風.
> 衣冠何處堆春草, 雞酒長年任野翁.
> 下馬一看思舊德, 浮名應與暮雲空.[22]

22. Quoted in Zhang Gun, *Jiangyin xian zhi* 8.14a. This poem is given with variant wording in Zhu Yu, *Chongxiu Piling zhi*, p. 1857. 人間不記吳王事, 江上今存季子宮/ 壞壁亂飄青蘇雨, 破檐時蕩白榆風/ 衣冠何處堆春草, 鷄酒長年任野翁/ 下馬一看思舊德, 浮名應與莫雲空.

During the Southern Song dynasty, the cult for Prince Jizha of Wu received imperial sponsorship, though it is not known what precise aspect of the cult first drew the attention of the court. During the Qingyuan 慶元 reign-period (1195–1200) of the Song emperor Ningzong 宋寧宗 (r. 1195–1225) the prince was enfeoffed with the title Zhaode Hou 昭得侯 (Enlightened and efficacious marquis). (The enfeoffment of the deified King Fuchai of Wu at approximately the same time is discussed in chapter 6.) In the case of Prince Jizha, the enfeoffment from the Song emperor may have resulted in the spread of the prince's cult beyond the immediate confines of the tomb site, but given the paucity of information concerning the precise date at which other temples were founded, it is not clear how the time frame of imperial sponsorship relates to the documented spread of shrines and temples dedicated to the prince during the Southern Song dynasty.

The first local gazetteer to describe the Changzhou area, including the site of the prince's tomb, was the *Xianchun Piling zhi* 咸淳毗陵志 (Gazetteer for Piling [County] from the Xianchun reign era, 1265–1274), compiled by the Prefect Shi Nengzhi 史能之. This gazetteer records the temples dedicated to Prince Jizha of Wu that had sprung up around Changzhou, and which stood within the area traditionally believed to have encompassed his fief of Yanling. At that time, there was a "Southern Temple" to Prince Jizha outside the eastern city wall of Jinling, a "Northern Temple" in Wujin County 武進縣, and a "Western Temple" at Qu'a 曲阿 in Runzhou 潤州. These three temples thrived in addition to the main foundation.[23] However, the main temple was traditionally by far the most important, thanks largely to its location right next to the tomb of Prince Jizha—and to the fact that it possessed the Ten-Character Stele (Shizibei 十字碑), an object of considerable interest to worshippers as well as tourists, as a direct historical link to both the prince and to Confucius. Within the cult for Prince Jizha, there seems to have been a consistent problem, in that shrines and temples built away from the tomb site were regarded as in some way unorthodox (and certainly were considered inferior): this apparently played a significant role in limiting the spread of the prince's cult throughout the imperial era.

23. Shi Nengzhi, *Xianchun Piling zhi*, p. 3574.

The 1503 Restoration

The history of the main temple dedicated to Prince Jizha is extremely vague prior to the Ming dynasty, although it is repeatedly said to have been an extremely ancient foundation. In the pre-Ming period, the temple to Prince Jizha is said to have been ruined and rebuilt a number of times, and also to have been moved from its original location. However, from the Ming dynasty onwards, the development of the temple is much more clearly described. The temple was completely rebuilt under the auspices of the Prefect Sun Yongbie 孫用別, in 1374.[24] The state of the temple at the beginning of the Ming dynasty should probably be understood in the context of the general decline and destruction that had ruined large swathes of southern Jiangsu Province at this time. This was in large part because the city of Suzhou, just to the south of the temple, had been the base of one of the unsuccessful contenders for power at the end of the Yuan dynasty, and because the city had been sacked after a ten-month siege. That was followed by large numbers of the local elite being forcibly removed and replaced by families loyal to the new dynasty.

This early fourteenth-century temple rebuilding would apparently survive for the next two centuries. In 1503, extensive renovations were undertaken under the auspices of the Censor Shi Lu 石祿 (1466–1524, *jinshi* 1499), the Prefect Lian Sheng 連盛 (*jinshi* 1468), and the District Magistrate Qiu Tai 丘泰 (*jinshi* 1496). To celebrate this occasion, these men commissioned a *ji* 記 or record of the occasion from Li Dongyang 李東陽 (1447–1516, *jinshi* 1463). Li Dongyang, one of the most distinguished scholars and officials of the day, was born in Beijing into a family of courtiers. An infant prodigy who was patronized by the emperor, he passed the *jinshi* exam at the age of just sixteen, an almost unparalleled achievement. Li Dongyang served in important official positions: for example, in the same year as he wrote the "Chongxiu Jizi miaobei [ji]" 重修季子廟碑[記] ([Record of the] restoration of the temple and stele of Master Ji), he represented the Hongzhi Emperor 明弘治 (r. 1488–1505) at the rededi-

24. Zhu Yu, *Chongxiu Piling zhi*, p. 1219.

cation of the main temple to Confucius in Shandong Province, following its restoration after the fire of 1499. In 1510, as Grand Secretary under the Zhengde Emperor 明正德 (r. 1506–1521), he was granted the extraordinary title of Specially Advanced Left Pillar of the State. Li Dongyang was also a significant literary critic and a respected calligrapher. (He retired in 1513.) The fact that the temple to Prince Jizha could command the services of so distinguished a statesman to write an account of its history is indicative of the wealth and importance of this foundation in the mid-Ming era.

Texts such as Li Dongyang's essay, written in highly formal classical Chinese and heavily larded with classical allusions, would have been incomprehensible to the vast majority of the population. At the time, there was a clear hierarchy in perceptions of poetry and prose written about an individual site. Inscriptions and literary responses by the emperor were extremely highly prized, as were works by officials and other members of the ruling elite. In the case of sites of religious significance, records by elite pilgrims and by famous members of the clergy were also of considerable importance. Even in instances where communities compiled records of local support, these records were frequently rewritten by the literati, out of concern that otherwise the text might be too vulgar.[25] This kind of literary patronage—recorded in local histories (and also sometimes inscribed in stone at the place concerned)—was of enormous importance for promoting the reputation of a particular site, and often went hand in hand with financial patronage. The gazetteers that record the history of Changzhou virtually all quote the text of Li Dongyang's essay, an indication both of his literary and cultural significance and of the luster that this shed on the temple to Prince Jizha. The text of Li Dongyang's essay is worth quoting in full, because it presents an extremely detailed account of the history of the temple as it was understood in the Ming dynasty, records the process by which the restoration was arranged and funded, and concludes with a remarkable and extremely unusual work of literature, a poem in the style of *Chuci* 楚辭 (Songs of Chu) on the subject of Prince Jizha:

25. Katz, *Images of the Immortal*, pp. 97–99.

The temple to Master Ji at Changzhou stands one *li* east of the county seat. His lordship Bai Ang, the Grand Guardian of the Heir Apparent and Minister of the Board of Punishments, used to read books there, and regretted its parlous condition. He [Bai Ang] told the Daoist clerics who lived there: "One day I will definitely repair it." His lordship passed the *jinshi* examinations in Dingchou year of the reign of the Tianshun Emperor (1457), and thereafter took a succession [of official posts] in the two capitals. Every time he made inquiries of one of his younger relatives or of a person from his hometown, he heard that [the situation of the temple] was getting worse, and he always carried this burden of worry. More than forty years later, in Wuwu year in the reign of the Hongzhi Emperor (1498), [Bai Ang] took the first opportunity to discuss this [matter] with the Censor, the Honorable Shi Lu. [Shi Lu] said: "That sacrifices are held here is [something that is] recorded in the classics, but government taxes have just been increased, so it would not be suitable to divert [the money] to other causes [such as repairing this temple]." His lordship [which may be either Bai Ang or Shi Lu, or possibly even both of them] then met the local officials and obtained a certain amount of their savings. He handed this [money] over to the Prefect, his lordship Lian Sheng, and to the Magistrate of Wujin, Qiu Tai (who chose the materials, kept the accounts, prepared things, and supervised the workmen as they gutted the old building and repaired it). The reason why the halls, corridors, and courtyards [of this temple] have been so frequently augmented is that when they are bare, they are extremely grand, and when they are painted, they are very beautiful. They set up an image [of the prince] and arranged the ritual vessels and other objects, and all those who had seen the old [temple] in a state of wrack and ruin were amazed. Yanling, where Wu enfeoffed [Prince Jizha] is in fact modern Wujin County. Seventy *li* northwest [of the county seat] at Jiyang Township there is the Ji Temple. Later on this land was under the administration of Jiangyin [County]. The inscription in the calligraphy of Confucius is located here. In the time of Tang Xuanzong, he [the emperor] ordered Yin Zhongrong to carve a replica of the inscription. In the time of Daizong, Xiao Ding (708–784), the Censor of Runzhou, [ordered it re-carved], and in the time of Huizong, Zhu Yan (*jinshi* 1076), the Magistrate of Changzhou, ordered it re-carved.

This temple was first built in the reign of Hongwu of the present dynasty. Afterwards it was repaired by the Prefect Mo Yu and the Magistrate Zhu Shu. They also made a replica of the old stele and placed it to one side of the main courtyard. In the two thousand and more years since the death of Master Ji, the temple has sometimes flourished and sometimes been in a state of ruin, and it has also sometimes been moved, but [the prince's] high and honorable reputation has never yet been destroyed. Master Ji is said to have stuck to his high principles and yielded the country to a better man; and he would not allow [the prospect of governing a kingdom of] one thousand chariots to affect his decision. He visited Lu and listened to music, and thus he knew the fates of the states [of the Zhou confederacy]. He visited the states of Qi, Zheng, Wei, and Jin, and thus understood their governments. He had audience with their ministers and determined what they were capable of. He was brilliant and admirable, conversable and well-informed, [his learning] was much more profound than ordinary people's, thus Confucius, in his wisdom, [recognized that the prince] was in harmony with the Rites to the point where he [Confucius] wrote an inscription to express this; given his exceptional intelligence, this can only be right. Those who criticize Master Ji disregard the fine reputation recorded [in ancient texts] after he visited [the state of Lu as an ambassador]; and [they] suspect that the prince yielded up the kingdom, thereby creating his reputation for wisdom, because he could not be bothered [with governing]; how can they say this! The *Chunqiu* records why he became a recluse. The *Li*[*ji*] and the inscription on his tomb state why he became illustrious. However, it is not possible to fully understand the reasons why he became a recluse, and the idea that he became illustrious is trusted without any proof; how is this possible! Yielding one's position to the better man is the most beautiful of virtues—if you know that yielding to the better man is the most beautiful of virtues then your family will not be ruined [by the kind of indifference shown] by the person of Qin to the one of Yue, and your people will not suffer the humiliation of becoming involved in the same kind of conflict as the Man and the Chu.[26] The sacrifices in

26. The term used here to describe indifference refers to the people of Qin and those of Yue. The most common form in which this expression appears is: *ruo Yueren shi Qinren zhi feiji* 若越人視秦人之肥瘠 (as if a person of Yue were to see whether a person of Qin were fat or thin) and speaks of the indifference felt by people to the sufferings of those geographically far removed from them. The popularity of this expression within literati discourse is generally associated with its appearance in one of Han Yu's 韓愈 (768–824) essays: "Zhengchen lun" 爭臣論 (Discourse on Competing Officials). Qian Zhonglian, *Han Changli shixinian jishi*

this temple are indeed an evocation of honesty and covetousness, upstanding principles and weakness, and as such are not without instruction for later generations. Everyone welcomes in their hearts an adherence to proper principles and a love of virtue. Besides which, private cultivation and respect [for the virtues] can take place anywhere! His lordship Bai [Ang] was an important official when he was younger, and in old age he sets the seal upon his reputation by restoring this ancient [temple] and encouraging scholars, all of which is thanks to the goodness of his heart. As for the merit of the Censor, the Prefect, and the Magistrate, it rests in their righteousness in loving virtue and in exalting [the wise], which is indeed correct. As for the restoration of this temple, the reasons why it had to wait until the present day have to be made known. [I, Li] Dongyang am a man of Chu, but even though I come from a different region, I am still moved by the righteousness [of loving virtue and exalting the wise]. Accordingly I record here past events so that they can be known to future [generations], that they, too, may from time to time restore [this temple]. Hence, I have composed a song of Chu as an offering to this deity. The text runs:

At dawn I stop my chariot east of the river,
At dusk I pluck fragrant blooms from the water.
I wait for his lordship,
My anxious heart is uneasy.
In the orchid hall with its cassia wood pillars,
The many-layered screens are wreathed in incense.
When his lordship returns,
My heart melts with delight.
Our nation is [ruled] by a branch of the Ji [royal clan],
Many times have older brothers yielded the title to the better man.
This beautiful young man,
Has every traditional characteristic of a crown prince.
In a time of great upheavals and massive change,
Fighting heroes contend over the Horizontal and Vertical Alliances.
Immovable, like a great rock on the hillside,
Watching the waters rolling ever-eastwards.
He [Prince Jizha] looked upon [a state of] one thousand chariots as
like a single hair,
He had no wish for high position.

14.9b. The Man and the Chu are the kingdoms based on the two horns of a snail and locked in endless vicious combat, as described in the *Zhuangzi*.

Throughout his life he had a great love of antiquity,
If we do not follow this man, then whom should we follow?
Though his abode during his lifetime was vulgar,
The honors received by his manes are abundant year after year.
I hope that he will be praised for one thousand years and one hundred generations,
And that sacrifices will be held without end.

常州季子廟在府治東一里. 太子太保刑部尚書白公昂嘗讀書其間, 慨其敝陋, 謂居守道徒曰: “吾他日必修之.” 公舉天順丁丑進士, 歷兩京不暇葺治. 每詢諸子弟及鄉之人問其益敝恒慨然于懷. 越四十餘年, 爲弘治戊午年, 始以屬諸巡按御史石君祿. 曰: “此有祀典所載. 第公賦方殷, 未易旁及.” 乃會諸官得嬴 [贏] 財若干. 以付知府連君盛,暨武進知縣丘泰, 簡材, 治籍, 庀物, 督工, 撤舊構而重修之. 堂廡庭所以次繼作, 屹然爲隆, 煥然爲華. 設像昭布禮器具列, 回視昔之頹垣敗宇者異矣. 按吳封于延陵, 實今之武進縣. 東北七十里暨陽鄉有季廟. 後其地屬于江陰. 孔子所書石刻在焉. 唐玄宗時, 命殷仲容摹刻之. 代宗時, 潤州刺史蕭定, 宋徽宗時, 知常州朱彥遞傳刻之.

國朝洪武間始建茲廟. 其後, 知府莫愚, 知縣朱恕修之. 又摹舊刻置于庭側. 自季子沒二千餘年廟幾興廢, 幾遷徙, 而其名號風節固未泯也. 夫稱季子者謂其執節讓國不以千乘動其心. 聘魯觀樂而知列國之故. 聘齊, 鄭, 衛, 晋, 而知其政. 見其臣而知其可與者. 其明膚通博, 出于人遠甚, 故以孔子之聖, 與其合禮至, 題辭以表之, 非其人之賢, 宜不得此. 議季子者, 乃以來聘書名之義, 疑其讓國爲賢者累, 殆亦有説焉! 然春秋書其隐然者也. 禮之所載與墓題之所識其顯然者也. 隐然者既未能以盡識, 顯然者不據而信之, 奚可哉! 夫讓德之美也, 苟知讓之爲美德, 則于處家必無秦越人相視之患, 于羣居必無觸蠻氏交戰之恥, 茲廟之祀, 固廉貪立懦之端, 其于世教不爲無助也. 秉彝好德, 人心所同. 况私淑景仰, 出乎其地也哉! 白公壯而用世, 老而完名, 募古力學, 盖其素志. 而御史之令, 郡守縣令之績, 于好德審尚之義, 亦有合焉. 茲廟之修若有待于今日不可以不識也. 東陽楚人. 雖殊地異境亦有感乎斯義. 因紀成事告諸來俾時修之. 且爲楚歌以祀神. 其辭曰:

朝弭節兮江東, 暮搴芳兮水中.
遲公子兮不來, 鬱予懷兮忡忡.
蘭堂兮桂宮, 幨裎兮數重.
公子兮歸來, 樂予心兮融融.
吾之國兮姬之宗, 紛伯仲兮讓侯邦.
彼美兮公子, 績太子兮遺風.
時震撼兮舂撞, 鬪雌雄兮兢衡從.
屹砥柱兮不動, 見東流兮淙淙.
眇千乘兮一毫, 亦無心兮鼎鐘.
生好古兮若渴, 匪斯人兮曷從.

人之居兮俗龐, 神之錫兮年豐.
願千秋兮百世咏, 報祀兮無終窮.[27]

The opening of Li Dongyang's essay records the lifelong interest felt by a local man, Bai Ang 白昂 (1435–1502, *jinshi* 1457), in the state of the temple. According to this account, the restoration of 1503 represents the fulfillment of a vow made more than forty years earlier, just before Bai Ang passed the *jinshi* examination and started on his stellar official career, which culminated in his appointment as Minister of the Board of Punishments (rank 2a). It is not certain why Bai Ang made the vow in the first place, or why he was so determined to carry it out. Probably, however, it is related to the status of Prince Jizha as a deity efficacious in examination success: a role that is attested to by a number of Ming dynasty gazetteers.[28] If this interpretation is correct, then his decision to restore the temple represents repayment of a longstanding debt to the deity. However, though Bai Ang's vow may have been the motive force behind the 1503 restoration, he was apparently not particularly closely involved in the process, and indeed he died before it was completed. In this case, the people who actually organized the collection of money, supervised the work, and paid for the whole project were not local men: rather, they were officials appointed to the region, such as the Prefect Lian Sheng who was a native of Yongnian County 永年縣 in what is now Hebei Province, and Magistrate Qiu Tai from Putian County 莆田縣 in Fujian Province. Looking at the whole history of the restoration project—with Li Dongyang's record of these events as the final stage—it may be said to represent an appropriation of the site for patronage by some of the most distinguished metropolitan officials of the day, with the active assistance of a number of local officials.

Though Li Dongyang was brought up in Beijing in a prominent court family, at the conclusion of this essay he identifies himself as a man of Chu, thus reflecting his family's origins in what is now Hunan Province. This reference to his southern origins is used to justify

27. Quoted in Zhang Kai, *Changzhou fu zhi xuji*, p. 231. This piece is included in the collected works of Li Dongyang, but it is given in a slightly abridged form. Zhou Yinbin, *Li Dongyang ji*, pp. 89–90.

28. Lu Xiong, *Suzhou fu zhi*, p. 581.

his decision to end his prose account of the restoration of the temple of Prince Jizha with a poem in the style of the *Chuci*. This is an extremely interesting choice, apparently made by Li Dongyang himself, which allowed him to commemorate the prince in an ancient and highly demanding literary form. This virtuoso ending not only gave Li Dongyang the opportunity to demonstrate his own erudition, but also imparts a highly "southern" flavor to the whole literary endeavor. Many imperial era writers wished to preserve in their works a sense of the foreignness of Wu, and to commemorate the brilliance with which Prince Jizha mastered the culture of the Zhou Central States. Li Dongyang however appears to be unique in his decision to laud the prince's understanding of Confucian principles in a southern literary form.

The Late Imperial History of the Temple

Shortly after the temple's 1503 restoration, at the beginning of the reign of the Ming Zhengde Emperor, the condition of the temple to Prince Jizha was again described as a cause for serious concern. However, it is unlikely that this statement should be taken at face value, particularly because no reason is ascribed for a sudden calamitous decline in the state of the temple. Local gazetteers state that in 1507, reportedly as a result of the parlous condition to which the temple had been reduced, District Magistrate Liu Hong 劉紘 (1478–1513, *jinshi* 1505), a young man in his very first official posting, ordered that a local man, Xia Lianghui 夏良惠, and unnamed others should rebuild the ruined temple. However, it would seem likely that what happened was a change of ownership of the temple, and that these building works were a part of this process. Three years later, in 1510, when the locals were presumably celebrating the completion of the restoration project, the new District Magistrate, Wang Ping 王鉼, was invited by a local resident, Yao De 姚德, to attend a sacrifice there.[29] As with the 1503 restoration, the 1510 project culminated with an

29. Zhang Kai, *Changzhou fu zhi xuji*, p. 213. The suggestion that the 1507–1510 "restoration" marks the take-over of the temple by a new group of owners, in this case locals taking over from officials temporarily appointed to the region, is derived from Vincent Goossaert's study of late imperial Daoists in Beijing, where a change in ownership was commonly associated with the "restoration" or "rebuilding" of

essay being commissioned from one of the most important literati of the day, the famous scholar and epigrapher Du Mu 杜穆 (1459–1525). Other essays written at around this time include the "Wu Jizi lun" 吳季子論 (Discourse on Master Ji of Wu) by Huang Fu 黃傅 (*jinshi* 1490), which may or may not have been commissioned in connection with one of the restorations which took place in the early sixteenth century, but which is certainly indicative of an increased interest in the site among members of the literati at this time.[30] Subsequently, during the reign of the Wanli Emperor 明萬曆 (r. 1572–1620), the temple was repaired twice. On the first occasion, in 1580, the restoration was the responsibility of the Prefect of Changzhou, Mu Wei 穆煒. On the second, in 1605, the repairs were carried out under the auspices of the District Magistrate, Yan Wenhui 晏文輝 (*jinshi* 1598).[31] However, neither of these occasions seems to have been marked by a specially commissioned essay.

For most of the Ming and much of the Qing dynasty, the temple to Prince Jizha was an extremely wealthy foundation, enriched by numerous donations. The increase in revenue during these dynasties made possible numerous refinements to the mausoleum complex. During the Qing dynasty the temple also attracted imperial patronage: for example, the Kangxi Emperor 清康熙 (r. 1662–1722) made a visit to the temple in 1680 during which he presented it an inscription in his own calligraphy recounting the virtues of Prince Jizha of Wu (*Rang de guang* 讓德光 [Yielding, virtuous, illustrious]). At the time of this imperial visit, the temple buildings associated with the tomb included the main hall, which housed a statue of Prince Jizha of Wu; in front of this was the pavilion which housed the Ten-Character Stele. There was also a further building, known as the Xie'en lou 謝恩樓 (Building raised in thanks for kindness), whose function is not recorded. Behind the main hall of the temple there were the Daoist clerics' quarters.[32] It is not known exactly why the Kangxi Emperor

---

what was actually a flourishing and well-maintained temple. Goossaert, *The Taoists of Peking*, pp. 50–51.

30. The text of Huang Fu's extended essay is quoted in Chen Yan'en and Li Zhaoluo, *Jiangyin xian zhi*, pp. 2342–47.

31. Liu Guangsheng and Tang Haozheng, *Chongxiu Changzhou fu zhi* 2.57b.

32. Chen Yan'en and Li Zhaoluo, *Jiangyin xian zhi*, p. 754.

particularly wished to visit this site, which lay somewhat out of his way. However, it is suggestive that in 1685, when the Kangxi Emperor published a selection of his favorite pieces of classical literature, among the choices from the *Zuozhuan* he included the passage describing Prince Jizha's visit to Lu (when the prince asked to listen to the music of the states of the Zhou confederacy).[33]

In 1751, the Qianlong Emperor 清乾隆 (r. 1736–1795) also visited the south on an imperial progress. Following in his grandfather's footsteps, the emperor presented Prince Jizha's temple with an inscription in his own calligraphy, reading: *Qing hui sheng wu* 清徽繩武 (Pure and honorable in imitation of the ancestors).[34] According to one Qing dynasty gazette, the temple was also restored during the reign of the Qianlong Emperor, under the auspices of District Magistrate Cai Peng 蔡澎, though it is not known if this restoration was directly connected with the emperor's visit.

In 1860, almost exactly one century after the temple enjoyed the glory of a personal visit from the Qianlong Emperor, practically everything—bar the Ten-Character Stele—was destroyed when the temple was burnt to the ground during the Taiping rebellion. This was part of a wave of destruction launched against religious sites in the Jiangsu region during the Taiping rebels' rule, and many important historical sites throughout the Jiangsu region were severely damaged at this time.[35] The temple was eventually rebuilt by public subscription in 1862.[36] This indicates a break with tradition, for all earlier restorations and rebuildings of the temple seem to have received official sponsorship, and perhaps even to have been initiated by local officials. The situation in the 1860s was, however, significantly different in that the general destruction caused by the Taiping Rebellion was so severe that official patronage, and indeed access to state funds, was hard to come by, particularly for what appears to have been a small local cult.

---

33. Kangxi Emperor, *Yuxuan guwen yuanjian* 3.15a–16b.

34. Gao Jin ed., *Nanxun shengdian*, p. 210.

35. Jiangsu ed., *Jiangsu wenwu zonglu*, p. 204. Jin Youli, *Taihu beikao*, p. 634, provides a discussion of the general decline in religious activity in the region in the wake of the Taiping rebellion. Even in the case of temples and shrines that survived, in many cases worship ceased in the aftermath of the rebellion.

36. Lu Sicheng and Li Nianyi, *Jiangling xian zhi*, p. 853.

As with the history of the temple buildings, virtually nothing is known about the nature of the sacrifices dedicated to Prince Jizha of Wu prior to the Ming dynasty. According to the *Chongxiu Piling zhi* 重修毗陵志 (Revised gazetteer for Piling) of 1484, it was customary for a pig to be sacrificed to Prince Jizha's memory every year, in the second *xun* 旬 (ten-day period) of the second lunar month.[37] The late Ming dynasty gazetteer—*Chongxiu Changzhoufu zhi* 重修常州府志 (Revised gazetteer for Changzhou Prefecture) compiled by Liu Guangsheng 劉廣生 and Tang Haozheng 唐鶴徵 (1538–1619, *jinshi* 1571) in 1618—stated that that the stele regularly received a sacrifice of wine from the gentlemen of the region.[38] A later account by a scholar-official native to the region, Zhang Gun 張袞 (1487–1564, *jinshi* 1521), found in the *Jiangyin xian zhi* 江陰縣志 (Gazetteer for Jiangyin County) records that sacrifices were held at the temple every spring and autumn. On these occasions, one pig and one sheep were sacrificed.[39] At the end of the nineteenth century, the Jesuit Albert Tschepe visited a number of sites around Changzhou, including the temple dedicated to the memory of Prince Jizha that stood beside his tomb in Shen'gang, as part of his research for his book, the *Histoire du Royaume de Ou*. His account of his travels in Jiangsu is particularly valuable, for it provides evidence of the popularity of the cult of Prince Jizha beyond the immediate confines of his tomb site and fief. According to Père Tschepe, he visited a number of "pagodas" dedicated to the prince, including two in Xiagang 夏港.[40] These minor sites had been little visited by famous tourists and scholars researching the life of the prince and hence had gone largely unrecorded. Père Tschepe also recorded that at the very end of the Qing dynasty, a festival was held in the memory of Prince Jizha at the main temple on the twenty-ninth day of the fourth month. Thus, though the temple seems never to have regained the status and wealth that it had during the High Qing era, in spite of the damage sustained during the Taiping rebellion, commemoration of Prince Jizha continued to the end of the Qing dynasty, and festivals continued to be held at the temple attached to his tomb.

---

37. Zhu Yu, *Chongxiu Piling zhi*, p. 1291.
38. Liu Guangsheng and Tang Haozheng, *Chongxiu Changzhou fu zhi* 2.57a.
39. Zhang Gun, *Jiangyin xian zhi* 8.3a.
40. Tschepe, *Histoire du Royaume de Ou*, p. 49.

The Ten-Character Stele

The early history of the Ten-Character Stele is extremely obscure. The first proper description of the stele and its inscription—attributed to the hand of Confucius himself—dates to the Song dynasty, though it makes reference to an early Tang dynasty account of the monument that does not survive. There are a number of tantalizing references in pre-Tang poems describing the temple to Prince Jizha of Wu, which may perhaps refer to the stele. The very earliest of these ambiguous references is found in a Chen dynasty (557–589) poem, entitled "Xingjing Jizi miao" 行經季子廟 (On passing by the temple to Master Ji) by Zhang Zhengjian 張正見 (d. c.569–582), a senior official who served in the court of Emperor Wu of the Liang dynasty 梁武帝 (r. 502–549):

Yanling's noble refusal [to take the throne] happened long ago,
His reputation is honorable and for generations sacrifices have continued.
The place is long gone where he abandoned gold in the road,
The pine tree mourns over the branch where he hung his sword.
Wild brambles encroach on the gushing spring,
Mountain rain wets the mossy stele.
There is another place for him to observe the customs,
Music is played, but no one understands it.
延陵高讓遠, 傳芳世祀移.
地絶遺金路, 松悲懸劍枝.
野藤侵沸井, 山雨濕苔碑.
別有觀風處, 樂奏無人知.[41]

The poet was clearly well aware of many of the stories found in ancient Chinese texts concerning the biography of Prince Jizha of Wu. The prince's actions as a gentleman in the Confucian tradition and his yielding of the throne of Wu to a better man are here portrayed as the motivations behind the cult. Prince Jizha's generosity to the deceased lord of Xu (who had so much coveted his fine sword) also finds a mention here, as does the prince's encounter with the Fur-Coated Elder. In each case, the passage of time since the events occurred is

41. Quoted in Liu Guangsheng and Tang Haozheng, *Chongxiu Changzhou fu zhi* 17.79b.

stressed. The poem concludes with a couplet suggesting that even after death, the prince would continue to observe the customs of the country; for him "another place" would represent the Underworld. In his absence, there is no one to understand the deep inner meaning of music when it is played. Prince Jizha's position as a consummate scholar of classical music is enshrined in this poem. From the point of view of scholars interested in tracing the early history of the Ten-Character Stele, it is the second line of the third couplet that is of the greatest interest. The terms used in this line are sufficiently vague that the moss-covered stele that is wet with mountain rain might either be a general reference to the appearance of stone monuments at this site, or a specific reference to the ancient Ten-Character Stele. Or indeed there may even have been no stone monuments present at all in this temple at this time: but Zhang Zhengjian was most likely aware of the common poetic conceit that bewailed the destruction of steles recording the deeds of good men of antiquity within the purlieus of abandoned temples, and he probably wished to include such a reference in his own work. This ambiguity ensures that this poem is not sufficiently explicit to stand as the earliest surviving reference to the Ten-Character Stele.

In spite of the paucity of the textual record concerning the early history of the Ten-Character Stele, it has been suggested that the stone was originally created by Wang Sengshu 王僧恕 in the Liang dynasty (502–556), though the source for this idea is not known.[42] As matters stand now, the first history of the stele and record of the text inscribed on its surface is found in the *Jigu lu* 集古錄 (Record of collected antiquities) by Ouyang Xiu 歐陽修 (1007–1072, *jinshi* 1030), which is a landmark in the study of Chinese epigraphy. This account suggests that the wording of the inscription by Confucius was handed down for generations before it was cut into stone. Ouyang Xiu also quotes an account attributed to the Tang dynasty calligrapher Zhang Congshen 張從紳 that states: "The old stone and mound had been destroyed, so in the Kaiyuan reign-period (713–741), the Emperor Yuanzong [apparently a mistake for Xuanzong, r. 712–756] ordered

---

42. Xie Chen, *Gouwu shi xinkao*, p. 111.

Yin Zhongrong [fl. early eighth century] to make a carved replica of the calligraphy, in order to preserve it." 舊石堙滅. 開元中元宗命殷仲容模搭其書以傳.[43]

This account states explicitly that by the beginning of the eighth century the "original" old stone (the date of which is not recorded) was no longer in existence, so an expert seal-script calligrapher was commissioned by the emperor to make a replica stele. This is also the earliest known reference to imperial interest in the commemoration of Prince Jizha, though a number of emperors in later dynasties would play a role in promoting the prince's cult or in enhancing monuments dedicated to his memory through the presentation of such gifts as imperial calligraphy. The *Jigu lu* is also the first text to transcribe the inscription in full: "Alas! This is the tomb of Master Ji of Yanling of Wu." 嗚呼! 有吳延陵季子之墓.[44]

The Emperor Xuanzong's commission to Yin Zhongrong to cut the words on the stone stele is interesting given the historical context of ongoing religious repression. At this time, the emperor was trying to bring the wealth and influence of the Buddhist church under state control by promulgating a succession of laws restricting its powers. At the same time, the emperor extensively patronized Daoist shrines and conducted a number of religious ceremonies such as the Feng 封 and Shan 禪 sacrifices on Taishan; and he also held a sacrifice at the main temple of Confucius in Shandong Province.[45] In any case, the policy of repressing local cults across the south seems to have fallen into abeyance by this time. Therefore, the emperor's commission of a new stele to grace the tomb of Prince Jizha was indicative of enduring official approval for this particular cult, while also marking a new focus in the attempts of the state to keep the religious life of the

---

43. Quoted in Ouyang Xiu, *Jigu lu*, p. 109. The text by Zhang Congshen from which this quotation is drawn was entitled: "Gaijian Wu Yanling Jizi miao ji" 改建吳延陵季子廟記 (A record of the rebuilding of the temple to Master Ji of Yanling in the kingdom of Wu), and does not survive. The composition of Zhang Congshen's essay has traditionally been associated with the 779 restoration of the temple and carving of a new stele by the Censor of Runzhou Xiao Ding. Zhonggong ed., *Jiangsu wenwu*, p. 186.

44. Ouyang Xiu, *Jigu lu*, p. 109.

45. Twitchett, "Hsüan-tsung (Reign 712–56)," p. 388.

nation within government-approved bounds. According to Ouyang Xiu, in the Zhengyuan 正元 reign-period (which appears to be a mistake for the Shangyuan 上元 reign-period, 760–761) in the reign of the Tang Emperor Suzong 唐肅宗 (r. 756–762), one Lu Guoqian 盧國遷 built a hall at the temple in which he set up a ten-character stele. This protective building may be connected with the weather damage that this stele was reported as having suffered at about this time. However, although the wording was the same, this particular stele was said not to be the stone featuring Yin Zhongrong's calligraphy.[46] It is not clear which of these two stones, if either, was the one that formed the centerpiece of the temple for so many centuries. This reference also points to an ongoing problem for anyone interested in researching the history of Prince Jizha's Ten-Character Stele: that is, there are a number of similar steles in the region. Although the Ten-Character Stele found at the tomb of Prince Jizha has always been the most famous, other similar steles are found across Jiangsu Province. The wording of these steles varies, and they are known in six-, ten- or twelve-character versions. Steles of this type have been recorded in Danyang County 丹陽縣, Liyang County 溧陽縣, Yixing County 宜興縣, and Jiangyin County.[47] The history of these other steles remains obscure, but it is likely that the carving of these stones reflects the great cultural importance of Prince Jizha of Wu in this region of China and a wish to lay claim to some part of his legacy.

The tradition that Confucius had written the words carved on the stone stele at the tomb of Prince Jizha was a source of inspiration for the Northern Song dynasty poet Mei Yaochen 梅堯臣 (1002–1060), in his poem "Fuzi zhuan" 夫子篆 (The sage's seal script). It is perhaps significant that Mei Yaochen was a close friend of Ouyang Xiu, and hence was likely to be aware of the inscriptions gathered for the *Jigu lu*. Given that this appears to be the very first work of literature to be directly inspired by the Ten-Character Stele, it is likely that Mei Yaochen drew the idea from his friend's research. This poem contains

46. Ouyang Xiu, *Jigu lu*, p. 109.
47. Xie Chen, *Gouwu shi xinkao*, p. 111.

striking images of the desolation and neglect of an ancient monument, again describing how care of monuments associated with Prince Jizha of Wu had been entrusted to ignorant peasants:

> The stele beside the tomb of Master Ji,
> Has been said from ancient times to bear the seal script of Confucius.
> From the beginning, the righteous ways of the Spring and Autumn period have been handed down,
> So these ten characters have remained un-erased.[48]
> Abraded and damaged, it has been left to the children of shepherds,
> [And has been] covered and scratched by the wild brambles.
> Alas! You men of later ages,
> The recording of ten thousand words is no light matter.
> 季札墓傍碑, 古稱尼父篆.
> 始沿春秋義, 十字固莫剗.
> 磨敲任牧童, 侵剝因野蘇.
> 嗟爾後之人, 萬言書不淺.[49]

Re-carving the Ten-Character Stele

In addition to all the problems raised by the extremely murky early history of the Ten-Character Stele and the existence of numerous near-duplicates, this monument is known to have been re-carved and embellished, and enhanced by the placement of further stone steles in its immediate vicinity. For example, in 779, during the reign of the Tang Emperor Daizong 唐代宗 (r. 763–779), Xiao Ding was Regional Chief of Runzhou (at that time Yanling County formed part of the administrative district of Runzhou). During this period, Xiao Ding ordered the carving of a second stele to ornament the temple, as a complement to the Ten-Character Stele, with an inscription of 360 characters arranged into twenty lines. This second stele has now been lost, and its exact wording never seems to have been

48. In later years, the stele would become known as the Ten-Character Stele. The development of this epithet seems to date to the Song dynasty, although it does not appear to have become common usage until the Ming.

49. Quoted in Liu Guangsheng and Tang Haozheng, *Chongxiu Changzhou fu zhi* 17.81a. Mei Yaochen also wrote a poem about the temple dedicated to Prince Jizha, entitled "Jizi Miao" 季子廟 (Master Ji's temple).

recorded. According to at least one gazetteer, the calligraphy on the Ten-Character Stele was re-cut at the same time.[50] Some two centuries later, in 1103 (during the Northern Song dynasty), the inscription was certainly re-carved by order of Zhu Yan, then the Administrator of Changzhou.[51] Zhu Yan also wrote the earliest surviving record of the history of the main temple to Prince Jizha of Wu, in which he bemoaned the building of a further temple to the prince in Qu'a (a site not intrinsically associated with Prince Jizha's memory).[52] Although this town did stand within what were believed to constitute the borders of Prince Jizha's former fief of Yanling, Zhu Yan nevertheless found the construction of a temple away from the site of the prince's tomb to be unacceptable—because the new site had no physical link with this great historical figure, and because there was thus no rationale for commemorating the prince in that location.

Nearly one century after Ouyang Xiu wrote the *Jigu lu*, a slightly different transcription of the wording of the Ten-Character Stele was given in the *Wujun zhi* by Fan Chengda 范成大 (1126–1193, *jinshi* 1154).[53] Likewise, the Southern Song dynasty gazetteer *Xianchun Piling zhi* transcribes the inscription on the stele in a slightly different version.[54] The fact that at least three different versions of the Ten-Character Stele inscription were in circulation during the Song dynasty is indicative of the interest aroused in this monument's inscription in the wake of its first publication in the *Jigu lu*. Scholarly interest was no doubt piqued, not just by the association of this monument with the figure of Prince Jizha of Wu, but also by the link with Confucius. Though both the *Jigu lu* and gazetteers such as the *Wujun zhi* would stress that it was the *wording* that was said to have been handed down from Confucius (rather than the characters themselves), many

---

50. Liu Guangsheng and Tang Haozheng, *Chongxiu Changzhou fu zhi* 2.57a.

51. One account dates this re-carving to the first year of the Chongning reign-period. Zhang Gun, *Jiangyin xian zhi* 2.25b.

52. Shi Nengzhi, *Xianchun Piling zhi*, p. 3574.

53. "When [Prince Jizha of Wu] died, Confucius wrote where he was buried: 'Alas! This is the tomb of the Gentleman of Yanling of Wu.' This has been handed down from one generation to the next to the present day." 其卒也, 孔子書其葬處曰: "嗚呼! 有吳延陵君子之墓." 至今傳於世. Fan Chengda, *Wujun zhi*, p. 302.

54. "Alas! This is the tomb of Master Ji of Yanling of Wu" 烏虖! 有吳延陵季子之墓. Shi Nengzhi, *Xianchun Piling zhi*, p. 3574.

later accounts would suggest that in fact the stele bore the calligraphy of the great sage. The Ten-Character Stele then became tied to a long tradition of apocryphal tales about Confucius that describe the sage as receiving a series of ambassadors from Wu, and in one case as travelling to visit King Goujian of Yue.

This can be seen in the 1510 essay "Yanling Jizi mubei kao" 延陵季子墓碑考 (Research into the stele from the tomb of Master Ji of Yanling), by Du Mu, which includes an interesting plea for the authenticity of this monument:

> I once read the *Yuejue* [*shu*] and saw that this text recorded that King Goujian of Yue personally begged for [advice] from the wise and sagacious. Confucius and his seventy disciples then presented the refined *qin* [music] of the former kings and rectified the rituals [of Yue] and its ancient music. If this is so, then Confucius must have passed through Wu on his way to Yue. This text does not seem to have been forged, so surely [the reason that this was not recorded in the *Shiji*] is that the Grand Historian did not have an opportunity to read it! Besides, in the Spring and Autumn period a person as wise as Master Ji must have met the Sage.
> 穆嘗讀越絶見其中載越王勾踐躬求賢聖. 孔子徒弟七十人奉先王雅琴治禮往奏. 則孔子固嘗歷吳至越. 其書近古言似非僞. 豈太史公未之見耶! 况春秋之時, 賢如季子固聖人之所與.[55]

The story mentioned in Du Mu's essay is found in the "Jidi zhuan" chapter of the *Yuejue shu*, and records how King Goujian of Yue summoned Confucius to his side, treated him with great respect, but ultimately was unable to find a use for the sage in the government of such a backward and remote kingdom. The great wealth and power

55. See Chen Yan'en and Li Zhaoluo, *Jiangyin xian zhi*, pp. 2168–69. Du Mu's position within the world of mid-Ming scholarship on the history and culture of the ancient kingdom of Wu is interesting. Although clearly very learned, and with an extremely strong intellectual interest in the history of the Wu region, his scholarship remained marginal and he was never invited to join any activities associated with the Wumen pai 吳門派 (Wu School), based in Suzhou and responsible for many major contemporary publications, including several gazetteers. This oversight seems to have been the result of Du Mu's association with the accusation that Tang Yin attempted to cheat in the 1498 *jinshi* examinations. Tang Yin, who was later very closely involved in many Wumen pai activities, was brought to the verge of suicide by the allegations. Chu-tsing Li, "Tang Yin," p. 1257.

of the king of Yue is stressed in this description, as well as the magnificence of the kingdom that he reigned over. However, at the same time, King Goujian and his people are presented as barbarians who are unable to appreciate the wisdom of Confucius. Much recent scholarship, both in China and the West, has focused on the "barbarian" associations of Confucius.[56] However in the case of this Han dynasty story, the meeting between these two famous men apparently represents the conflict between powerful barbarian military might (symbolized by the figure of the great King Goujian), and gentle, refined Zhou cultural supremacy (embodied by Confucius). The story ends in mutual incomprehension and refusal to engage:

> Goujian attacked Wu, and was hegemon over the lands east of the pass.[57] He went to Langya and built the Guantai (Observation tower).[58] The tower was seven *li* in circumference, and from it you could look out over the Eastern Sea. He had eight thousand suicide troops and three hundred warships. A short time later, he personally invited wise men and sages to come to his court.[59] Confucius brought his seventy disciples, and carried an elegant lute. He rectified the rituals, and then went to offer his advice. Goujian then put on the armor of Ciyi, he buckled on the sword Buguang, and grasped the lance Wulu.[60] He sent out three hundred suicide troops, and made

---

56. Eno, "The Background of the Kong Family of Lu and the Origins of Ruism"; Wilson, "Ritualizing Confucius/Kongzi."

57. Some scholars, such as Yu Jidong, *Yuejue shu quanyi*, p. 164, have interpreted this as a reference to the Hangu 函谷 pass. This would have made King Goujian of Yue hegemon over virtually every state of the Zhou confederacy with the exception of Qin. King Goujian's hegemony is mentioned in a number of ancient Chinese texts, such as for example *Shiji* 41.1746, which records that the Zhou king gave him a mandate and a gift of meat, but there are no references to the extent of his dominance.

58. According to the *Zhushu jinian* 竹書紀年 (Bamboo Annals), the move of the capital to Langya in fact only took place in 468 BCE, during the reign of King Goujian's son. *Zhushu jinian* B.19a. A discussion of various theories about the movements of the Yue capital in the late Spring and Autumn and early Warring States can be found in Đao, *Yuenan gudai shi*, pp. 78–79.

59. *Guoyu*, p. 635 ("Yueyu shang").

60. The *Wudu fu* by Zuo Si, refers to Yangyi 睗夷 armor and Bolu 勃盧 lances. *Wen xuan*, p. 72. In the commentary on this phrase, Li Shan 李善 quotes this section of the *Yuejue shu*, but with slightly different wording: "The king of Yue then put on the Yangyi armor, and grasped the Bolu lance" 越王身被睗夷之甲, 扶勃盧之矛. In

them line up in battle formation below the pass. Confucius then arrived in Yue in state. The king of Yue said: "Good, good. What are you going to teach me?" Confucius replied: "I can explain the Way of the Five Emperors and the Three Kings; therefore, I packed up my fine lute, and came to your majesty's home." Goujian sighed deeply and said: "The people of Yue are weak and stupid. They live on dry land but travel by water. Boats are their chariots and oars are their horses: when they travel it is as if they are drifting on the wind; once they set off they are hard to stop. Besides which, it is the nature of the Yue people to keep their weapons ready, and they have no fear of death. Do you think you can change this?" Confucius then said goodbye, and none of his disciples were able to stop him.

句踐伐吳, 霸關東, 從瑯琊起觀臺, 周七里, 望東海. 死士八千人, 戈船三百艘, 居無幾躬求賢聖. 孔子從弟子七十人奉先王雅琴治禮往奏. 句踐乃身被賜夷之甲, 帶步光之劍, 杖物盧之矛, 出死士三百人爲陣關下. 孔子有頃姚稽到越. 越王曰: "唯唯! 夫子何以教之?" 孔子對曰: "丘能述五帝三王之道. 故奉雅琴至大王所." 句踐喟然嘆曰: "夫越性脆而愚. 水行而山處, 以船爲車, 以楫爲馬. 往若飄風, 去則難從, 銳兵任死, 越之常性也. 夫子異則不可?" 於是孔子辭. 弟子莫能從乎.[61]

The story of Confucius's meeting with King Goujian is also given in the *Wu Yue chunqiu*. In this case, the story is apparently quoted practically verbatim from the *Yuejue shu*.[62] This story seems to have been a southern tale, associated with the ancient Jiangnan region, and does not seem to have made its way out of the confines of the Wu-Yue area, even after the unification of China. This story was never included among compilations of tales about Confucius, nor was it apparently ever generally accepted as part of the standard biography of the sage.

The way Du Mu uses this story in his essay is therefore interesting, for he ignores all the problematic issues raised by the tale in favor of a series of assertions of a remarkably specious logic: if Confucius travelled to Yue to see King Goujian, then the sage would have had to pass by Wu. If he passed by Wu, he would have wanted to stop off and see the famously wise Prince Jizha. If he met Prince Jizha,

---

this case the two names are most likely to refer to two tribal peoples: the Yangyi and the Bulu 卜盧. Knechtges, *Wen xuan or Selections of Refined Literature, vol. 1*, p. 408.

61. *Yuejue shu*, p. 58 ("Jidi zhuan").

62. *Wu Yue chunqiu*, pp. 176–77 ("Goujian fa Wu waizhuan").

Confucius would naturally have taken the time to write his epitaph, and thus the text which was traditionally said to have come from the hand of the great sage must indeed have emanated from the brush of Confucius.

The essay by Du Mu revised the transcription of the calligraphy on the stele—returning to the form first given by Ouyang Xiu, rather than using the Southern Song dynasty versions put forward by Fan Chengda or Shi Nengzhi. Subsequent accounts have tended to follow the reading given by Du Mu. An exception to this rule appears in the "Shizi bei lun" 十字碑論 (Discourse on the Ten-Character Stele) by the distinguished local scholar, Hanlin Academician, and Donglin martyr Miao Changqi 繆昌期 (1562–1626, *jinshi* 1613), who preferred Fan Chengda's reading.[63] In the Ming dynasty, during the reign of the Zhengtong Emperor 明正統 (r. 1436–1449), the calligraphy on this monument was again re-carved under the auspices of the Prefect Mo Yu 莫愚. After re-cutting of the main inscription, in addition to the "Confucian" text on the Ten-Character Stele in seal script, the stone was given a further inscription in modern characters: "Confucius wrote the inscription for the stele on Master Ji of Wu's tomb. In the eighth year of Zhengtong (1444), the Prefect Mo Yu had it re-cut on the stone." 孔子題吳季子墓碑. 正統八年知府莫愚摹刻于石.[64]

The inscription on the Ten-Character Stele is not recorded as having been re-cut between 1444 and its destruction in 1937. The 1444 re-carving of the stele was one small part of a much wider program of restoration of the temple dedicated to Prince Jizha that was undertaken at this time by the Prefect Mo Yu and the District Magistrate of Wujin County, Zhu Shu. The two men were also responsible for the re-carving of the numerous stone inscriptions that ornamented

63. Miao Changqi's essay was reprinted in Chen Yan'en and Li Zhaoluo, *Jiangyin xian zhi*, p. 2348. The destruction of the Dongling faction in 1625–1626, and the death of Miao Changqi under torture is documented in Dardess, *Blood and History in China*. Tiger Hill was to become strongly associated with the Donglin cause, given that a number of the lesser martyrs (those who died in Suzhou rather than being transported to the capital for execution) were buried there in the "Five Men's Tomb" (Wuren mu 五人墓). Xu Song and Zhang Dachun, *Baicheng yanshui*, p. 37.

64. Tschepe, *Histoire du Royaume de Ou*, p. 49.

the main hall.[65] Their efforts were intended to remind visitors of the great antiquity of the place, and of the numerous distinguished patrons the temple had attracted during its long history. Sadly, at the end of the Ming dynasty, the Ten-Character Stele was smashed to pieces during a storm. Apparently, the stele was already in extremely bad condition at this time—hardly surprising for a monument that may have been a thousand years old at the time. Subsequently, the stone was reassembled and mortared together again.[66]

It was clearly a matter of considerable pride to be involved in the restoration of the temple. The inscriptions—recorded on the stele itself and housed in the main hall of the temple until it was destroyed during the Taiping rebellion—described previous re-carvings of the stone, rebuildings of the monument, and visits by dignitaries who wished to pay their respects to the famous Prince Jizha of Wu. These inscriptions provide an invaluable record of the history of the temple and of the Ten-Character Stele, quite apart from the essays included in gazetteers. The importance of these secondary inscriptions was well known and they were themselves carefully preserved. Thus, during the Qing dynasty, in 1800, an inscription recording an earlier undated restoration of the temple's Ten-Character Stele by Zheng Man 鄭鄤 (1594–1639, *jinshi* 1622) of Wujin County was repaired by order of then District Magistrate Liu Shoutai 劉守泰.[67] As a local, Zheng Man may have felt a strong link with Prince Jizha of Wu, and perhaps associated his success in the *jinshi* examinations with his worship at this temple. Be that as it may, the paucity of records about this particular restoration of the Ten-Character Stele may be derived from Zheng Man's unfortunate end; he was convicted of a lack of filial piety after beating his mother with a stick, and was dismembered on the execution grounds.

Although the vast majority of recorded enhancements and restorations of monuments commemorating Prince Jizha of Wu were sponsored by officials and members of the ruling elite, an important and often ignored part was also played by local people. The best-recorded

65. Liu Guangsheng and Tang Haozheng, *Chongxiu Changzhou fu zhi* 2.57a.
66. Zhang Gun, *Jiangyin xian zhi*, 8.3a.
67. Chen Yan'en and Li Zhaoluo, *Jiangyin xian zhi*, p. 753.

participation of local people in the cult of Prince Jizha of Wu came in the wake of the Taiping rebellion, when so many religious buildings had been destroyed, and when official participation in temple reconstruction was at a minimum. Were it not for this local interest in rebuilding the temple dedicated to the prince's memory, it would not have been re-erected. Although famous visitors were in a position to record their impressions and to participate actively in embellishing the temple with their calligraphy and writings, local people were crucial for the day-to-day maintenance of the site, and they were no doubt the major participants in worship during its millennia of existence.

The Temple to Prince Jizha at Jiujinfeng

Throughout the imperial period, people claiming descent from great historical figures of the Spring and Autumn period were closely involved in the commemoration of these personages. Individuals claiming to be family members of a famous historical figure could expect to play a key role in determining the location of temple sites, and the manner of worship there. For example, in the city of Suzhou, on a number of occasions families claiming descent from the famous loyal minister, Wu Zixu, played an important part in the development of shrines dedicated to his memory within the city walls—sometimes choosing the location of a shrine. For example, the intervention of a "descendant" named Wu Yuancui 伍袁萃 (*jinshi* 1580) in 1612 was to prove crucial in the process that saw the shrine to Wu Zixu at the Pan Gate 盤門 (originally founded in 426 by the Magistrate Xie Xun 謝詢) moved to its present location. The fact that Wu Yuancui held the office of Assistant Administration Commissioner (Canyi 參議), rank 4b, no doubt did not hurt his cause, but his rank alone would probably not have been sufficient to order such a major change to such a venerable and important local foundation without the added authority of his status as a family member.[68] Another example of this

68. Wu Naifu, "Suzhou gu Panmen yu Wu Zixu," pp. 8–9. The same article cites another example of the treatment of the deified Wu Zixu, this time by a non-relative. When the Prefect of Suzhou, Kuang Zhong 况鐘, visited the Xu Gate temple during the reign of the Ming Zhengtong Emperor (r. 1435–1449), he decided that the image installed there, representing Wu Zixu looking out for the arrival of

kind of situation is the role played the great scholar Sun Xingyan 孫星衍 (1753–1818, *jinshi* 1787) in the commemoration of the famous general Sun Wu. Sun Xingyan, who claimed to be a descendant in the fifty-seventh generation of the author of the *Sunzi bingfa*, was closely involved in a number of early nineteenth-century efforts to remember Sun Wu, including the designation of a specific tomb site and location where he is said to have drilled the palace women of King Helü of Wu. Sun Xingyan was also responsible for the erection of a small monument at Tiger Hill opposite the tomb of King Helü that was dedicated to the memory of his ancestor.[69] His status as a descendant was apparently crucial in overcoming opposition to his building plans.

Of all the members of the Wu royal house, Prince Jizha was the only one to have such putative descendants involved in the building of monuments dedicated to his memory. Given that a number of additional shrines were built by individuals who said that they were descended from the prince, these religious foundations had a very different status from those constructed at his tomb or in the surrounding area. The temple most closely associated with the descendants of Prince Jizha of Wu was that at Jinjiufeng 錦鳩峰 on Wushan 吳山. This temple was said to have originally been founded in 779 by Xiao Ding, a man who played a major part in promoting the cult of Prince Jizha during the Tang dynasty, and who is mentioned above in connection with the re-carving of the Ten-Character Stele. This temple subsequently fell into disuse and was eventually completely forgotten, its location lost. However, worship of members of the ruling house of Wu is known to have continued at Jiujinfeng. In 1252, during the Southern Song dynasty, a temple at Jiujinfeng (dedicated jointly to the memory of Zhongyong and Prince Jizha) was restored by the Judicial Commissioner Pan Kai 潘凱 (*jinshi* Shaoding 紹定 reign-era, 1228–1233). The relationship, if any, between this Southern Song dynasty temple and the one from the Tang dynasty is unknown.

---

the Yue army, was not respectful, so he ordered a new statue carved to show Wu Zixu in a seated position. A change of this nature, though significant for the appearance of the temple and popular perception of the deity, did not require anything other than money and perhaps the authority of an official position to achieve.

69. Li Jiaqiu, "Sun Wu yu Gusu," pp. 377–80.

During the Yuan dynasty, in the fifth year of the Zhiyuan 至元 reign-period (1340), a temple dedicated solely to Prince Jizha of Wu was established at Jiujinfeng by a man claiming descent from the prince, an individual named Wu Fengchen 吳逢辰.[70] Although descendants of the prince played a crucial role in building and restoring this temple it cannot be described as a true family temple. As is clear from the records of the history of this foundation, its management was a collective affair, involving local people, officials serving in the region, members of the national ruling elite, and family members. It would seem likely that it was a source of considerable pride that descendants of Prince Jizha of Wu remained closely involved with the foundation, but they apparently did not control the way their ancestor was remembered and worshipped at the temple at Jinjiufeng. However, this may simply reflect a failure on their part to pass the official examination or to achieve a bureaucratic office—which would mean that they were unable to impose their wishes on other (wealthier and more powerful) patrons and donors to the temple.

The foundation at Jinjiufeng was not unique in maintaining a link with descendants of the prince; the same was true of the Yanling Jizi ci 延陵季子祠 (Shrine to Master Ji of Yanling) at Yixing County, founded in 1682. It was originally built by a man named Wu Heng 吳珩, who claimed to be descended from Prince Jizha, and was subsequently restored by one of Wu Heng's descendants, Wu Shimin 吳時敏, in 1785.[71] The paucity of detailed records makes it unclear to what extent the patronage of the Wu family was significant for attracting donations from other patrons. Nor is it clear how much individuals from the Wu family were able to use their patronage of these temples and shrines to enhance their status within the region (that is, by making the local community accept their claim to be descendants of the great Prince Jizha of Wu).

The history of the temple at Jiujinfeng is exhaustively described in the Qing dynasty gazetteer edited by Li Mingwan 李銘皖 and Feng Guifen 馮桂芬 (1809–1874, *jinshi* 1840): the *Suzhoufu zhi* 蘇州府志

70. The name of the founder of this temple is given in Ning Yunpeng et al., *Suzhou fu zhi* 36.15a.

71. See the Ming dynasty gazette for Yixing county by Chen Linwei 陳遴瑋 and Wang Sheng 王升, quoted in Wu wenhua yanjiu cujinhui ed., *Gouwu shi ji*, p. 429.

(Gazetteer of Suzhou Prefecture). After the initial foundation of the temple by Wu Fengchen, subsequent restorations and enhancements were largely the responsibility of local officials. For some reason, at the beginning of the Ming dynasty, in 1369, the temple was temporarily rededicated to the worship of Wu Taibo. Wu Taibo was always a much more popular deity than Prince Jizha, and numerous temples dedicated to him (including a number which are of great antiquity) are known across Jiangsu Province. Temples dedicated to the founder of the state of Wu tend to either use his name, or they were called Zhide Miao 至德廟 (Temple of the supreme virtue). It is not clear when worship at this temple reverted to Prince Jizha of Wu, but by the end of the Ming dynasty the prince was again receiving sacrifices at Jiujinfeng. Then in 1629, the local magistrate Shi Yingxuan 史鷹選 was joined by a descendant of Prince Jizha named Wu Ercheng 吳爾成 to organize a restoration of this temple. Wu Ercheng was at this time the abbot of the Shangbao Temple 尚寶寺 in Nanjing.[72] The temple to Prince Jizha was again restored in 1690, the twenty-ninth year of the reign of the Kangxi Emperor, by Wu Shiyan 吳時雁, who also claimed descent from Prince Jizha of Wu.[73] Although all the members of the Wu family involved with the temple at Jiujinfeng from the time of its founding in the Yuan dynasty until the early Qing restoration would claim descent from Prince Jizha, it is unfortunately not known if they were related to each other: this makes it unclear if many branches of the Wu clan were involved or just a single family.

Like the main temple dedicated to the prince at the site of his tomb, this temple was also destroyed in 1860 during the Taiping rebellion. Local people rebuilt the temple, and worship began again in 1869, but it was not restored fully to its former glory until 1875. That was the year that the Governor of Anhui Province, Wu Yuanbing 吳元炳 (?–1886, *jinshi* 1860), decided to sponsor a major program for rebuilding the temple, and to make significant expenditure on

72. No biographical information is available about Wu Ercheng, but he is thought to have been the older brother of Wu Erxun 吳爾壎 (?–1645). Wu Erxun, *jinshi* 1643, drowned himself in a well at Yangzhou when the Manchu forces took the city. He was therefore regularly numbered among the martyrs of the collapse of the Ming dynasty.

73. Li Mingwan and Feng Guifen, *Suzhou fu zhi*, p. 1038.

decoration.[74] Although the surname Wu might suggest that the Governor was interested in claiming a link between his own family and that of Prince Jizha of Wu, in fact this seems not to have been the case. In the end, the temple at Jiujinfeng, though temporarily rededicated to another more important deity during the early Ming dynasty, was to maintain an enduring association not only with Prince Jizha of Wu but with many generations of his descendants. The history of this temple shows that just as local officials were interested in promoting the worship of one of the great Confucian heroes of ancient China, members of the Wu family were greatly concerned to assert their links with the royal family in general and to Prince Jizha in particular. Their expenditure on patronage can be explained in terms of family piety, and also by the increase of their own status should they successfully assert kinship with such a famous historical figure.

Other Temples and Shrines Dedicated to Prince Jizha

As mentioned above, the temple dedicated to the memory of Prince Jizha of Wu at the site of his tomb was part of a small constellation of related religious foundations, of which the shrine at Jiujinfeng is by far the best recorded and the most interesting, thanks to its ongoing association with people claiming descent from the prince. One of the earliest references to the existence of a wider cult is found in the *Wujun tujing xuji* by Zhu Changwen.[75] By the time of the Southern Song dynasty, there were three recorded shrines to Prince Jizha of Wu in the region around Changzhou, in addition to that found near his tomb. One of these additional shrines had been built on the east side of the local Confucian academy. This building was erected by Zhang Shouxiao 張守孝 during the Chunxi 淳熙 reign-period of the Southern Song Emperor Xiaozong 宋孝宗 (r. 1163–1189). A second shrine was erected in conjunction with a temple to Prince Jizha outside the eastern city wall at Jinling. Another shrine was built by a former Magistrate of Jinling, Zhao Yan 趙彥, and this was to become one of

---

74. This account of the restoration of the temple dedicated to Prince Jizha of Wu at Jiujinfeng is taken from the 1933 gazette for Wu county by Wu Xiuzhi 吳秀之, quoted in Wu wenhua yanjiu cujinhui ed., *Gouwu shi ji*, p. 428.

75. Zhu Changwen, *Wujun tujing xuji*, p. 26.

the best recorded of the subsidiary shrines dedicated to Prince Jizha, because it was described by Ye Shi 葉適 (1150–1223, *jinshi* 1178), in his essay: "Jizi ci ji" 季子祠記 (Record of the shrine of Master Ji).[76]

In addition, a shrine not specifically identified by location, which was dedicated to the memory of Prince Jizha (possibly one of the above, or possibly an otherwise unrecorded site), is mentioned in the poem by the Song dynasty poet and monk Zongle 宗泐 (1317–1391, original name Zhou Jitan 周季潭) entitled "Yanling Jizi ci song Zhang Shou" 延陵季子祠送張守 (Saying goodbye to Zhang Shou at the shrine of Master Ji of Yanling):

> Yanling is an ancient and famous commandery,
> Master Ji has a shrine here.
> Old trees meet in front of the steps,
> The long river rolls past outside the door.
> A reputation for kindness has been passed down to later ages,
> The virtue of yielding is inherited from former lords.
> The prefect is departing to take up another position,
> May he respect and reward the wise even more.
> 延陵古名郡, 季子有祠宮.
> 古木階前合, 長河户外通.
> 仁風垂後代, 讓德繼先公.
> 太守之官去, 褒賢禮更崇.[77]

This poem is closely related to the ones written by visitors to the main temple of Prince Jizha at his mausoleum complex, thanks to its references to the antiquity of the cult dedicated to the prince, and its awareness of biographical details recorded in ancient texts. However, such poems provide little evidence of more than the existence of certain buildings at the time of writing; they are vehicles for the poet to display his learning of the classics and his appreciation of the virtues of the famous Prince Jizha, rather than an attempt to record the landscape before his eyes.

During the Qing dynasty, more shrines dedicated to the memory of the prince were recorded in the Changzhou region: one at the

---

76. The three shrines are mentioned in Shi Nengzhi, *Xianchun Piling zhi*, p. 3574. Ye Shi's essay on the history of the last of these is reprinted in Liu Guangsheng and Tang Haozheng, *Chongxiu Changzhou fu zhi* 19.9a–10b.

77. Quoted in Zhu Yu, *Chongxiu Piling zhi*, p. 1936.

county seat, and one in the town of Xiagang.[78] The subsequent history of these buildings is not known, and they appear not to have been mentioned in any later gazetteer. Likewise, the Qing dynasty gazetteer for Wujin County records the presence within the county borders of both a temple and a shrine to the memory of Prince Jizha.[79] According to the Qianlong-era *Shandong tongzhi* 山東通志 (Comprehensive gazetteer for Shandong Province) published in 1736, at this time there was a shrine dedicated to the memory of the prince at Anping zhen 安平鎮, beside the Guajian tai (Hanging sword tower). This foundation is supposed to have been extant at least as far back as the beginning of the Ming dynasty, because the Hongwu Emperor 明洪武 (r. 1368–1398) is said to have presented the shrine with a plaque reading: "Jiaxian" 嘉賢 (Excellent and wise).[80] Nevertheless, it would seem that in spite of the prince's fame as one of the great Confucian heroes of antiquity, shrines and temples dedicated to his memory were mostly confined to a very small area, being grouped around his tomb, or located within the boundaries of his former fief, with only a few being built outside this region.[81]

The existence of all these shrines raises the question of what worshippers at such sites were praying for. The writings of literati visitors to these shrines and of officials in whose jurisdiction they were located provide but scant information about the direction of worship of Prince Jizha. As mentioned above, it is recorded in one Ming dynasty gazetteer for Suzhou that a temple in the city dedicated to Prince Jizha, under his alternative title of Master Ji of Yanling, was the site used by students at the Confucian academy when they wished to pray prior to examinations. This seems to have come about because Prince Jizha was believed to be an efficacious deity for examination success,

78. Chen Yan'en and Li Zhaoluo, *Jiangyin xian zhi*, p. 754.

79. Wang Zusu et al., *Wujin xian zhi*, p. 356.

80. Du Zhao, *Shandong tongzhi* 21.43a.

81. Hansen, *Changing Gods in Medieval China*, pp. 189, 194. In the first instance, the temple dedicated to the prince known as the Xi Wu Jizi Miao 西吳季子廟 (Temple to Master Ji of the Western Wu) in Guian County 歸安縣 was recorded as having purchased land between 1241 and 1252. In the second case, the temple dedicated to Wu Xi Ji Wang 吳西季王 (King Ji of the Western Wu) in Changxing County 長興縣 was enhanced by a new inscription, presented between 1131 and 1162.

a conclusion presumably drawn from his uncanny ability to discern the secret meanings of traditional Zhou music. While this gives some indication of the reasons why members of the literati and prospective members of the ruling elite would wish to worship the prince, it gives but little indication of what local worshippers sought through their practices, because the vast majority of these ordinary people can have had no interest in examination success. Although the city of Suzhou was certainly big enough, and was a sufficiently important educational center during the Ming dynasty to support a students' temple, this does not explain the survival for many centuries of the numerous other religious foundations dedicated to Prince Jizha of Wu. Thus, commemoration of the prince perhaps simply reflected his importance as a powerful figure from the history of this region.

Conclusion

The existence of the temples and shrines dedicated to the memory of Prince Jizha of Wu serve to indicate the enduring importance of local cults after the unification of China, and indeed throughout the imperial period. A number of Chinese emperors, from the Tang Emperor Xuanzong to the Kangxi Emperor in the Qing dynasty, are known to have displayed a personal interest in commemorating the prince. This imperial interest was sporadic, for Prince Jizha of Wu was not a figure of such great cultural and historical importance as to attract lasting patronage from the emperors of China; nevertheless, it is still indicative of the enduring power of the prince's legend. Whatever the level of imperial interest, however, the temple and tomb complex were certainly famous enough to attract the interest of the national elite. Throughout the imperial period, some of the greatest scholars and officials in China went out of their way to visit and to patronize the temples raised to the prince. These officials wrote about their visits; they presided over restorations and rebuildings of the memorials; and they took an interest in recording the history of the temple, tomb, and steles. Local officials and important families also took great pride in associating themselves with the prince's cult. There was clearly considerable prestige to be garnered from an association with the development and preservation of temples and shrines dedicated to Prince Jizha of Wu.

In addition to the scholars and officials of the national elite, and the local officials appointed to the region, monuments raised to the memory of Prince Jizha also attracted the interest of a succession of poets and artists. Some of them were local men, who were drawn to a major local tourist spot that was a site of great historic interest. Some were officials, on tours of duty, or enjoying their retirement, and this group sometimes overlapped with the group described above. Others were famous artists and poets, able to indulge their own interests in visiting such a well-known site, or men specially commissioned to add to the beauties of the spot. They came to re-cut the inscription on the steles, and to decorate the purlieus of the temple with further inscriptions. They described visits to these shrines and temples, the stele and the tomb in verse and prose. Although none of the most famous Chinese poets apparently ever wrote about the memorials built to Prince Jizha, these less well-known voices should still be seen as adding considerably to the fame of these monuments. In spite of the convention in *huaigu* literature of portraying visits as spontaneous or unexpected, it is clear that the goal of many literati visitors was to visit sites associated with Prince Jizha. This can be seen in the poem by the Ming dynasty literatus Sun Yiyuan 孫一元 (1484–1520), entitled "You Wu" 遊吳 (On travelling through Wu):

> Though dressed in coarse cloth, my heart is ever stout,
> Hemp binds the hilt of my sword, but I sing freely.
> I wander through the country of the kings of Wu,
> I have come to seek out the tomb of Master Ji.
> 裋褐心愈壯, 蒯緱歌自聞.
> 薄遊吳王國, 來尋季子墳.[82]

The final social group of importance in the commemoration of Prince Jizha of Wu was comprised of local people. They were the vast majority of those who attended the festivals celebrated at his shrines and temples; and they must also have paid for the majority of the restorations and rebuildings. Their role in the history of these monuments went largely unrecorded, though occasionally the contribution of an important individual might be described in a gazetteer. Naturally, it was the enduring interest of the local population in

82. Sun Yiyuan, *Taibai shanren man'gao* 7.835.

maintaining their historic links with Prince Jizha that has preserved these memorials to the present day.

The importance of the monuments raised to the memory of Prince Jizha of Wu lies in their complex history. These temples and shrines were dedicated to a historical figure who represented a meeting of cultures: a member of a southern ruling house, Prince Jizha's wisdom and profound knowledge of Zhou culture won him the respect of the great lords of the Zhou confederacy. During the imperial period, at a time when other local cults in the south were viciously suppressed, that of the prince remained untouched. The continued reverence shown to the memory of Prince Jizha of Wu throughout the imperial period is indicative of enduring interest in the legend of Master Ji of Yanling. In his study of Chinese popular religion, Stephan Feuchtwang noted: "The beings celebrated and pictured in Chinese local festivals are addressed as actual historical persons . . . Very often they are . . . They are often martyrs, but to a loyalty, not a faith—loyalty to friends, loyalty to principles of behavior, loyalty to an emperor or dynasty, loyalty to family line and its honor."[83]

Prince Jizha's staunch upholding of his principles, his devotion to the interests of his family and his people, have ensured that he is worshipped in temples and shrines in the Jiangnan region to the present day.

83. Feuchtwang, *The Imperial Metaphor*, p. 3.

5

The Tomb at Tiger Hill

After the death of King Helü of Wu, he was buried at a site outside the walls of his capital, at a place named Huqiushan 虎丘山, or Tiger Hill. Although King Helü has generally been regarded as the very greatest of all the kings of Wu, he was the subject of remarkably few commemorative structures in the imperial era and only one important site was associated with his memory: his tomb. It is not clear why there should be this paucity of known sites linked with important events during his lifetime and a subsequent lack of commemorative temples and shrines. It is certainly the case that many Wu royal sites that might be regarded as jointly associated with both King Helü and his son, King Fuchai, in fact seem to have become most strongly linked to the doomed last king of Wu. The immensely successful King Helü seems to have been a much more difficult subject to romanticize than was King Fuchai of Wu—and thus the penultimate king of Wu was the subject of considerably less attention in literati culture during the imperial era. Because he lacked the spectacular and attention-grabbing flaws of his successor, King Helü of Wu was significantly less interesting to later poets and scholars.

The "Ji Wudi zhuan" chapter of the *Yuejue shu* provides an extensive record of those buildings and sites that in the Han dynasty were believed to be associated with King Helü. The discussion below focuses on those sites that are either explicitly said to have been built by King Helü, or those where the context determines that the king of Wu mentioned as commanding their construction must be King Helü. Although some other entries in the *Yuejue shu* chapter refer generally to the activities of the kings of Wu at particular sites, and may hence be assumed to apply to King Helü of Wu as well, these entries are not considered here. The landscape features considered in the "Ji Wudi zhuan" chapter can be roughly grouped into four different categories. The first is royal residences, of which two are mentioned:

> The Helü Gong (King Helü's palace) was located at Gaoping Village.
> 闔廬宮在高平里.[1]

> The Gucheng (Old walled city) was the secondary residence built by King Helü of Wu for his concubines. It stands seventy *li* out of town (29.05 km).
> 古城者吳王闔廬所置美人離城也. 去縣七十里.[2]

In addition to the royal residences, there are a number of secondary structures that must have been associated with the royal palaces, for they were described as necessary for provisioning them. These include two icehouses, which would have provided fresh food for the royal table, and an area where deer were raised:

> The mound outside the outer city wall by the Changmen (Chang Gate) was Helü's icehouse.
> 閶門外郭中冢者闔廬冰室也.[3]

> The mound outside Wumen (Wu's gate) was Helü's icehouse.
> 巫門外冢者闔廬冰室也.[4]

> Mihucheng (Deer lake walled city) was the place where Helü raised deer, and it is located fifty *li* from town (20.75 km).
> 麋湖城者闔廬所置麋也. 去縣五十里.[5]

The second important group of sites associated with King Helü of Wu and recorded in the *Yuejue shu* are tombs. Not only is the king's own tomb mentioned in the "Ji Wudi zhuan"; but the work also provides details about the graves of his children, one of his daughters-in-law, one of his generals, and a number of his aristocrats. The description of King Helü's tomb at Tiger Hill that is given in the *Yuejue shu* will be considered in more detail below. In the case of the graves of the king of Wu's relatives and associates, these individuals are identified with respect to their relationship to the great king of Wu; even the princes and princesses of Wu are not differentiated by having their

---

1. *Yuejue shu*, p. 9 ("Ji Wudi zhuan").
2. Ibid., p. 14 ("Ji Wudi zhuan").
3. Ibid., p. 11 ("Ji Wudi zhuan"). For references to the use of *bingshi* 冰室 (icehouses) as cool places for the storage of food in ancient China; see *Zuozhuan*, pp. 1248–1250 (Zhao 4); Sterckx, "Food and Philosophy in Early China," p. 36.
4. *Yuejue shu*, p. 12 ("Ji Wudi zhuan").
5. Ibid., p. 13 ("Ji Wudi zhuan").

personal names recorded. The only person who served King Helü of Wu whose name is specifically mentioned in the context of his tomb is the great general and military strategist Sun Wu:

> The Tomb of Helü's Children is located on the road leading north out of the Changmen. It is located below a pond forty-eight *bu* across (68 m), and the water is two *zhang*, five *chi* deep (5.76 m). The pond here is sixty *bu* across (85 m) and the water is one *zhang*, five *cun* deep (2.43 m). The spirit road leads southwards from the temple road, and goes on to the Guxumen. [The tomb] is six *li* in circumference (2.49 km). There were dancing cranes in the Wu marketplace, and they killed the living to serve the dead.
> 闔廬子女冢在閶門外道北. 下方池廣四十八步, 水深二丈五尺. 池廣六十步, 水深丈五寸. 隧出廟路以南通姑胥門. 幷周六里. 舞鶴吳市, 殺生以送死.[6]

> The Great Tomb Outside Wumen is the grave of the king of Wu's client Sun Wu, who came from Qi. It stands ten *li* outside town (4.15 km). [Sun Wu] was good at the military arts.
> 巫門外大冢, 吳王客齊孫武冢也. 去縣十里. 善爲兵法.[7]

---

6. Ibid., p. 11 ("Ji Wudi zhuan"). In his commentary on the opening phrase of this entry, Qian Peiming, *Yuejue shu zhaji*, p. 7, suggests that it refers to the grave of a *nüzi* 女子 (daughter) of the king of Wu rather than his *zinü* 子女 (children). There are many references in imperial era Chinese texts to the story of a daughter of the king of Wu who committed suicide, and the closing line of this entry seems to refer to the story found in the *Wu Yue chunqiu*, p. 53 ("Helü neizhuan"), which describes how on her death, cranes danced in the marketplace of Wu, and then the people followed the birds out of the city, where they were then entombed with the princess. Apparently the *Yuejue shu* did at one time contain a specific reference to the death and burial of this princess, but it has been lost from the transmitted text. As an alternative to Qian Peiming's suggestion that this whole entry refers to the death of the princess of Wu but has become corrupt, I would suggest that it is also possible that two entries have become conflated. There seems to be no reason why two different sets of dimensions should be given for this water feature, which suggests that the text is corrupt at this point. Furthermore, there are persistent reports in imperial era texts that King Helü of Wu's children were buried in a great mortuary complex at Jiangyin County. Yue Shi, *Taiping huanyu ji* 92.18b; Ye Wenxian, *Wuguo lishi yu Wu wenhua tanmi*, p. 115.

7. *Yuejue shu*, p. 12 ("Ji Wudi zhuan"). This place is now identified with the Sundun 孫墩 (Sun's mound) at Huxiaocun 虎嘯村, thanks to the efforts of the Qing dynasty scholar Sun Xingyan 孫星衍 (1753–1818), who in 1800 travelled to Suzhou to find sites associated with Sun Wu. Li Jiaqiu, "Sun Wu yu Gusu," pp. 377–8; Gu Lu, *Tongqiao yizhao lu*, p. 39. The site is now marked with a stele reading: *Wu wang ke Qi Sun Wu zhong* 吳王客齊孫武冢 (The tomb of Sun Wu of Qi, the client of the king of Wu). Wu Enpei, *Gouwu wenhua de xiandai chanshi*, p. 435.

Qimen (Qi Gate) [was so named] because Helü attacked Qi and won a great victory. He [Helü] took the daughter of the king of Qi hostage, and built the Qimen for her. It was constructed on the wastes of Shuihai. This tower was built on the left of Chedao and on the right of Shuihai, and stands seventy *li* from town (29.05 km). The girl from Qi missed her homeland so much that she died, and they buried her at Yuxishan.
齊門. 闔廬伐齊大克, 取齊王女爲質子, 爲造齊門. 置於水海虛. 其臺在車道左, 水海右. 去縣七十里. 齊女思其國死, 葬虞西山.[8]

Fuhoushan (Cherishing-the-aristocrats mountain) was set aside by order of Helü for the burial of members of the aristocracy, and stands twenty *li* from town (8.3 km).
撫侯山者故闔廬治以諸侯冢次. 去縣二十里.[9]

The third group of sites associated with the great King Helü of Wu are the city walls that he ordered to be built; his fortified encampments and harbors; and structures associated with his weapons-making program. King Helü was clearly deeply concerned not only about the defensive capabilities of the capital and key strategic sites within his kingdom, but he must also have believed that his country should maintain a high degree of military capability, and that it should be constantly prepared for war. These twin concerns are recorded in numerous ancient texts, and can also be seen in the descriptions of various urban and military sites that were constructed during his reign, as recorded in the "Ji Wudi zhuan:"[10]

The Main City Wall of Wu is forty-seven *li*, two hundred and ten *bu* and two *chi* in circumference (19.8 km). There are eight land gates and two of them have towers. There are eight water gates. The southern wall is ten *li*, forty-two *bu*, and five *chi* long (4.2 km). The west wall is seven *li* one hundred and twelve *bu*, and three *chi* long (3.07 km). The north wall is eight *li*, two hundred and twenty-six *bu*, and three *chi* long (3.6 km). The east wall is eleven *li*, seventy-nine *bu*,

8. *Yuejue shu*, p. 12 ("Ji Wudi zhuan"). According to the *Wu Yue chunqiu*, p. 66 ("Helü neizhuan"), the daughter of the lord of Qi particularly asked to be buried at Yuxishan, because it was on the road to Qi. There is a strong local tradition associating Yuxishan with Yushan 虞山 in Changshu County 常熟縣, but in spite of exhaustive searches no trace of any ancient tomb has been found here. Ye Wenxian, *Wuguo lishi yu Wu wenhua tanmi*, p. 67.

9. *Yuejue shu*, p. 13 ("Ji Wudi zhuan").

10. Chen Huixing, "Wu Yue chunqiu de moulüe sixiang," pp. 64–65.

and one *chi* long (4.68 km). It was constructed by Helü.[11] The outer city wall of Wu is sixty-eight *li*, sixty *bu* in circumference (29.61 km).
吳大城, 周四十七里二百一十步二尺. 陸門八, 其二有樓. 水門八. 南面十里四十二步五尺, 西面七里百一十二步三尺, 北面八里二百二十六步三尺, 東面十一里七十九步一尺. 闔廬所造也. 吳郭周六十八里六十步.[12]

The Eastern Wu Walled City was an encampment built by Helü on a royal progress, and it stands twenty *li* out of town (8.3 km).
居 (吳) 東城者, 闔廬所遊城也, 去縣二十里.[13]

The Wastes of Gan Village Forge was the place where Helü forged the Gan Jiang sword. Ou Ye had three hundred boys and girls [working for him].[14] It is located two *li* out of town (0.83 km), and to the south it reaches to the river.
千 (干) 里廬虛者闔廬以鑄干將劍. 歐冶僮女三百人. 去縣二里, 南達江.[15]

---

11. Lu Guangwei, *Wudi ji*, p. 15, states specifically that this wall was built in the sixth year of King Jing of Zhou 周敬王 (514 BCE). Recent excavations of the walls of Suzhou are discussed in Zou Houben et al., *Jiangsu kaogu wushinian*, pp. 190–93. Some scholars believe that the Wu Walled City mentioned here is nothing to do with the present city of Suzhou, which they argue was not founded until the Han dynasty. Instead they suggest that the Wu Walled City was in fact located at Lingyanshan. Lu Xuemei and Qian Gonglin, "Chunqiu shidai Wudacheng weizhi zaikao."

12. *Yuejue shu*, p. 9–10 ("Ji Wudi zhuan"). Yinong Xu, *The Chinese City in Space and Time*, p. 43, discusses the layout of the city, reconstructed according to the dimensions given in this chapter of the *Yuejue shu*.

13. *Yuejue shu*, p. 10 ("Ji Wudi zhuan"). The original text of the *Yuejue shu* reads Judongcheng 居東城, however this is being read as Wudongcheng 吳東城 following the commentary by Liu Dianjue, *Yuejue shu zhuzi suoyin*, p. 5, n. 9. The remnants of a number of defensive encampments built by the kings of Wu survive to the present day, though they have been impossible to identify conclusively with those described in the "Ji Wudi zhuan." Zhang Shangjin et al., *Wujin xian zhi*, pp. 708–9.

14. The original text of the *Yuejue shu* names this site as Qianli 千里 (Qian Village), however the character Qian should probably be read as Gan 干, as in the surname of the famous swordsmith Gan Jiang. Liu Dianjue, *Yuejue shu zhuzi suoyin*, p. 5, n. 10. I would suggest that the character *lu* 廬 (hut) should be read as *lu* 爐 (forge). Earlier accounts of these events have Master Ou Ye as a craftsman from Yue, and Gan Jiang from Wu. However by the Eastern Han dynasty these two individuals had become linked and Master Ou Ye was often described as Gan Jiang's teacher. The development of their initially separate legends is described in Liu Dunyuan, *Meishu kaogu yu gudai wenming*, pp. 512–16.

15. *Yuejue shu*, p. 11 ("Ji Wudi zhuan").

> Lixicheng (Boat stream walled city) was where Helü anchored his boats, and it was founded by Helü.
> 欐溪城者闔廬所置船宮也. 闔廬所造.[16]

> Lishi (Brave knights) outside the Loumen was built by Helü in order to defend against the Waiyue.
> 婁門外力士者, 闔廬所造以備外越.[17]

> Wucheng (Martial walled city) north of the Lou[men] was built by Helü to defend against the Waiyue. It stands thirty *li* from town (12.45 km). Today it is a township.
> 婁北武城闔廬所以候外越也. 去縣三十里. 今爲鄉也.[18]

Finally, King Helü of Wu was involved in the construction of a number of prestigious buildings. For example, the construction of the famous Gusu Tower 姑蘇臺 (named in the "Ji Wudi zhuan" account as the Guxu Tower 姑胥臺), is traditionally said to have been ordered by King Fuchai of Wu, in an extravagant gesture of confidence following his comprehensive defeat of the forces of King Goujian at Kuaiji. However, according to the account given below, building activity at this site in fact commenced during the reign of King Helü, and involved a major intervention in the landscape. Given the strong association of the Gusu Tower with King Fuchai of Wu, this site will be considered in more detail in chapter 6. However, the "Ji Wudi zhuan" clearly associates at least some phases of this prestigious project (and the enormous changes to the landscape that were wrought) with King Helü of Wu:

> The Road with Nine Bends outside Xumen was built by Helü so he could travel to Guxu [Gusu] Tower, in order to gaze over Lake Tai and inspect his populace. It is located thirty *li* from town (12.45 km).
> 胥門外有九曲路闔廬造以遊姑胥之臺, 以望太湖中, 闚百姓. 去縣三十里.[19]

The road with nine bends leading to the Gusu Tower was not the only prestigious project undertaken during the reign of King Helü. The "Ji Wudi zhuan" also records the construction of an ambassadorial residence, no doubt intended to impress visitors from other states with the power and wealth of the kingdom of Wu. Such a construction is

---

16. Ibid., p. 13 ("Ji Wudi zhuan"). There is good reason to believe that part of this entry is missing. Zhang Zongxiang, *Yuejue shu jiaozhu* 2.7a.
17. *Yuejue shu*, p. 12 ("Ji Wudi zhuan").
18. Ibid., p. 14 ("Ji Wudi zhuan").
19. Ibid., p. 12 ("Ji Wudi zhuan").

evidence of the importance that the kings of Wu attached to their diplomatic relations with other rulers, which is also attested to in a number of ancient historical texts—though diplomacy is not usually mentioned as one of King Helü's interests:

> Wulicheng (Shaman boat walled city) was built by Helü as a separate residence for ambassadors visiting from the feudal lords. It stands fifteen *li* outside town (6.23 km).
> 巫欐城者闔廬所置諸侯遠客離城也. 去縣十五里.[20]

In spite of this wide array of sites that were associated with the penultimate king of Wu in the Han dynasty, interest in the majority of these places quickly faded. Some of these sites continued to be mentioned in gazetteers during the imperial era, but commemoration of King Helü, and nostalgic tourism that paid tribute to the king quickly came to be focused only upon his tomb at Tiger Hill. There seems to be no evidence that shrines or temples of any kind were erected to the memory of King Helü during the imperial era, in stark contrast to the situation with his uncle, Prince Jizha, and his son, King Fuchai, both of whom were worshipped in the region of their former homes. It also contrasts with the situation pertaining to King Helü's most important general and senior advisor, Wu Zixu, who was worshipped across southern China as a river deity. The reasons that King Helü of Wu was not the subject of a local cult are obscure, particularly given that so many of members of his family, including his younger brother, King Fugai, are known to have been commemorated in temples and shrines in the Suzhou area and beyond. This lack of shrines and temples dedicated to a man of such great historical significance is highly striking, but seems to have gone completely unremarked by scholars.

The Burial of King Helü of Wu

After his death—following a chance and apparently insignificant injury sustained at the battle of Zuili—King Helü of Wu's body was taken home for burial, and he was interred at Tiger Hill. The motive

20. Ibid., p. 13 ("Ji Wudi zhuan"). The kingdom of Wu is known to have undertaken an active program of diplomacy in the late Spring and Autumn period, their most famous ambassador being Prince Jizha. However virtually nothing is known about reciprocal diplomatic visits, though an embassy from Jin Pinggong 晉平公 (r. 557–532 BCE) to Wu is mentioned in the *Shuoyuan*, p. 223 ("Zhengjian").

for this particular choice of burial site is not known; however, some scholars have suggested that this had earlier been the site of one of his summer palaces.[21] The location and appearance of the tomb, and the rich grave goods associated with the burial of the greatest king of Wu, were first recorded in the "Ji Wudi zhuan" chapter of the *Yuejue shu*, and this account was of great importance in determining subsequent interpretations of this landscape throughout the imperial era:

> The tomb of King Helü lies outside the Changmen. It is called Tiger Hill. It is below a pond sixty paces across. The water is one *zhang*, five *chi* deep (approximately 3.5 meters). [He is buried inside] three bronze coffins. The [mercury] pool [inside] the tomb mound is six *chi* across (approximately 1.5 m). Jade ducks swim there. Three thousand swords of Bianzhu, and three thousand other items, as well as the swords [named] Shihao and Yuchang are there. A hundred thousand men were employed to build it. They piled up so much earth that you can see the edge of Lake [Tai]. Three days after they buried him, a white tiger appeared above it [the tomb]. Therefore it is called Tiger Hill.
> 闔廬冢在閶門外. 名虎丘. 下池廣六十步, 水深丈五尺. 銅槨三重. 澒池六尺. 玉鳧之流, 扁諸之劍三千, 方圓之口三千. 時耗、 魚腸之劍在焉. 十萬人築治之. 取土臨湖口. 葬三日而白虎居上, 故號爲虎丘.[22]

This account introduced a number of important features into the story of the burial of King Helü at Tiger Hill. The first is the location of the tomb within the context of other landscape features mentioned. The grave is clearly described as being situated below a pond; this body of water would henceforward become the major focus of visits to King Helü's tomb, of commemorative inscriptions for the great king of Wu, and of attempts to rob the grave.[23] The account given here also stresses both the great wealth buried with King Helü and the enormous efforts made to construct a tomb suitable to such an important monarch. There are frequent references in the poems and essays of imperial-era literati visitors to Tiger Hill to the riches

21. Xie Xiaosi, *Suzhou yuanlin pinshang lu*, p. 176.

22. *Yuejue shu*, p. 11 ("Ji Wudi zhuan").

23. Some writers in the imperial period recorded a minor tradition that the tomb of King Helü was in fact located beneath the Fatang 法堂 (the hall where Buddhist scriptures are recited) of the temple that crowns Tiger Hill. Zhang Defu et al., *Changzhou xian zhi*, p. 1008.

found in this tomb—in particular to the presence of the famous swords from the kingdom of Wu, and the jade ducks swimming on a pool of mercury. The fact that King Helü of Wu was buried with swords inspired many literary responses—which range from the highly critical comments (given that burying swords with the dead is pointless, because there are no enemies in the underworld to be killed this way), to highly exoticized accounts that interpret the presence of swords as a sign of the military might and martial prowess of the ancient southern kingdom of Wu. This latter response is particularly important given that up until the archaeological discoveries of the late twentieth century, no genuine Wu swords were known to exist, leaving the writers' imagination unfettered by anything other than the sword legends recorded in ancient texts.

Although modern geological surveys have determined that Tiger Hill is in fact a natural feature of the landscape, many imperial-era Chinese texts, drawing on the account of the construction of the tomb found in the *Yuejue shu*, suggested that the hill was an artificial mound.[24] The problem of relating the description found in the *Yuejue shu* with the fact that Tiger Hill is, in fact, a natural landscape feature has recently become the subject of much scholarly controversy, particularly in the wake of archaeological discoveries in both Jiangsu and Zhejiang Provinces. In recent years a number of tombs have been excavated in Jiangsu, most notably tomb D9M1 at Zhenshan 眞山, and the great tomb at Beishan, Dantu County, which are believed to be those of members of the Wu royal house. The location of these tombs at the very top of the mountain (along with the positioning of associated contemporary graves along the ridges) is suggestive of a completely different kind of burial practice: that is, different from the previous assumption that the tomb of King Helü was in fact placed below a pond at the base of a cleft in the rocks, approximately half-way up Tiger Hill.[25] Regardless of whether this

---

24. Li Yuqing, *Jiangsu mingcheng lu*, p. 167.

25. The mortuary complex at Zhenshan consists of fifty-seven tombs dating from the Spring and Autumn period to the Han dynasty, of which the vast majority predate the unification of China. Tomb D9—which occupies the highest position at the peak of the mountain—is among the oldest, though this once magnificent burial was looted in antiquity. This is thought to be a royal tomb and has been

description of the construction of the tomb was historically accurate, the grave at Tiger Hill was frequently cited in ancient texts as an example of unwarranted extravagance: for example Han Ying 韓嬰 (c. 200–c. 120 BCE), the author of the *Hanshi waizhuan*, condemned the expensive and wasteful burial of King Helü.[26] Like the authors of the "Ji Wudi zhuan" it seems that he believed that Tiger Hill was artificial, and that he disapproved of the massive effort he thought had been expended on the construction of this tomb (an action for which King Fuchai received all the blame).

The description of King Helü's tomb given in the *Yuejue shu* is also the locus classicus for the story of the naming of Tiger Hill. The original name of this hill is given in many imperial era gazetteers as Haiyongshan 海涌山 (Bubbling sea hill), and the much more famous name was said to have come from the appearance of the tiger at this site in the wake of the burial of King Helü.[27] The story of the white tiger is known in many different versions, but the earliest accounts always stated that the tiger appeared almost immediately after the king of Wu's funeral. The White Tiger is an animal of considerable mystical significance; together with the Green Dragon, Dark Warrior, and Red Bird, it is one of the four directional spirits, being associated with the West. The White Tiger governs seven of the twenty-eight lunar lodges, again associated with the West. In addition to that, the White Tiger was traditionally associated with the Chinese constellation Shen 参 (Tri-star)—the three stars of Orion's belt—and worshipped as the guardian spirit of warriors. According to the *Shiji*: "Shen is the White Tiger . . . Below there are three stars lined up [in a constellation]

---

tentatively identified as the grave of King Shoumeng of Wu. Suzhou bowuguan et al., *Zhenshan Dongzhou mudi*. An alternative candidate for being the tomb of King Shoumeng of Wu was excavated at Qinglongshan 青龍山, Ningzhen 寧鎮. Wu Enpei, *Gouwu wenhua de xianzai chanshi*, pp. 142–3. The tomb at Beishan in Dantu County has been assigned as that of King Yumei of Wu, on the basis of the inscribed bronzes excavated from this site. Dantuxian, ed., *Dantu xian zhi*, p. 765; Xie Chen, *Gouwu shi xinkao*, p. 47.

26. *Hanshi waizhuan*, p. 353 (10.14).

27. The earliest surviving reference to the name Haiyongshan is found in Lu Guangwei, *Wudi ji*, p. 62. According to Zhu Changwen, *Wujun tujing xuji*, p. 41, this earlier name was recorded in a text by Wang Xun 王珣, one of the Jin dynasty owners of the site, in his book entitled *Shanming* 山銘 (Mountain inscriptions).

called Fa, and they are in charge of matters of warfare and death." 參爲白虎 . . . 下有三星, 兑, 曰罰, 爲斬艾事.[28]

As a result of the association of the White Tiger with military matters, this animal also frequently figured on military banners.[29] Perhaps significantly, the White Tiger was a common figure in tomb paintings, often appearing either with the other three directional spirits, or with its fellow denizen of the West, the Queen Mother.[30] It is clear that the appearance of a white tiger above King Helü's tomb was an event full of numinous importance, but the precise significance of this manifestation is unclear. The earliest references to the meaning of the appearance of this white tiger are generally attributed to the *Wu Yue chunqiu*. Although the present transmitted text of the *Wu Yue chunqiu* makes no mention of the burial of King Helü and the appearance of a white tiger above the tomb, numerous quotations in later texts suggest that it did originally contain a story of this kind.[31] Some of these quotations are very close in wording to the description of the tomb of King Helü found in the *Yuejue shu*: this is not surprising given that these two texts are believed to be closely related. However, the *Wu Yue chunqiu* also provides a new strand to the story, suggesting that the white tiger was the visible manifestation of the essence of the treasures buried with this great king: "The *Wu Yue chunqiu* says: 'Three days after they buried him [King Helü], the pure essence of the metal floated upwards and became a white tiger, which crouched on the tomb mound; therefore it is called Tiger Hill.'" 吳越春秋云: "葬之三日, 金精上揚, 爲白虎據墳, 故曰虎丘."[32]

A further quotation from the *Wu Yue chunqiu*, which is also not found in the present transmitted text, describes the tomb of the penultimate king of Wu as being extremely rich and containing the very finest grave goods, of a quality that justified supernatural apparitions. This account does not make any mention of the weaponry that fea-

---

28. *Shiji* 27.1306. The *Hou Hanshu* 30B.1063 also refers to the connection between the White Tiger constellation and military matters: "Fa is the White Tiger, and this lunar lodge is in charge of military matters" 罰者白虎, 其宿主兵.

29. *Liji*, p. 55 ("Quli shang" 曲離上).

30. He Xilin, *Gumu danqing*, pp. 16, 31, 36, 49, 57.

31. *Wu Yue chunqiu*, pp. 263–4 ("*Wu Yue chunqiu* yiwen" 吳越春秋佚文).

32. Quoted in Lu Guangwei, *Wudi ji*, p. 62; Fan Chengda, *Wujun zhi*, p. 554.

tures so prominently in the description given in the *Yuejue shu*, which might be seen as appropriate to such a martial king; but instead focuses on the extravagant luxuries interred with the penultimate king of Wu: "King Helü of Wu was buried lavishly with rich ornaments, beautiful women were interred alive with him, and many treasures were massed around him. For several centuries afterwards, sacred cranes flew over the forested valleys, and a were-tiger howled on the mountain." 吳王闔閭崇飾厚葬, 生埋美人, 多葬寶物. 數百年後, 靈鶴翔于林壑, 神虎嘯于山丘.[33]

This is a unique reference to human sacrifice taking place at the burial of the king of Wu. There are a number of other ancient texts that made reference to this practice in the kingdom of Wu, but little is known about this aspect of their culture.[34]

Understanding the frequency with which the riches buried with King Helü of Wu were mentioned in ancient Chinese texts is crucial for interpreting later accounts of this site. The reason that so many attempts were made during the early imperial era to find and rob the tomb can directly be traced to these early references, which provide not only apparently detailed and accurate information concerning the location of the tomb, but also indicate the wealth to be found within. Likewise, many of the literati tourists who would record their impressions of Tiger Hill during the imperial era were drawn not only by their wish to see a site of great historical importance—the tomb of the great King Helü of Wu—but also by a romantic interest in a place associated with such wealth and such power. Without the presence of the very finest and most precious of ancient swords buried deep within, without the jade ducks swimming for eternity on a lake of mercury in a dark and silent tomb, without the mysterious apparition of the white tiger, Tiger Hill would have lost a large part of its appeal.

---

33. This short passage is given as a quotation from the *Wu Yue chunqiu* (though it is not found in the transmitted text) in Gu Derong and Zhu Shunlong, *Chunqiu shi*, p. 498.

34. A unique reference to this practice is found in the *Shizi* 尸子, p. 19 ("Guangze" 廣澤). "In the kingdoms of Wu and Yue, they use servants and concubines as human sacrifice, and when the Central States heard about this, they thought that it was wrong" 夫吳越之國以臣妾爲殉. 中國聞而非之.

Tiger Hill in Imperial Era Gazetteers

Many imperial era gazetteers clearly draw upon the account given in the *Yuejue shu* in describing the historical significance and hidden treasures of Tiger Hill. However, by the time the *Wudi ji* (which provides the next important and detailed account of Tiger Hill) was complied during the Tang dynasty, this site had already acquired other connotations and associations that would also significantly affect perceptions of this place. Although the majority of the *Wudi ji*'s entry concerning Tiger Hill is concerned with the burial of King Helü and the subsequent legends associated with it, by the time this text was written, the burial place had also become a religious site, home to a large and wealthy Buddhist temple. Furthermore, another tomb in the area had also became a place of pilgrimage for romantically minded visitors: that of a young local woman named Hu Zhenniang 胡貞娘 (also given as Zhenniang 眞娘) who had committed suicide rather than allow herself to be forced into prostitution:

> [Tiger Hill] was originally the rural retreat of the Jin dynasty Minister of Education Wang Xun (349–400) and his younger brother the Minister of Works Wang Min (351–388) and in the second year of the Xianhe reign-era (327), they gave their mountain homes to become the East and West Temples, and established a religious foundation on this hill. To one side of the temple there is the tomb of Zhenniang, an exceptionally beautiful woman of the [Tang dynasty] kingdom of Wu. Talented men who have travelled to this place have written many poems [on the rocks] above her tomb. There was a Provincial Graduate named Tan Zhu (*jinshi* 841) who wrote a poem [about this] and afterwards people gradually rested their brushes.
> 其山本晋司徒王珣與弟司空王珉之别墅, 咸和二年捨山宅爲東西二寺, 立祠於山. 寺側有貞娘墓, 吳國之佳麗也. 行客才子多題詩墓上. 有舉子譚銖作詩一絶, 其後人稍稍息筆.[35]

35. Lu Guangwei, *Wudi ji*, pp. 62–3. The tomb of Zhenniang is also described in Gao Deji, *Pingjiang jishi*, pp. 143–4. This Yuan dynasty account explains the importance of the site for literati visitors, and notes the number of inscriptions around her tomb. The name of the Provincial Graduate is here incorrectly given as Tan Yan 譚彦 and his verse dated to 756–7. His poem reads: "There are many tombs below Tiger Hill,/ Surmounted by sad pines and catalpas./ What makes people of

The date given here for the Wang brothers' generous gift of their homes in order to form a religious foundation is clearly wrong, but is repeated in virtually all accounts of these events.[36] Although the story of the burial of King Helü of Wu found in the *Wudi ji* was derived from the *Yuejue shu*, the later gazetteers and local histories that presented this information in a more accessible form than the original Han dynasty text were to prove far more influential in encouraging tourism and determining which sites visitors to Tiger Hill wished to see. This can be seen from the reports of visitors who mention exactly which books they were using as travel guides.[37] Very few visitors seem to have been guided by the "Ji Wudi zhuan," though many were aware of the information contained therein through quotations and popularizations published in later gazetteers.

The next two major accounts of the history and cultural significance of Tiger Hill are found in gazetteers dating to the Song dynasty. The earlier of the two is Zhu Changwen's *Wujun tujing xuji*, which describes Tiger Hill under two separate classifications. The entry under "Shan" 山 (Mountains) describes Tiger Hill as the tomb of King Helü of Wu, but then goes on to discuss the derivation of the name and alternative names for this site.[38] In the entry under "Siyuan" 寺院 (Temples and monasteries), the work gives considerable detail about the buildings of the Yunyansi 雲岩寺 (Cloud cliff temple)

this age value sex so highly,/ That they only write poems on the tomb of Zhenniang?" 虎丘山上冢纍纍, 是處松楸盡可悲. 何事世人偏重色, 眞娘墓上獨題詩?

36. This can be seen in a number of references to these events quoted in this chapter. However, in one account Jin Chengdi 晋成帝 (r. 326–42) is said to have given Tiger Hill to the Wang family in 327. Gao Deji, *Pingjiang jishi*, p. 143. An interesting account of the process by which Tiger Hill was given to the Buddhist church by the Wang brothers can be found in Gu Yilu, *Huqiushan zhi*, p. 171, which states that they were so impressed by a monk from Suzhou, named Zhudaoyi 竺道壹, that they made the gift in the middle of the Taihe 太和 reign-era (366–70).

37. For example Zhou Bida 周必大, in his *Wujun zhushan lu* 吳郡諸山錄 (Record of the mountains of Wu Commandery) specifically mentions that his visit to Tiger Hill was assisted by his readings from Zhu Changwen's *Wujun tujing xuzhi*. Zhou Bida, *Wujun zhushan lu*, p. 811.

38. Zhu Changwen, *Wujun tujing xuji*, pp. 40–41.

at Tiger Hill—the religious foundation developed by combining the temples founded by Wang Xun and Wang Min:

> In the middle of the temple, there is the Pavilion Housing Imperial Calligraphy,[39] the Officials' Lodge, the White Cloud Hall, and the Five Sages Tower; when you climb up to look at the view it is extremely beautiful. In addition, there are the halls that house ancestral portraits of the Grand Master of Remonstrance Chen Shenghua (939–1006), the Hanlin Academician Wang Yucheng (954–1001, *jinshi* 983), the Junior Grandee Ye Can, and Auxiliary Academician Jiang Tang (980–1054, *jinshi* 1008). In front of the temple there is the Hall where Shenggong expounded and the place where the senior monk, Master Zhudao, recited the sutras. There is an old story that Shenggong set up stones to be his listeners and broke off a branch of a pine tree to be his pointer.[40] The Tiger Leap Spring and Lu Yu's (733–804) Spring are still extant.
> 寺中有御書閣, 官廳, 白雲堂, 五聖臺, 登覽勝絶. 又有陳諫議省華, 王翰林禹偁, 葉少列參, 蔣密直堂眞堂. 寺前有生公講堂, 乃高僧竺道生談法之所. 舊傳生公立片石以作聽徒, 折松枝而爲談柄. 其虎跑泉, 陸羽泉, 見存.[41]

---

39. This building housed three hundred scrolls written by Emperor Zhenzong of the Song dynasty, as described below. The Pavilion Housing Imperial Calligraphy was destroyed by a fire in the early Yuan dynasty. The site is now thought to be occupied by the Imperial Stele Belvedere (Yubei ting 御碑亭), which houses inscriptions in the calligraphy of the Kangxi and Qianlong Emperors. Suzhoushi Huqiushan fengjingqu guanlichu, *Wuzhong diyi mingsheng-Huqiu*, p. 41.

40. Supposedly when Shenggong expounded on the Buddhist scriptures, even the rocks were moved to agree. These events inspired many poems about Tiger Hill, such as the Song dynasty poem by Yang Bei 楊備 entitled "Qianrenzuo" 千人坐 (Thousand-man seat): "Rising above the sea, is the famous mountain Tiger Hill,/ Traces of Shenggong's presence have been preserved to the present day./ In those days when he expounded the sutras, one thousand men sat [and listened]/ You could even see the rocks by the cliff face nod their heads" 海上名山即虎丘, 生公遺跡至今留. 當年說法千人坐, 曾見巖邊石點頭. Quoted in Fan Chengda, *Wujun zhi*, p. 232. This interpretation of the site is marked by the use of the term *zuo* 坐 (seat) rather than *shi* 石 (rock), and is preserved in the still-extant inscription "Qianrenzuo" by the Ming dynasty magistrate for Suzhou, Hu Zuanzong 胡纘宗 (1480–1560, *jinshi* 1508). Dong Shouqi, *Huqiu*, p. 40.

41. Zhu Changwen, *Wujun tujing xuji*, p. 35.

Of particular interest in this account is the reference to the springs found on Tiger Hill, for this would add yet another dimension to representations of this site in the imperial era: for following the association of this hill with Lu Yu, the founder of tea culture in China, Tiger Hill became a major attraction for gourmets who wished to sample tea brewed with these famous waters.[42] The *Wujun tujing xuji* account does not mention the presence of Zhenniang's grave here, and the author seems to have been little interested in the association of this site with King Helü, focusing instead on giving a detailed account of the religious buildings erected at Tiger Hill and associating the site with near-contemporary figures of importance rather than with historical individuals from the distant past. This reflects the author's own interests, and gives the *Wujun tujing xuji* its distinctive character.

The second important Song dynasty account of this site is given by Fan Chengda in the *Wujun zhi*, which includes a chapter on Tiger Hill that describes this place both as a historical site and as the location of an important religious foundation. What is unique among early accounts of Tiger Hill is that Fan Chengda emphasizes the importance of this place as a beauty-spot, worth visiting purely for its scenic attractions and literary associations, among which he specifically mentions the prose writings of Wang Yucheng and the poetry of Su Shi 蘇軾 (1037–1101, *jinshi* 1057).[43] Although the *Wujun tujing*

---

42. See for example Chen Jian, *Huqiu chajing zhubu*. This book assesses the applicability of the guidelines for tea appreciation set out in the *Chajing* 茶經 (Classic of tea) to the teas grown at Tiger Hill and brewed with its waters.

43. Wang Yucheng claimed descent from the Wang family who originally gave Tiger Hill to the Buddhist church. This is mentioned in the poem "Deng Huqiushan" 登虎丘山 (Climbing tiger hill): "Lichen-covered walls surround the verdant slopes;/ It was once the Bubbling Sea Hill of earlier days./ This beautiful peak is completely enclosed by the temple;/ They would not want this refined spot polluted by ordinary people./ The grass by Sword Pond stays green even in the depths of winter;/ Moss has speckled the rocky seat since ancient times./ I love the home of my Jin dynasty ancestors,/ Every time I come here I find it easy to forget to go back" 薜墻圍著碧孱顏, 曾是當年海湧山. 盡把好峯藏寺裏, 不教幽境落人間. 劍池草色經冬在, 石坐苔花自古斑. 珍重晉朝吾祖宅, 一回來此便忘還. Quoted in Fan Chengda, *Wujun zhi*, p. 229.

xuji had already mentioned the beauties of Tiger Hill, Fan Chengda was the first to foreground this interpretation of the site, giving it precedence over any considerations of religious or historical interest, and indicating a handful of named sites to which visitors to Tiger Hill should bend their footsteps: "[Among other sites] this mountain also has the Rock on which the King of Qin Tested his Sword, the Nodding-Head Rocks, the Laughing Spring; these are all scenic spots on this mountain. Those who know about these matters say that the famous mountains of the empire don't match up to their reputations, it is only Tiger Hill where what you see exceeds what you have been told." 又有秦王試劍石, 點頭石, 憨憨泉, 皆山中之景. 好事者云: 天下名山, 所見不及所聞, 獨虎丘所聞不及所見.[44]

Individual buildings and sites at Tiger Hill are discussed separately in other chapters of the *Wujun zhi*. For example, in the chapter entitled "Guowai si" 郭外寺 (Temples outside the city walls), the Yunyan Temple is mentioned as a must-see for travelers to the region (presumably as tourists rather than as pilgrims, though the two groups may have overlapped significantly).[45] In the chapter "Guji" 古迹 (Ancient remains), Fan Chengda noted the presence of ancient pine trees at Tiger Hill, which could still be viewed as late as the end of the Tang dynasty and which were supposed to be remnants of the gardens planted at this site by the Wang brothers.[46] Unusually, the *Wujun zhi* specifically mentions that these pine trees were no longer present at the time of writing—though many other gazetteers misled and irritated readers (who were attempting to use them as guidebooks) by referring to buildings and vistas long destroyed as though they were still extant.

Over the course of centuries, many locations on Tiger Hill acquired multiple meanings, depending on the interpretations of

44. Fan Chengda, *Wujun zhi*, p. 224. As noted by Timothy Brook, *The Confusions of Pleasure*, p. 182, later on in the imperial era it would become common for eight or ten vistas to be singled out at a particular site as most worthy of the visitors' notice. This much more ancient account only mentions three individual vistas; however, by the time of the Ming dynasty, Tiger Hill would have acquired innumerable famous beauty spots.

45. Fan Chengda, *Wujun zhi*, p. 484.

46. Ibid., p. 115.

individual scholars and literati. For example, the Qianrenshi 千人石 (Thousand-man rock) is an extensive bare granite outcrop located in front of Sword Pond on the side of Tiger Hill. This vast rock has been variously interpreted in the writings of imperial era scholars and literati: sometimes as a religious site (since it was supposedly one of the places on Tiger Hill where Shenggong expounded the sutras); and sometimes as a historical site, because (according to other accounts), it was the place where the workmen who built the tomb of King Helü of Wu were massacred once construction was completed: "Some people say: King Helü of Wu employed one thousand workmen, and when they constructed the tomb, they included many traps and pitfalls. When the tomb was finished [the king of Wu] was afraid that they would reveal their secrets. He planned to entice all the workmen to this spot, and then [he] killed them, in order to ensure their silence. Afterwards later generations called this rock the One-Thousand Man Rock." 或云: 吳王闔閭顧匠千人, 興工築墓, 中多機關. 墓成恐露秘密. 設計盡誘工匠於此, 而殺之, 以滅其口. 後人遂名此石曰: 千人石.[47]

For those visitors indifferent to its religious associations, or lacking any interest in experiencing the macabre thrill of visiting the site of an ancient massacre, Thousand-Man Rock was also occasionally promoted as a beauty spot in its own right, or as the perfect place to view other more famous vistas at Tiger Hill. It is this interpretation that can be seen in the eponymous Tang dynasty poem by Jia Dao 賈島 (779–843), which links the Thousand-Man Rock with the next and much more famous site on the itinerary of tourists to Tiger Hill: the waters covering the tomb of King Helü of Wu at Sword Pond:

Advancing to Thousand-Man Rock,
I lower my head to admire the hundred foot pines.
This green pool hides precious swords,
This cold mountain stream is the abode of a hidden dragon.
上陟千人坐, 低窺百尺松.
碧池藏寶劍, 寒澗宿潛龍.[48]

47. This legend is an extremely late addition to the lore relating King Helü of Wu to the landscape features of Tiger Hill. This particular version of the story comes from Lu Xuanjing, *Huqiushan xiaozhi*, p. 14.

48. Quoted in Dong Shouqi, *Huqiu*, p. 148.

Clearly an ancient and venerable site such as Tiger Hill generated many associations and interpretations, which were not mutually exclusive, and therefore a visitor might be attracted by several different aspects at once. It is, however, certainly the case that some reasons for visiting Tiger Hill were seen as more respectable than others: there are for example very few poems written after the famous complaint by Tan Zhu that explicitly mention an interest in seeing the tomb of Zhenniang, though it was a major site of literati pilgrimage and the subject of many poems in the Tang dynasty.[49] Likewise, although it is known that many people were attracted to visit Tiger Hill by the shopping opportunities, this aspect of the site is virtually never mentioned in the surviving literature, except occasionally by literati annoyed by the presence of vulgar visitors. Poems by visitors expressing an interest in the historical significance of Tiger Hill are comparatively well preserved, and frequently mention both the presence of King Helü's tomb, and the Buddhist Yunyan Temple as the key attractions. These works codify the subject of literati tourism to Tiger Hill in the imperial era, and hence attempt to exclude other interpretations of the site, and other types of attraction. These writings also seek to give cultural value to literati responses to the site, while denigrating the experiences of other types of visitors, particularly those stigmatized as vulgar.

The way in which a literati visitor could travel to Tiger Hill to see the sights—and then transform this experience into a poetic response—is first described in detail in Ming and Qing dynasty ac-

---

49. A large number of Tang dynasty poems on the subject of Zhenniang's short and unhappy life written by visitors to her tomb survive; these include "He Letian ti Zhenniang mu" 和樂天題眞娘墓 (Written on the tomb of Zhenniang in company with [Bai] Letian (i.e., Bai Juyi) by Liu Yuxi 劉禹錫 (772–842, *jinshi* 793), "Zhenniang mu" 眞娘墓 (The tomb of Zhenniang) by Bai Juyi (772–846, *jinshi* 800) himself, "Huqiu shan Zhenniang mu" 虎丘山眞娘墓 (The tomb of Zhenniang at Tiger Hill) by Shen Yazhi 沈亞之 (fl. 825), "Zhenniang mu" by Li Shen 李紳 (*jinshi* Yuanhe reign-era, 806–21, d. 846), "He ren ti Zhenniang mu" 和人題眞娘墓 (Written on the tomb of Zhenniang with a companion) by Li Shangyin 李商隱 (c. 813–58), "Ti Zhenniang mu" 題眞娘墓 (Written on the tomb of Zhenniang) by Luo Yin 羅隱 (833–909) and so on. Though later poems on the same subject by equally eminent poets are known, there seems to be a significant reduction in quantity after the Tang.

counts. The diary account quoted below comes from the *San Wu youlan zhi* 三吳游覽志 (Record of a journey to three cities in Wu) by the Ming-Qing transition era poet and song-writer Yu Huai 余懷 (1616–96), recording his travels from Nanjing to Suzhou, Songjiang 松江, and Taicang 太倉 in the year 1650. This is a particularly interesting account, given that it juxtaposes the diary entry containing a factual account of the trip and the poem that Yu Huai wrote on this occasion, transmuting his mundane visit into a literati experience. From the diary entry, it is clear that Yu Huai had an extremely enjoyable trip to Tiger Hill, largely given over to eating and shopping. The poem, on the other hand, expresses the kind of sentiments appropriate to a member of the literati on a visit to such an important historical and religious site; Yu Huai makes reference to a number of different aspects of the site, possibly including (through the mention of "looking back at remote antiquity" *wang zhonggu* 望終古) the fact that this site had once been a summer palace for King Helü of Wu and later the site of his grave:

> Fifth day. Sunny. The boat passed by Tiger Hill, so I wandered around outside the gate to the mountain, and decided that I would buy a hermitage in which to rest for six months, eating my fill of loquats and bayberries.[50] At the mere thought, I could not avoid salivating. On this day I heard a golden oriole singing, and ate cherries and sugarcane, and bought some fresh high-quality mountain tea. This evening I saw the new moon, and wrote "A Song on the Spring Green at Tiger Hill:"
>
> One tree-covered peak shows a high craggy outline;
> Even the bells and stone chimes in pagoda and temple are overgrown with lichen.
> Walking back and forth by the temple gate I look back to remote antiquity;
> Cloth sails filled with wind ceaselessly scud across the waters.
> Remote cliffs are drenched in mists, until it seems like a still-damp painting,
> The cranes fly from the cold gulf, which is verdant throughout the year.
> At the distant halls and towers the green sets off the red,

---

50. The term used here to describe staying for six months is derived from the *Zhuangzi*, p. 4 ("Xiaoyao you" 逍遙遊), which describes the migration of the great *peng*-bird, which flies ninety thousand *li* before resting.

Baby orioles left alone sing at dawn and at dusk.
In old age, I drift on the spring waters in my solitary boat,
The oarsman hurries on, speeding my journey.
The spirits of the mountains laugh at my vulgarity;
I love the mountain spirits, so full of sentiment through the ages.
The [leaves] of the luxuriant trees seem to dance before my eyes;
The abundant breeze of the first month of summer sends an additional blessing.[51]
On Thousand-Man Rock an old flute song sounds,[52]
An old man enjoys an inexpressible pleasure in this.

初五. 晴. 舟過虎丘, 徘徊山門外, 擬買一庵作六月息, 飽餐枇杷、楊梅, 此時未免作道逢麯車想也. 是日聞黃鸝聲, 啖櫻桃、甘蔗, 買新芥茶. 晚見初月. 作 《虎丘新綠歌》:
鬱然一丘高嵯峨, 鐘磬塔廟依藤蘿.
躑躅寺門望終古, 布帆風飽無停波.
栖崖濕雲畫欲滴, 鶴飛澗冷經年碧.
迢遞樓臺綠映紅, 新鶯寂寂鳴朝夕.
老我孤舟春水生, 榜人刺促催我行.
山靈笑我俗如此, 我愛山靈長有情.
婆娑茂樹猶在眼, 孟夏滔滔送餘善.
千人石上舊笙歌, 老子於玆興不淺.[53]

The Baicheng yanshui Account

The Qing dynasty local history entitled *Baicheng yanshui* 百城烟水 (The city wreathed in mist), by Xu Song 徐崧 and Zhang Dachun 張大純, contains an extensive account of the historical associations,

---

51. This is an allusion to the line: *Lingfeng song yushan* 泠風送餘善 (The gentle breeze sends an additional blessing) from the poem "Guimaosui shichun huaigu Tianshe" 癸卯歲始春懷古田舍 (Cherishing antiquity at Tianshe at the beginning of spring in Kuimao year, 403) by Tao Yuanming 陶淵明 (365–427). Sun Junxi, *Tao Yuanming ji jiaozhu*, p. 17.

52. This seems to be an allusion to the way that the Mid-Autumn Festival was celebrated at Tiger Hill at this time; there is a famous description of the festival by Yuan Hongdao 袁宏道 (1568–1610) who visited the site intending to enjoy the flute music and singing performed on this occasion, only to find out that the presence of an official dampened the festivities. His account refers to a visit made to Tiger Hill in the year 1597. Yang Jialuo, *Yuan Zhonglang quanji*, *Youji* 遊記.1. This account is translated in Strassberg, *Inscribed Landscapes*, pp. 305–7.

53. Yu Huai, *San Wu youlan zhi*, p. 852.

buildings, vistas, and sights of Tiger Hill up to the reign of the Kangxi Emperor, and indeed it seems to be the first gazetteer written for the Suzhou region that attempts to provide a comprehensive catalog of this site. This attempt at listing all the famous sites, both past and present, is in contrast to the account given in the *Gusu zhi* 姑蘇志 (Gusu [Suzhou] gazetteer), the Ming gazetteer for Suzhou widely regarded as the best of the many produced during that dynasty, which lists a number of the same sites as the *Baicheng yanshui* in its description of Tiger Hill, but concludes with the words: "The remaining scenic sites are so numerous that it is impossible to record them all" (*Ta shengchu shang duo bu neng xi zai* 他勝處尚多不能悉載).[54] The description given in the *Baicheng yanshui* is worth quoting in full, for it demonstrates the significant increase in the quantity of recommended points of interest for visitors and pilgrims that had occurred over the course of the Ming dynasty. The following account names seventy-two individual sites on Tiger Hill thought to be of interest to the visitor, of which fifteen are specifically stated to no longer be extant at the time of writing. These seventy-two sites are grouped into three main types: key sites that the visitor would have to pass on their arrival by road, ancient remains, and famous sites. They include both natural features of the landscape such as rocks, springs, and trees, as well as monuments and shrines. This description contains both a main text and additional notes, indicated in the translation below by different font size:

> Tiger Hill has another name: Haiyong (Bubbling sea), and stands seven *li* from the Chang gate [to the city of Suzhou]. It is one hundred and twenty *chi* high, and two hundred and ten *zhang* round. There is a tradition that King Helü of Wu was buried at its foot, and they used the swords of Bianzhu, Yuchang, and three thousand others as funerary goods. About three days later, the essence of the metal floated upwards to form a white tiger, hence the name. To begin with, Mr. Bai's Embankment had not yet been built, and so [Tiger Hill] stood among the flat fields and was just a hill. To the south there is the mountain road, but Bai Juyi (772–846, *jinshi* 800) dug a canal which runs north-south, in order to connect to the Grand Canal. He also dug a moat the whole way round the foot of the mountain. Now the mountain

54. Wang Ao 王鏊 et al., *Gusu zhi* 8.3b.

road approaches from the west, [and you pass] Laughing Spring: this is a relic of Kankanzunzhe of the Liang dynasty. There is an inscription by Lü Shengqing (*jinshi* 1070). Sword-Testing Rock: the center is split as though it has been cleaved.[55] There is also an inscription here by Lü Shengqing dated to the Shaosheng reign-era (1094–97). Some say that this [is associated with] the First Emperor of Qin, others say that it is the king of Wu. Thousand-Man Rock: originally named Thousand-Man Seat. This great rock slopes gently across several *mu*, and then turns into steep crevasses. There is a tradition that it is the place where Shenggong expounded on the sutras. Nodding-Head Rocks: the strange monk Zhudaosheng expounded on the sutras here, but people did not believe him, so he collected some rocks to be his disciples and discussed *prajñā* with them, and the rocks all nodded their heads. White Lotus Pool: one hundred and thirty *bu* across, it begins beside the cliff-edge rocks and in the middle there is an underwater rock. They say that when Buddhist doctrine is recited, the lotuses growing in the pool put out flowers with one thousand petals. Nurturing Cranes Torrent: this is by White Lotus Pool, and they say that the Daoist Qingyuan raised cranes here.[56] The monk Nanyin constructed a pavilion [here]. Sword Pond: it is said that Helü is buried here. The two cliffs are precipitous and the waters of this spring are deep, but there was a crossbeam like a bridge, fitted level into two holes, and above there was a windlass to draw water. This has now been destroyed. Some say that the emperor of Qin dug up the mountain to get the swords, others say that it was Sun Quan who cut [this crevasse], and the place where he dug then became a deep pool. Yan Zhenqing (709–85, *jinshi* 734) wrote the four characters "Tiger Hill Sword Pond."[57] Lu Yu's Stone Well: above the north side of Sword Pond. The mouth of this well is square, and more than one *zhang* across, and there are stone walls on all four sides, which at the bottom join to the stone floor. The waters are sweet and pure;

---

55. This rock is usually said to have been split by the First Emperor of Qin. According to some accounts he was testing his sword, according to others he was frightened by the appearance of a tiger and hit the rock by mistake.

56. An account of the visit of the Daoist Master Qingyuan to Tiger Hill can be found in Gong Mingzhi, *Zhongwu jiwen*, pp. 56–57.

57. Yan Zhenqing, scion of an immensely distinguished literati family, was noted during his lifetime for the strict uprightness of his character and his bravery in the face of considerable danger during the course of his official career. His biography and the subsequent promotion of his calligraphy as a model for imitation are considered in McNair, *The Upright Brush*. In fact only half this inscription is now believed to have been written by Yan Zhenqing. The other two characters are attributed to the Yuan dynasty scholar and calligrapher Zhou Boqi 周伯琦 (1298–1369). Gu Jiegang, *Suzhou shizhi biji*, p. 101.

hence it has been graded as the third best spring. In the third year of the Shaoxing reign-era (1133), the senior monk Rubi first cleaned out [this site] and dug down through more than five *zhang* of mud that was blocking [the spring], and then water gushed out of the rock. It has the common name of Guanyin Spring. The Prefect Shen Kai (*jinshi* 1161) put up a building to cover it, and built a pavilion to one side, but afterwards they were destroyed again. In the middle of the reign of the Zhengde Emperor (r. 1506–21) in the Ming dynasty, the magistrate of Changzhou, Gao Di (*jinshi* 1514) again cleaned out the spring, and he built the two pavilions: Ranked Spring and Imbibing Purity. There is a record of this by Wang Ao. Now it has become blocked again. Master Ying's Tiger Spring: the Liang dynasty monk Huiying dug out stones to make a well, and the waters bubbled up for three *zhang*. Some say that a tiger ran away because of this, and hence it is named Tiger-Leap Spring. It is a spring that wells up from the foundations of the granary on the back slope of the mountain. Shenggong's Pool; above the western peak. Basin-Washing Pool: located south of the Arhat Tower. Liberation Pool, Washing-Inkstones Pool: these two pools were still extant in the Eastern Jin dynasty, but they have now disappeared. Refining-Cinnabar Well: located south of the Returning-Immortal Path. Stepping-Stone Rock: Li Ao (772–841, *jinshi* 798) in his *Lainan lu* (Record of a journey to the south) [mentions] seeing the Stepping-Stone Rock.[58] Iron Flower Cliff: located beside Sword Pond. Returning-Immortal Path: traditionally said to have been on the southwest side of the mountain. In the Jin dynasty, Wang Xun and his younger brother, Wang Min, at one point took possession of the mountain to make a rural retreat, and they each built a house. In the second year of the Xianhe reign-era, these [separate residences on either side of] Sword Pond were both established as the Eastern [temple] and Western [temple]. In the Tang dynasty, to avoid a name taboo, it was called Martial Hill Temple, and had the alternative name of the Temple of Requiting Kindness. In the Huichang reign era (836–40), they [the Eastern and Western temples] were destroyed, and afterwards [the two foundations] were united into one. In the Song dynasty, in the middle of the Zhidao reign-era (995–97), the Prefect Wei Xiang submitted a memorial about repairing the pagoda at Cloud Cliff Temple: built during the Sui dynasty.[59] According to the *Wujun zhi*: "When they first laid the foundations for the pagoda, when they dug down they found a Buddhist relic, and from the clear air there was the sound of

58. The original reference is given in Li Ao, *Lainan lu*, p. 381.

59. A pagoda was first built at Tiger Hill in 608, constructed by order of the Prefect Li Xian 李顯. The present structure dates to 978. Shi Jianhua et al., *Suzhou gucheng de baohu yu gengxin*, p. 30.

heavenly music, and the wells resounded for three days."[60] By imperial decree [the temple] was given the Belvedere for Storing the Sutras. They have the decrees by Yingzong (r. 1064–67) and Shenzong (r. 1068–85) commanding the bestowal of sutras. Among ancient remains there are the Twin Halls of the Liang dynasty: located in front of the main hall, these two small halls faced each other. Rebuilt by a monk in the middle of the Chunxi reign-era (1174–89), they have now been destroyed. Shenggong's Exposition Tower: [the name of this site was written] in seal script by Li Yangbing (fl. 756) of the Tang dynasty, each [character] carved on [one of] four separate stones.[61] Some say that this was from the brush of Lord Cai, the Loyal and Kind. Gu Mei (fl. 1650s) did research on this: Shenggong's Exposition Tower is mentioned in Liu Mengde's *Jinling wuti* (Five inscriptions on Jinling), and this poem was originally written about Jinling and has nothing to do with Tiger Hill. Later generations borrowed this story [and told it about] Tiger Hill.[62] There are actually two different sites, an Exposition Hall, and an Exposition Tower. Midday Pavilion: this has the alternative name of Daytime Moon [Pavilion], both are derived from a line by Fu Huimeng: "To one side the bright moon tarries in the daytime sky." Flower-Rain Pavilion: this looks down on Thousand-Man Rock. The name comes from the poem by Fang Zitong: "Shenggong was a miraculous teacher,/ When he spoke on Buddha's law the flowers fell like rain."[63] It has now been destroyed. Overlooking-the-Sea Hall: according to a gazetteer, the ruins [of this building] are above Sword Pond. Ancient Firs: there is a tradition that these were planted by Wang Min, and they were still extant at the end of the Tang dynasty. Imperial Calligraphy Belvedere: [this refers to] three hundred scrolls in the imperial calligraphy of Song Zhenzong (r. 998–1022). At the beginning of the Jingyou reign-era (1034–37), an edict ordered that a duplicate copy should be kept at a famous mountain. There is a tradition that [this belvedere] was at the Eastern Courtyard, some say that the Śubha-vyūha-rāja Pavilion occupies its old location.[64] Illumination Pavilion: located behind the Doctrinal Hall. Lord Chen's Hall: in the second year of the Longxing reign-era of the

---

60. This quotation is not found in the transmitted text of the *Wujun zhi*.

61. Li Yangbing, a cousin of the poet Li Bai 李白 (701–62), is today remembered best as a fine seal-script calligrapher. Zhou Zumo, "Li Yangbing zhuanshu kao." He also played an important role in the compilation of the first edition of the collected works of Li Bai, and is mentioned numerous times in his poetic works.

62. *Quan Tang shi* 365.4118. The poem concerned is actually entitled: "Shenggong jiangtang" 生公講堂 (Shengong's exposition hall).

63. The poem from which this quotation was derived is no longer extant.

64. The Śubha-vyūha-rāja is a Bodhisattva whose name only appears in the "Lotus Sutra."

Song dynasty (1162), Chen Fuwen gave two hundred thousand cash [for a structure to be made] connecting the two sheer cliff faces, and constructed a building above it, forming a well that would facilitate drawing water, and therefore it is known as Lord Chen's Hall. This was replaced with stone beams by Zhi Zhangong. The Small Wu Pavilion: located at the southeastern corner of the temple, it is called the Small Wu Assembly Room in Zhu [Changwen, styled] Lepu's text. Mr. Zhang [wrote a] sign: "Heaven Reveals its Plans." Thousand-Mile Cloud: located in front of the old Courtyard, it was built in the eighth year of the Xianchun reign-era of the Song dynasty (1272) by the monk Dehou, and he took the name from [Su] Dongpo's poem: "The clouds and rivers are beautiful for a thousand miles."[65] Five Worthies Tower: [located] at the western end of the peak. Sutra Translation Tower: located southeast of Shenggong's Pool, there is a story that in the Jin dynasty an Indian monk retranslated the Lotus Sutra here. Arhat Taking-Buddhist-Vows Tower: located west of Sutra Translation Tower, there is a story that in the past an Arhat took his Buddhist vows here. Wang Xun's Qin Tower: there is a tradition that this was at the base of the pagoda. He Yin's (446–531) Exposition Hall: located in the Western Temple. Mountain Viewing Hall: located behind the Doctrinal Hall, beside the Illumination Pavilion, this has now become the Shrine to Five Worthies. Communicating-with–the-Hidden Hall: located in the Western Monastery, it was the abode of Master Yin Hejing (1071–1142).[66] Lankavatara Chamber: located at the old eastern courtyard.[67] As for famous sites, there is the Enlightenment-Rock Pavilion: this was the Obtaining-Spring Hall, to the left of Sword Pond. Great Wu Pavilion: to the left of the Five [Worthies] Tower, they used three pillars in the construction of this pavilion. Respecting-Su Hall: located east of the Heavenly Kings Hall, there is a tradition that this was the old site of the [Su] Dongpo Hall. In the Ming dynasty during the reign of the Jiajing Emperor (r. 1522–66), it was built by Hu Zuanzong (1480–1560, *jinshi* 1508). Plum Flower Hall: below this hall there is the Monastic Rules Hall, and it was built by the monk Yuanxiao. Eastern Mountain

---

65. This line is found in the poem "Huqiu si" 虎丘寺 (The temple at Tiger Hill). Feng Yingliu et al., *Su Shi shiji hezhu*, pp. 538–40.

66. The name of this hall is apparently derived from the title of the Han dynasty rhapsody, the "Youtong fu" 幽通賦 (Rhapsody of communicating with the hidden), written by Ban Gu on the death of his father. *Wenxuan*, pp. 193–7. For a translation of this rhapsody, see Knechtges, *Wen xuan or Selections of Refined Literature, vol. 3*, pp. 82–103.

67. The name of this room is derived from the Lankavatara Sutra, which is one of the most important texts of Chan Buddhism. As a Chan Buddhist foundation, the Yunyan Temple at Tiger Hill would have had such a site.

Temple: dedicated to Wang Xun, also known as the Duanbo Temple. Western Mountain Temple: located on the flat land to the west of the Mountain Gate, [this temple is] dedicated to Wang Min. Temple to King Guan: built by Zhang Guowei (1594–1646, *jinshi* 1622), the Grand Coordinator in the reign of the Chongzhen Emperor (r. 1628–44). Shrine to Master Yin Hejing: dedicated to the Song dynasty Confucian scholar Yin Tun, a native of Luoyang, who lived in the Western Monastery at Tiger Hill, and the tablet [above the door] read: "Studio of Three Awe-inspiring Things."[68] In the seventh year of the Jiading reign-era (1208–24), the Prefect Chen Fu and others visited the Western Monastery and [ordered] the construction of a shrine on some empty land. There is a record of this by Huang Jin. After two years, the disloyal minister Meng You (1156–1217) moved the building to the upper courtyard, south of the Communicating-with-the-Hidden Hall. In the second year of the Duanping reign-era (1235), the Assistant Director of the Palace Library Cao Bin (1170–1249, *jinshi* 1203) moved the shrine to the Confucian Academy. There is a record of this by Liu Zai (1167–1240, *jinshi* 1190). At the beginning of the Yuan dynasty, it was taken over by monks, and in the first year of the Yanyou reign-era (1314) they moved [the shrine] and rebuilt it in Changzhou county, north of the Black Magpie Bridge. Later on [this shrine] was destroyed. At the beginning of the Ming dynasty, it was moved back to its old location in the Western Monastery when they built Hejing's Reading Tower, and in the third year of the reign of the Jiajing Emperor (1524), the Prefect Hu Zuanzong again built a shrine next to the tower, which has now been destroyed. Shrine to the [Grand Master] for Closing Court Chen: dedicated to the Song dynasty Prefect Chen Shenghua. Shrine to the Junior Grandee Ye: dedicated to the Song dynasty Prefect Ye Can, this shrine is located east of Thousand-Mile Cloud. At the beginning of the reign of the Jiajing Emperor, [this shrine] was rebuilt by Hu Zuanzong. Shrine to the Palace Librarian Yao: dedicated to the Song dynasty Prefect Yao Hui. These three shrines mentioned above were established by local people in the fifth year of the Qiandao reign-era (1169), and there is a record of this by the Head of the Confucian School, Chen Bozhen (*jinshi* 1194), but they have now all been destroyed. Shrine to the Grand Master of Remonstrance Wei: dedicated to the Song dynasty Prefect Wei Xiang. Shrine to the Hanlin Academician Wang: dedicated to the Song dynasty Magistrate of Changzhou, Wang Yucheng. Shrine to Director of the Criminal Administration Bureau Kang: dedicated to the Song dynasty Prefect Kang Xiaoji. Shrine to

---

68. The name of this studio is a reference to the *Analects*, where Confucius stated that there were three things of which a gentleman should be in awe: the commands of Heaven, great men, and the words of sages. *Lunyu*, p. 177 ("Jishi" 季氏 16.8).

Academician Jiang: dedicated to the Song dynasty Prefect Jiang Tang. Shrine to Kaiping, the Loyal and Martial King: in the first year of the Wu dynasty (1363), Chang Kaiping received orders to attack [Zhang] Shicheng, and he stationed [his army] at Tiger Hill, but the temple was not harmed by the soldiers and hence they built this shrine though it has now been destroyed. Shrine to the Cultured and Supportive Lord Zhou: the lord was governor of Wu for nineteen years, and he memorialized to reduce taxes by more than seven hundred thousand *dan*. Shrine to Five Worthies: in the twenty-sixth year of the reign of the Wanli Emperor (1598), the Magistrate of Changzhou, Jiang Yingke (*jinshi* 1592), rebuilt this and the Mountain Viewing Hall. [This shrine is] dedicated to Wei Yingwu (737–791?), Bai Juyi, Liu Yuxi (772–842, *jinshi* 793), Wang Yucheng, and Su Shi. [Jiang] Yingke wrote a record about this, which was engraved on stone. Shrine to Three Worthies: located on the western peak, dedicated to Fan Zhongyan (989–1052, *jinshi* 1015), Hu Gongyuan, and Yin Tun of the Song dynasty. It was constructed in the middle of the reign of the Jiajing Emperor by Wu Yipeng (1460–1542, *jinshi* 1493), and there is a record by Shen Ruoshui (1466–1560, *jinshi* 1505).[69] Shrine to the Cultured and Resolute Lord Shen: still extant. Hungry Ghosts Altar: located to the left, inside the three gates. Tomb of Zhantai Mieming: there is a tradition that when Zhang Shicheng built the city walls, in the earth at Tiger Hill they found an engraved stone, which read: "Tomb of Zhantai Mieming."[70] Tomb of Zhenniang: located on the eastern peak. The *Yunxi youyi* (Friendly discussions at cloud stream) says: "Miss Zhenniang of Wu died, and was buried at Tiger Hill. In her time she was compared to Su Xiaoxiao, and many visitors wrote inscriptions on her tomb." The Tomb of the Solitary Lord: commemorated by a ghost's poem. Eastern Peak Cottage, the Chamber where Miaoxi Read the Sutras, the Tomb of the Martyr Yang: he had the personal name Chun, and died in battle at the end of the Yuan dynasty. Mandarin Ducks Grave: at the end of the reign of the Chongzhen Emperor, the child bride Miss Yang buried her husband, then she carved the two characters "Mandarin Ducks" on the tombstone and cut her throat. Zibo Court: this is the place where the great master Daguan was tonsured. Stone Guanyin Hall, Little Wudang: located on the back of the mountain. Shrine to the Two Masters of the Cheng Family: built in the reign of the Kangxi Emperor (r. 1662–1722) by Cheng Wenyi.

---

69. There is an extant "Sanxianci ji" 三賢祠記 (Record of the shrine to three worthies) by Shen Ruoshui, but it describes a religious site in Fuzhou 撫州 in Jiangxi Province. Lin Tinggang and Zhou Guang, *Jiangxi tongzhi* 131.59b–62a.

70. Tantai Mieming was the name of one of the disciples of Confucius. *Lunyu*, p. 59 ("Yongye" 雍也 6.14); *Shiji* 67.2205. His tomb was more commonly associated in pre-Ming sources with Tantai Lake. Lu Guangwei, *Wudi ji*, p. 41.

Shrine to the Four Wise Governors: dedicated to Xia Yuanji (1366–1430, *juren* 1390), Zhou Chen (1381–1453, *jinshi* 1404), Wang Shu, and Hai Rui (1514–87). This was built by the Governor Tang Bin (1627–87, *jinshi* 1652). Combined Shrine for Yao Ximeng (1579–1636, *jinshi* 1619), Wen Zhenmeng (1574–1636, *jinshi* 1622), and Chen Renxi (1581–1636, *jinshi* 1622).[71] Shrine to the Loyal and Supportive Lord Cai Maode (1586–1644, *jinshi* 1589). Shrine to the Cultured and Tranquil Lord Xu Qian (1597–1645, *jinshi* 1628). Shrine to the Two Masters of the Jiang family: the older brother [was named] Cai (1607–73, *jinshi* 1631), the younger brother [was named] Gai (1614–43, *jinshi* 1640), and they were natives of Laiyang who had come to live in Wu.

虎丘, 一名海涌, 去閶門七里. 高一百三十尺, 周二百十丈. 相傳吳王闔閭葬其下, 以扁諸之劍魚腸三千殉焉. 越三日, 金精上揚爲白虎, 故名. 初時, 白堤未開, 山在平田中, 一丘耳. 南是山徑, 白居易鑿渠以通南北, 而達於運河; 又緣山麓, 鑿水四周. 今山徑自西入, 有憨憨泉, 梁時䤈䤈尊者遺迹. 有吕升卿題字. 試劍石, 中開如截. 亦有紹聖年吕升卿題字, 或云秦始皇, 或云吳王. 千人石, 本名千人坐. 大石盤陀數畝, 高下如刻削. 相傳生公講經處. 點頭石, 夷僧竺道生講經於此, 人無信者, 乃聚石爲徒, 與談般若, 石皆點頭. 白蓮池, 周百三十步, 巉石邊出而中有磯. 云説法時池生千葉蓮花. 養鶴澗, 在白蓮池, 云清遠道士養鶴於此. 僧南印構亭. 劍池, 謂闔閭葬處. 兩崖陡削, 泉水中深, 横架如橋, 平穿兩孔, 上置轆轤汲水, 今廢. 或云秦皇鑿山求劍, 或云孫權穿之, 其鑿處遂成深澗. 顔眞卿書: '虎丘劍池,'四字. 陆羽石井, 旁劍池北上. 井口方丈餘, 四傍石壁, 下連石底, 泉甘冽, 即所品第三泉也. 宋紹興三年, 主僧如璧始淘去淤泥五丈許, 泉出石脉中, 俗名觀音泉. 郡守沈揆作屋覆之, 構亭於旁, 其後復廢. 明正德中, 長洲令高第重疏汩洳, 構: '品泉,' '汲清,' 二亭. 王鏊記. 今復淤. 響師虎泉, 梁僧惠響鑿石爲井, 泉涌三丈. 或謂虎爲之跑, 因名虎跑泉, 山後倉基上濆泉也. 生公池, 在西嶺上. 洗盋池, 在羅漢臺南. 放生池, 洗硯池, 二池東晋時尚存, 今湮. 鍊丹井, 在回仙徑南. 走砌石, 李翺來南錄觀走砌石. 鐵花岩, 在劍池側. 回仙徑, 相傳山之西南是. 晋王珣與弟珉嘗據丘爲别墅, 已而各捨宅, 咸和二年, 即劍池分建東西二寺. 唐避會諱名武丘寺, 一名報恩寺, 會昌間毁, 後合爲一. 宋至道中, 知州事魏庠奏改雲岩寺塔, 隋時建. 《吳郡志》云: '初立塔基, 掘得一舍利, 空中天樂鳴, 井中吼三日.' 敕賜藏經閣, 有英宗、 神宗頒賜經敕. 其古迹有梁雙殿, 在大殿前, 二小殿相對. 淳熙中有僧修建, 毁之. 生公講經臺, 唐禮陽冰篆, 分刻四石. 或云蔡忠惠公筆. 顧湄考: 生公講堂, 劉夢德"金陵五題"也, 詩本爲金陵而作, 與虎丘無涉, 後人影借爲虎丘故實. 分列講亭、 講臺二條. 可中亭, 一名: '可月.' 亦傳會夢得: '一方明月可中亭'之句. 花雨亭, 下臨千人坐, 取方子通: '生公天人師, 説法花雨墮'語, 今廢. 望海樓, 志云劍池上廢址是. 古杉, 相傳爲王珉所植, 唐末猶在. 御書閣, 宋眞宗御書三百卷, 景祐初詔以其副藏于名山, 相傳在東方丈, 或云妙莊嚴閣, 即其

71. This shrine commemorates three important late Ming officials, all from the city of Suzhou. It seems to have been sheer coincidence that they all died in the same year.

故址. 致爽閣, 在法堂後. 陳公樓, 宋隆興二年, 陳敷文出錢二十萬, 跨兩崖, 建樓其上, 爲井幹以便汲, 因名陈公樓. 石梁則霌公改爲之. 小吳軒, 在寺東南隅, 朱樂圃文稱: '小吳會,' 張氏名: '天開圖畫.' 千頃雲, 在舊方丈前, 宋咸淳八年僧德厚建, 取東坡詩: '雲水麗千頃' 語. 五聖臺, 山絕頂. 翻經臺, 在生公池東南, 相傳晉時梵僧于此重譯 《法華經》. 羅漢受戒臺，在翻經臺西, 相傳昔有羅漢於此受戒. 王珣琴臺, 相傳塔基是. 何胤講堂, 在西寺. 平遠堂, 在法堂後致爽閣旁, 今爲五賢祠. 通幽軒, 在西庵, 即尹和靖先生寓舍. 楞伽室, 在舊東方丈. 名迹則有悟石軒, 即得泉樓, 在劍池左. 大吳軒, 在五臺之右, 爲樓三楹. 仰蘇樓, 在天王殿東, 相傳爲東坡樓舊址, 明嘉靖間, 俱胡纘宗建. 梅花樓, 樓下有戒珠堂, 僧圓曉建. 東山廟, 祀王珣, 名短簿祠. 西山廟, 在山門西平壤, 祀王珉. 關王廟, 崇禎間巡撫張國維建. 尹和靖先生廟, 祀宋儒尹焞, 洛陽人, 寓虎丘西庵, 牓曰: 三畏齋. 嘉定七年, 郡守陳芾等度西庵空地建祠. 黄軨記. 後二年, 貳卿孟猷改建於上方通幽軒之南. 端平二年, 秘書丞曹豳易祠爲書院. 劉宰記. 元初爲寺僧所據, 延祐元年移建長洲縣治東烏鵲橋北, 後廢. 明初仍於西庵故址建和靖讀書臺, 嘉靖三年郡守胡纘宗復於臺右建祠, 今廢. 陳朝散祠, 祀宋知州陳省華. 葉少列祠, 祀宋知州葉参, 祠在千頃雲之東, 嘉靖初胡纘宗重建. 姚秘閣祠, 祀宋郡守姚憲. 已上三祠, 乾道五年郡人立, 教授陳伯震記, 今皆廢. 魏建議祠, 祀宋知州魏庠. 王翰林祠, 祀宋長洲令王禹稱. 康都官祠, 祀宋知州事康公孝基. 蔣學士祠, 祀宋知州事蔣公堂. 開平忠武王祠, 吳元年常開平奉命討士誠, 駐虎丘, 寺得免兵燹, 因爲立祠, 今廢. 周文襄公祠, 公撫吳十九年, 奏減糧額七十餘萬石. 五賢祠, 萬曆二十六年, 長洲令江盈科即平遠堂新建, 祀韋公應物，白公居易, 劉公禹錫, 王公禹稱, 蘇公軾, 盈科有記, 勒石. 三賢祠, 在西嶺, 祀宋范公仲淹, 胡公瑗, 尹公焞. 嘉靖間吳公一鵬建, 湛公若水記. 申文定公祠, 時行. 郡厲臺, 在三門内左偏. 澹臺滅明墓, 相傳張士誠築城, 虎丘土中得石刻, 曰: '澹臺滅明之墓.' 眞娘墓, 在東嶺上. 《雲溪友議》云: "吳門女郎眞娘死, 葬虎丘山. 時人比之蘇小小, 行客題墓甚多." 幽獨君墓, 有鬼詩. 東嶺草堂, 妙喜看經室, 楊烈士墓, 名椿, 元末戰死. 鴛鴦冢, 崇禎末, 倪妻楊氏葬夫, 鑿鴛鴦二字於壙石, 遂自剄. 紫柏院, 達觀大師剃度處. 石觀音殿, 小武當, 在山後. 二程夫子祠, 康熙間程文彝建. 四賢撫祠, 祀夏原吉、周忱、王恕、海瑞. 巡撫湯斌建. 姚希孟, 文震孟, 陳仁錫 合祠, 蔡忠襄公祠, 懋德. 徐文靖公祠, 汧. 二姜先生祠. 兄埰，弟垓, 萊陽人, 僑居吳門.[72]

There are some seventy-two sites mentioned by name in this Qing dynasty account. Of these thirty-six are clearly religious sites, of which fourteen are Buddhist, and twenty-two are dedicated to the memory of historical individuals important in the history and culture of the city of Suzhou. There are also a number of historical sites mentioned, of which five are tombs. Of the nine religious figures mentioned by name, by far the most important is Shenggong, who is also referred to by his alternative appellation of Zhudaosheng, and who is

72. Xu Song and Zhang Dachun, *Baicheng yanshui*, pp. 25–28.

associated with five separate sites. The most significant members of the laity, at least according to this account, are the Wang brothers, who once owned the whole of Tiger Hill, and the Ming dynasty Prefect Hu Zuanzong who is said to have been involved in the construction or restoration of three buildings in and around the temple. Tiger Hill clearly attracted a wide variety of important patrons who supported the building and renovation of monuments. The patronage of three Song dynasty emperors is recorded in this account, since the *Baicheng yanshui*, completed in 1690, does not record the visit of the Kangxi Emperor to Suzhou in 1689. (Interestingly no mention is made of Ming dynasty imperial interest in this site, though prose essays by the Zhengtong and Wanli emperors would be anthologized in the 1767 gazetteer for Tiger Hill, which is discussed in more detail below.)[73] Excluding members of the clergy, a further sixty-two individuals are mentioned in this account either as the subject of commemorative structures or as patrons: these individuals came from many eras, ranging in date from the Spring and Autumn period to the early years of the Qing. Three of them were recluses, living in the Suzhou region: He Yin of the Age of Disunion; and the Jiang brothers of the Ming-Qing transition era. A number of individuals mentioned were natives of Suzhou or the surrounding region who held high office in the national government: for example Fan Zhongyan of the Song dynasty, or the triumvirate of Yao Ximeng, Wen Zhenmeng, and Chen Renxi during the late Ming. Others commemorated in this account of Tiger Hill were officials who served for part of their careers in Suzhou: this group includes Bai Juyi, Wei Yingwu, and Chen Shenghua. Of the officials and locals mentioned by name in this account, at least twenty-eight had passed the *jinshi* examinations, indicating the importance of Tiger Hill as a site for commemorating the literati, as well as a focus for their cultural interests.

For an ambitious official, patronage of the monuments at Tiger Hill was apparently a relatively secure route to both high social status and lasting commemoration, a fact that was probably reflected in the

73. Gu Yilu, *Huqiushan zhi*, pp. 747–48.

price of adding a new structure to these already-crowded hillsides. This, however, remains one aspect of the matter that is almost entirely unelucidated by surviving gazetteers and local histories. There seem to be virtually no records that describe how a particular individual came to be buried or commemorated at Tiger Hill, and likewise nothing seems to be known about the financial arrangements that saw a monument first erected and then repaired and preserved for future generations.[74] While the religious buildings on Tiger Hill could rely on the contributions of pious pilgrims and wealthy Buddhist patrons in nearby Suzhou, it is not at all clear who was responsible for maintaining the tombs, the shrines commemorating local officials and examination successes, or any of the other monuments built here. This no doubt accounts for the considerable number of buildings that eventually collapsed, or were rededicated to a more famous individual. Only the most important or lucky literati figures could expect their shrines to be maintained for generation after generation, particularly at a place with such stiff competition for attention.

The 1767 Gazetteer for Tiger Hill

From the Ming dynasty onwards, gazetteers were written that focused upon a particular area, rather than describing a region, a county, or a city. There are a number of such gazetteers for Tiger Hill, of which the earliest known example is the *Huqiushan zhi* 虎丘山志 (Gazetteer for Tiger Hill) by Wang Bin 王賓 in two *juan*, preface dated 1483. This was followed by Wen Zhaozhi's 文肇祉 gazetteer of the same name, an updated and revised version in four *juan*, preface dated 1578. This later publication is of particular interest for the history of tourism to this site, given that the author was the grandson of Wen Zhengming 文徵明 (1470–1559), and one of the clear aims of

74. A rare exception is the tomb of three women of the Ji 姬 family, where it is recorded that they were buried on Tiger Hill through the good offices of Chen Renxi. Gu Yilu, *Huqiushan zhi*, p. 140. McNair, *Donors of Longmen*, provides a fascinating study focusing on religious patronage and the expense of adding shrines to a desirable grotto complex in the Northern Wei and Tang dynasties. In the case of the Longmen grottos, there is considerable evidence that erecting a shrine would exhaust a family's resources or consume a donor's entire life-savings. .

this book was to preserve the *Wumen pai* or Wu School interpretation of Tiger Hill as a focus of literati activity, rather than popular tourism or indeed religious pilgrimage.[75] The first gazetteer for this site produced during the Qing dynasty was written in the reign of the Kangxi Emperor, and again used the same title. This gazetteer in ten *juan* was produced by Gu Mei 顧湄. However, the single most important gazetteer for Tiger Hill was the *Huqiushan zhi* 虎邱山志 (the title preserves the Qing dynasty taboo on the character Qiu 丘, since it was the personal name of Confucius), preface dated 1767, in twenty-four *juan*, produced by Gu Yilu 顧詒祿. The significance of this gazetteer is due not just to its length, though this does allow for a much more detailed account of the site, including comprehensive and extensive coverage of the literature written about Tiger Hill. Although many gazetteers preserve the perspective of a particular individual or group in any appended anthology of literature, Gu Yilu's *Huqiushan zhi* attempted to provide a relatively unbiased survey of writings about this important focus for literati tourism.

This gazetteer features a particularly interesting section on the presence of ghosts on Tiger Hill—an unusual aspect of the site to be recorded in such detail, but one that is apparently derived from Fan Chengda's *Wujun zhi*, which contains a similar collection of tales. It is hardly surprising that ghosts should appear in such a storied spot, though the absence of references to this subject in earlier gazetteers makes it unclear where many of these accounts come from, or how old these stories are. As might be expected in a spot that had for more than one thousand years been such a strong focus of literati interest, the ghosts that appeared at Tiger Hill often did so purely in order to inscribe verse on the stones of this famous site. For example, the Qing dynasty *Huqiushan zhi* account reads:

> In the thirteenth year of the Dali reign-era of the Tang dynasty, a ghost wrote a poem on one of the rock faces, and signed itself the Solitary Lord. This poem was very melancholy. There was also a poem replying to [that of the] Solitary Lord's. Li Daochang, the Surveillance Commissioner of Suzhou, thought the whole affair was most

75. Clunas, *Fruitful Sites*, pp. 135–36.

> peculiar, so then he reported it [to the emperor] and received an imperial command to perform a sacrifice.[76] A few days after the sacrifice was performed, both poems disappeared, but later on, another quatrain mysteriously appeared. North of this mountain temple there are two tomb mounds that are extremely high, and overgrown with brambles, weeds, and vines. Even inquiring among the oldest residents, no one knows who is buried there. Up to the present day they are still there.
> 唐大曆十三年, 虎邱寺有鬼題詩石壁之上, 自稱幽獨君. 其詞悽惋又有一詩答幽獨君. 蘇州觀察使李道昌異其事, 遂具奏聞, 敕令致祭. 祭後二詩沒不見, 復隱出詩一絶. 山寺之北有二墳甚高大荊榛叢蔚. 詢之耆艾莫知何人所葬. 至今猶存.[77]

This is by far the most famous of the ghost inscriptions associated with Tiger Hill, and one of the few to be mentioned in previous gazetteers. The earliest references to this story are found in the Song dynasty

---

76. The text of Li Daochang's oration at this ceremony is preserved in the *Quan Tang wen* 458.4678. "Alas! Tombs and mounds [survive] through the ages, but once a person has passed away, they never reappear. Who were you, my lord? Clearly you were trained in the composition of poetry, but when did you die? Which family did you belong to? Did you hold government office? Of which immortal palace are you now a denizen? Alone in your tomb, you must spend every day in sadness. [Your poem] is not recorded on paper, but appeared mysteriously on the rock face. In this Elysium in the third month, green grass [meets] the trailing willow branches; golden orioles warble deliciously, and the cry of the gibbon tugs at the heartstrings. You do not sign your surname or style, leaving us to determine your wisdom and quality. Alas, how sad! Let us bewail this former worthy. It is all in vain to be recorded in the classics and histories; the dead will never return. Green pines on every slope [clothe the] crags of these verdant mountains" 嗚呼! 萬古邱陵, 化無再出. 君是何人? 能閑詩筆, 何代而亡, 誰人子侄? 曾作何官, 是誰仙室? 寂寞夜臺, 悲乎白日, 不向紙上, 石中隱出. 桃源三月, 綠草垂楊. 黃鶯百囀, 猿聲斷腸. 不題姓字, 寧辨賢良. 嗚呼痛或! 吧惜先賢. 空傳經史, 終無再還. 青松嶺上, 嵯峨碧山.

77. Gu Yilu, *Huqiushan zhi*, p. 205. The three poems and Li Daochang's text are included in Fan Chengda, *Wujun zhi*, pp. 605–6. There are a number of extant works which used the same rhyme scheme; see for example Pi Rixiu "Zhuihe Youdujun shi ciyun" 追和幽獨君詩次韻 (A later poem harmonizing with the rhymes found in the Solitary Lord's work); and Lu Guimeng "Ci Youdujun yun" 次幽獨君韻 (Harmonizing with the rhymes of the Solitary Lord). *Quan Tang shi* 609.7030 and 619.7128 respectively. Chen Zhongxiu, *Tangdai heshi yanjiu*, p. 63, one of the few scholars to have studied the poems inspired by the Solitary Lord's work, incorrectly states that the original poems are no longer extant.

Wujun tujing xuji, and the tale is also mentioned in the *Zhongwu jiwen* 中吳紀聞 (Records of the Wu region).[78] The mention of the two tomb mounds however does not appear in pre-Qing versions of this story. Poems inscribed on rock faces, in this case supposedly above Sword Pond, were ephemeral at the best of times unless recorded and published, or incised into the stone. This is even more true in the case of verses attributed to ghosts, a genre of considerable popularity from at least the time of the Tang dynasty, but such verses were liable to disappear suddenly, without waiting to be erased by the passage of time. This short tale, which bemoans the death of a talented man and the ignorance of later generations that are unaware of his brilliance, is typical of this type of ghost story.[79] Though the Solitary Lord's verses disappeared after just a few days, they were remembered in a more permanent form in the eponymous poem by Yang Bei inscribed on a stone stele at Tiger Hill:

> Sometimes metal survives when books are destroyed and stone cliffs are blotted out by cloud,
> Who is this man named the Solitary [Lord]?
> Deep in spring, plants cover the road lined with pine trees,
> In the underworld, poetry still has the power to move the ghosts and spirits.
> 金見書殘石壁雲, 一名幽獨彼何人.
> 春深草没松門路, 泉下詩猶感鬼神.[80]

To return to the subject of the 1767 *Huqiushan zhi*, this gazetteer contains an anthology of poetry and prose on the subject of Tiger Hill that is the most comprehensive and authoritative produced to date. This makes it possible to perform a comparative analysis, to see the development of the site as a focus for literati tourism over the course of the centuries. In table 4, the number of poets and writers are arranged by dynasty, and the number of literary works of each type is then given in brackets. Clearly, this anthology is significantly weighted

---

78. Zhu Changwen, *Wujun tujing xuji*, p. 77; Gong Mingzhi, *Zhongwu jiwen*, p. 57.

79. Zeitlin, "Disappearing Verses," gives an interesting account of the history of the production of ephemeral writings on walls and rock faces in China, and the association of this genre with ghosts and suicidal women.

80. Quoted in Fan Chengda, *Wujun zhi*, p. 606.

Table 4. Literary works of the 1767 *Huqiushan zhi* by dynasty.

	Poets	Prose writers	Writers of both poetry and prose	Total
Liang	—	2 (2)	—	2 (2)
Chen	2 (2)	1 (1)	—	3 (3)
Sui	—	1 (1)	—	1 (1)
Tang	26 (46)	2 (2)	—	28 (48)
Song	86 (107)	10 (11)	5 (18)	101 (136)
Yuan	90 (113)	1 (1)	—	91 (114)
Ming	168 (271)	16 (16)	8 (31)	192 (318)
Qing	224 (296)	5 (5)	7 (29)	236 (330)
Total	596 (835)	38 (39)	20 (78)	654 (952)

in favor of poetry; at least in part, this is no doubt due to simple constraints of space, since prose works are much longer. This ensures that only the most significant prose works are preserved in the *Huqiushan zhi*, though a much wider variety of poetry is given (including some poems that were apparently chosen more for curiosity value than for any literary merit). However, scattered through this anthology are works by some of the finest poets and prose writers in Chinese history: texts that no doubt served to add great luster to Tiger Hill and that clearly supplied important models for later authors. As evidenced by this anthology, there is a clear and steady increase in the number of literati writing on the subject of Tiger Hill over the course of history, apparently unaffected by dynastic change. This increase is unlikely to be simply the function of better rates of survival for more recent works of literature. More probably, it is the outcome of a wide variety of factors: including the promotion of Tiger Hill as a focus for literati culture in successive dynasties; increased tourism and ease of travel to this site (particularly from the Ming dynasty onwards); the development of a major publishing industry based in Suzhou; the importance of that city from the Song dynasty onwards as one of the great centers of learning of imperial China; and the patronage of both emperors and important local officials.[81]

81. The commercial importance of Suzhou in the late imperial period is exhaustively documented in Marmé, *Suzhou*.

The vast majority of the works of poetry and prose included in this gazetteer was clearly written by male members of the literati elite. Of these, by far the most significant in terms of the number of works included is Gao Qi 高啓 (1336–74), the famous Yuan-Ming transition era poet and native of the Suzhou region, who is represented by twenty-two poems. This places him far ahead of the next-most prolific writers included in the *Huqiushan zhi*, the Ming dynasty literatus Shen Zhou 沈周 (1427–1509), represented by twelve poems, and the Qing dynasty literatus Shen Deqian 沈德潜 (1673–1769, *jinshi* 1740), represented by eight poems and two essays. Both of these men were also natives of the Suzhou region, indicating the importance of locals in establishing and preserving the reputation of Tiger Hill. This anthology appears to consistently give local writers precedence over the famous scholar-officials who served for part of their careers in Suzhou or the surrounding region, and who visited Tiger Hill as tourists—a group represented by such luminaries as Bai Juyi, five of whose poems are included, Su Shi who has three poems and one essay, or Yuan Hongdao 袁宏道 (1568–1610, *jinshi* 1592) who has one poem and one essay.

In addition to the works of members of the male literati elite, this anthology also includes a number of poems by religious figures (as might be expected from a publication from such a significant Buddhist foundation), ghosts, foreigners, and women. Their small contribution to the 1767 *Huqiushan zhi* can be seen in table 5, and consists exclusively of poetry on the subject of Tiger Hill; no prose writings are included except those written by male literati. It is worth noting that this table excludes the writings of the Qing Kangxi and Qianlong emperors, given that their works are found in a separate chapter of the *Huqiushan zhi*, representing their significance as poems by regnant members of the imperial house. Because the two emperors are given a separate status in the text itself, it would seem inappropriate to attempt to allocate them to either the category of writings by the literati, or by foreigners. This is particularly true given that the way a ruling emperor experienced sites like Tiger Hill was completely different from other visitors: that is, he responded to the lessons of history to be garnered in such important places in a way

Table 5. Types of authors of the 1767 *Huqiushan zhi* by dynasty.

	Men	Women	Clergy	Ghosts	Foreigners
Liang	2 (2)	—	—	—	—
Chen	3 (3)	—	—	—	—
Sui	1 (1)	—	—	—	—
Tang	22 (40)	—	2 (3)	2 (3)	—
Song	97 (126)	—	4 (10)	—	—
Yuan	76 (97)	—	15 (17)	—	—
Ming	178 (298)	2 (4)	11 (15)	—	1 (1)
Qing	231 (322)	2 (2)	3 (6)	—	—
Total	610 (889)	4 (6)	35 (51)	2 (3)	1 (1)

distinct from other members of the ruling elite. This issue will be discussed in more detail in the section concerning Qing imperial poetry on the occasion of visiting sites associated with King Fuchai of Wu.

The results seen in table 5 raise a number of interesting questions. The first concerns the decline of poetry written by members of clergy that can clearly be seen in the figures for the Qing dynasty. This does not appear to represent a concomitant decline in the writing of poetry on the religious significance of this site by members of the laity, and, at present, the reason for this change is unknown. It is worth noting that just as the laity wrote poems about the religious significance of Tiger Hill, monks also wrote poems concerning the historical associations of this site, including the presence of King Helü of Wu's tomb and its rich grave goods. This can be seen in the poem entitled "Huqiu" by a Yuan dynasty monk whose name in religion was Wan 琬:

A soaring rock face cleft for a thousand feet,
Below there are the pitch-black waters of Sword Pond.
The aura of death here prevents the dragons from playing,
This cold steel cannot be transmuted by the earth.
Above the tomb of the king of Wu you can hear the howling of dark foxes,
Beside Shenggong's Tower cold gibbons cry.
The old monk awakes from his meditations in the temple hall at dawn,
The sound of the windlass escorts the mountain moon to the west.

飛厓裂斷一千尺, 下有劍池深黑色.
殺氣禁絶蛟龍游, 鐵花秀冷土不融.
吳王冢上玄狐悲, 生公臺畔寒猿啼.
老僧禪起洞堂曉, 聲動轆轤山月西.[82]

The figure for foreigners given here, as indicated above, is somewhat problematic. Only one individual in the whole of this massive anthology of literature is specifically designated as non-Chinese: a monk named Tianxiang 天祥 who came from Japan. This figure is, however, certainly incorrect, for it is clear that a number of individuals who contributed works of literature to the *Huqiushan zhi* anthology, though not clearly identified as such, were in fact of non-Chinese descent. For example, from the section on Yuan dynasty poetry, Sa Dula 薩都剌 (1272–1340, *jinshi* 1327, also known by his Chinese name: Sa Tianxi 薩天錫) represents a particularly interesting example. A Muslim of Central Asian descent, his original surname of Dānishmand (Dashiman 答失蠻) reflects the high status and educational attainments of his family. This was not belied by Sa Dula himself, a Hanlin Academician, who eventually retired to Hangzhou after a highly distinguished career. Likewise Ang Ji 昂吉 (*jinshi* 1348), who held various mid-level bureaucratic posts in the Jiangnan region, including Administrative Supervisor (Lushi canjun 錄事參軍) of Shaoxing, was in fact of Xixia ancestry though his family was at that time resident in the Suzhou region.[83] It seems that for the High Qing compiler of the *Huqiushan zhi*, the examination success and subsequent bureaucratic careers of these individuals placed them firmly within the category of the Chinese literati elite, regardless of their actual ethnic and cultural background. The Japanese monk is therefore exceptional, for though he shows considerable mastery of the rules of poetic diction and the cultural connotations of Tiger Hill in his poem, the inclusion of his work in this anthology was nevertheless dependent on his status as a visitor from Japan.

---

82. Gu Yilu, *Huqiushan zhi*, p. 401.

83. The poems by Sa Dula and Ang Ji are quoted in ibid., pp. 361–62, and 376–77 respectively.

The small number of poems written by women is unsurprising, as is the fact that these works are found only in the Ming and Qing dynasty sections. All four women whose works are included in this anthology seem to have been members of literati families, though this is made explicit only in the case of one of the women poets mentioned, where Lu Su 陸素 from the Qing dynasty is specifically described by Gu Yilu as a *guixiu* 閨秀 (a young unmarried woman of good family). No further biographical information seems to be available for her, or for the other female Qing dynasty poet included here, Gong Jingzhao 龔静照. Of the two Ming dynasty women poets, Zhu Guiying 朱桂英 (dates unknown) seems to have been known only for one single poem "Ti Huqiu bi" 題虎丘壁 (Writings on a wall at Tiger Hill)—whose title is given in this gazetteer simply as "Huqiu"—which was also included in a number of Ming dynasty anthologies of women's writings.[84] The other Ming dynasty woman poet included is the much more significant figure of Xu Yuan 徐媛 (fl. 1590s), a native of the city of Suzhou. Xu Yuan is represented by three poems in the *Huqiushan zhi* anthology. Two of these poems, "Zhoubo Huqiu" 舟泊虎丘 (Sailing to Tiger Hill) and "Huqiu huaigu" 虎丘懷古 (Nostalgia at Tiger Hill) are also found in contemporary anthologies of women's writings; the third, entitled "Sianxiang niangzi" 似安鄉娘子 (The woman from Sian town), is apparently otherwise unknown:[85]

The waves flow gently past, driven by drizzle and a light breeze,
Carrying wine, we journey beyond the suburbs in search of flowers.
The overgrown Wu palace seems a half-forgotten dream,
Boats made of magnolia wood now fill Bai [Juyi's] canal.
雨微風細漾輕流，載酒尋芳郊外游.
花草吳宮渾一夢，白公堤畔木蘭舟.

By the clear stream there is a small pavilion, a shelter in the rain,
My eyes follow the spring sails that send the rain on its way.
The bones of Zhenniang here turned to cold dust,

84. Ibid., p. 553. The same poem is found in Zhong Xing, *Mingyuan shigui* 30.18a; Wang Duanshu, *Mingyuan shiwei chubian* 6.20a.

85. For example both these poems were anthologized in Zhong Xing, *Mingyuan shigui* 33.18a–18b.

The fallen petals have all gone by autumn in this old palace.
清溪小築雨中樓, 目送春帆帶雨流.
自古眞娘冷香骨, 殘英飛盡故宮秋.

When Shenggong expounded on Buddhist doctrine the stones nodded their heads,
Scriptures were translated in the fragrant rain on this dark and desolate hillside.
The swords in this pond leap up, their dragon-like patterns roar,
In the quiet night in an empty forest the mountain ghosts are sad.
説法生公石點頭, 翻經香雨黯荒邱.
池中劍躍龍文吼, 静夜林空山鬼愁.[86]

This poem seems to blend the personal experience of a rain-soaked journey to Tiger Hill with a melancholy reflection on the fates of historical individuals associated with this site, men and women, religious figures, kings, and high officials. The mode that this woman poet uses to describe her emotions on considering such a storied spot as Tiger Hill makes no reference to her gender; indeed such poems could easily have been written by a male member of the literati elite from any time after the Tang dynasty. The only somewhat unusual feature of these poems is the reference to the figure of Zhenniang—though this beautiful and ill-fated local girl was a popular subject of poetry in the Tang dynasty, comparatively few Ming dynasty poets make reference to her. There is, however, no sense in which Xu Yuan's poem is informed by any kind of feminist sympathy or fellow feeling. Zhenniang's sufferings are part of the literary associations in which Tiger Hill is so rich, just like the stories of King Helü of Wu's swords or the famous Buddhist monks that once lived there.

Robbing the Tomb at Tiger Hill

The tomb of King Helü at Tiger Hill was of great importance both in the development of a local identity and in the history of tourism in the Jiangsu region. Only a handful of readily identifiable sites survived into modern times from the Spring and Autumn period king-

86. Gu Yilu, *Huqiushan zhi*, pp. 554–55.

dom of Wu: some lengths of pounded earth wall and a couple of tomb sites. These few remains were the oldest accessible signs of human habitation in the region; they were indisputably ancient, and they provided a link with a proud, independent past.[87] The locations of even earlier Wu sites, such as the tomb of Wu Taibo, the supposed founder of the state, were highly controversial, with a number of places claiming the honor. This dispute meant that any connection with this remoter past was extremely tenuous, and so was unsatisfactory to many people. During the Imperial period, numerous scholars, historians, artists, and poets would visit Tiger Hill to meditate on the wealth, power, and importance of King Helü as well as his enduring cultural legacy because this was a place where it was possible to feel a close connection with one of the great figures of classical antiquity.

By all accounts there have been a number of deliberate attempts to gain access to the tomb of King Helü since he was laid to rest in 496 BCE, and there have been persistent stories that his grave was looted in antiquity. First, the tomb was reportedly desecrated in 473 BCE, when the troops of Yue finally conquered the kingdom of Wu. This is perhaps the least well-recorded attack on the grave, since the only reference to the desecration of King Helü's tomb by the Yue army is recorded in a marginal note attributed to Liu Xiang 劉向 (79 BCE–8 CE), apparently commenting on the description of the tomb recorded in the *Yuejue shu*: "Liu Xiang of the Han dynasty wrote in a commentary: 'King Helü of Wu contravened the Rites, and was buried lavishly. A decade or so later, the people of Yue took him [out of his tomb].'" 漢劉向《疏》云: "吳王闔廬違禮, 厚葬. 十餘年間, 越人發之."[88]

Subsequently the grave was said to have been attacked in 210 BCE by the First Emperor of China. The First Emperor wished to rob it of the treasure it contained, particularly the fine swords thought to have been buried with the king of Wu: however, he was prevented

87. This point is eloquently put in the gazette for Suzhou incorporated into the *Yongle dadian* 永樂大典 (Yongle encyclopedia); *Suzhou fu zhi*, p. 1.

88. Quoted in Lu Xiong, *Suzhou fu zhi*, p. 1787.

from doing so either by the appearance of a tiger or by the gushing forth of a spring (which became the source of Sword Pond). An attempt to break open the grave of King Helü of Wu is also said to have been made by Sun Quan 孫權, the founder of the Wu dynasty (r. 222–52), and again this was said to have been foiled by the gushing of the spring that formed Sword Pond. As a result of these traditions of successive attempts to break open the tomb, it has proved very difficult indeed to apportion blame for the desecration of this important grave, as can be seen from the following gazetteer entry in which the reader is left to make up his own mind: "Liu Xiang of the Han dynasty wrote in a commentary: 'Within a dozen or so years the people of Yue had thrown him out [of his tomb].' The [*Wu*]*di ji* says: 'The Emperor of Qin threw him out.' The [*Taiping*] *huanyu ji* says: 'Sun Quan threw him out.'" 漢劉向《疏》言: "十餘年間越人發之." 《地記》言: "秦皇發之." 《寰宇記》言: "孫權發之."[89]

In fact, as will be seen below, the final quotation is incorrect. The wording has been changed to make it fit with that given in the other quotations. The original text made clear that the verb *fa* 發 referred to the digging of a pit to attempt to gain access to the tomb, not to a desecration of the grave itself. It is evident that there was unanimity among later historians and commentators that at some point in the distant past, the tomb of King Helü was opened, presumably with the aim of desecrating or robbing the tomb. However, there was no agreement over when this event had taken place, or which powerful and famous ruler was responsible. After the supposed attack by Sun Quan, the tomb seems to have lain largely undisturbed for many centuries, until the Song dynasty when on a number of occasions and for different reasons the entrance to the tomb was investigated. Subsequently during the Ming dynasty, in 1512, a group of literati from Suzhou conducted an amateur excavation of the tomb. Since that date, the tomb of King Helü of Wu has continued to be an important historical site famed for the riches hidden within, and remains a source of fascination for many visitors to Tiger Hill today.

89. Wang Bin, *Huqiushan zhi*, *Wuwang Helü mu* 吳王闔閭墓.1a.

The First Emperor of China Attempts to Rob the Tomb

The earliest known reference to an attempt made by the First Emperor of Qin to rob the tomb of King Helü of Wu at Tiger Hill is found in the Tang dynasty gazetteer, the *Yuanhe junxian tuzhi* by Li Jifu. As with other accounts, this text makes it clear that this was merely one of many attempts to break into the tomb and that these repeated attacks resulted in permanent changes to the landscape of Tiger Hill: "Tiger Hill lies eight *li* northwest of the county [of Wu, present day Suzhou] . . . The Emperor of Qin dug up its rare and precious objects. No one knows what was found there. Sun Quan opened it, and again he did not get anything. The place where he dug is now a deep spring." 虎丘山在縣西北八里. . . . 秦皇鑿其珍異, 莫知所在, 孫權穿之, 亦無所得. 其鑿處, 今成深澗.[90]

The historical veracity of the story of the First Emperor's attempted tomb-robbery is dubious. The First Emperor did make an imperial progress through Wu, which is mentioned in his biography in the *Shiji*.[91] This progress took place in the last year of his life, in 210 BCE; however, there is no mention in any surviving historical texts of a visit to Tiger Hill, and the First Emperor's supposed attack on the tomb was not recorded until one thousand years after his death. However, it is worth noting that at this time the swords said to have been buried with King Helü would still have been an important treasure worth the effort and odium of tomb robbing to acquire. Given the importance of these weapons in Wu culture, it is entirely possible that the First Emperor of China would have wished to gain possession of those buried with the great King Helü in order to enhance his grip on power in the south. The swords of Wu were their royal regalia, and could be seen as giving their possessor a right to rule these lands.

According to the Tang dynasty gazetteer, the *Wudi ji*, the First Emperor's attempt to rob the tomb was thwarted by a supernatural apparition. As with the appearance of the white tiger above the tomb a few days after King Helü's burial, the tiger that foiled the First

90. Li Jifu, *Yuanhe junxian tuzhi*, p. 601.
91. *Shiji* 6.263.

Emperor of Qin's attempt to break open the tomb seems to have been understood as a manifestation of the essence of the precious swords within:

> The First Emperor of Qin went east on an imperial progress, and arrived at Tiger Hill, where he tried to get the Wu king's precious swords, but a tiger [appeared and] crouched down opposite the tomb. The First Emperor attacked it with his sword, but did not get it; by mistake he struck a stone instead. The tiger ran west for twenty-five *li*, and then suddenly disappeared. . . . The swords were never again captured, so then they turned the pit [which had been dug] into a pond, and called it Sword Pond.
> 秦始皇東巡, 至虎邱, 求吳王寶劍, 其虎當墳而踞. 始皇以劍擊之, 不及, 誤中于石. 其虎西走二十五里, 忽失. . . . 劍無復獲, 乃陷成池, 故號劍池.[92]

In the imperial era, many visitors to Tiger Hill made reference to their belief that the tomb below the waters of Sword Pond was empty, and the swords that had once been buried with the king of Wu had "escaped."[93] Since at least the Eastern Han dynasty, the tomb of King Helü of Wu has been said to be located below a pond, originally unnamed but now generally known by the appellation, Sword Pond. Many texts describe this water feature not as an original part of the landscape of Tiger Hill, but as being formed by a spring that was discovered as a result of attempts to dig out the grave. As indicated in the passage quoted above, the creation of this body of water was frequently associated with the efforts of the First Emperor of Qin to rob the tomb. According to the *Wudi ji*, the pond was created after the robbery had failed. Left with a deep pit, the decision was made to turn it into a decorative feature. However, according to the *Wujun tujing xuji*, the pond itself (rather than the appearance of a supernatural tiger) played a key part in thwarting the First Emperor's

92. Lu Guangwei, *Wudi ji*, p. 62.

93. See for example the Ming dynasty poem supposedly written above Sword Pond by a literati visitor to the site and quoted in the Qing dynasty local history by Zhang Zilin, *Honglan yicheng*, p. 269: "The Yuchang sword has flown away,/ [Sword] Pond is empty and its stones have grown chill./ The ancient paulownias have grown to one hundred feet tall,/ When it rains at night they drip with a cold fragrance" 飛去魚腸劍, 池空石氣凉. 古桐高白尺, 宿雨滴寒香.

plans to rob the tomb, for the earth split to prevent him from stealing King Helü of Wu's precious swords.[94]

The First Emperor of China was by later accounts spectacularly unlucky in his attempts at tomb robbing. According to the different accounts of what occurred at Tiger Hill, either he was frightened off by the sudden appearance of a supernatural tiger guardian of the tomb or he was prevented from gaining access by a sudden gush of water from the spring that subsequently formed Sword Pond. Likewise, it was said that when the First Emperor opened the tomb of Confucius at Qufu 曲阜, all he found was an inscription prophesying his own imminent demise.[95] The story of Sun Quan's attempt to rob the tomb at Tiger Hill seems to have been derived from that of the First Emperor of Qin, and hence is considered here as an updating of what was clearly a very popular tale. The earliest reference to Sun Quan's attempt to rob the tomb of King Helü of Wu is found in the Song dynasty general gazetteer covering the whole of the Chinese empire, the *Taiping huanyu ji* 太平寰宇記 (An account of the world in the time of the Taiping reign-era, 976–83). This text described the creation of Sword Pond as follows: "This mountain gulf was opened by Sun Quan, when he sought the treasures of Helü." 山澗是孫權所掘, 求闔閭寶器.[96]

It is significant that the tale of Sun Quan creating Sword Pond post-dates the reference to this site in the "Ji Wudi zhuan" chapter of the *Yuejue shu* and in the *Wu Yue chunqiu*, both of which recorded the presence of this water feature in the Eastern Han dynasty. There is no mention in the *Wushu* 吳書 (History of Wu) section of the *Sanguo zhi* 三國志 (Records of the Three Kingdoms) that Sun Quan ever visited Tiger Hill, let alone dug for treasure there. Very little information seems to have been recorded about Sun Quan's supposed robbery of the tomb of King Helü of Wu. Only a handful of texts mention this story, and mostly they refer back to the *Taiping huanyu ji* as the source of the tale. Given the similarities recorded between the

94. Zhu Changwen, *Wujun tujing xuji*, p. 41.
95. Murray, "Varied Views of the Sage," p. 241, fig. 5.23.
96. Yue Shi, *Taiping huanyu ji* 91.7a.

tale of the First Emperor of China's attempt to rob the tomb and that of Sun Quan, it would seem likely that the second is merely an updating of the first for a new audience.

Song Dynasty Investigations of the Tomb

During most of the early imperial era, King Helü's grave was apparently largely ignored as a target of robbery. However, during the Song dynasty two events occurred which resulted in an upsurge of interest in the tomb at Sword Pond. The first was a flood, which resulted in ancient objects being washed out of the tomb; the second event was a drought that revealed a cleft in the rock, interpreted by contemporary observers as the entrance to the tomb of King Helü. The first of these events is by far the most obscure. The only surviving account of these events comes from a commentary on the works of the Song dynasty poet Jiang Tang, a native of the city of Changzhou in Jiangsu Province. (As mentioned in a number of imperial era gazetteers translated above, the literatus Jiang Tang was the focus of a commemorative shrine at Tiger Hill, indicative of a strong association with this site.) According to this, a sudden change in conditions at Sword Pond resulted in an important discovery: "In the Huangyou (1049–53) reign period of the Song [Emperor Renzong (r. 1023–63)], the spring [that feeds] Sword Pond gave a sudden gush, and a number of bamboo strips were discovered. They were all inscribed with red ink and had ancient reign-titles." 宋皇祐間劍池泉湧. 得竹簡數片. 皆朱書有古年號.[97]

This passage provides an interesting pre-modern account of someone discovering ancient objects at Tiger Hill. It may not have been the treasures recorded in ancient texts, but there is nothing intrinsically unlikely about such light objects as bamboo strips being washed out of place by a sudden flood. Other than this brief account, nothing more is known of the fate of the bamboo strips found at Tiger Hill. However, this may be the original source of a supernatural story recorded in a Qing dynasty local history, the *Wuyu* 吳語 (Stories of Wu) published in 1771 by Dai Yannian 戴延年 (fl. 1761–87):

97. Quoted in Gu Yilu, *Huqiushan zhi*, p. 221.

> Sword Pond at Tiger Hill is so deep that it cannot be plumbed. Some years ago, a round piece of wood was suddenly washed out, and someone picked it up and took it home. In the middle of the night it suddenly started glowing so that it lit up the whole room, and so he thought it was unnatural and chopped it up. Later on, making inquiries about it from an old monk on the mountain, [the monk stated] that this was called "Night Shining Wood" and that when the king of Wu was buried, two pieces of Night Shining Wood [were interred with him], and now the piece that had floated out was one of them. [The finder] was sad about this and left. However, located below such a weight of water, who knows how it could float up to the surface, and although this was a funerary object, it is not recorded in any record or tradition, so who knows where the old monk got his information from!
> 虎丘劍池, 其深莫測. 數年前忽浮圜木一枝, 有人取之以歸, 中夜忽然光明滿室, 異而斧之. 後詢諸山中老僧, 是名夜光木, 吳王殉葬時有夜光木二枝, 今浮出者, 其一也. 其人爲之慨然而去. 然重泉之下, 不知何以浮出於外，而殉葬之物, 傳記不載, 老僧不知其何所據也.[98]

From the Age of Disunion onwards, once Tiger Hill had become the site of a Buddhist temple, members of the literati elite turned their attention to efforts to beautify Tiger Hill, and succeeding generations ordered commemorative inscriptions, pavilions, steles, and so on to be erected there. Many of these enhancements were placed around Sword Pond, reflecting the generally-held belief that this marked the site of the entrance to the Wu king's tomb. The supposed entrance to the tomb of King Helü of Wu was very rarely accessible, because it took an extremely dry summer to stop the springs filling Sword Pond. However, in the Song dynasty there was such a drought, as a result of which the level of Sword Pond fell and what was believed to be the entrance to the tomb of King Helü of Wu was suddenly visible below the surface of the water: "In the Song dynasty, in Wuzi year, there was a sudden drought, and in the middle [of Sword Pond] there could be seen a stone doorway. In the end a diver was sent down to investigate it, but he only saw two short pieces of poetry above the

98. Dai, *Wuyu*, p. 253. Dai Yannian's dates of activity are derived from Zhang Huijian, *Ming Qing Jiangsu wenren nianbiao*, pp. 1137–1241.

door, and that is all." 宋戊子歲, 忽乾暵, 中見石扉. 游人競下探之, 惟見石扉上題詩二絕而已.[99]

During this Song dynasty drought, the level of water in Sword Pond did not fall sufficiently to allow open access to the entrance, thus only a diver could get to the door. The most detailed account of these events is found in the *Wumen biaoyin* 吳門表隐 (An exposition of the gates of Wu), a Qing dynasty text by Gu Zhentao 顧震濤 (1790–?). This text specifically dates the drought to 1228, the first year of the Shaoding reign-period (1228–33) of the Song Emperor Lizong 宋理宗 (r. 1225–64), and quotes the two verses of poetry mentioned above, which were said to have been inscribed over the entrance to King Helü's tomb:

Climbing a tower to look at the moon, the sea mist is dark,
Sword Pond has no bottom, [its waters] lap at the rocks.
The old monk is only afraid that the mountain will be carried away,
As the sun goes down he goes first to lock the gate to the temple.
望月登樓海氣昏, 劍池無底浸雲根.
老僧只恐山攜去, 日落先教鎖寺門.

The swords have gone, the pond is empty, and the waters run cold,
Travelers arriving here lean against the railings.
As the years pass, the affairs of the world crumble and wear away,
Only the green mountains appear the same as before.
劍去池空一水寒, 游人到此憑闌干.
年來世事銷磨盡, 只有青山依舊看.[100]

Bizarrely, the first of these two poems has ended up being attributed to Gao Qi, a native of Suzhou and the most high-profile casualty of the first Ming emperor's well-known suspicion of intellectuals from that city. This poem is indeed found in his eighteen-*juan* collected works, entitled *Daquan ji* 大全集 (Great collected writings) under the title "Huqiu si" 虎丘寺 (Temple at Tiger Hill). However, this attribution is clearly incorrect, since this poem was first recorded

99. Quoted in Gu Lu, *Tongqiao yizhuo lu*, p. 541.

100. Quoted in Gu Zhentao, *Wumen biaoyin*, pp. 107–8. This pair of poems is given with very minor variations in the wording (*Lao seng zhi kong shan yi qu* 老僧只恐山移去 rather than *lao seng zhi kong shan ji qu* 老僧只恐山攜去) in Zhang Zilin, *Honglan yicheng*, p. 276.

in the Tang dynasty, in the collected works of Zhang Ji 張籍 (c. 766–c. 830), entitled *Zhang Siye ji* 張司業集 (The collected writings of Director of Studies Zhang).[101] The second of these poems is elsewhere attributed to a Song dynasty poet named Xu Xin 徐忻, and entitled "Jianchi" (Sword Pond). Other versions of this poem give the last line somewhat differently: Only the green mountains are still good to look at calmly 只有青山好静看.[102] There is in fact a genuine poem by Gao Qi carved in seal-script on the cliff face above the waters of Sword Pond, entitled "Helü mu" 闔閭墓 (The Tomb of [King] Helü), which clearly indicates his familiarity with both the *Yuejue shu* account of the construction of the tomb, and certain later legends about it:

> Mercury forms a sea that touches the Yellow Springs,
> The labor of constructing one tomb employed ten thousand soldiers in digging.
> There are exaggerated tales of hidden traps to hinder thieves and robbers,
> It is difficult for rotten bones to be transformed into an immortal being.
> On an empty mountain the tiger leaves after the autumn winds arrive,
> At the abandoned belvedere the sound of a crow greets the moon at night.
> You should know that in the underworld there are no enemy kingdoms,
> Why would you need to bury three thousand swords?
> 水銀爲海接黄泉, 一穴曾勞萬卒穿.
> 謾説深機防盜賊, 難令枯骨化神仙.
> 空山虎去秋風後, 廢榭烏啼夜月邊.
> 地下應知無敵國, 何須深葬劍三千.[103]

101. Zhang Ji, *Zhang Siye ji* 7.21a. Wu Qiming, *Suzhou shiyong*, p. 115, argues that the attribution to Gao Qi is correct, and that the confusion stems from the gazetteer for Tiger Hill compiled by Gu Mei, where this poem was incorrectly ascribed to Zhang Ji.

102. Hu Zi, *Tiaoxi yuyin conghua*, p. 362. Li E ed., *Songshi jishi*, p. 984, gives the attribution of this poem to Xu Xin and the alternative version of the final line.

103. Quoted in Gu Yilu, *Huqiushan zhi*, p. 422.

In the opening couplet of this poem Gao Qi relies heavily on the earliest account of the construction of this tomb, found in the *Yuejue shu*, which describes the sea of mercury inside the grave, on which jade ducks were set afloat. However, he reduces the massive number of workmen who were said to have worked on this site from one hundred thousand men to ten thousand. Where the description of the tomb found in the *Yuejue shu* informs the first couplet, the second seems to be more closely related to ancient accounts of the tomb of the First Emperor of China, which also contained such a mercury "sea." There are no early texts that record any kind of hidden traps in the tomb of King Helü, but this was an important feature of the tomb of the First Emperor, which was said to contain crossbows aimed to kill anyone attempting to gain access to the treasures buried within.[104] When the funeral ceremonies were completed, the artisans that constructed these traps were said to have been cruelly entombed with the body of the First Emperor, lest they should reveal the secret of how to access the tomb. From at least the Ming dynasty onwards, popular legends concerning the burial of King Helü seem to have been significantly affected by a confusion with the much more famous tomb of the First Emperor; this can also be seen in the late imperial tradition mentioned above that the workers who built the penultimate king of Wu's tomb were massacred at Thousand-Man Rock.

The drought in the Song dynasty lowered the level of Sword Pond sufficiently that a cleft in the rocks could be seen below the waters. It would, however, not be until the Ming dynasty that a drought of sufficient severity occurred to dry out the pond completely, thus allowing visitors free access to this site. This would be the first time in recorded history that anyone had the opportunity to explore the access tunnel to the tomb of King Helü of Wu.

---

104. *Shiji* 6.265.

The Ming Dynasty Drought

In 1512, during the reign of the Zhengde Emperor, there was a period of unprecedented drought in southern Jiangsu Province and Sword Pond was completely dried out. This would have been a considerable surprise to local people because these waters had traditionally been said to be bottomless. An opening in the rocks, assumed by all visitors to Tiger Hill to be the entrance to the tomb of King Helü of Wu, was revealed at the northern end of the pond, a place known as Sword Point (Jianjian 劍尖). This place is now marked with a Ming dynasty inscription commemorating the occasion, which reads: "When the waters of Sword Pond dry out, the entrance to the tomb of the king of Wu is revealed." 劍池水涸, 見吳王墓門.[105]

A party of local literati, led by one of the most important men in Suzhou, the retired scholar and statesman Wang Ao 王鏊 (1450–1524, *jinshi* 1475) and including the painter Tang Yin 唐寅 (1470–1524), and the poet and artist Wen Zhengming, set out from Suzhou in order to investigate the site. Wang Ao was noted for his antiquarian interests—particularly in sites associated with the great kings of Wu—and hence could be expected to take advantage of such a unique opportunity. At Sword Point, they found a triangular passage. Exploring this passage further, they discovered a small, reddish skull. When this find was announced to the authorities, they were recorded as taking a most dim view of the scholars disturbing the tomb of a great king: "For the physical remains of former kings to be exposed to the light of heaven and the changing seasons is the greatest crime it is possible for later generations to commit." 先王遺骸, 暴露在光天化日之下, 是後人之莫大罪過.[106]

Given the official disapproval expressed concerning their actions, it is not surprising that there are very few surviving textual accounts of Wang Ao's investigation of the tomb passage—though there are a number of stone inscriptions that record visits to Tiger Hill on the

---

105. Li Yuqing, *Jiangsu mingcheng lu*, p. 168.
106. Quoted in Wu Qu, *Gusu yeshi*, pp. 8–9.

occasion of the 1512 drought by Wang Ao and other contemporary literati, local officials, and members of the local elite. The extent of damage done to the tomb of King Helü of Wu by pillaging and robbery in antiquity is unknown; however, the magistrate who reprimanded the Suzhou literati for disturbing the tomb clearly thought that the skull they had found was that of the penultimate king of Wu. It is likely that had the exploration of the passage been carried out by someone less socially prominent than Wang Ao, particularly given the extremely dim view taken of disturbing tombs in Ming law, this person's actions would have been judged much more harshly. What happened later to the skull found in the passage below the waters of Sword Pond is unknown, and was apparently not recorded in any Ming dynasty text.

There is only one brief description of this Ming dynasty investigation of the tomb of King Helü of Wu, since presumably the censure that this amateur archaeology attracted discouraged other eyewitnesses from writing about the events. However Wen Zhengming wrote a short introductory preface to his poem about the drought at Tiger Hill: "Huqiu Jianchi dong shuihao chikong. Yu wangguan fushi" 虎丘劍池冬水涸池空. 余往觀賦詩 (In the winter the waters dried up and the lake was empty at Sword Pond on Tiger Hill. I went to look at it and composed this poem):

> There is a tradition that Sword Pond at Tiger Hill is too deep to be plumbed. Old gazetteers record that the Emperor of Qin broke open Helü's tomb, and dug out the mountain in order to get his swords. The place that he dug has since become a deep pool. Wang Yucheng made the inscription at Sword Pond, criticizing the mistake [of old gazetteers, and arguing that this is a natural landscape feature]. In the winter of Xinwei year of the Zhengde Emperor, the waters dried up and the lake was empty, and a stone cleft was revealed, and no one knew where it ended. I went to see it, and composed a poem. I gave this verse to my fellow-tourists to respond to with the same rhyme, thus my poem has been transmitted:
>
> The king of Wu has been buried for several thousand years,
> The water level drops and the pond empties, and so we find the bricks of his tomb.
> Who in the underworld still has need for precious swords?
> I have already seen with my own eyes the mulberry plantations and fields.

Golden ducks are solitary and still through many kalpas,[107]
The stone cleft that stands revealed is a way to paradise.
Where can one find a [Wang Yucheng] to discourse on past matters?
Cold sunshine and wisps of azure mist spread across the hill.

虎丘劍池相傳, 深不可測. 舊志載秦皇發闔廬墓, 鑿山求劍. 其鑿處遂成深澗. 王禹偁作劍池銘, 嘗辨其非. 正德辛未冬水涸, 池空, 得石闕中空, 不知其際. 余往觀之, 賦詩. 貽同游者和而傳焉.

吳王埋玉幾千年, 水落池空得墓磚.
地下誰曾求寶劍, 眼中吾已見桑田.
金鳧寂寞随塵劫, 石闕分明有洞天.
安得元之論往事, 滿山寒日散蒼煙.[108]

There are two contemporary stone inscriptions at Tiger Hill that record the impressions of other visitors who came to see the entrance to the tomb. The first, an inscription in ten lines, commemorates a visit by literati clearly associated with Wang Ao and his friends:

In the first month of the seventh year of the Zhengde Emperor, the local gentlemen Wang Shanchun, Hou Quan, Ren Yunfan, and Zu Yuzhi climbed Tiger Hill. At that time the waters of [two illegible characters, from context Sword Pond] had dried up, so it was said that we could see the dark palace of King Helü. What had been a mystery for a thousand years was laid bare in one morning, how sad! [Four illegible characters] we looked reverently upon the inscriptions in the hall, and visited [the site] with the Tutor to the Heir-Apparent Wang Ao, the Provincial Graduate with the Highest Honors Tang Yin, the Filial and Incorrupt Chen [two illegible characters], and the Tutor to the Heir-Apparent's son [two illegible characters] Yanling.

---

107. According to the *Yuejue shu*, King Helü of Wu was buried with jade ducks floating on a lake of mercury. It is possible that Wen Zhengming was thinking of this reference when he composed his poem; however, it is also possible that this is another instance of a description of the tomb of the penultimate king of Wu that has been infected by accounts of the burial of the First Emperor. There is a famous Jin dynasty story of just such a golden duck: "In the first year of the Baoding reign era (266), Zhang Shan was Prefect of Rinan and some people from that commandery presented him with a gold duck. Zhang Shan was an exceptionally learned man and he investigated its age, only to discover that this was in fact a gold duck from the tomb of the First Emperor of Qin" 寶鼎元年, 張善爲日南太守郡, 民有得金鳧以獻. 張善該博多通, 考其年月, 即秦始皇墓之金鳧也. Wang Jia, *Shiyi ji* 5.6a.

108. Wen Zhengming, *Wen Zhengming ji*, p. 232.

正德七年正月，郡士王山椿、侯權、任雲藩、祖與之登虎丘．于時□□水涸，傳觀闔閭之幽宮，千年神密，一朝顯露，可悼而已．庭字利瞻，同游．少傅王鏊、解元唐寅、孝廉陳□□、少傅之子□□延齡.[109]

The second inscription, in this instance recording the visit of local officials to Tiger Hill on account of the drought in 1512, reads:

> The Magistrate of Changzhou, Wu Xi, the Magistrate of Wu, Hu Wenjing, and the Magistrate of Kunshan, Fang Hao (*jinshi* 1508), heard that Sword Pond had dried up, and the entrance to the king of Wu's tomb could be seen, so we all came to see it. A deep mystery for ten thousand years, one morning became something that men could pry into. Surely this is fate! Now it has been hidden [again]. The fourteenth day of the second month of the seventh year of the reign of the Zhengde Emperor.
> 長洲令吾翕、吳令胡文静、昆山令方豪聞劍池枯，見吳王墓門，偕往觀焉，萬年深閟，一旦爲人所窺，豈非數耶！今掩藏之．正德七年上月前一日.[110]

The Ming dynasty drought represents a unique occasion during the imperial era when the waters of Sword Pond dried up sufficiently to allow access to the supposed tomb entrance. The number of surviving references to this event suggests that it resulted in an enormous upsurge of interest in visiting the tomb of King Helü of Wu. This would however not be the last time during the imperial era that this site was investigated. The Qing dynasty gazetteer, the *Wumen biaoyin*, which also records the discovery of the bamboo slips in the Song period, mentions another undated investigation of what was

---

109. The text of this inscription is quoted in Jiangsu wenwu zonglu bianji weiyuanhui ed., *Jiangsu wenwu zonglu*, p. 153. The name given for Wang Ao's son in this inscription is known to be wrong: his name was Wang Yanling 王延陵. This was not the only inscription on Tiger Hill recording a visit by Wang Ao. Another inscription, commemorating a visit by Wang Ao and Tang Yin in 1505, is described in Gu Zhentao, *Wumen biaoyin*, p. 107, where it is mentioned as one of the three important inscriptions found on the rocks at Sword Pond, together with the seal script characters "Jianchi" (Sword pond) from the brush of the Yuan dynasty calligrapher Zhou Boqi, and the four characters "Fenghe yunquan" 風壑雲泉 (Wind-blown valley and cloudy waters) by the Song dynasty calligrapher Mi Fu 米芾 (1051–1107).

110. Jiangsu wenwu zonglu bianji weiyuanhui ed., *Jiangsu wenwu zonglu*, p. 153.

believed to be the entrance to the tomb. In this case, the cause of the attempt was a tragedy: "Some years ago, someone fell into Sword Pond [and drowned]. The chief monk ordered a man who was good at diving to tie a rope around himself and go down to get the body. It was found in an empty cave in the deep ravine. There was an entrance in this place. Surely this cannot be the site of the tomb of Helü!" 往歲有墮劍池者. 主僧俾善匿水人繩貫而下求其尸. 乃在一嵌巖空洞中. 其處宛有門户. 即闔閭所葬處邪![111]

From other records that described the death of the unfortunate man who fell into Sword Pond and drowned there, it would seem that these events took place in the reign of the Emperor Daoguang of the Qing dynasty 清道光 (r. 1820–50). No precise date was given for the drowning of this person, but the local magistrate responded to the death by ordering that Sword Pond should be fenced off.[112] This appears to be the last time the waters were investigated during the imperial era, and seems to have aroused a similar sense of amazement as did the explorations during the Ming dynasty drought. For all that every major account of the tomb of King Helü placed it below Sword Pond, the times when the cleft in the rocks was actually visible seems to have startled all that saw it. Viewing the still waters was an aesthetic experience hallowed by poetic and cultural associations stretching back over many centuries; seeing the rocky passageway was an exceptional opportunity accorded to very few to experience a genuine connection with the penultimate king of Wu.

It would seem likely that the short but exciting appearance during the Ming dynasty drought of the supposed entrance to the tomb of the great King Helü of Wu in an area with a long tradition of local pride in the chief figures of its glorious past resulted in an upsurge of interest in visiting Tiger Hill. During the Ming dynasty, Suzhou had become one of the wealthiest areas in China, and a mecca for internal tourism. Many members of the local elite had come to see the incursions of tourists as a great imposition: they believed that the

---

111. This account, supposedly from an unnamed old gazetteer, is quoted in Gu Yilu, *Huqiushan zhi*, p. 223.

112. Gu Lu, *Tongqiao yizhuo lu*, p. 3.

tourists (who were themselves unable to appreciate the sights) prevented others from enjoying them properly by their very presence.[113] Wang Ao, Tang Yin, and Wen Zhengming were at the heart of a movement to reclaim Tiger Hill as a local attraction and a focus of local pride. Beginning with their efforts, from the late Ming dynasty onwards Tiger Hill was increasingly understood as an important historical site in the literati imagination, and it became a focus for a reinvigorated interest in the events of the classical past. From the Ming dynasty onwards, Suzhou was one of the most important tourist destinations in China and many visitors went on to travel to Tiger Hill. The universal nature of the appeal of this site was revealed by the comments of the Qing dynasty author Li Liufang 李流芳 (1575–1629) in his *Jiangnan woyou ceti ci* 江南臥游册題詞 (Collected remarks by a Jiangnan aesthete): "Tiger Hill is good by moonlight, it is good in the snow, it is good in the rain, it is good on a spring dawn, it is good in summer, it is good in crisp autumn weather, it is good when the leaves fall from the trees, it is good when the sun sets, it is always good except when tourists trample round indiscriminately." 虎丘宜月, 宜雪, 宜雨, 宜春曉, 宜夏, 宜秋爽, 宜落木, 宜夕陽, 無所不宜, 而獨不宜于游人雜踏之時.[114]

Conclusion

The tomb of King Helü of Wu at Tiger Hill is one of the best recorded mausoleum sites in China. It has never been lost. For the last two thousand years the vicissitudes undergone by this site have been recorded in considerable detail, in local and national histories, in the works of great poets and scholars, and in gazetteers. In antiquity, rumors of the vast wealth buried with this great king attracted a succession of unscrupulous monarchs to the tomb and they attempted to open it and gain access to this treasure. Although there are no reports of the tomb being emptied of any specific items once said to have been interred there, the persistent reports of ancient robberies suggest that the site was thoroughly plundered in antiq-

113. Brook, *The Confusions of Pleasure*, pp. 174–82.

114. Quoted in Shan Gu, *Suzhou yaowang Gusu tai*, p. 174.

uity. Once men no longer sought the treasures to be found below the waters of Sword Pond, Tiger Hill increasingly became a focus of literati activity, and an association with this site became an important asset to be prized. The commemorative shrines erected here to both scholar-officials local to the region and those who served for part of their careers in Suzhou or the surrounding area are indicative of the importance accorded to Tiger Hill in the literati imagination.

In addition to the historical significance accorded to Tiger Hill, it was also a focus of religious pilgrimage from the Age of Disunion onwards, as the site of the Yunyan Temple. Many literary works on the subject of Tiger Hill would make reference both to the historical and religious importance of this place. From the Song dynasty onwards, Tiger Hill was also frequently described as an area of outstanding natural beauty, worth visiting for this quality alone. Although some accounts of this site attempt to present one particular reason for visiting as of paramount importance, and one interpretation of Tiger Hill as the most correct and refined, in fact many visitors no doubt had complicated reasons for wishing to travel there, in which the religious and historical significance of the site was only enhanced by its fame as a beauty spot and the opportunities to eat, drink, and shop which abounded in the vicinity. Without this plethora of attractions to be found within its purlieus, Tiger Hill could not have been such an important tourist attraction as it was throughout the imperial era.

The tomb at Tiger Hill has always been more than just the last resting place of the greatest king of Wu. The historical and cultural importance of this site is not really affected by the fact that the tomb has never been successfully explored, and the treasures within lie beyond the powers of later generations to visualize. The tomb has a symbolic importance; it is one of the few tangible reminders of southern independence and power, and virtually the only monument to survive from that time at the end of the Spring and Autumn period when Wu was one of the most powerful states in the Chinese world and when the rulers of Wu imposed their will on the lands to the north. The unique status of this tomb, as one of the few places where the visitor can experience a true connection to the past greatness of the kingdom of Wu, has gone far to ensuring its enduring popularity as a tourist destination. Though many have attempted to rob the tomb of the material goods buried with the king, they have paradoxically merely served to keep the memory of the wealth and power of the ancient kingdom of Wu alive, and enhanced the importance of Tiger Hill within the cultural history of China.

6

Numinous Cliff and Gusu Tower

During the imperial era numerous scholar-officials and members of the literati elite visited the famous attractions in and around the city of Suzhou that were associated with the late Spring and Autumn period state of Wu, and these visitors would be crucial for development of the tourism industry in the region. Men of this class would have been fully aware of the historical importance of these places through their readings of the Chinese classics, and they were also virtually the only people with the financial resources, the interest, and the incentive to travel for pleasure. Their travel accounts, prose-writings, and poems defined tourism as an elite activity, and established certain locations as cultural markers. In order to be considered truly well travelled and sophisticated, it became necessary to have visited famous historical sites—and perhaps even more importantly—to have composed essays or poetry on the subject. The importance of literati writings in creating the reputation for particular sites (for example, places of great natural beauty or historical interest) can hardly be overstated. The writings and poems of earlier visitors served both to establish and to popularize locations as tourist attractions, a relationship that has occasionally been explicitly described: "The fame of mountains and rivers is mostly due to outstanding people. Before Su Shi's excursion, the Red Cliff was just another stupid rock. Since Su Shi toured it, although the terraces are ruined and the pavilions are damaged, Red Cliff is still a famous mountain."[1]

Over the centuries, countless visitors were drawn to the famous sites in and around the city of Suzhou that were traditionally as-

1. This statement was made by the Qing dynasty poet and essayist, Dong Yining 董以寧 (1629–70), and is quoted in Meyer-Fong, *Building Culture in Early Qing Yangzhou*, p. 25.

sociated with the romantic figure of the last monarch of the kingdom of Wu, King Fuchai. Two of these sites, and these perhaps the best known, are examined in this chapter: Numinous Cliff and Gusu Tower. These two places are significantly different from the sites associated with Prince Jizha of Wu and his nephew King Helü that were discussed in previous chapters. The structures associated with Prince Jizha represent a largely local commemoration of a great historical figure, since they are generally located within the confines of his fief, and specifically in the environs of his tomb. Similarly, commemoration of King Helü of Wu seems to have been focused almost exclusively on the site of his tomb, which was also a place where visitors could feel a real link with the king when they gazed down upon the waters covering the entrance to his grave. The situation with respect to King Fuchai of Wu is somewhat different. Although a number of ancient historical texts mentioned the location of his tomb, this did not lead to a specific site being designated as his resting place. There seems to have been no tradition of visiting the tomb of King Fuchai, nor of any commemorative structures associated with a grave site such as a temple or shrine. This means that, unlike the situation with respect to his father and great-uncle, interested visitors had no opportunity to experience a tangible association with King Fuchai by making a journey to a site physically linked to the last king of Wu. All the possible alternatives—the palaces where King Fuchai once lived and the gardens where he wandered with the beautiful Xi Shi—were destroyed in 473 BCE at the time of the conquest by the kingdom of Yue.

Visitors to Lingyanshan or Numinous Cliff Mountain had the luxury of actually having a physical site to go to: Numinous Cliff Mountain stands southwest of Suzhou, within easy reach of any tourist to the city. Although no trace remains of the Wu royal palace or gardens that once stood there, the mountain itself was traditionally noted for its many beautiful vistas, and as with Tiger Hill, has been prized since at least the Song dynasty for the aesthetic experience that it offers to the cultured visitor. From the earliest detailed records of the sites at Numinous Cliff—and in spite of the comprehensive destruction of all the buildings of the Wu royal palace by time or by military action—there has nevertheless been a strong tradition that certain spots around the mountain are locations specifically associated with King Fuchai of Wu and Xi Shi. The fact that this site had been ruined in antiquity means that tourism to Numinous Cliff in the imperial era was suitably shot through with melancholy to serve as a good subject for *huaigu* writings. This place had once been rich and luxurious, and had been destroyed; this had once been royal pleasure grounds, and was now reduced to more plebeian status; this had been the scene of King Fuchai's romance with the fabled beauty Xi Shi, but both lovers were long dead. This perspective was articulated by the Qing dynasty poet Fan Zhongyue 樊鍾岳, in his poem: "Lingyan huaigu" 靈巖懷古 (Cherishing antiquity at Numinous Cliff):

> This place of scenic beauty has survived for a thousand autumns,
> But where to look for the Wu palace?
> Pavilions and towers remain from the abandoned garden,
> Deer step out from the dense forest.
> The Fragrant Canal is muffled in green moss,
> The empty corridors are thick with fallen leaves.
> Ever since the woman who washed silk (Xi Shi) departed,
> Her sorrowful memory has endured to the present day.
> 勝蹟千秋著, 吳宮何處尋?
> 亭臺餘廢苑, 麋鹿出荒林.
> 香逕青苔冷, 空廊落葉深.
> 浣紗人去後, 遺恨到於今.[2]

The case of Gusu Tower, however, is significantly different from that of Numinous Cliff, or indeed any of the other sites discussed in this book. Not only was the tower destroyed in antiquity, but the location of this structure was also lost in the mists of time.[3] In spite of many efforts to rediscover this site, which represents not only the most famous prestige building project undertaken in the ancient kingdom of Wu but also the scene of many important events in the last years of

---

2. Quoted in Zhang Yiliu, *Suzhou Lingyanshan zhi*, p. 223.

3. Some scholars argue that the reference made by Sima Qian to his visit to Gusu: "[I] climbed Gusu and gazed out at the Five Lakes" (*shang Gusu wang Wuhu* 上姑蘇望五湖) means that the location of this mountain was still known in the Western Han dynasty. If that is so, the information was lost shortly afterwards. Yue Junjie et al., *Suzhou wenhua*, p. 18. The original reference is given in *Shiji* 29.1415. Wu Enpei, *Gouwu wenhua de xianzai chanshi*, p. 96, discusses the loss of information concerning Wu royal sites in the early imperial era.

King Fuchai's life, it has remained elusive. The writings of literati on the subject of the Gusu Tower may therefore be said to push the possibilities of the *huaigu* genre to the limit, for they describe a place that can only be visited in the pages of books. In the case of both Numinous Cliff and Gusu Tower, the literati who wrote about them were dependent on descriptions found in texts written many centuries after the fall of the kingdom of Wu. However, in the case of Numinous Cliff, it was possible to refresh and revitalize images of the place by reference to subsequent developments at the site and descriptions of its contemporary appearance. The works that describe Gusu Tower on the other hand are purely exercises in the imagination, and hence the poetry and prose written on this subject suffers from a certain lack of originality and spontaneity.

Numinous Cliff Mountain and Gusu Tower drew many different responses from the literati that wrote about them, not least thanks to the ambiguity inherent in the situation. As much as the literati might wish to try to recreate the glamour of these places during the reign of King Fuchai, they could only invent their own interpretations of these vanished splendors. Given that the earliest descriptions of these sites and the luxurious appointments that characterized them during the decadent reign of the last king of Wu date to the Age of Disunion, some seven centuries after the buildings were destroyed, the best that any literati could hope to achieve was an imaginary account based upon an older imaginary account. The palaces and towers of the last king of Wu conjured up in imperial era poetry and prose are as invented as any castle in the air.

Numinous Cliff Mountain

Numinous Cliff Mountain, now situated within the ever-encroaching western suburbs of the city of Suzhou, is supposedly the site of one of the oldest known royal gardens in China. The early history of this site is extremely confusing. This place is not mentioned in any ancient Chinese text, and, strikingly, is missing from the account of the historical geography of the kingdom of Wu recorded in the *Yuejue shu*. However, it would appear that this omission is the result of textual loss, and a number of imperial era texts contain quotations attributed to ancient texts that describe the building works undertaken by the Wu royal house at Numinous Cliff.[4] From the Tang dynasty onwards Numinous Cliff Mountain was frequently described by scholars as the site of the Wu Gong 吳宮 (Wu palace), a summer palace constructed by King Helü of Wu. None of the landscaping appears to have survived from the garden of the Spring and Autumn period, with a possible exception of some of the wells, but this site has reputedly been preserved as a green space since that time. Although there seems to be general agreement that King Helü was the first monarch to build a palace and lay out gardens at Numinous Cliff Mountain, there seems to have been some confusion about the function played by this place during his reign, as described by the Song dynasty gazetteer, the *Wujun tujing xuji*. The problem seems to be derived from the description of the peripatetic lifestyle of the ancient kings of Wu that is found in the "Ji Wudi zhuan" chapter of the *Yuejue shu*, which records these monarchs as constantly in motion. By the time of the Song dynasty, this had apparently led to the development of a number of different stories about the significance of various major sites in and around the city of Suzhou: "It has been popularly rumored that the old capital of Wu stood [here] . . . but this is wrong. . . . There is a story that Helü ruled from inside the city walls during the autumn and winter, and in the spring and summer, he ruled from outside the city walls (i.e., while resident in a summer palace such as this)." 而流俗或傳吳之故都在[此] . . . 非也 . . . 故傳闔廬秋冬治城中, 春夏治城外.[5]

---

4. Many gazetteers contain a reference to a line lost from the present text of the *Wu Yue chunqiu*, which refers to the Wu royal sites here. Wang Ao et al., *Gusu zhi*, vol. 3, p. 112.

5. Zhu Changwen, *Wujun tujing xuji*, p. 6. The original reference from the *Yuejue shu*, p. 9 ("Ji Wudi zhuan") reads: "In the autumn and winter the seat of government was inside the city walls, in the spring and summer, the seat of government was at Guxutai (Gusu tower). In the mornings [the king] ate breakfast at Niushan (Knot mountain), in the evenings he travelled to Xumu. He shot arrows at Qupo (Archery bank) and raced past Youtai (Travelling tower), enjoying himself at Shicheng (Stone walled city). He also raced his dogs at Changzhou (Long marsh)" 秋冬治城中, 春夏治姑胥之臺. 旦食於紐山, 晝遊於胥母, 射於鷗陂, 馳於遊臺, 興樂石城, 走犬長洲. Xie Chen, *Gouwu shi xinkao*, p. 66, suggests that King Fuchai of Wu, for the last decade of his reign, divided government between Gusu Tower and Numinous Cliff.

Although the Wu Palace at Numinous Cliff Mountain was one of King Helü's summer residences, this place was never particularly strongly associated with him. However, King Helü's son and heir, King Fuchai, developed particularly close links with this royal palace and garden. When King Fuchai inherited the throne, he made his summer residence here: the famous Guanwa Gong 館娃宮 (Lodging-beauties palace). This was surrounded by one of the famous pleasure gardens of the ancient world and possibly the first planted garden in China, the Wutong Yuan 梧桐園 (Paulownia garden).[6] While King Helü's Wu Palace was not mentioned until the Tang dynasty, the first reference to King Fuchai's Lodging-Beauties Palace is found in the *Fangyan* 方言 (Regional speech) dictionary by Yang Xiong 楊雄 (53 BCE–18 CE), which provides a gloss on the Wu dialect word *wa* 娃.[7] The somewhat bizarre fact that the first reference to this site is made in a dictionary suggests that it was still extremely famous in the Han dynasty, though the corresponding literary references have not survived. Thus the Lodging-Beauties Palace was first mentioned in Chinese literature in the "Wudu fu" by Zuo Si.[8] In a passage describing the celebrations for a successful hunt, the king is said to have ordered female musicians to entertain his guests here. It is not clear whether the Lodging-Beauties Palace was the same building as King Helü's Wu Palace and the royal residence was simply renamed, or whether King Fuchai of Wu rebuilt or improved the palace here and the name change commemorated a redevelopment of the site.

---

6. The earliest surviving reference to this place seems to be found in Ren Fang, *Shuyi ji* B.11a, which also provides the famous description of the Lodging-Beauties Palace translated below. The *Shuyi ji* provides no description of the Paulownia Garden, other than to record its existence, the fact that it was constructed by King Fuchai of Wu, and that it was also occasionally known as Mingqin chuan 鳴琴川 (Singing-Qin stream). A number of imperial-era texts also quote two lines from a Yuefu 樂府 (Music bureau) poem where the rest does not survive: *Wu gong qiu, Wu wang chou* 梧宮秋, 吳王愁 (In autumn in the palace by Paulownia [garden], / The king of Wu is sad). Tao Zongyi, *Shuofu* 105.15b; Qian Gu, *Wudu wencui xuji* 11.39a. The suggestion that this was the first proper planted garden to be constructed in China is derived from Cao Lindi, *Gusu yuanlin yu Zhongguo wenhua*, p. 3.

7. *Fangyan* 2.13.

8. *Wenxuan*, p. 75; Knechtges, *Wen xuan or Selections of Refined Literature, vol. 1*, p. 421.

Throughout the imperial era, when considering the history of Numinous Cliff Mountain, the majority of poets chose to understand it as the scene of the ill-fated romance between King Fuchai of Wu and Xi Shi. However, occasionally there are works that evoke the lines in the "Wudu fu" describing the Lodging-Beauties Palace as a place of limitless extravagance and luxury where guests of the king of Wu's were entertained with music and dance. In poems of this type, the pleasure grounds at Numinous Cliff Mountain are portrayed as a dangerous fulfillment of male fantasy. In the work of the Tang dynasty poet Yin Yaofan 殷堯藩 (*jinshi* Yuanhe 元和 reign-era 806–20) it is this aspect of the site that is paramount, as can be seen from the poem "Wu Gong" 吳宮 (The Wu palace):

The king of Wu loves singing and dancing,
Night after night he gets drunk with his beauties.
On seeing the sun, he blows out the red candle,
As [the servants] sweep up jade and filigree jewels with the dust.
He might as well have made Goujian a hegemon,
He did not trust the wisdom of [Wu] Zixu.
Do not ask after the wilds of Changzhou,
Desolate through the endless years.
吳王愛歌舞, 夜夜醉嬋娟.
見日吹紅燭, 和塵掃翠鈿.
徒令勾踐霸, 不信子胥賢.
莫問長洲草, 荒涼無限年.[9]

The behavior described in this poem was typical of that indulged in by doomed Chinese rulers. It was part of the stereotype that the last ruler of a line would be debauched: surrounded by women and overindulgent in alcohol. Such lack of self-control on the part of the monarch made the destruction of Wu by Yue only too comprehensible for a later audience. Music was also traditionally seen as a significant factor in the decline of a state: the inner workings of a kingdom were believed to be revealed through the songs of the people, and important personality traits were thought to be shown in musical performance. As would be repeatedly stressed in poems of this kind, by the imperial era

9. Quoted in Fan Chengda, *Wujun zhi*, p. 104. This particular poem is also included in the important anthology of verse about Suzhou, the *Wudu wencui* 吳都文粹 (Literary classics from the Wu capital). Zheng Huchen, *Wudu wencui* 3.41b.

desolation had overtaken the places where King Fuchai had once indulged himself. The palace where the king had once held court (whose glamour was encapsulated in the image of the jade and filigree jewels fallen to the ground) now lay in ruins. The portrayal of this site as a wilderness must be understood as a poetic conceit, for in fact from the Age of Disunion onwards, Numinous Cliff Mountain was the site of a highly successful and thriving Buddhist community.

At various times in its history Numinous Cliff Mountain has been known by other names, including Yanshishan 硯石山 (Inkstone mountain), and Shigushan 石鼓山 (Stone drum mountain).[10] The first of these names seems to have been derived from a type of stone found at this mountain, for which the site was apparently already famous in antiquity. This seems to be the oldest name for the mountain, and according to the *Taiping yulan* 太平御覽 (Imperial readings from the Taiping reign era [976–83])—quoting a lost line from the *Yuejue shu*: "The people of Wu constructed Lodging-Beauties Palace at Inkstone [Mountain]" (吳人於硯石[山]置館娃宮).[11] This name was still used occasionally as the primary designation for this site long after the designation of Numinous Cliff had become generally accepted, which apparently reflects the importance of the term as the original name of this mountain.[12] The second and much less common name for the mountain came about as a result of the presence of an ancient stone drum. According to the Tang dynasty gazetteer, the *Wudi ji*: "The Wu gazetteer says: 'This drum will sound when there are troops about.' In the second year of the Longan reign-period of the Jin dynasty (398), the bandit Sun En (d. 402) raised a rebellion and the drum sounded." 《吳志》云: "其鼓有兵則鳴." 晉隆安二年, 賊孫恩作亂, 鼓鳴.[13]

---

10. These alternative names are not only frequently mentioned in imperial era gazetteers, they are also periodically found in literary works on the subject of Numinous Cliff; see for example the essay entitled "Lingyan ji" 靈巖記 (A record of Numinous Cliff) by Yuan Hongdao, quoted in Yang Xunji et al. eds., *Wuzhong xiaozhi congkan*, pp. 288–89.

11. Li Fang et al., *Taiping yulan* 46.341. This line is also quoted in a number of later accounts, including Wang Jian, *Song Pingjiang chengfang kao*, p. 261.

12. Ouyang Xun, *Yiwen leiju*, p. 143.

13. Lu Guangwei, *Wudi ji*, p. 67. Sun En was a native of the city of Langya in Shandong province. He raised a Daoist-inspired rebellion in the south against the

Although these early references to Numinous Cliff Mountain in general, and to Lodging-Beauties Palace in particular, no doubt reflect contemporary interest in this site, and its ongoing importance in the early imperial era, two texts were to be of particular significance in the subsequent portrayal of this site in later literature. The first dates to the Liang dynasty (502–56), and is found in Ren Fang's 任昉 (460–508) *Shuyi ji* 述異記 (Record of strange things): "The Lodging-Beauties [Palace] Pavilion [was built with] bronze gutters and jade pillars. The beams and pillars of the palace were all ornamented with pearls and jade." 館娃閣銅溝玉檻. 宮之楹檻皆珠玉飾之.[14]

This description, penned many centuries after the palace had been destroyed, was to become one of the most famous accounts of its beauties. Virtually all subsequent descriptions of the Lodging-Beauties Palace can be traced back, either in theme or in wording, to the account given in the *Shuyi ji*. This brief description came to represent all the luxuries that could be found in the residence of a pleasure-loving monarch at the end of the Spring and Autumn period.[15] Although many later accounts of the Lodging-Beauties Palace and its surrounding gardens are much longer than the *Shuyi ji* description, and although they might enlarge on the vast sums of money expended on the place and on the decadent lifestyle of the last king of Wu, these accounts add little of fundamental importance to the earlier text. The *Shuyi ji* description, as the dominant account of this site, ensured that Numinous Cliff was understood as the site of an ancient pleasure palace. This would have largely discouraged the acceptance of alternative interpretations sanctioned by earlier texts, for example, that the palace was important as a seat of government during the time of King Fuchai, and a place where crucial decisions affecting the destiny of nations were taken. As a result, in addition to the consistent theme that this was a place given over to sybaritic living and

---

rule of Sima Yuanxian 司馬元顯 (382–402), who acted as regent for the severely disabled Emperor An of the Jin dynasty 晉安帝 (r. 397–419). After a number of naval battles, Sun En was defeated, and he drowned at sea. The appalling violence that marked the Sun En rebellion is discussed in Shek, "Sectarian Eschatology and Violence," pp. 104–5.

14. Ren Fang, *Shuyi ji* A.9a.

15. Wu Qu, *Gusu yeshi*, p. 16.

decadent luxuries, Numinous Cliff is also regularly presented as a feminized site: as the abode of Xi Shi and the other beauties that entertained King Fuchai of Wu and distracted him from his official duties.

The second important text to determine later imperial era representations of Numinous Cliff is the first gazetteer to give a detailed description of the site and its historical significance: the *Wujun tujing xuji*. This account would largely decide what subsequent literati tourists wanted to see, and how they would interpret the site in their own literary works. Given its importance, this entry is worth quoting in full:

> On the mountain peak there are three ponds, one is called Moon Pond, [one] is called Inkstone Pond, and [one] is called Enjoying-the-Flowers Pond. Even in a drought they never dry up, and water mallows grow there that are very beautiful.[16] These ponds were dug during Wu times. There is an ancient tradition that Qin Tower stood on top of the mountain, and there is also Echoing-Step Corridor, which is sometimes called Singing-Step Corridor. They used elm and catalpa [planks] to cover the ground, and when Lady Xi [Shi] walked along it there was a sound, hence the name.[17] Below there is a rocky chamber, which is still extant; and there is a legend that the king of Wu imprisoned Fan Li here. Where the mountain peaks meet, there is the Huo Village. Rocks are quarried here that are used to make inkstones, and the fame of these inkstones is well deserved. I once climbed the slopes of Numinous Cliff Mountain, looked down on Lake Tai, and gazed upon the Dongting islands in that vast expanse of water, and at a glance I could see one thousand *li*. Verdant cliffs and emerald embankments lay like gems between the waves; it really was an exceptionally beautiful vista.
> 山頂有三池, 一曰月池, 曰硯池, 曰玩華池. 雖旱不竭, 其中有水葵甚美, 蓋吳時所鑿也. 山上舊傳有琴臺. 又有響屧廊, 或曰鳴屐廊. 以楩梓藉其地. 西子行則有聲, 故以名云. 下有石室, 今存, 俗傳吳王囚范蠡之地.

16. This line seems to refer to a passage in the *Wudi ji*: "On top of [Numinous Cliff] Mountain there is a pond, and even in a drought it does not dry up. In this pond they grow very beautiful water mallows, and in the summer they eat them, to get rid of the heat, in the Wu region this is considered an excellent plant." 山上有池, 旱亦不涸. 中有蒓甚美, 夏食之, 則去熱, 吳中以爲佳品. Lu Guangwei, *Wudi ji*, p. 67.

17. The identification of *pian* 楩 as elm (*ulmus macrocarpa*) is derived from Gao Mingqian et al. eds., *Zhiwu gu Hanming tukao*, p. 383.

山相連屬, 有(山+隻)村. 其山出石, 可以爲硯, 蓋硯石之名不虛也. 嘗登靈岩之巔, 俯具區, 瞰洞庭, 烟濤浩渺, 一目千里. 而碧岩翠塢點綴於滄波之間, 誠絶景也.[18]

From the time of the Northern Song dynasty when the *Wujun tujing xuji* was written, there was a significant divergence in the two main traditions for interpreting the role played by Numinous Cliff Mountain during the kingdom of Wu. According to the minor tradition, this mountain was the site of the king of Wu's summer palace, and hence a seat of government. The major tradition describes Numinous Cliff as the site of a pleasure palace where the last king of Wu diverted himself in the company of his favorite Xi Shi, one of the most famous beauties of ancient China. This romantic tradition would always significantly outweigh the popularity of the other, and the vast majority of imperial era references to Numinous Cliff describe it as King Fuchai's pleasure dome. This may of course represent a significant distortion of the actual contemporary role of this site in the history of the kingdom of Wu.

The problem for all imperial-era visitors to Numinous Cliff, who were hoping to capture some sense of the romance of the last years of the kingdom of Wu, was that there was nothing there to see. Unlike other sites such as Tiger Hill, where there was a well-defined area traditionally said to be the tomb of King Helü, tourists to Numinous Cliff had no focus for their interest. Given that every vestige of the Lodging-Beauties Palace had vanished at the time of the conquest of Wu by the kingdom of Yue, early descriptions of the palace and its surroundings became correspondingly more important. The significance of these two descriptions of the Numinous Cliff—that of the *Shuyi ji* focusing on the lost splendors of the Lodging-Beauties Palace, and that of the *Wujun tujing xuji* discussing the sights to be seen by contemporary visitors—can be seen from their influence on numerous later works of literature. To quote merely one example, in the *Xin lieguo zhi* 新列國志 (New history of the kingdoms and states [of the Eastern Zhou]), Feng Menglong 馮夢龍 (1574–1645) drew on both of these accounts when creating his description of the summer palace of King Fuchai of Wu and its environs:

---

18. Zhu Changwen, *Wujun tujing xuji*, p. 43.

It is said that when [King] Fuchai favored Xi Shi, he ordered Wangsun Xiong to build the Lodging-Beauties Palace especially [for her] on top of Numinous Cliff.[19] It had bronze gutters and jade pillars, and was ornamented with pearls and jade; it was a place where his concubine could relax and enjoy herself . . . .Gao Qi's "Guanwa Gong shi" (Poem on the Lodging-Beauties Palace) reads:

At the Lodging-Beauties Palace there is a Lodging-Beauties Pavilion,
Its painted beams pierce the heavens and cleave the mountains.
How bitter that it was not high enough then,
That they could look into the distance and see the arrival of the Yue troops!

On top of this mountain there is Enjoying-the-Flowers Pond, and Enjoying-the-Moon Pond. There is also a well, which they call the King of Wu's Well; the well water is pure and blue; Xi Shi sometimes used the reflections in the water [as a mirror] when she was putting on her makeup. Fuchai stood by her side and personally arranged her hair. Yang Bei wrote a poem that reads:

Stones and bricks lie abandoned beside the ancient tower,
Cold shadows on these limpid waters form a shining mirror.
Whose face was here reflected as she rearranged her golden hairpins?
See her rouge carried along the Yue river![20]

There is also a cave called the Xi Shi Cave, Fuchai and Xi Shi sat together here.[21] Outside the cave there is a stone with a small depression in it, this is now popularly known as Xi Shi's footprint. Gao Qi wrote a poem that reads:

The moss grows thickly beside the spring pool in the ruined palace,
I will never see her silk skirt come sweeping across the ground.
And yet maybe Xi Shi has become a fairy,
Living in her own palace inside this cave.

---

19. Wangsun Xiong (also known as Wangsun Luo 王孫駱/雒 or Gongsun Xiong 公孫雄) was an important figure at King Fuchai of Wu's court mentioned in a number of ancient texts. *Guoyu*, p. 606 ("Wuyu"); *Shiji* 41.1744; *Yuejue shu*, p. 39 ("Qingdi"). For some reason Feng Menglong favored the version of the name given in the *Lüshi chunqiu*, p. 97 ("Dangran" 當染). The association of Wangsun Xiong with the building of the Guanwa Gong seems to be unique to the *Xin lieguo zhi*.

20. This would seem to be a feminization of the Yuelaixi 越來溪 (literally Yue access river), that is, the route taken by the army as they launched their attack on Wu. Zhengxie ed., *Shihu shang Fangshan*, pp. 21–22.

21. Xi Shi's cave is first mentioned as one of the sights at Numinous Cliff in the Southern Song dynasty. Fan Chengda, *Wujun zhi*, p. 105.

[King Fuchai] also once played the *qin* with Xi Shi at the mountain's peak, now there is a Qin Tower [here]. Zhang Yu (1333–85) wrote a poem that reads:

Divining the future,
This beauty was predestined to enter the kingdom of Wu.
Today on this mountain beneath the moon,
All I hear is the cawing of the crows at night.

且說夫差寵幸西施, 令王孫雄特建館娃宮於靈巖之山. 銅溝玉檻, 飾以珠玉, 爲美人遊息之所 . . . 高啓"館娃宮詩"云:

館娃宮中館娃閣, 畫棟侵雲峰頂開.
猶恨當時高未極, 不能望見越兵來.

山上有翫花池, 翫月池. 又有井名吳王井. 井泉清碧, 西施或照泉而妝. 夫差立於旁, 親爲理髮. 楊備有詩云:

石甃遺縱旁古臺, 一泓寒影鑒光開.
何人照面金釵落? 曾見越溪紅粉來.

又有洞名西施洞, 夫差與西施同坐於此. 洞外石有小陷, 今俗名西施跡. 高啓有詩云:

廢宮春水長蒼苔, 不見羅裙拂地來.

只恐西施是仙子, 洞中別自有樓臺.
又嘗與西施鳴琴於山巔, 今有琴臺. 張羽詩云:

坐鼓朱晬日, 玉人方入吳.
於今山月下, 惟聽夜啼烏.[22]

Given the destruction of the Lodging-Beauties Palace in antiquity, the site could only be visited in the literary imaginings of poets and writers. Regardless of this fact, and in spite of the paucity of reliable information about the original appearance of the palace, imperial-era writers continued to be inspired by its legendary beauties, and many visitors travelled to see this famous site. Though certain parts of this site, such as the Echoing-Step Corridor, were not described in the records until at least a thousand years after the fall of the kingdom of Wu and the destruction of the Lodging-Beauties Palace, these accounts inspired countless works of literature. However, the lack of any connection with reality often gives these poems and essays a lurid and exaggerated quality, and this is coupled with a tendency to

22. Feng Menglong, *Xin lieguo zhi*, pp. 986–87.

substitute name-dropping for any genuine reflections on the appearance of the place and its historical significance, something that is not found in the works of literature written about other famous Wu historical sites.[23] A good example of this is the poem "Xiangxie Lang" 響屧廊 (Echoing-step corridor) by the local Yuan dynasty poet, Gu Ying 顧英 (1310–69):

Day after day, deep in the palace, [Fuchai] does not awaken from his drunken stupor,
The beautiful [Xi Shi] steps gracefully as though walking amid flowers.
After giving [the sword] Zhulou to his loyal minister [Wu Zixu],
The fall of a leaf startles the king from his dreams.
日日深宮醉不醒, 美人嬌步蹋花行.
屬鏤賜與忠臣後, 葉落君王夢亦驚.[24]

Though in many literary works about Numinous Cliff, the ultimate fate of King Fuchai and his court hangs over the images of pleasure and debauchery like the sword of Damocles, very few imperial-era writers would actually confront the issue of how to portray the tragic end of the kingdom of Wu. It seems that the intrusion of images of carnage and bloodshed into a place so strongly associated with luxurious living was a juxtaposition too daring or disturbing for most imperial-era writers. As a result, very few literati make explicit reference in their work to the death and destruction that accompanied the fall of the kingdom of Wu. One of the exceptions was the Tang dynasty poet Pi Rixiu 皮日休 (c. 834–83, *jinshi* 867), in his work entitled "Yong Guanwa gong 咏館娃宮" (Commemorating the Lodging-beauties palace), which imagines this site overrun by the forces of King Goujian of Yue:

In the middle of the night, the [Lodging] Beauties Palace becomes a battlefield,

23. A rare example of a successful fusion of present experience with the glamorous and romantic past is found in the essay "Lingyan huaijiu ji" 靈巖懷舊記 (A record of cherishing the past at Numinous Cliff) by the local poet Tang Chuanying 湯傳楹 (1620–44), which describes leaving the temple precincts at dusk and hearing the sound of the sand of the mountain path being crunched by clogs (which is likened to the clinking of the jewellery of a beautiful woman as she hurries in pursuit). 昏黄出寺門, 從山前大徑下. 屐齒與沙相嚙, 珊珊自鳴, 疑美人環佩釧釵聲追於後也. Quoted in Wang Xiqi ed., *Xiaofanghu zhaiyu dicong chaoxuan*, p. 922.

24. Quoted in Su Wenlian, *Suzhou shici*, p. 179.

The stench of blood still mingles with the incense lit for a banquet.
Xi Shi has no time to relight the broken lamps,
Yet she cries a few tears for her husband, the king.
半夜娃宫作戰場, 血腥猶雜宴時香.
西施不及燒殘燭, 猶爲君王泣數行.[25]

Numinous Cliff Temple

As with Tiger Hill, Numinous Cliff Mountain was in private ownership during the Age of Disunion, prior to becoming a religious foundation. The presence of a Buddhist temple at this site must in large degree be responsible for its preservation as a green space to the present day. At the end of the Eastern Jin dynasty, when Numinous Cliff Mountain was owned by one of the most senior ministers of the day, the Defender-in-Chief Lu Wan 陸玩 (278–342), he determined to give the site to the Buddhist Church.[26] The temple that still crowns this hill was founded at the beginning of the Liang dynasty in the Tianjian reign-period (502–19), on the site of Lu Wan's former home. Since then, the temple at Numinous Cliff Mountain has undergone a number of name changes. Originally the temple was known as Xiufengsi 秀峰寺 (Flowering peak temple), then at some point in the Tang dynasty it was renamed Lingyansi 靈巖寺 (Numinous Cliff temple). It was known by two names in the Southern Song dynasty: Han Qi Wang Gongdesi 韓蘄王功德寺 (Han, King of Qi's successful virtue temple) and Xianqin chongbao chanyuan 顯親崇報禪院 (Glorifying the family and worshipping reciprocity Chan monastery).[27] Since the end of the Southern Song dynasty, the temple has been known by the name it holds today: Lingyanshansi 靈巖山寺 (Numinous Cliff Mountain temple). The temple remains a very important southern Chinese Buddhist foundation, and its architecture is of considerable interest. The temple's pagoda, known variously as Lingyanta 靈巖塔 (Numinous Cliff pagoda) or Baota 寶塔 (Treasure pagoda) was built in the seventeenth year of the Shaoxing reign-period in the Southern Song (1147), and is a significant surviving example of Southern Song Buddhist architecture in the region.

---

25. Quoted in Wang Suijin, *Wu Yue wenhua shihua*, p. 30.
26. Lu Guangwei, *Wudi ji*, p. 67.
27. Fan Chengda, *Wujun zhi*, p. 488.

This is supposedly not the first pagoda built here, since according to the Qing dynasty gazetteer, the *Wumen biaoyin*, the Zhuanta 磚塔 (Brick pagoda) had earlier stood to the west of Qin Tower. (The relative location of this earlier pagoda and the present structure is not clear.) This older pagoda was built by order of Sun Chengyou 孫承祐 in 977, in memory of his older sister who had married into the Qian 錢 ruling house of the Wu-Yue kingdom.[28]

The changes of name for the temple at Numinous Cliff Mountain would seem to be of great importance. There are no surviving accounts recording the exact nature of the worship that took place at the temple when it was known as Flowering Peak Temple, but some of the later changes in the name of this temple certainly reflected changes in the dedication of the worship. The site has been dedicated to Buddhist worship for most of its history, with the exception of a brief hiatus during much of the Southern Song. At this time the temple was temporarily dedicated to the memory of one of the greatest military heroes of the day, Han Shizhong 韓世忠 (1089–1151).[29] It would seem that the temple complex was known by two names during the Southern Song, both of which commemorate this change of worship. One name made obvious the new dedication of the temple, for it was known as Han, King of Qi's Successful Virtue Temple. This name recorded Han Shizhong's posthumous title, granted in 1168 by the Emperor Xiaozong. However, this seems to have been a short-lived name change. For most of the Southern Song dynasty, and indeed, according to one account, from the middle of the Shaoxing reign period onwards, the name of the temple was said to have been Glorifying the Family and Worshipping Reciprocity Chan Monastery.[30] Although this name suggests a discontinuation of worship of Han Shizhong and a return to the original dedication of the temple, it seems that in fact the

---

28. Gu Zhentao, *Wumen biaoyin*, p. 152.

29. Deng Guangming, *Han Shizhong nianpu*.

30. The statement that this second Southern Song dynasty name for the foundation at Numinous Cliff Mountain had already been developed in the Shaoxing reign-era is made in an essay by Sun Di 孫覿 entitled "Zhiji Pusa dian ji" 智積菩薩殿記 (A Record of the Zhiji Bodhisattva Hall), quoted in Fan Chengda, *Wujun zhi*, p. 489.

name represents a phase in which Buddhist worship was combined with an ongoing commemoration of Han Shizhong. It was only at the end of the Southern Song dynasty that worship of this important historical figure ceased at Numinous Cliff.

It is interesting that a Buddhist foundation that had presumably been doing reasonably well in attracting worshippers and donors chose to change dedication to the worship of a recently deceased individual. It is likely that the temple's finances were in a good state at the beginning of the Southern Song dynasty, given that just a few years before the change of dedication, they could afford the construction of the magnificent pagoda that still dominates the site. It is therefore unlikely that the temple was in a particularly parlous state, or that it needed to change the dedication in the hope of attracting new patrons. However, the authorities in charge may have felt that a temple dedicated to the great patriot and general, Han Shizhong, who was in fact buried at the foot of Numinous Cliff Mountain, would be a greater draw for pilgrims than the original dedication of the site. The importance of Han Shizhong to the establishment of the Southern Song dynasty made it entirely appropriate that the ancient temple that stood near the site of his tomb should be rededicated to his memory. However, the temple at Numinous Cliff Mountain only retained this dedication for a short space of time before it reverted to Buddhist worship. No reasons for this change have been recorded, but it would seem likely that it coincided with the gradual eclipse of Han Shizhong's reputation by that of Yue Fei 岳飛 (1103–42).

The *Wujun zhi* provides an interesting encapsulation of the different aspects of Numinous Cliff Mountain in the Southern Song dynasty. The site is mentioned under a number of different categories, including "Ancient Remains," "Mountains," and "Temples." In the chapter entitled "Ancient Remains," four sites on Numinous Cliff Mountain are mentioned as vestiges of the Lodging-Beauties Palace: the Qin Tower, Xi Shi's Cave, Inkstone Pond, and Enjoying-the-Flowers Pond. Following this, there are entries for the King of Wu's Well, Echoing-Step Corridor, and Paulownia Garden. In the chapter entitled "Mountains," Fan Chengda quotes extensively from a text named the *Wudi ji* 吳地記 (Record of the lands of Wu), attributed to a man named either Dong Jian 董監 (as here) or Dong Lan 董覽 (as he is named in a variety of later gazetteers).[31] This early account of the historical geography of the Suzhou region has unfortunately not survived, but quotations such as this in the *Wujun zhi* ensured it would have an ongoing impact on literary representations of Numinous Cliff Mountain:

> The [*Wudi ji*] also says: "There is a stone citadel at Inkstone Mountain that stands ten *li* from Gusu Mountain, and Helü (clearly a mistake for Fuchai) kept beautiful women from Yue here. On top [of the mountain] there are two pools, and the water mallows grown in these pools are used as tribute. This is now [known as] Numinous Cliff Mountain." The above was all recorded by Dong Jian. The *Wu Yue chunqiu* and the *Wudi ji*, and many other books all say: "There is a mountain west of Helü's city which is called Inkstone Mountain. It is three hundred and sixty *zhang* tall, and is shrouded in mist for three *li*. It stands thirty or forty *li* from Wu county, and on top there is Wu's Lodging-Beauties Palace, Qin Tower, and Echoing-Step Corridor. This mountaintop has Xi Shi's Cave, the Inkstone Pond, and the Enjoying the Moon Pond. Water-mallows grow in the ponds on the mountaintop; in the summer they can expel the heat, and in the autumn they expel cold. Every year [this plant] is sent as tribute to the palace from Wu, after it has been dried. These pools never dry up even in times of drought, but the water mallows cannot now be picked. Below Qin Tower there is a great reclining pine tree whose trunk lies flat on the ground, and [its] two great branches soar upwards intertwining to form a canopy-like cover; the people of Wu think it is an auspicious omen. In successive years it was struck by lightning, and so one branch has died. Looking down from the mountain you can see Lake Tai and the two Dongting islands, like lush emerald and jade flecks set in an ocean of silver; it really is the most beautiful vista in the world."
> [《吳地記》]又云: "硯石山有石城, 去姑蘇山十里. 闔閭養越美人於此. 上有兩湖, 湖中有蒓充貢. 按此即今靈岩山." 以上皆董監所記. 今按《吳越春秋》《吳地記》等書云: "闔閭城西有山, 號硯石山, 高三百六十丈, 去入烟三里. 在吳縣西三十里. 上有吳館娃宮, 琴臺, 響屧廊. 山上有西施洞, 硯池, 玩月池. 山頂之池有葵蒓, 夏能去熱, 秋則去寒. 吳中每年暴乾供進. 其池至旱不竭, 葵蒓今不復采. 琴臺下有大偃松, 身卧於地, 兩頭

31. Li Fang et al., *Taiping yulan* 56.387; Peng Dayi, *Shantang sikao* 29.2b.

崛起, 交蔭如蓋, 不見根之所自出. 吳人以爲奇賞. 比年雷震, 一枝已瘁. 山下平瞰太湖及洞庭兩山, 滴翠叢碧在白銀世界中. 亦宇内絶景."[32]

The constant references to the availability of water—particularly, in this case, to a pond that never dries up, and to the types of plants grown on the mountain—may seem peculiar to modern readers, but this reflects a longstanding trend in gazetteer writing that would become superseded in the course of the Southern Song dynasty by a more "people-centered" approach, as the focus shifted from the facts of physical geography to a concentration on famous local historical personages, and to the reaction of visitors to these celebrated figures.[33] For some reason, gazetteer descriptions of Numinous Cliff Mountain seem to have been exceptionally conservative, preserving references to the flora of this site long after such a style of description had become unfashionable, and indeed long after water mallow was no longer grown in these ponds. It may perhaps be a reflection of the extent to which descriptions of Numinous Cliff relied on fiction: where so many of the famous sites on the mountain were imaginary, it became tempting to dwell on an aspect of the place that was entirely genuine.

As with Tiger Hill, there is a long tradition of literature that contrasts the past history of Numinous Cliff with its subsequent role as a major Buddhist center. In the case of Numinous Cliff, the juxtaposition of the two images—the past when the exquisitely luxurious palace here was the scene of the famous romance between King Fuchai and Xi Shi, and the present where monks who had forsaken the world flocked here—provided a strong sense of the passage of time and the change in destiny. For many writers, the poignant contrast offered by the peaceful temple and monastery with the bloodstained romance that took place here in antiquity was an important source of

---

32. Fan Chengda, *Wujun zhi*, pp. 208–209. When this passage is quoted in the official history of Qianlong's southern tours, the *Nanxun shengdian* 南巡盛典 (The magnificent record of the southern progresses), the word silver (*baiyin* 白銀) is replaced with glass (*boli* 玻璃). Gao Jin et al., *Nanxun shengdian*, p. 1875. The glamorous image evoked here is clearly derived from the earlier description found in the *Wujun tujing xuji*, translated above.

33. Hargett, "Song Dynasty Local Gazetteers," p. 428.

inspiration for their works. This theme can be found in the poem by Su Shunqin 蘇舜欽 (1008–49), a resident of Suzhou during the last years of his life, entitled "You Lingyan" 遊靈巖 (Travelling to Numinous Cliff):

From ancient times, the rise and fall [of kingdoms] saddens us
The white-haired monk turns back to shut the temple gate.
The Yue minister [Fan Li, vanished into] mist and waves; the wild goose leaves in vain,
In the palace and belvederes of the king of Wu the monkeys half-cry.
The spring breeze seems as of old, and the flowers seem to smile,
Past affairs leave many vestiges, but stones cannot speak.
Only [Master Ji of] Yanling ran away,
An old man [living among] clear winds and high bamboos.
古來興廢亦愁人, 白髪僧歸掩寺門.
越相煙波空去雁, 吳王宮闕半啼猿.
春風似舊花猶笑, 往事多遺石不言.
唯有延陵逃遁去, 清風高節老乾坤.[34]

One of the famous sights at Numinous Cliff Mountain, recorded in numerous imperial era texts, was the Wuwang jing 吳王井 (King of Wu's well). Confusingly, since at least the time of the Ming dynasty there have been two wells at Numinous Cliff, one circular and one octagonal, both of which are now known as the King of Wu's Well.[35] According to the 1947 gazette, the *Suzhou Lingyanshan zhi* 蘇州靈燕山志 (Gazette for numinous cliff mountain at Suzhou) only the round well, also known as the Richi 日池 (Sun pond) should correctly be known as the King of Wu's Well. The octagonal well, also known as the Yuechi 月池 (Moon pond), is more properly known as the Zhiji Jing 智積井 (Zhiji [Bodhisattva] well).[36] However, the as-

34. Quoted in Niu Ruolin, *Wuxian zhi* 3.5a. This poem is also quoted in Qian Zhonglian, *Suzhou mingsheng shici xuan*, p. 81, under the title "You Lingyan si" 游靈巖寺 (Travelling to Numinous Cliff temple).

35. The earliest reference to this pair of wells seems to be in Wang Ao's *Gusu zhi*, vol. 3, p. 119. This pair of wells is also described in Yuan Hongdao's essay: "Lingyan ji." Yang Xunji et al. eds., *Wuzhong xiaozhi congkan*, p. 288.

36. Zhang Yiliu, *Suzhou Lingyanshan zhi*, pp. 8–9. The temple at Numinous Cliff Mountain has a particularly strong link with the Zhiji Bodhisattva since he is said to have arrived from the West at the end of the Eastern Jin dynasty and founded this monastery outside Suzhou. Subsequently it was said to have housed an impor-

sociation of both wells with the sybaritic last king of Wu is recorded in the "Wuwang jing shi" 吳王井詩 (Poem on the king of Wu's well) by Zhang Xizuo 張錫祚 (1672–1724), which again implicitly contrasts the turbulent events of the reign of King Fuchai, many of which were enacted at Numinous Cliff, with the current peace of the Buddhist monastery:

> The bones of the king of Wu have already turned to dust,
> His traces remain at the two wells.
> The waters are deep and still,
> For years they have been exceptionally pure.
> The mountain monk looks down at the old brick wall around the well,
> Suddenly his lone reflection appears clearly.
> 吳王骨已枯, 遺蹟存雙井.
> 水空無波瀾, 歲久逾清冷.
> 山僧臨古甃, 倏然淨孤影.[37]

This poem juxtaposes the tumultuous figure of King Fuchai of Wu, whose foolish decisions ruined his country and brought about his own death, with the quiet contemporary individual, the mountain monk. Both occupy the same physical space, yet time and character ensure that their experiences are completely different. The most important of the Yuan-Ming transition-era poets from Suzhou, Gao Qi, also wrote poems on the subject of the King of Wu's Well. For example, in his poem entitled "Wuwang Jing" he described the way that a water feature once used by a decadent monarch in his pleasure palace later on became devoted to holy purposes. Here a feminine, bustling, and decadent past is contrasted with a masculine, quiet, religious, and restrained present:

> Once like a mirror it reflected palace beauties,
> Their jade hands pulling the ropes [wet] with dew.
> Today the mountain is deserted, and a man draws water,

---

tant relic of the bodhisattva: a footprint. Fan Chengda, *Wujun zhi*, p. 488. Other Song dynasty accounts mention the annual festival held for the bodhisattva that involved eating *zongzi*, a celebration particularly dear to old women from the Suzhou region. Gong Mingzhi, *Zhongwu jiwen*, p. 32.

37. Quoted in Zhang Yiliu, *Suzhou Lingyanshan zhi*, p. 9. The author of this poem, Zhang Xizuo, is buried at the foot of Numinous Cliff Mountain. Zhou Hongdu, *Lingyanshan*, pp. 96–98.

One cold jarful for the flowers offered before the Buddha.
曾開鑑影照宮娃, 玉手牽絲帶露華.
今日空山人自汲, 一瓶寒供佛前花.[38]

Numinous Cliff in Ming and Qing Gazetteers

The most significant Ming dynasty gazetteer for Suzhou and the surrounding region was the *Gusu zhi* produced under the auspices of Wang Ao, one of the greatest scholar-officials ever produced by the region, and native of the island of Dongshan 東山 in the middle of Lake Tai. The very title indicates that it was written with a specific purpose in mind, for Gusu is the oldest known name for this region of China, and probably predates the founding of the city of Suzhou itself, conventionally dated to 514 BCE. By using this ancient name, it is clear that Wang Ao intended to focus on one specific aspect of the city's history: its glorious past as the capital of the independent kingdom of Wu. One of Wang Ao's aims in sponsoring the *Gusu zhi* was to assert the importance of Wu culture for the city of Suzhou in particular, and also for China as a whole. This approach ran directly counter to the attitudes prevailing during the Ming dynasty, during which (when ancient regional cultures were discussed at all) commentators tended to denigrate Wu and Yue for failing to make a lasting contribution to mainstream traditional Chinese civilization. Whereas the kingdom of Chu had provided the "Lisao" 離騷 (Encountering sorrow), and other major literary works preserved in the *Chuci*, contemporary Ming scholarship tended to regard the ancient kingdoms of Jiangnan as inferior, since they were thought to have left no significant cultural legacy.[39]

Work began on the *Gusu zhi* in around 1504, when the Prefect of Suzhou, Lin Shiyuan 林世遠, approached Wang Ao with the sugges-

---

38. Xu Song and Zhang Dachun, *Baicheng yanshui*, p. 95. An alternative translation of this poem is given in Chaves, *The Columbia Book of Later Chinese Poetry*, p. 126.

39. This attitude is strongly expressed in the introduction to the *Wu Yue shi* 吳越史 (History of Wu and Yue), a compilation of ancient texts produced at the end of the Ming dynasty by He Yunzhong 何允中 (*jinshi* 1622). He Yunzhong, "Wu-Yue shi xu," 1a.

tion that he should write a new gazetteer for Suzhou. It is not clear how much work was done by Wang Ao personally, particularly given his return to official duties as the Grand Councilor in Beijing in 1506, while the gazetteer was being produced. Wu Kuan 吳寬 (1435–1504, *jinshi* 1472) in the months before his death presided over the first draft of this work, and his name appears as the chief editor, though this may have been an affectionate gesture honoring a great scholar and close personal friend. The actual writing of the *Gusu zhi* was apparently entrusted to a number of Wang Ao's clients, including Du Qi 杜啓 (*jinshi* 1474), Pu Yingxiang 浦應祥, Zhu Yunming 祝允明 (1460–1526), Cai Yu 蔡羽 (*gongsheng* 1522), Wen Zhengming, Zhu Cunli 朱存理 (1444–1513), and the local scholar Xing Can 邢参. However, there can be no doubt that the directing intelligence behind the *Gusu zhi* was that of Wang Ao himself. His influence can clearly be seen throughout the book, in particular his determination to document the cultural legacy of Wu, and ascribe ancient roots to contemporary monuments and vistas. For example, in the introduction to the section on ancient remains, the ongoing importance of Wu culture to the people of Suzhou was stressed:

> Throughout history we have moved through the cycle of waxing and waning. Every single thing that we have been left by our ancestors is treasured by people today. Even if nothing is left but the ruins of an ancient city, it is often the case that when going past we hesitate and cannot bear to leave. Surely this is because the rise and fall [of this kingdom] is so moving. There are many ancient remains in Wu, from the time of Taibo to the present day. These have been carefully recorded in texts, for the edification of researchers in the future.
>
> 古今之在天地之間猶旦暮也. 而古人所遺, 每爲今人重. 雖故城坵隴, 往往 過之爲躊躇而不忍去. 豈非以其興廢存亡之足感邪. 吳自太伯迄今其間古 跡多矣. 悉記于篇以備後之考者.[40]

The *Gusu zhi* is an interesting phenomenon, in that, although it fits the standard format of a Ming dynasty gazetteer, in content it is much closer to a private gazetteer. This is hardly surprising, since in the preface Wang Ao lists the earlier works that had inspired his own:

40. Wang Ao et al., *Gusu zhi*, vol. 3, p. 95.

the *Yuejue shu* by Yuan Kang and Wu Ping and the *Wu Yue chunqiu* by Zhao Ye from the Han dynasty, the *Wudi ji* by Lu Guangwei from the Tang dynasty, the *Wujun tujing xuji* by Zhu Changwen, the *Zhongwu jiwen* by Gong Mingzhi, and the *Wujun zhi* by Fan Chengda from the Song dynasty, and the *Suzhou fu zhi* 蘇州府志 (Gazetteer of Suzhou Prefecture) by Lu Xiong 盧熊 (1331–80) from the Ming dynasty. Of these, only the last is an official gazetteer. The *Gusu zhi* is a landmark in research into the history of the city of Suzhou. Through its careful appraisal of both private and official gazetteers, it functioned as an important addition to the many major local histories produced about the city and surrounding region since the Eastern Han dynasty. The city of Suzhou has an exceptionally well-recorded historical geography, and a wealth of writings survive about the culture, customs, and intellectual heritage of the region. Wang Ao's gazetteer revived interest in the history and cultural legacy of the city at a time when this was under threat from the predominance of commercial interests.[41] The *Gusu zhi*, which is well-researched and generally free from the extravagant claims found in Wang Ao's other writings on the historical geography of the region, would stand as the finest Ming gazetteer about Suzhou.[42]

Numinous Cliff is mentioned several times in different chapters of the *Gusu zhi*. In the chapter entitled "Mountains," the description of Numinous Cliff places this site firmly in an antiquarian context.

---

41. Suzhou was the site of the most significant Confucian academy in China, which produced four hundred and eighty-six *jinshi* between the Song dynasty and the Qing, of whom more than twenty were Zhuangyuan 壯元 or first-place graduates. This total far outweighs the success of any other academy, and would ensure that Suzhou was enormously influential in the direction and trends of traditional Chinese education and scholarship. Shi Jianhua et al., *Suzhou gucheng de baohu yu gengxin*, p. 19. The Confucian academy was merely the apex of the local educational system; during the Ming and Qing dynasties, the six counties of the greater Suzhou region produced more than four thousand *juren*, more than one thousand five hundred *jinshi* (an estimated one-sixth of China's examination successes during this period are thought to have come from this area). Jiang Hui, *Jinfen renjian*, p. 48.

42. Wang Ao made some extremely extravagant assertions, which were aimed at demonstrating the importance of the legacy of the ancient kingdom of Wu for contemporary Suzhou, and claimed the survival of many sites from that time (based on the most tenuous evidence, or sometimes on no evidence at all). Milburn, "Image, Identity, and Cherishing Antiquity."

Although the religious significance of the monastery at Numinous Cliff is not ignored, the emphasis is consistently placed upon the romantic association of the site with King Fuchai of Wu and Xi Shi:

> Numinous Cliff Mountain stands south of Tianping Mountain. It has the alternative name of Stone Drum Mountain . . . .There is also the Stone Horse, which from a distance looks like a man riding a horse. The Lodging-Beauties Palace was located here. Xi Shi's Cave, the Echoing-Step Corridor, Perfume Stream, and the King of Wu's Well are all remains from this [palace].[43] For more details see the chapter "Ancient Remains." On top of the mountain there was the Qin Tower, and the carved characters [of this name] are still extant. There is also the Inkstone Pond, and the Enjoying-the-Flowers Pond. On the crest of the mountain there is the Stone Pond, and there is a tradition that water mallows grew there, though they are not to be seen now. Numinous Cliff Temple is located here. Recently it was destroyed by fire, and only one pagoda survives.
> 靈巖山在天平山之南. 一名石鼓山 . . . 又有石馬, 望如人騎. 館娃宮在焉, 西施洞, 響屧廊, 香水溪, 吳王井, 皆其跡也. 其詳互見"古跡." 山巔有琴臺, 刻字猶存. 又有硯池, 翫花池. 山頂有石池. 相傳生葵蒓, 今不復見. 靈巖寺在焉. 今燬, 惟一塔存耳[44]

The description given in the *Gusu zhi* of Numinous Cliff Mountain differs little from those written in earlier centuries, except in the burgeoning interest in the strangely shaped rocks found here, an aspect of the site that would be explored in much greater detail in Qing dynasty gazetteers, most notably the *Baicheng yanshui*. This description

---

43. According to Wang Ao et al., *Gusu zhi*, vol. 3, p. 121, the Perfume Stream was the place inside the ancient palace complex where Xi Shi bathed. The existence of this place seems to have escaped many scholars, but it appears that the earliest reference to this place was in Ren Fang's *Shuyi ji*. This line is not found in the transmitted edition of the text, but is quoted in a number of imperial era texts, such as the work of the Qing dynasty scholar Chen Houyao, *Chunqiu Zhanguo yici* 52.47a. In some later texts, this water-feature is confused with the Jianjing 箭涇 (Arrow canal), also known as the Caixiang jing 採香涇 (Picking scents canal) which was supposedly built by King Fuchai of Wu to connect his pleasure palace at Numinous Cliff with the waters of Lake Tai. This mistake can be seen in the 1687 comprehensive gazetteer for the region, the *Jiangnan tongzhi* 12.17b.

44. Wang Ao et al., *Gusu zhi*, vol. 1, pp. 678–79. This disastrous fire is elsewhere dated to the reign of the Hongzhi Emperor, in other words to just prior to the writing of this gazetteer. Ibid., vol. 2, p. 700.

of Numinous Cliff modestly does not mention a contribution made by Wang Ao himself, when he provided the calligraphy for an inscription at Qin Tower: *Wuzhong shengji* 吳中勝蹟 (A scenic ancient ruin of Wu).[45] As befits someone with such a strong interest in the ancient history of the kingdom of Wu, who visited many sites associated with its kings, Wang Ao is known to have written several poems on the subject of Numinous Cliff, including the "Lingyan huaigu" 靈巖懷古 (Cherishing antiquity at Numinous Cliff):

> Where is Fuchai's hegemony now?
> Deer walk alongside the Fragrant River and Qin Tower.
> The green mountains on the horizon encircle this ancient kingdom,
> In the deepest night the bright moon catches on an overgrown hill.
> The sound of waves has not washed away the hero's regrets,
> The colors of the grass still preserve the beauty's shame.
> Do not feel too melancholy about the Wu palace,
> From antiquity to the present day such [destruction] has been
> commonplace.
> 夫差霸業今何在? 香徑琴臺鹿自游.
> 天際青山還故國, 夜深明月有荒丘.
> 濤聲不盡英雄恨, 草色猶含粉黛羞.
> 莫爲吳宮多悵望, 今來古往總悠悠.[46]

The *Gusu zhi* also mentions Numinous Cliff in the chapter on temples. This account is interesting for it is the first surviving record to describe a strong association between the Tang dynasty Chancellor Lu Xiangxian 陸象先 (665–736) and the religious foundation at Numinous Cliff.[47] The link between this individual and Numinous Cliff was subsequently described in much more detail in the *Baicheng yanshui* account, which is translated below. According to the *Gusu zhi*, by this point in the Ming dynasty Lu Xiangxian had come to dominate discourse about the development of Numinous Cliff Temple, and many individual buildings around the mountain were seen as spe-

---

45. Zhang Yiliu, *Suzhou Lingyanshan zhi*, p. 2.

46. Quoted in Niu Ruolin, *Wuxian zhi* 3.8a. This poem was also later included in the revised version of the *Wudu wencui* by Qian Gu 錢穀 (1508–72), entitled *Wudu wencui xuji* 吳都文粹續集 (A Supplement to the literary classics from the Wu capital). Qian Gu, *Wudu wencui xuji* 19.35b–36a.

47. Wang Ao et al., *Gusu zhi*, vol. 2, p. 700.

cifically linked to him. This left no room for other important patrons to be mentioned, such as Lu Wan, who gave the land to the Buddhist church in the first place, or Han Shizhong, who was a significant donor to the temple during his lifetime and was buried at the foot of the mountain after his death.

After the *Gusu zhi*, one of the single most significant descriptions of the sights to be seen at Numinous Cliff Mountain is found in the Qing dynasty gazetteer, the *Baicheng yanshui*. Much of this account draws upon earlier gazetteers, but some of the information given is unique. This is particularly true of the description of the rocks found on this mountain, an aspect of the site that really does not seem to have interested earlier gazetteer writers or literati visitors. It is extremely striking that this account makes virtually no reference to the historical significance of Numinous Cliff Mountain, though the omission of any extensive discussion of the association of this place with Fuchai and Xi Shi within the prose text is to a certain extent rectified in the selection of poetry given subsequently. As with the previous extracts from this book, the authors' marginal comments will be given in a smaller font:

> Numinous Cliff Mountain stands thirty *li* west of the city [of Suzhou], and the remains of the Lodging-Beauties Palace are located here. The highest point [on the mountain] is named Qin Tower. There are two wells on the mountain, the round one represents Heaven; the octagonal one represents Earth. There is a stone chamber, which is traditionally said to be Xi Shi's Cave. There are four ponds, Bathing-the-Flowers, Heaven, Washing Inkstones, Bathing-the-Moon. There are eighteen strange rocks, two Stone Drums, Stone Quiver, Drunken-Monk Rock, Stone Lizard, Longevity Star (Canopus) Rock, two stone towers [named] "Wrapped in Cloud" and "Gazing at the Moon" at Buddha Cliff, Stone Belvedere, Buddhist Robe Rock, Stone Chignon, Stone City, Numinous Fungus Rock, Stone Horse, Carp Rock, Offering-Flowers Rock, Sutra Library Stone Screen, Kitten Rock. Of these only Numinous Fungus Rock is of the most superior kind, and hence the name of Numinous Cliff. On the western side they quarry inkstones, now [known as] Huo Village Rock, and so one alternative name [for this place] is Inkstone Mountain. After the Jiajing period of the Ming dynasty [the quarry] was repeatedly bought and sold, this rocky vista has been semi-destroyed. In the winter of Guichou year of the reign of Wanli, Ma Zhijun (1588–1625, *jinshi* 1610) of the Customs House launched a subscription to buy

[the quarry] and give it back to the Buddhist monastery. [The temple] was first established at the end of the Eastern Jin dynasty. There is a tradition that this was Lu Wan's home that he gave to the church. During the Tianjian reign era of the Liang dynasty Zhiji achieved enlightenment. There was a strange monk who entered [the temple] to rest and during the night he painted his portrait on the wall and then left. A foreign monk said: "This is a portrait of the Bodhisattva Zhiji of the Western lands." Later on the younger brother of Lu Xiangxian became critically ill, and a monk drank a cup of water only to spit it out all over him which cured him.[48] When he [Lu Xiangxian's brother] thanked him, [the monk] would not accept it, and said: "I am a monk from Numinous Cliff, and in a past life you held my place." When they went to visit him they were not able [to see him], so all they could do was make a statue of him. The Lu family bestowed five hundred thousand cash [on the temple]. This is recorded in the "Essay on the Śramana monk Zhixian of the Wu-Yue Kingdom." In the Tang dynasty it was named Numinous Cliff Temple, and Lu Xiangxian built the Zhiji [Bodhisattva] Hall, and the Reflecting-Space Pavilion. In the Song dynasty the Prefect Lord Yan submitted a memorial to change [the name of the temple] to Flowering Peak Chan Buddhist Monastery, which refers to the fact that the [numinous] fungus flowers three times a year.[49] In the middle of the Shaoxing reign era, the [Commandery] Prince of Xian'an, Han [Shizhong] performed a sacrificial ceremony here for good luck, and changed the name to Glorifying the Family and Worshipping Reciprocity [Monastery]. The Elder Zhine rebuilt the Zhiji Hall, and Sun Di wrote a record of this, and at the same time he built the Five Acmes Hall.[50] In the second year of the Taiping xingguo reign-era (977), the high official Sun Chengyou built a brick pagoda of nine stories [here] to the memory of his older sister, the wife of a member of the Qian royal

48. Lu Xiangxian is known to have had two brothers, Lu Jingqian 陸景倩 and Lu Jingrong 陸景融, both of whom also became senior government officials. It is not known which one of them is meant here.

49. Zhang Yiliu, *Suzhou Lingyanshan zhi*, p. 19, identifies this individual as Yan Zhizhi 晏知止, who during the Yuanfeng reign-era (1078–85) was responsible for developing the monastery as a Chan Buddhist foundation.

50. The name of this hall, the Wuzhi Tang (Five acmes hall), seems to be derived from a quotation from the *Liji*, in which Confucius describes how *zhi* 志 (the human mind), *shi* 詩 (song), *li* 禮 (ritual), *le* 樂 (happiness), and *ai* 哀 (sorrow), when taken to their extreme point encompass the entire world. *Liji*, p. 858 ("Kongzi xianju" 孔子閑居).

family. Sun wrote a record of these events himself.[51] In the Ming dynasty the Hongwu Emperor bestowed a tablet [reading] "Requiting the Nation Perpetual Blessing Chan Buddhist Temple." In the reign of the Wanli Emperor, Vice-Prefect Shen Yaozhong rebuilt the Reflecting Space Pavilion. In the past there used to be the Mysterious Void Monastery, which was built by Han [Shizhong], the king of Qi.[52] Resembling-the-Ancients Pavilion was built by Lu Xiangxian.[53] These have both been destroyed. In the Song dynasty, Yuanzhao (d. 1099) spent his final years and died at this mountain pagoda, and his body is preserved incorrupt here.[54] In the third year after Cishou became abbot, he carved the characters "Wrapped in Cloud Tower" onto stone and composed a hymn. A gazetteer was written by the local man Huang Xiyuan.[55] In Yichou year of the reign of the Shunzhi Emperor in the Qing dynasty, they invited the Chan Buddhist Master [Li] Jiqi (李繼起), [whose name in religion was Hong]chu (弘儲) to undertake a program of reform whereby after ten years all the ruined [buildings] had been reconstructed and a vast Chan Buddhist monastery had been

51. Sun Chengyou's record, and that written by Sun Di mentioned above, are both included in the *Gusu zhi* anthology of literature on Suzhou and its environs. Wang Ao et al., *Gusu zhi*, vol. 2, pp. 700–703.

52. The name of this religious foundation is originally derived from the *Laozi* 老子, which says: "To look but not to see is called *yi*, to listen but not to hear is called *xi*." 視而不見名曰夷，聽而不聞名曰希. *Laozi Daodejing* A.87. From this, the term *xiyi* 夷希 later came to be understood as referring to the mysterious boundaries of perception, hence the translation here: "Mysterious Void."

53. The name of this pavilion, Xiangxian, refers to the name which was given to Lu Xiangxian by the Tang Emperor Ruizong 唐睿宗 (r. 684–90, 710–12). Lu Xiangxian's original name was Lu Jingchu 陸景初, but the emperor is said to have renamed him "Resembling the Ancients" in honor of his great scholarship and upright character.

54. Yuanzhao's name before taking his religious vows was Guan Zongben 管宗本, and he was a native of Wuxi in Jiangsu province. He divided his career between Suzhou's Ruiguang si 瑞光寺 (Auspicious light temple), where his popularity brought great prosperity to this foundation, and Hangzhou, where he acted as spiritual advisor to Emperor Shenzong (r. 1067–85). Zhou Hongdu, *Lingyanshan*, pp. 113–16.

55. Huang Xiyuan's book, entitled *Lingyanshan zhi* 靈巖山志 (Gazetteer for Numinous Cliff Mountain) in eight *juan*, does not survive, but it is recorded in Huang Yuji, *Qianqingtang shumu* 8.31b.

created.[56] To begin with he built the Hall for Expounding Doctrine and the Main Hall, and for the celebrations for his fiftieth birthday in Jiawu year, he built the two pavilions "Heavenly Mountain" and "Receiving Mercy." At this time Chen Huangshi built the Compassion Pavilion, and the Xi family from Dongting [Island] built the Maitreya Hall. The master also completely rebuilt the Five Acmes Hall, Chan Buddhist Hall, Fasting Hall, Complete Reflection Great Mirror Hall, Square Kitchen, and the monks' own living quarters. His successors were Tang Yinggao, and Bei Muqian, [at which point] Provincial Governor Mu built the Bell Hall,[57] the monk Jianqing, who rebuilt the Main Hall and the Maitreya Hall, Qu Ximing and Tong Shihong, who built the Prolonging Longevity Hall.

靈岩山, 去城西三十里, 館娃宮遺址在焉. 其突起者名琴臺. 山有二井, 圓象天, 八角象地. 石室一, 傳西施洞. 池四, 澣花, 上方, 洗硯, 澣月. 石之奇巧者十有八, 石鼓二, 石射堋, 醉僧石, 石鼉, 壽星石, 佛日岩, '披雲' '望月' 二臺, 石樓, 袈裟石, 石髻, 石城, 靈芝石, 石馬, 槎頭石, 獻花石, 藏經石幢, 猫兒石. 惟靈芝石爲最, 故名靈岩. 西產硯石, 即穫村石. 一名硯石山, 明嘉靖後屢經購采, 石景半廢. 萬曆癸丑冬椎部馬之駿捐贖歸僧寺. 始建於東晋末. 相傳陸玩捨宅. 梁天監間智積顯化. 有異僧入憩, 夜畫其象於壁而去. 胡僧曰: "此西土智積菩薩象也." 又唐陸象先弟遘危疾,一僧索杯水喘之而瘳. 謝, 弗受, 曰: "我靈岩僧, 他日當過我." 訪之不得, 惟象肖焉. 陸施錢五十萬. 載吳越國沙門智賢文. 唐名靈岩寺, 陸象先建智積殿, 涵空閣. 宋郡守晏公奏改秀峰禪院, 以芝三秀. 紹興中賜咸安王韓公薦先福, 更號顯親崇報. 長老智訥重建智積殿. 孫覿記. 幷建五至堂. 太平興國二年, 藩臣孫承祐爲姊錢王妃建磚塔九級. 孫自有記. 明洪武賜額: '報國永祚禪寺.' 萬曆間, 沈郡丞堯中重建涵空閣. 舊有希夷觀, 韓蘄王建, 象先亭, 陸象先建. 俱廢. 宋圓照本晚終是山塔全身焉. 慈受深主席三年, 刻披雲臺字於石, 作頌, 有里人黃習遠志. 清順治己丑延繼起儲禪師行化. 十年之後, 百廢具舉, 爲禪刹巨觀. 初建法堂正殿. 甲午五十壽, 建'天山' '慈受' 二閣. 又陳皇士建大悲閣. 洞庭席氏建彌勒殿. 師又建五至堂, 禪堂,

56. A short biography of Hongchu, who successfully administered the Numinous Cliff Monastery through the difficult years following the establishment of the Qing dynasty in spite of his openly avowed Ming loyalist sentiments, is given in Zhou Hongdu, *Lingyanshan*, pp. 116–17.

57. Governor Mu is identified by Zhang Yiliu, *Suzhou Lingyanshan zhi*, p. 19, as Mu Tianyan 慕天顏 (1624–96, *jinshi* 1655), a native of Gansu province, whose early career postings included time as the Jiangsu Provincial Administration Commissioner (Buzhengshi 布政使), at which point he became a patron of the monastery at Numinous Cliff. After an exceptionally brilliant official career, which culminated with the Kangxi Emperor placing him in charge of the campaign against Wu Sangui, Mu Tianyan retired to Suzhou.

齋堂, 圓照大鑒堂, 方丈厨庫, 寮舍畢備. 繼住者, 曇應杲, 卑牧謙, 慕撫軍建鐘殿, 僧鑒青, 重修正殿, 彌勒殿, 去息溟, 童石宏也, 建延壽堂.[58]

This particular account provides something of a corrective to the *Gusu zhi*. Where the *Gusu zhi* emphasizes the importance of Numinous Cliff Mountain as a site associated with King Fuchai of Wu and his Lodging-Beauties Palace, to the virtual exclusion of other interpretations, the *Baicheng yanshui* gives much greater attention to its role as a famous and ancient Buddhist monastery. Likewise, where the *Gusu zhi* references to the temple mention only Lu Xiangxian's association with the site and his patronage of it, this account is more nuanced, referring to other important figures like Han Shizhong, and discussing the role played by both clergy and lay individuals in the erection of new buildings and the reconstruction and renovation of old ones. Whereas the portrayal of Tiger Hill in the *Baicheng yanshui* focuses on literati activity, the religious role of the temple at Numinous Cliff Mountain seems to have been extremely important in the late imperial era, and hence receives priority in the *Gusu zhi*. The vast majority of sites individually named in this gazetteer are recorded for their religious significance, while only four may be said to represent structures associated with the kings of Wu.

Although apparently an extremely wealthy foundation, the temple at Numinous Cliff has undergone many vicissitudes during its long history. It is clear that with the exception of the pagoda, all the other buildings at this site were repeatedly destroyed. The *Gusu zhi* passage translated above mentions a fire in the reign of the Hongzhi Emperor, a conflagration that spared only the pagoda. This fire is rarely mentioned in later accounts—which instead tend to emphasize the destruction experienced by the monastery in a terrible fire that occurred during the summer of 1587, as a result of a lightning strike. All the wooden buildings, the vast majority of the temple complex, were destroyed, and the pagoda was severely damaged. However, a monk named Puhan 普含 was able to save the temple's most precious relic,

58. Xu Song and Zhang Dachun, *Baicheng yanshui*, pp. 96–97.

a tooth of the Buddha, which is still housed in the pagoda.[59] From the tenor of the remarks made in the *Baicheng yanshui*, the monastery must have experienced serious destruction at around the time of the Ming-Qing transition, though it is not at all clear what exactly happened or who was responsible. This account stresses the importance of the chief monks, who united under a charismatic abbot to undertake a major program of institutional reform and rebuilding. It is perhaps also significant that Numinous Cliff received its first imperial visitor during the reign of the Kangxi Emperor, which can only have enhanced the reputation of its abbot and speeded the process of reconstruction and renovation.[60] The temple at Numinous Cliff subsequently also became a favorite destination on the southern tours of the Qianlong Emperor. This resulted in many significant changes to the site, which included the erection of a travelling palace to accommodate the imperial visitor and his entourage during his stay. No trace of this structure has survived, since its destruction in 1860, at the time of the Taiping Rebellion. These imperial visits will be discussed in more detail in the following section.

Qing Imperial Visits to Numinous Cliff Temple

In the Qing dynasty, both the Kangxi Emperor and his grandson, the Qianlong Emperor, made visits to Numinous Cliff Mountain, which ranked as one of the major tourist attractions beyond the city walls of Suzhou. Both commemorated the occasion of their visit in verse, like so many other literati visitors before and after them. However, though in some ways the response of regnant members of the Qing imperial house was conditioned by their readings of ancient historical texts, and classic poetry and prose (a quality which they held in common with other educated visitors to this site), their experience of travel to Numinous Cliff was in other ways constrained—and perhaps enhanced—by their special status. Where members of the literati elite, no matter how distinguished and important, would

59. The most detailed account of the fire is given in Zhang Yiliu, *Suzhou Lingyanshan zhi*, p. 20.

60. The significance for the monastery of the visits by the Kangxi emperor is discussed, ibid., p. 20.

by and large have to take a site like Numinous Cliff as they found it, there is considerable evidence that well-travelled emperors like Kangxi and Qianlong did not actually see the same things as other visitors. Not only were the sites selected for imperial visits tidied up for the occasion, sometimes significant changes were made which altered the landscape irrevocably. This was particularly true during the reign of the Qianlong Emperor, who sometimes announced years in advance precisely what locations he wished to see: this allowed time for massive renovations and, in some cases, for the complete reconstruction of important cultural sites (occasionally in a totally different location from the original).

To cite the example of Numinous Cliff, the visit of the Kangxi Emperor in 1689 resulted in a decision to significantly change access to the site by the construction of a new ingress route: the Yudao 御道 (Imperial way). It was this road, covered for the occasion with cloth awnings, which the Kangxi Emperor took up to the temple on the rain-soaked day that he visited this famous site, and which is recorded in his poem, "Deng Lingyan" 登靈巖 (Climbing Numinous Cliff):

A fine numinous drizzle scatters the spring mist,
I hold the reins; I bend carefree steps towards the emerald peaks.
The rolling waters of the Perfume River shine like an arrow,
The collected rocks around the Qin Tower are as powerful as fists.
These mountains all stand beyond the verdant vines,
A myriad wells are located in front of my colorful banners.
I have heard that this used to be the garden of the Wu palace,
Bells and stone chimes resound in the empty space of the Brahma Hall.
霏微靈雨散春煙, 按轡逍遙步翠巔.
香水通流明若箭, 琴臺列石勢如拳.
諸峰盡在青蘿外, 萬井全依綵仗前.
聞是吳宮花草地, 空餘鐘磬梵王筵.[61]

61. Kangxi Emperor, *Shengzu Renhuangdi yuzhi wenji*, *wen* 文 2, 43.8a. For a detailed account of the Kangxi Emperor's visit to Suzhou, and his visit to Numinous Cliff on the fifth day of the second lunar month (24th February according to the Western calendar), including his presentation to the monks of an inscription in imperial calligraphy reading: Luancui 巒翠 (Peaks of emerald). See Zhang Dachun, "Gusu caifeng leiji" 5.42b. Although this text was reprinted in the *congshu* 叢書 (collectanea) edited by Wang Jiaju 王稼句 entitled *Suzhou wenxian congchao chubian*

Like his grandfather, the Qianlong Emperor would visit Numinous Cliff Mountain on a number of his southern progresses, and would leave a much greater mark on the landscape, given that he had a travelling palace erected there. This was in accordance with the usual pattern of imperial visits to the most important tourist attractions in China, in which local officials would arrange for two temporary palaces to be erected (one in an urban area, and one at a site of special scenic and historical interest).[62] On the Qianlong Emperor's first visit in 1766, he commemorated the occasion by composing a cycle of eight poems on the subject of Numinous Cliff. Each individual poem celebrated a famous site (such as the Lodging-Beauties Palace, Qin Tower, Echoing-Step Corridor, Reflecting-Space Pavilion, the King of Wu's Well, Inkstone Pond, and Picking-Fragrance Canal); and the vast majority of these sites were clearly associated with King Fuchai of Wu. The Qianlong Emperor also presented Numinous Cliff Mountain Temple with a number of inscriptions in his own calligraphy, including one reading: *Wu yuan xiang lin* 吳苑香林 (The Wu garden fragrant forest). This first cycle of poems, written to match rhymes set by Shen Deqian, is rich in allusions to the historical significance of Numinous Cliff, but fails to develop any theme that could not equally well have been expressed by another imperial-era literati poet. For example, the first poem in this sequence is entitled "Guanwa gong" (Lodging-beauties palace), and contains no reflection of the special status of the poet:

Seeking afresh the Inkstone path,
The spring flowers dance in the wind.
In the past this was the site of the Lodging-Beauties [Palace],
Now this is where sacrifices are made to the Buddha.
The pure sounds of sutras are lost among cloudy pines,
Quiet incense floats over the dikes and the altar of earth.
Here I can rest for a moment,

蘇州文獻叢鈔初編 (A first collection of literary works about Suzhou) published by the Guwuxuan chubanshe in 2005, this particular essay was for some reason omitted.

62. Wang, "Paradise for Sale," p. 75. For the Qianlong Emperor's second southern progress, two palaces were erected at Suzhou (one inside the city walls and one at Numinous Cliff Mountain), and similar pairs of palaces were built at Hangzhou and Nanjing.

Why should I think about the ancient past?
石硯徑重尋, 春花風自舞.
昔日館娃處, 今時選佛土.
清梵落雲松, 静香飄埭社.
於此暫息心, 何必論前古?[63]

The second poem in this cycle is entitled "Qintai" (Qin tower), and again shows no evidence of the Qianlong Emperor regarding his own special status as requiring anything other than a highly conventional response to his visit to Numinous Cliff. As with the poem cited above, there is nothing here that could not equally well have been written by another High Qing literati poet:

From western Shu (Sichuan) to eastern Lu (Shandong),
The name Qin Tower is widely found.
At this lake there is another [such structure]:[64]
A ruin said to date to the time of King Helü.
The wind in the pines gives a soughing sound,
The mountain torrent foams without cease.
I think about Sanlang's (Tang Xuanzong) melody,[65]
On listening to it, I already want to fall asleep.
西蜀及東魯, 琴臺名紛然.
此胡亦有之, 蹟傳闔閭年.
松風寫謖謖, 峽水常湲湲.
想彼三郎流, 聽之早欲眠.[66]

The sensibilities reflected in these poems are similar to those found in the works of other members of the literati elite, and can be said to

63. Gao Jin et al., *Nanxun shengdian*, p. 138.

64. This line of the poem is extremely difficult to interpret. All versions of this poem have identical wording: *Ci hu yi you zhi* 此胡亦有之, but in this translation I have read *hu* 胡 as *hu* 湖 (lake) on the grounds that this would seem to make more sense in the context.

65. Tang Xuanzong is said to have composed a song entitled "Guanghan you" 廣寒遊 (Wandering in a lunar palace), also known as the "Qingdu yin" 清都引 (Heavenly capital prelude). Xiao Luan, *Xingzhuang taiyin buyi*, p. 320. This piece of music, when known under the latter title, is also occasionally attributed to the famous late Southern Song *qin* master Mao Minzhong 毛敏仲. Huang Xian, *Wugang qinpu*, p. 382. Though apparently very popular in the Ming dynasty and included in many texts, this particular piece is usually thought to have fallen out of favor in the early Qing dynasty.

66. Gao Jin et al., *Nanxun shengdian*, p. 138.

be closely related to a theme developed in both poetry and prose about Numinous Cliff from the Song dynasty onwards (when the site was first promoted as a beauty spot worth visiting for its fine vistas rather than for its historical associations).

The Qianlong Emperor would write a completely different kind of poetry on the occasions of his later visits to the Jiangnan region. The change in the Qianlong Emperor's response to this site can clearly be seen by comparing the poems written on the occasion of his first visit in 1766 with those composed nearly thirty years later, when the now-aged emperor had an entirely different reaction to seeing scenes associated with the last king of Wu. The Qianlong Emperor would stay at his temporary palace at Numinous Cliff Mountain on his southern progresses in 1778, 1779, and 1793. On the occasion of his last visit, in 1793, he again wrote a cycle of poems on the subject of the different sights of Numinous Cliff Mountain. This second cycle of poems mirrors exactly the subject matter and titles of the cycle written on the occasion of his first southern tour: hence they are a fruitful source of comparison. As in the 1761 cycle, the first poem in the 1793 cycle is entitled "Guanwa gong":

> Four plans deluded the heart of [the king of] Wu,
> [Women dressed in] silk and gauze were taught to sing and dance.
> Where could you learn such looks and bearing?
> Some say these city walls are just old earth.
> [Fan] Li presented [Xi Shi] and Zixu gave his warnings,
> [King Fuchai] did not listen to his words at all.
> I write verse about the Lodging-Beauties [Palace],
> So I take warning from the mirror of ancient history.
> 四計惑吳心, 羅穀教歌舞.
> 容步於何習, 或曰城古土.
> 蠡獻子胥諫, 弗聽其言杜.
> 伊人詠館娃, 戒之在鑑古.[67]

In the 1793 cycle of poems, the Qianlong Emperor's verse is strikingly different from other poetic responses to this site, including his own verses from earlier visits. The Qianlong Emperor here presents himself as a monarch-poet, and so his response to seeing the place

67. Ibid., p. 555.

where King Fuchai of Wu had once held court is conditioned not just by his awareness of the cultural and literary significance of the site, but also by his rank and responsibilities. For the Qianlong Emperor, King Fuchai's example was a warning from history: although other people might have blamed the last king of Wu for neglecting his duties to spend time with a beautiful woman, very few would have taken the legend of the Lodging-Beauties Palace in the personal way indicated by the last line. This poem was written by a ruler, visiting a site particularly connected with a doomed king—and this history had resonances for the aging emperor that it would not have had for other literati visitors, no matter how distinguished or important. As a hereditary monarch, the Qianlong Emperor seems at this time to have been particularly sensitive to the travails of other earlier rulers. A similar sensibility can be seen in the second poem of the 1793 cycle, again entitled "Qin Tai":

> The seven stringed [*qin*] is indeed an ancient instrument,
> However, the age of this tower is not certain.
> Could it have been built in the era of King Helü?
> Or constructed in the time of King Fuchai?
> Time moves on just like the shining moon,
> Though people leave, the spring still flows.
> But when the recluse arrives,
> Bending his arm, he sleeps with his head pillowed on it.
> 七絃實古器, 斯臺未恰然.
> 抑于闔閭代, 抑在夫差年.
> 世遷猶月白, 人去餘泉湲.
> 但供幽客至, 曲肱時枕眠.[68]

The Qing emperor's visits to the south and his repeated stays at temporary palaces at some of the most famous tourist attractions of the Jiangnan region was clearly a source of considerable local pride. The itineraries of the emperor were carefully recorded in the local histories, and the poems written on these occasions would only have served to highlight the importance of these sites that had once seen the glories of the independent state of Wu.[69] However, though at first glance their literary works might appear to be highly conventional,

68. Ibid., 556. The last line of this poem quotes the *Lunyu*, p. 70 ("Shuer" 7.16).
69. Li Mingwan and Feng Guifen, *Suzhou fu zhi*, p. 191.

in fact this is not the case. The writings of emperors reveal the special circumstances in which they travelled to see these famous sites, which were cleared of other tourists, perhaps even with brand new monuments and vistas constructed specifically for the pleasure of the imperial visitor. In the case of the Qianlong emperor, his later poems clearly reveal his unique status as a regnant monarch surveying sites associated with a failed regime and a doomed king.

Gusu Tower

The word *tai* 臺 has frequently been translated either as a tower or terrace. In the Spring and Autumn period these buildings were constructed to allow rulers to survey their domains, and to strike awe into their enemies. Towers of this kind were often built as part of palace complexes, but were also constructed in conjunction with parks or gardens, and as such might also fulfill the function of hunting lodges. The erection of such a building represents a major project, since it often involved making significant changes to the landscape in order to build up suitable foundations. The construction of such buildings in the Spring and Autumn period signaled an important change in the perception of what constituted a prestigious ritual or ceremonial center. Older palaces and official spaces occupied enormous areas of land; significant ceremonies were concealed from view, and the emphasis was on enclosure and solemnity, which added to the mystique of the ruling elite. The building of towers, on the other hand, represented not just the power and authority of the ruling elite in terms of the spatial area they could command, but it also represented their conquest of a third dimension: the air. Lest this assertion might seem to be exaggerated, it is worth noting that this interpretation of such buildings was recorded in many Han dynasty accounts.[70] However, since the architectural knowledge of the time did not admit the building of multi-story structures, these towers were constructed around a core of pounded earth. This then gave the external appearance of a much

70. Wu, "Art and Architecture of the Warring States Period," pp. 669–73. The account of a tower reaching to the floating clouds is found in the *Xinyu*, p. 134. Meanwhile, the *Xinxu*, p. 165 ("Cishe" 刺奢), describes the Zhongtian tai 中天臺 (Piercing heaven tower), which was constructed in the kingdom of Wei.

taller structure than was actually the case. Given that the height of these buildings was their most important characteristic, I have consistently translated the term *tai* as "tower."[71]

Building a tower of this kind was once the prerogative of the Son of Heaven. This was the place that he communed with Heaven, and received its mandate.[72] However, in the Spring and Autumn period, as the feudal lords increasingly encroached upon the privileges of the Zhou king, they began to construct their own towers. There are numerous references in historical texts to the towers that were constructed by the lords of the Zhou confederacy during this period. The very first non-royal towers were recorded in the *Chunqiu*, when in 663 BCE Lord Zhuang of Lu 魯莊公 (r. 693–662 BCE) built himself no less than three towers. The first, known as the Quantai 泉臺 or Kuiquantai 逵泉臺, was built in the spring of that year outside the city of Lang 郎. In the summer, a second tower was built at the city of Xue 薛. In the autumn, the third tower was built at the city of Qin 秦.[73] Lord Zhuang of Lu's example in building his own towers was enthusiastically followed by a number of his peers. For example according to the *Zuozhuan*, in 645 BCE Lord Mu of Qin 秦穆公 (r. 659–621 BCE) also constructed a tower.[74]

Occasionally there are references in ancient texts to the trouble that could be caused by the construction of towers—for these projects often involved major changes to the landscape as a suitably grand approach was designed and the pounded-earth core constructed. In 556 BCE, Huang Guofu 皇國父 of the state of Song became the prime minister of that state and decided to build a tower for his ruler, Lord Ping of Song 宋平公 (r. 575–532 BCE). It was recorded that so many men were drafted in to work on this great project that it

71. There are no references in any surviving ancient text to the dimensions of the Gusu Tower. However, the 凸-shaped pounded earth bases of a handful of Yue towers survive in Fujian province and the dimensions of a couple of King Goujian of Yue's towers are given in the "Jidi zhuan" chapter of the *Yuejue shu*. These vary enormously in size from 60 m^2 to 440 m^2, which presumably reflects some difference in function. Milburn, "The Towers of Yue."

72. Wang Yi, *Yuanlin yu Zhongguo wenhua*, p. 36.

73. *Chunqiu*, pp. 248–49 (Zhuang 31).

74. *Zuozhuan*, p. 358 (Xi 15).

interfered with the harvest.[75] However, this is an unusual account of the human costs of such a project. The majority of references to these towers in ancient texts describe their social function: as places from which the lords of the Zhou confederacy surveyed their domains or set out on hunts; and as places where they met to feast with noble companions. Constructing these towers garnered considerable prestige, and this was the aspect that occurred most frequently to those who commissioned the building of towers, and whose views were recorded in ancient texts.

Although many feudal lords and rulers in the Spring and Autumn period would construct towers for themselves, a few towers of outstanding magnificence would be built during this time. Among these famous buildings was the Zhanghua Tower 章化臺 constructed in Chu and the Gusu Tower built in the state of Wu. Building a tower like this, which involved large numbers of construction workers and which completely changed the landscape of the area, was an important prestige project showing the wealth and power of the country. It is not known which monarch of Wu was responsible for the construction of the Gusu Tower because in ancient texts both King Helü and King Fuchai of Wu were credited with ordering that it be built. It would seem that the older tradition attributed the construction of the Gusu Tower to King Fuchai of Wu, who was famous among later generations as a creator of gardens and as a devotee of projects aimed at changing the landscape of his kingdom. According to the *Zuozhuan*, in a highly illuminating passage comparing the characters and conduct of these two kings of Wu, this was all part and parcel of the last king of Wu's luxurious and wasteful tastes:

> Zi Xi (a grandee of Chu) said: "In the past King Helü's food did not have complex flavors, when he sat down it was not on a thick mat, he did not live in a house [built] on a platform, his utensils were not lacquered red or inlaid, his palace did not have a pavilions, his boat and chariot were not ornamented; and as for his clothes and personal property, he chose carefully but did not select anything extravagant. . . . Now I have heard that Fuchai has towers, pavilions, embankments, and lakes wherever he stays; when he spends the night he has women of noble and humble birth with him; when

75. Ibid., pp. 1032–33 (Xiang 17).

> he travels for one day, everything that he wants must be provided, and his playthings must follow him; he collects rare and strange items, and is interested in spectacles and music; he regards the people as his enemy and every day uses them for some new caprice."
>
> 子西曰: "昔闔廬食不二味, 居不重席, 室不崇壇, 器不彤鏤, 宮室不觀, 舟車不飾, 衣服財用, 擇不取費 . . . 今聞夫差, 次有臺榭陂池焉, 宿有妃嬙, 嬪御焉; 一日之行, 所欲必成, 玩好必從, 珍異是聚, 觀樂是務, 視民如讎, 而用之日新."[76]

This speech was indicative of the way that the posthumous reputations of King Helü and King Fuchai were rearranged. It is clear from historical records that a number of major building and landscaping projects that today are associated with the last king of Wu were in fact begun during the reign of his father. However, King Fuchai was the last king of his line, and therefore it was imperative for him to have done something wrong—that is, to lose the Mandate of Heaven. Therefore, the most extravagant projects undertaken in the last years of the kingdom of Wu were attributed to King Fuchai; and these major building works were said to have alienated him from his people. The conflicting accounts of who was actually responsible for the construction of the Gusu Tower resulted in considerable confusion for later scholars. This is sometimes resolved by crediting both King Helü and King Fuchai with a role in the building of the tower. For example the Tang dynasty encyclopedia, the *Yiwen leiju* 藝文類聚 (Collection of literature arranged by category), states that the tower was first built in the reign of King Helü and then made higher and embellished under King Fuchai. This text is also unique in that it attributes a specific date to the commencement of work on the Gusu Tower: the eleventh year of the reign of King Helü or 504 BCE.[77] Regardless of who was ultimately responsible for commissioning the construction of the Gusu Tower, building it was a major effort and this aspect dominates the discussion of it found in ancient texts. Many ancient Chinese texts record the criticisms leveled at rulers who built towers for their extravagance and their general disregard

76. Ibid., pp. 1608–1609 (Ai 1).

77. Ouyang Xun, *Yiwen leiju*, p. 1119. This reference is here attributed to the *Wudi ji*.

for the well-being of their people, and King Fuchai was no exception. The "Wuyu" chapter of the *Guoyu* records how the king of Wu was criticized by Wu Zixu for his landscaping projects: "Now, your Majesty has already changed the works of Gun and Yu, in making the high higher (i.e., building towers) and making the low lower (i.e., having lakes dug), and you have exhausted the people with [the building of] Gusu [Tower]." 今王既變鯀, 禹之功, 而高高下下, 以罷民於姑蘇.[78]

The *Mozi* also contains references to the burden placed on the people of Wu by the building of Gusu Tower, stating that even after seven years of labor the tower that King Fuchai had commissioned was not completed.[79] Such a statement should, however, not be taken at face value, particularly given the extensive discourse in the *Mozi* concerning different aspects of the extravagance of the ruling elite, arguing that it is immoral to spend money on luxuries in a world of want, where people are dying of starvation. In this context such a prestigious project as the Gusu Tower would be an obvious candidate for criticism, and the expense in human labor and resources would be exaggerated for rhetorical effect. It is striking that over time the amount of work said to have gone into building the Gusu Tower increased, as indeed did the distance that could be seen from the top. Thus, by the time of the Tang dynasty it was said that the construction of the tower took nine years to complete: "Gusu Tower stood thirty-five *li* to the southwest of Wu county. Helü built it, and they labored for nine years to finish it. This tower stood three hundred *zhang* high, and from it you could look into the distance for three hundred *li*, and they made a road with nine bends in order to climb up to it." 姑蘇臺在吳縣西南三十五里. 闔閭造. 經營九年始成. 其臺高三百丈, 望見三百里 外, 作九曲路以登之.[80]

According to some ancient accounts, the Gusu Tower was not merely an unwarranted extravagance on the part of the last king of Wu, but also part of a cunning ploy by his greatest enemy to destroy him and his kingdom. The "Jiushu" chapter of the *Yuejue shu* de-

78. *Guoyu*, p. 599 ("Wuyu").
79. *Mozi*, p. 138 ("Feigong zhong").
80. Lu Guangwei, *Wudi ji*, p. 38.

scribes how the construction of Gusu Tower was used by King Goujian as part of his strategy for destroying the enemy kingdom: by giving exceptionally fine timbers, felled in the forests of Yue, to the king of Wu, King Goujian hoped to tempt the king into ordering the construction of this exceptionally expensive and unpopular "prestige project." Again, the emphasis in this depiction of the construction of the tower is on King Fuchai's inhuman lack of consideration for the suffering of his people, and his folly in falling into the simple trap laid for him by his inveterate enemy in spite of the remonstrance of his loyal minister, Wu Zixu:

> Then [King Goujian] made his people [cut down] beautiful trees, ornamenting them with white jade discs and inlaying them with gold in the form of dragons and serpents. Afterwards he sent Grandee Zhong to present them to Wu. . . . The king of Wu was very pleased. Shen Xu (Wu Zixu) remonstrated: "This is not right. Your Majesty must not accept this. In the past Jie built the Numinous Gate and Zhou built Deer Tower.[81] As a result, *yin* and *yang* were not in harmony, and the five grains did not ripen in season. Heaven sent down disasters so that their countries were ruined and they died. If your majesty accepts this, it will cause disaster in the future." The king of Wu did not listen to him, but accepted [this present] and built the Guxu (Gusu) Tower. For three years they gathered the building materials and then after a further five years it was completed. From this eminence you could see two hundred *li*. [Passers-by] wept to see the dead bodies along the roads.
> 於是作爲策楯, 嬰以白璧, 鏤以黃金, 類龍蛇而行者. 乃使大夫種獻之於吳 . . . 吳王大悅. 申胥諫曰: "不可. 王勿受. 昔桀起靈門, 紂起鹿臺, 陰陽不和, 五穀不時, 天與之災, 邦國空虛, 遂以之亡. 大王受之, 是後必有災." 吳王不聽, 遂受之而起姑胥臺. 三年聚材, 五年乃成. 高見二百里. 行路之人, 道死尸.[82]

---

81. Jie was the evil last king of the (mythical) Xia dynasty, Zhou the evil last king of the Shang dynasty. These highly stereotyped figures have standard biographies in the *Shiji* 2.88, 3.105–108. The Lingmen or Numinous Gate is not described in any other ancient text, but the Deer Tower was a byword for extravagance in ancient China.

82. *Yuejue shu*, p. 83 ("Jiushu" 九術). Qian Peiming, *Yuejue shu zhaji*, p. 38, suggests an amendment of the original text, so that it reads *dao si xiang ku* 道死巷哭 (the streets [were full of] dead bodies and the lanes [resounded with the sound of] weeping).

This text adds several new dimensions to the construction of the Gusu Tower: first, that King Fuchai of Wu seems to have intended it as a physical representation of his authority, and particularly of his triumphant conquest of the kingdom of Yue (as demonstrated by the use of timber from Yue in the building); and secondly, that for King Goujian this was one step in his plan for revenge. Both these aspects of the history of the tower would be developed by subsequent texts. For example, the quality of the timber that was supplied by the people of Yue, and the extensive workmanship that they expended on it before presenting it to Wu for use in building this tower is vividly described in the *Wu Yue chunqiu*. According to this account the timber used was of such fine quality that only supernatural intervention could explain its appearance:

> The king of Yue then sent out more than three thousand woodcutters to go into the mountains and cut down trees. For one whole year they found nothing suitable. The woodcutters thought of returning home, they were all resentful and homesick, and so they sang the "Plaint of Travelers through the Woods." One night, Heaven created a pair of miraculous trees, twenty hand-spans across and four hundred (Chinese) feet tall. The *yang* tree was a catalpa tree and the *yin* tree was a *nan*-burl tree. They worked [the wood] cunningly and carefully, regulated by the compass and plumb line. They carved it on a turntable and smoothed it down with planes. They decorated it with red and blue [paintwork], and ornamented it with auspicious signs. They adorned it with white jade discs and inlaid it with gold. [The wood] had the forms of dragons and serpents, and the ornamental patterns seemed alive.
>
> 越王乃使木工三千餘人入山伐木, 一年, 師無所幸. 作士思歸, 皆有怨望之心, 而歌木客之吟. 一夜天生神木一雙, 大二十圍, 長五十尋. 陽爲文梓, 陰爲楩柟. 巧工施校, 制以規繩. 雕治圓轉, 刻削磨礱. 分以丹青, 錯畫文章. 嬰以白璧, 鏤以黃金, 狀類龍蛇. 文彩生光.[83]

This passage may be seen as developing the theme of the influence of the Mandate of Heaven in the events in the kingdoms of Wu and Yue. This is referred to a number of times in ancient Chinese texts: Heaven delivered King Goujian of Yue into the hands of King Fuchai; and by refusing to take his life and instead allowing him to re-

83. *Wu Yue chunqiu*, p. 143 ("Goujian yinmou waizhuan").

turn to his kingdom, King Fuchai may be said to have lost the Mandate of Heaven. In the discussions of what to do with King Fuchai after his capture, consideration of the Mandate of Heaven was very important—for any attempt by King Goujian to argue in favor of sparing his enemy's life was countered by his ministers with this argument. As this description of the timbers presented to Wu by King Goujian makes clear, Yue, too, spent vast resources on the construction of Gusu Tower, ornamenting their finest timbers with gold and jade. Yet at no stage are they criticized for doing so, though the luxury of the Gusu Tower was a byword for many centuries. As the *Wu Yue chunqiu* makes clear, Yue's expenditure represents an outlay sanctioned by Heaven for which they will reap a great reward; Wu's is merely extravagance. It is worth noting that in some later versions of this story, King Goujian's involvement in the construction of the Gusu Tower is completely omitted, and it is King Fuchai alone who is said to have been responsible for this great extravagance.[84] It is then the last king of Wu who tormented his people by forcing them deep into the forests to find the very finest of timbers, and then compounded his errors by expending the resources of his kingdom in decorating them with gold and pearls.

In the imperial era, a further minor tradition (again with mildly supernatural overtones) would be developed concerning the timbers from which the Gusu Tower had been built. This story is found in the *Taiping huanyu ji*, and is repeated in a number of other texts from the Song dynasty onwards. Here the construction of the Gusu Tower was used to explain the name of a lake and river in the vicinity of Suzhou: the Meiao hu 梅澳湖 (Plum bank lake) and the Meixi 梅溪 (Plum stream): "In the past, there were plum trees [here]. The kingdom of Wu cut down these trees to make beams for the Gusu Tower. Afterwards they suddenly sank [below the waters]. Up to the present time [the river] beside this lake is still known as 'Plum Stream.'" 昔有梅樹. 吳國採爲姑蘇臺梁. 後忽于此沈. 至今湖側猶有梅溪.[85]

The *Yuejue shu* also contains a number of other important references to the construction of Gusu Tower. As mentioned in the chapter on

84. Li Fang et al., *Taiping yulan* 47.346.
85. Yue Shi, *Taiping huanyu ji* 96.16a.

King Helü of Wu and Tiger Hill, the "Ji Wudi zhuan" chapter includes an extensive list of buildings in and around the capital of the kingdom of Wu that were specifically associated with this monarch (including the road with nine bends leading up to the tower). The *Yuejue shu* also includes a much more important story in the "Qingdi" chapter, which would have a significant impact in later representations of Gusu Tower in imperial era literature. This tale records a conversation at court between King Fuchai of Wu, Prime Minister Pi, and Wu Zixu, which led to a serious disagreement between the latter pair. The issue that provoked their argument was King Fuchai's determination to provide famine relief for the kingdom of Yue, which had announced that they were suffering from starvation:

> Shen Xu said: "I have heard that when a sage is in a crisis situation, he is not humiliated by accepting the position of a vassal to another person, but his ambitions can still be seen. Now the king of Yue has quietly humbled himself before you, he has submitted to becoming a vassal, he performs all the necessary rituals and more, but your majesty does not understand how to interpret [his actions]. This is why you believe that you have conquered and overawed him. I have heard it said that a wolf's cub keeps a wild heart, and an enemy cannot become a friend.[86] A rat may forget the wall, but the wall does not forget the rat, and the people of Yue have certainly not yet forgotten about Wu![87] I have heard it said that when justice wins, then the altars of soil and grain are secure; but when flattery wins, the state altars are in danger. I was a minister in the government of the late king. If I had been disloyal and untrustworthy, I would not have been a minister in the government of the late king. Has your majesty never considered the way in which King Wu attacked [King] Zhou [of the Shang dy-

86. The expression *langzi yexin* 狼子野心 (a wolf's cub has a wild heart) was proverbial in ancient China, and is found in texts such as the *Zuozhuan*, p. 679 (Xuan 4), p. 1493 (Zhao 28); *Guoyu*, p. 587 ("Chuyu xia"). This expression seems to have been a southern one, generally associated with the kingdom of Chu.

87. The rhetoric found in this chapter of the *Yuejue shu* is marked by the use of apothegm, whereby proverbs are cited suggesting that conventional wisdom is on the side of the speaker. Interestingly, many of the proverbs cited in the *Yuejue shu*, including this one about the wall and the rat, are unique to this text. This rhetorical technique is particularly common in the *Zhanguo ce*. Goldin, *After Confucius*, p. 82.

> nasty]? Only a few years from now deer and wild boar will trample across the site of Guxu tower."
>
> 申胥曰: "臣聞聖人有急, 則不羞爲人臣僕, 而志氣見人. 今越王爲吾浦伏約辭, 服爲臣下, 其執禮過, 吾君不知省也而已, 故勝威之. 臣聞狼子野心, 仇讎之人, 不可親也. 夫鼠忘壁, 壁不忘鼠; 今越人不忘吳矣! 胥聞之, 拂勝, 則社稷固. 諛勝, 則社稷危. 胥, 先王之老臣, 不忠不信, 則不得爲先王之老臣. 君王胡不覽觀夫武王之伐紂也? 今不出數年, 鹿豕遊於姑胥之臺矣."[88]

In many accounts of the collapse of the kingdom of Wu King Fuchai is reduced to the level of a puppet, manipulated by his prime minister, who was acting at the behest of the kingdom of Yue. Wu Zixu then comes to represent not only an exceptionally intelligent man, but also one whose prescient and loyal warnings were ignored for the most venal of reasons: his opponents had accepted bribes from the enemy. Though this passage—in which King Fuchai, Prime Minister Pi, and Wu Zixu all present their different points of view—would have little impact on the portrayal of the conflict between the kingdoms of Wu and Yue in literati writings of the imperial era, the image with which Wu Zixu concluded his speech (that is, of wild animals walking through the ruins of the Gusu Tower) was widely adopted.

One of the few later works of literature to make extensive use of imagery derived from this passage in the *Yuejue shu* is the Qing dynasty poem "Jinfan jing" 錦帆涇 (Brocade sail canal) by the Qianlong Emperor, which takes its title from one of the more romantic names for the canal which ran outside the citadel of the city of Suzhou. This name is supposed to have commemorated the silk sails of the royal boat used by the kings of Wu that was anchored there when the royal family was in residence. This canal, destroyed in 1931, used to run along the site of what is now Jinfan lu 錦帆路, in the center of Suzhou. (Though no trace now remains of the ancient Suzhou citadel, which was destroyed at the beginning of the Ming dynasty, its walls are thought to have run roughly along what is now Jinfan lu, Shizi lu 十梓路, Gongyuan lu 公園路, and Yanqiao xiatang

88. *Yuejue shu*, p. 36 ("Qingdi").

言橋下塘.)[89] The Qianlong Emperor's poem is notable not only for its references to the wild animals ranging around the Gusu Tower, but also for its remarkable third line, a direct quotation from the "Qingdi" chapter of the *Yuejue shu*:

> The silk brocade sails hang high on the wave-tossed painted boat,
> Helü's banquets were extremely refined.
> The rats may forget the wall but the wall does not forget the rats,
> In the end deer and wild boar roam at [Gu]xu Tower.
> 高挂錦帆漾彩舟, 闔閭宴樂極風流.
> 鼠忘壁壁不忘鼠, 終致胥臺鹿豕遊.[90]

In the poem "Gusu huaigu" 姑蘇懷古 (Cherishing antiquity at Gusu) by the Ming dynasty poet Qian Fuxiang 錢復享, the conventional image of wild animals occupying the ruins of the Gusu Tower was turned on its head. This poem describes the place where the tower once stood and the wilderness that had grown up at the site where King Helü had once surveyed his kingdom and where King Fuchai had caroused with the beautiful Xi Shi. However, the contrast is not made with the animals that walk here, but instead with the total absence of any sign of life other than the presence of the poet and the partridges (a conventional symbol of homesickness) crying in the undergrowth:

> How many times have spring breezes [blown] the willow trees of
> Helü's walled city?
> The mountains are distant and the tower high; I look out at emptiness.
> Deer do not come here and the people have also left,
> The partridges cry where the Wu palace stood.
> 闔廬城柳幾春風, 山遠臺高望眼空.
> 麋鹿不來人亦去, 鷓鴣啼處是吳宮.[91]

---

89. The date of the filling in of this canal is given in Pan Junming, *Zicheng*, p. 26. The original location of the ancient walls of the citadel is derived from Yue Junjie et al., *Suzhou wenhua*, p. 7.

90. Quoted in Gao Jin et al., *Nanxun shengdian*, p. 313.

91. Quoted in Qian Gu, *Wudu wencui xuji* 11.19a. The reference to partridges here may be an allusion to the famous poem "Yuezhong langu" 越中覽古 (On [Visiting] Yue and contemplating antiquity) by Li Bai: "King Goujian of Yue, having crushed Wu, turned back,/ His righteous knights went home, all dressed in silk brocade./ The palace women, like flowers, filled the bright halls,/ But now only partridges fly here." 越王勾踐破吳歸, 義士還家盡錦衣. 宮女如花滿春殿, 只今惟有

As with the Lodging-Beauties Palace at Numinous Cliff, the accounts of the Gusu Tower written in the Age of Disunion were the first to try and quantify the conspicuous consumption represented by such a major project. Although there were numerous earlier references to the amount of work that went into the tower and the enormous amount of time it had taken to build, to the dissatisfaction of the people of Wu concerning this expensive project, and to the choiceness of the materials used, it is only from the Eastern Han dynasty onwards that writers began to describe the kind of luxury that King Fuchai was trying to create. The first aspect of the building of the Gusu Tower to be described in detail was the quality and workmanship involved in producing the timbers that came from Yue, which were ornamented with jade and gold inlay. This description was first recorded in detail in the *Wu Yue chunqiu*, and might be seen as representative of the extravagance of the whole project. In the Age of Disunion, this description was enhanced by accounts that focused on other aspects of Gusu Tower, and stressed the elaborate and expensive pleasures available at this site. Again, as in the case of Lodging-Beauties Palace, a particularly important and influential description of Gusu Tower was given by Ren Fang in the *Shuyi ji*: "His palace women numbered several thousand. On top (of the tower) and to one side there was the Chunxiao Gong (Spring night palace), where he drank all night long, and he had wine holders made that held one thousand *dan* of wine. Fuchai made Heaven Lake; and on the lake he had a green dragon boat built, and he filled the boat with female musicians. Every day he went on river excursions with Xi Shi." 宮妓數千人. 上別立春宵宮, 爲長夜之飲, 造千石酒鍾. 夫差作天池, 池中造青龍舟, 舟中盛陳妓樂. 日與西施爲水嬉.[92]

The precise motive for the king of Wu to build the Gusu Tower is not made clear in any ancient text. Possibly this is because the Gusu Tower was actually built over the course of many years, during the reigns of several kings of Wu: and each king would have had a different

---

鷓鴣飛. Qu Tuiyuan and Zhu Jincheng eds., *Li Bai ji jiaozhu*, p. 1292. The important role played by Li Bai (the first major Tang poet to travel to this part of eastern Zhejiang) in constructing the literary reputation of a number of ancient Yue sites is considered in Zou Zhifang, "Zhedong Tang shi zhi lu," pp. 266–67.

92. Ren Fang, *Shuyi ji* A.8a.

motivation for the construction of this major project. The tower is in turn described as an extravagant prestige project, a symbol of the conquest of Yue by Wu, as the site of King Fuchai's banquets, and as the seat of his government. However, according to the *Taiping huanyu ji*, in a version of the story occasionally repeated in later accounts, this building was erected with a very specific purpose in mind: to cheer up Xi Shi from her homesickness by allowing her to look towards the kingdom of Yue.[93] In this case, the role of the Gusu Tower seems to have become conflated with that of the Qi Gate to the Wu capital, which was supposedly built by King Helü of Wu for his homesick daughter-in-law, to allow her to look at the road home to Qi. This interpretation, apparently of little significance in the overall cultural history of Gusu Tower since it is so rarely mentioned, nevertheless makes the site even more romantic, as a symbol of the love and concern felt by the king of Wu for his beloved.

Endgame at the Gusu Tower

A number of ancient Chinese historical texts and imperial era gazetteers record that Gusu Tower played an important role in the last days of the kingdom of Wu. There seem to have been two main traditions developed. The first was that the Yue army attacked Wu, took Crown Prince You of Wu prisoner, and burned the Gusu Tower in an act of revenge for their terrible humiliation at Kuaiji at the very outset of their long campaign of conquest. The second tradition states that King Fuchai of Wu spent his final days in residence at the tower, planning his doomed resistance to the onslaught of the Yue army. The first of these traditions seems to be the older, and was first recorded in the "Wuyu" chapter of the *Guoyu*, an account that dates the burning of the tower to 482 BCE, the year following the defeat of the state of Qi in the battle of Ailing:

> Following that [defeat], the king of Yue commanded Fan Li and She Yong to lead the army out to sea and then up the Zhe and Huai Riv-

---

93. Yue Shi, *Taiping huanyu ji* 91.13b. The same story is also given in Peng Dayi, *Shantang sikao* 172.9a–9b, in which it is cited as an example of the great favor shown by King Fuchai of Wu to Xi Shi.

ers, in order to cut off the route [home] to Wu. They defeated Crown Prince You at Shixiongyi. King Goujian of Yue then led the Central Army up the Zhe River to make a surprise attack on Wu, whereupon they entered the outer city wall, burned the Gusu [Tower], and sailed away the Great [Royal] Ship.
于是越王句踐乃命范蠡, 舌庸, 率師沿海泝淮以絶吳路. 敗王子友于姑熊夷. 越王句踐乃率中軍泝江以襲吳, 入其郛, 焚其姑蘇, 徙其大舟.[94]

This account is supplemented by that of the *Zuozhuan*, which allows for a much more precise dating of these events to a few days before the meeting held at Huangchi. According to the *Zuozhuan*, King Goujian of Yue attacked Wu in a pincer movement on Bingzi day of the sixth month. He himself was in command of the northern column of the army; two individuals named Chou Wuyu 疇無餘 and Ou Yang 謳陽 were in command of the southern column. These individuals are identified in the Du Yu commentary as grandees of the kingdom of Yue.[95] Watching them from the banks of the Hong 泓 River were Crown Prince You, Prince Di, and two Royal Grandsons: Miyong and Shouyuyao. In the absence of King Fuchai of Wu, the defense of the realm would fall upon the shoulders of these men. In the first battle, which took place on Yiyou day outside the walls of the Wu capital, the Royal Grandson Miyong and Prince Di, in joint command of a force of five thousand men, fought the southern column of the Yue army, and captured their two commanders, Chou Wuyu and Ou Yang. This victory would be short-lived. The same day the northern column of the army arrived under the command of King Goujian himself, and Prince Di was charged with holding his ground. The following day, on Bingxu day, a much more serious battle was fought, in which the Wu army was comprehensively defeated, and Crown Prince You and the Royal Grandsons, Miyong and Shouyuyao, were all captured. The day after that, the Yue army entered the Wu capital.[96] No mention is made in the *Zuozhuan* account of the burning of the Gusu Tower; instead, it focuses on giving a day-by-day account of

94. *Guoyu*, p. 604 ("Wuyu"). The same story is given with some minor variations in the *Wu Yue chunqiu*, p. 87 ("Fuchai neizhuan").

95. Du Yu, *Chunqiu jingzhuan jijie*, p. 1790, n. 2.

96. *Zuozhuan*, pp. 1676–77 (Ai 13).

the progress of the battle and the fates of the most senior commanders. However, if the Gusu Tower was intended to represent the humiliating subordination of the kingdom of Yue, there is nothing intrinsically unlikely that the victorious army, on the occasion of its first great incursion into Wu, would take the time to go and put this monument to the torch.

In addition to this, there is a longstanding tradition that Gusu Mountain, the site of the Gusu Tower, played an important role in the final days of the kingdom of Wu. Ancient historical texts record how King Fuchai of Wu, accompanied by a handful of loyal guards, was trapped in his capital as the Yue army encircled his city—though the king was able to break through the siege before the city fell. However, in the imperial era, a tradition developed whereby King Fuchai of Wu was said to have left his capital before the siege, and that Gusu Mountain was his base during his final last-ditch attempts to preserve his kingdom from the invading forces. This tradition is recorded in the Song dynasty gazette for Wu Commandery, the *Wujun tujing xuji*, which specifically claims that King Fuchai was resident outside the city during the last weeks of his life: "Fuchai lived at Gusu Mountain, and fought a series of battles to the northwest until he was defeated at Gansui. Fuchai then fell on his sword and died, and the king of Yue ordered his soldiers to each bring a basket of earth to bury him at Beiyou at Qinyuhang Mountain." 夫差栖於姑蘇山, 轉戰西北敗于干遂. 夫差既伏劍死. 越王令干戈人以一壥土葬之秦餘杭山卑猶.[97]

It is interesting that this account states that King Fuchai was resident at Gusu Mountain, rather than Gusu Tower. This may accurately reflect the fact that the tower had been burned nearly a decade earlier. This tradition develops a certain symmetry within the portrayals of King Goujian of Yue and King Fuchai of Wu. Just as King Goujian had once been forced back into the mountain fastness of Kuaiji, a sacred site for his people, the king of Wu was based at Gusu Mountain in the last days of his life (at a place of great significance

97. Zhu Changwen, *Wujun tujing xuji*, p. 67. This account of the burial of King Fuchai of Wu is clearly based upon the description given in the *Yuejue shu*.

for his people, and the location of the Gusu Tower, a monument to their military prowess).

Although thousands, if not tens of thousands of pieces of poetry and prose were written during the imperial era on the subject of the lost glories and vanished splendors of the Gusu Tower, there seem to be virtually no literati works with commemorate the importance of this place as the last abode of King Fuchai of Wu, or which mention its destruction at the hands of the people of Yue. The Gusu Tower is consistently presented as the luxurious abode of King Fuchai of Wu and the beautiful Xi Shi when they were both at the height of their powers, when this place was a scene of music, dancing, and drunken pleasure. There seems to have been virtually no room in this highly dominant tradition for any alternative interpretations of this site. Although descriptions of the glamour and luxury of the Gusu Tower drew much of their power from the reader's knowledge of the blood-stained end which awaited its denizens, this is rarely mentioned in imperial era poetry. The destruction of the kingdom of Wu was mostly left as an "absent presence" to give poignancy to the literary works that described the famous historical sites once inhabited by King Fuchai of Wu and Xi Shi. There were a few poets who did make reference to the oncoming cataclysm; for example the Tang dynasty poet Cao Ye 曹鄴 (*jinshi* 850) in his work entitled "Gusu tai" speaks of the sound of war drums breaking into the pleasure seekers' laughter, and the terrible carnage that accompanied the fall of the kingdom:

In the Wu palace, before the wine has been fully drained,
Another banquet is held at Gusu Tower.
Beautiful women leave tearfully,
Even at midnight the Chang Gate is open.
Facing each other they sing and dance,
But in the midst of their revelry they hear the sound of battle drums.
The [women] are scattered like stars to every corner of the heavens,
Blood flows through the streets.
Once past, they are forever consigned to history,
The tower has vanished, its denizens have not returned.
From time to time one hears that in these fields,
People pick up golden hairpins.

吳宮酒未消, 又宴姑蘇臺.
美人和淚去, 半夜閶門開.
相對正歌舞, 笑中聞鼓鼙.
星散九重門, 血流十二街.
一去成萬古, 臺盡人不回.
時聞野田中, 拾得黃金釵.[98]

Unlike the situation pertaining to other Wu royal sites, the imaginations of imperial-era writers could not be refreshed or invigorated by a visit to the site of the Gusu Tower. Since every trace of this tower was lost in antiquity, they could only occasionally find inspiration from contemplating the contemporary appearance of the city of Suzhou. As a result, there are very few poems which juxtapose the Gusu Tower with any references to the poet's own experiences. A rare exception is the poem entitled "Gusu tai" by the Song dynasty poet Su Jiong 蘇炯:

The grass covers these ruins just like snow covers the mountain peaks,
The blue and red [evening clouds] fall over the towers and palaces of the king of Wu.
Outside the Gusu gate, as I anchor my boat for the night,
Sadly I listen to the Hanshan [Temple's] midnight bell.
草滿污萊雪滿峰, 吳王臺殿落青紅.
姑蘇門外連宵泊, 愁聽寒山半夜鐘.[99]

The Gusu Tower Lives On

The Gusu Tower was destroyed, at the latest, in 473 BCE, at the time of the conquest of Wu by Yue. The majority of ancient Chinese historical texts do not record the exact fates of individual buildings as the kingdom of Wu was overrun by the forces of King Goujian of Yue: their focus is on what happened to key individuals, in particular King Fuchai of Wu and Prime Minister Pi. The vast majority of imperial-era gazetteers do not discuss the issue of the destruction of this tower and give no details about exactly when it vanished. Indeed, many major gazetteers for the city of Suzhou make no reference to the Gusu Tower at all. This may perhaps reflect its status as an imaginary construct, destroyed before any accurate description was made,

98. This poem is quoted in Wang Ao et al., *Gusu zhi,* vol. 3, p. 108.
99. Su Qiong, *Lengranzhai shiji* 7.12b.

vanished so early that even the location of the site where it stood was soon forgotten. One of the few gazetteers to specifically mention the fate of the Gusu Tower in terms derived from ancient historical texts seems to be Wang Ao's *Gusu zhi*, which records that it was destroyed after the defeat and capture of Crown Prince You of Wu in an account that is clearly linked to the description of the events given in the *Guoyu* and *Zuozhuan*.[100] Though the destruction of the Gusu Tower by fire at the time of the first invasion of Wu by Yue is the older tradition, a second story concerning the fate of this building was recorded in the *Wujun zhi*. In this Song dynasty gazetteer, a quotation is given from a text called the *Jianjie lu* 鑒誡錄 (Account of the mirror of admonitions), which states that the Gusu Tower was destroyed for the sake of building materials that were then used in a temple dedicated to King Fuchai of Wu: "The *Jianjie lu* says: 'The story has been handed down for generations that this temple was built with wood that came from chopping up the Gusu Tower.' In the Tang dynasty the presented-scholar Chen Yu (*jinshi* 792) once wrote [a poem about] the temple to Fuchai." 《鑒誡錄》云: "世傳此廟折姑蘇臺木創成." 唐陳羽秀才嘗題夫差廟.[101]

Chen Yu, a native of the city of Suzhou, wrote a surviving *jueju* on the subject entitled "Ti Fuchai miao" 題夫差廟 (On the temple to King Fuchai), also sometimes known by the alternative title "Jing Fuchai miao" 經夫差廟 (On passing by the temple to King Fuchai), which certainly records the use of timbers from Gusu Tower in the construction of a temple dedicated to the memory of the last king of Wu:

> Gusu Tower was built with timbers over a thousand years old,
> It was cut down to make the Fuchai Temple to house his numinous
> spirit.
> Banners are lonely, covered in dust,
> I do not know for whom the flutes and drums are played.
> 姑蘇臺上千年木, 刻作夫差廟裏神.
> 幡盖寂寥塵土滿, 不知簫鼓樂何人.[102]

---

100. Wang Ao et al., *Gusu zhi*, vol. 3, p. 105.

101. Fan Chengda, *Wujun zhi*, p. 166.

102. He Guangyuan, *Jianjie lu*, p. 67. The alternative title to this poem and a version of the text with slightly different wording is found in Li Fang ed., *Wenyuan yinghua* 320.15a.

The present text of the *Jianjie lu*, although it quotes Chen Yu's poem, contains no other references to the chopping down of the Gusu Tower to build a temple dedicated to King Fuchai. It is possible that the current version of the *Jianjie lu* is corrupt, since there is a persistent tradition from at least the Tang dynasty onwards that the original timbers from Gusu Tower were reused at some point after the fall of Wu to build a temple to the last king. This is in direct contradiction with the tradition that Gusu Tower was burnt when Wu fell. The poem by Chen Yu also represents one of only two works of literature on the subject of the temple dedicated to King Fuchai of Wu to be widely anthologized during the imperial era. The other, by Zhang Yong 張咏, entitled "Fuchai miao" 夫差廟 (The temple to Fuchai), lacks any overt reference (other than in its title) to the commemoration of the last king of Wu in the vicinity of the ancient Gusu Tower:

> Good or evil actions can make you secure or put you in danger,
> He did not trust a loyal and good [man] but gave employment to Bo Pi [instead].
> Ever since antiquity every household has its own beauty,
> Why should anyone blame the destruction of the kingdom on Xi Shi?
> 由來邪正是安危, 不信忠良任伯嚭.
> 自古家家有容冶, 何須亡國殢西施?[103]

---

103. Both this poem and Chen Yu's are quoted following the entry for the temple to King Fuchai of Wu in Fan Chengda, *Wujun zhi*, p. 166. Fan Chengda, as a more modest man than many gazetteer writers, did not include his own poem on the subject, "Ti Fuchai miao" 題夫差廟 (On the temple to King Fuchai," which is given in his collected works: "Releasing the enemy at [Kuai]ji Mountain created a disaster,/ Greed for victory over the Upper States was even more reckless./ He did not know that he was raising a tiger and bringing ruin upon himself,/ Until he found the fish he had no sense of impending doom./ In his dreams he saw catalpas growing in the rear garden,/ He lived to see deer climb the high tower./ After a thousand ages only the regrets of his loyal minister endure,/ Transformed into the snowy waves of the flowing river" 縱敵稽山禍已胎, 垂涎上國更荒哉. 不知養虎自遺患, 只道求魚無後災. 夢見梧桐生後圃, 眼看麋鹿上高臺. 千齡只有忠臣恨, 化作濤江雪浪堆. Fan Chengda, *Fan Shihu ji*, p. 385. The reference to the fish in this poem seems to belong to a later legend concerning the conflict between Wu and Yue. King Fuchai at one time had King Goujian pinned down and sent him a gift of a salted fish to represent his plight. King Goujian responded with the present of a fresh carp, to symbolize his intention to fight on, and the Wu army withdrew. This legend, apparently only recorded at the end of the imperial era, is discussed in

Gazetteers for the Suzhou region would record that by the Song dynasty there were two major temples dedicated to King Fuchai in the vicinity of the Gusu Tower: one northeast of the city that was traditionally identified as being associated with Gusu Mountain, and the other in Changshu County, that was founded by a Buddhist monk Li Zezheng 李則正 in the Xining 熙寧 reign-period (1068–76).[104] The first temple was that supposed to have been built with the remains of the Gusu Tower. In the Ming dynasty the existence of a third major temple dedicated to the last king of Wu was recorded: this temple was built in Xin'an Village 新安鄉 in Kunshan County 昆山縣.[105] The Qing dynasty gazetteer for Suzhou (compiled in 1874) stated that a temple dedicated to the memory of King Fuchai of Wu had once stood on to the northeast of Gusu Mountain, in this text called Guxu. However, by the nineteenth century, this temple had been destroyed, and all traces of where it had once stood were lost.[106] The paucity of these references seems to indicate that commemoration of King Fuchai of Wu was not a particularly widespread or well-established local cult. As a result of this, the history of worship in these temples is extremely difficult to trace.

By far the best-recorded temple dedicated to the memory of the last king of Wu stood in the city of Hangzhou. This foundation was established in the fifth year of the Chunhua 淳化 reign era (994) by the prefect Wang Huaji 王化基 (944–1010, *jinshi* 977). In the third year of the Qiandao 乾道 reign era (1167) it was restored by the Military Commissioner, Zhou Cong 周淙. In the sixth year of the Qingyuan reign era (1200), King Fuchai of Wu was given the title of the Marquis of Benevolent Response, Peaceful Succor, Trusting Assistance, and

---

Schoppa, *Song Full of Tears*, p. 61. The reference to catalpas refers to a story found in the "Ji Wuwang zhanmeng" chapter of the *Yuejue shu*, in which King Fuchai of Wu dreamed (among various other things) of the trees growing unpruned in his garden and requested first Prime Minister Pi and then Gongsun Sheng to divine if it was auspicious or not. The final couplet refers to the fact that Wu Zixu was an important water deity in the Wu region throughout the imperial era.

104. This was not the only temple built by Li Zezheng. He is also credited with rebuilding a temple dedicated to King Goujian of Yue in the same county. Lu Xiong, *Suzhou fu zhi*, pp. 583–84.

105. Wang Ao et al., *Gusu zhi*, vol. 2, p. 531.

106. Li Mingwan and Feng Guifen, *Suzhou fu zhi*, p. 1059.

Illustrious Protection (*Shanying anji fouyou xianwei hou* 善應安濟孚佑顯衛侯). The granting of such a title, indicating the assumption of this deity into the imperially sponsored pantheon, would normally have been followed by an official program of temple building, as shrines dedicated to this god were then built in other major cities.[107] In fact, this seems not to have been the case in this instance, and the commemoration of King Fuchai of Wu remained a strictly local cult, confined to a handful of temples in the Jiangnan region. Then in the ninth year of the Chunyou 淳祐 reign period (1249), this temple was completely rebuilt by a junior member of the Song imperial family, the Military Commissioner Zhao Yuchou 趙與籌 (1179–1260, *jinshi* 1221). The name of this temple, Zhaoji miao 昭濟廟 (Temple of enlightened succor) in use from the Southern Song dynasty onwards gives no overt indication of its significance as a major foundation dedicated to the memory of King Fuchai of Wu, and in a subsidiary fashion, to Wu Zixu as well.[108]

Many ancient accounts of the conflict between the two ancient kingdoms of Wu and Yue stress their ongoing links and the frequent symmetry of their experiences. The ingrained animosity between the two kingdoms seems not to have overridden this continued intimate connection. Thus, in the case of the construction of the Gusu Tower, cunningly worked timbers taken from the forests of Yue were sent by King Goujian to Wu to delude his greatest enemy. These Yue timbers, having once been used by King Fuchai of Wu in building the Gusu Tower, were then subsequently taken down and reused in the construction of a temple dedicated to his memory after the conquest of his kingdom.

---

107. Watson, "Standardizing the Gods" p. 300.

108. The history of this temple is given in identical terms in the Song dynasty gazetteer for Hangzhou by Qian Shuoyou, *Xianchun Linan zhi* 71.2b; and in the Qing dynasty local history by Di Junlian, *Haitang lu* 12.25b. The former gazetteer suggests that though other local histories, in particular the Chunyou reign-era gazetteer for Lin'an, state that the primary deity to whom this temple was dedicated was King Fuchai, in fact the deity concerned was a local water god subsumed into the historical figure of the last king of Wu. This type of conflicting dedication, though using a much more famous and important example, is discussed in Miller, *The Divine Nature of Power*.

Gusu Station and the New Gusu Tower

The tower built by the last kings of Wu as a potent expression of their wealth and power is referred to in ancient and imperial era texts either as the Gusu Tower, or by the name Guxu. This difference in nomenclature, though minor, nevertheless indicates an enduring problem. From the very earliest times, there seems to have been confusion about the origins of the name of Gusu Mountain, with many authorities understanding it as Guxu Mountain (named in honor of King Helü's loyal minister Wu Zixu). It is certainly the case that the mountain was thought to stand beyond the Xu Gate of the city of Suzhou. However, modern scholarship has indicated that in antiquity Gusu was phonetically identical with the word Gouwu—that is, to the tribal name of the Wu people.[109] It would therefore seem likely that the name of this mountain referred to the people who lived in the region, rather than to the minister Wu Zixu. As a result of the confusion between Gusu and Guxu, the Xu Gate came to be particularly associated with the ancient tower, and thus in the Song dynasty, the prefect Wang Huan 王喚 ordered the construction of a new Gusu Tower here, which was completed in 1144. At that time, the Xu Gate was impassable, having been bricked up in 1084. The Xu Gate is shown clearly on the engraved map of Suzhou completed in 1229 under the auspices of the then-prefect of the city Li Shoupeng 李壽朋, with the new, two-story Gusu Tower built on top of it.[110] This new tower was built to facilitate viewing the scenery from a vantage point high above the great city walls of Suzhou. Just to the north of this new Gusu Tower was a complex of buildings, including a station for passing official travellers, the Gusu Guan 姑蘇館. This was one of the most impressive government hostels south of the Yangtze at the time of its construction, and a regular staging post for official visitors travelling to the Southern Song capital at Lin'an. In addition to its official function, this place became a popular site for

109. Shang Zhitan, "Wuguo ducheng de bianqian ji Helü jiandu Suzhou de yuanyou," p. 8.

110. Xu, *The Chinese City in Space and Time*, p. 117, fig. 4.9 gives a detailed image of this section of the map. The history of the creation of this map, and details of the 1917 re-carving, are given in Hu, *Visible Traces*, pp. 176–77.

taking leave of friends, and many literati travelled here in order to see off officials departing on tours of duty. For example, it is recorded that Fan Chengda spent seven days at the Gusu station, saying goodbye to his friends before leaving for an official posting in Guilin.[111]

Both the new Gusu Tower and the Gusu Station were restored in 1266. The Xu Gate was finally unblocked in 1352, after the discovery of a stone inscribed with the name of the gate, which was interpreted as an omen requiring the restoration of the original function of this gate.[112] There had long been debate over the practicalities of reopening Xu Gate for traffic into the city. However, this had always previously been postponed due to the presence of the magnificent Gusu Station immediately adjacent to the gate, which would have had to be at least partially demolished to make access to the gate possible. It is not clear how the buildings of the station and the new Gusu Tower were affected by the decision to reopen the gate. Nevertheless, the station remained in use well into the Ming dynasty, and its role as the site of many a leave-taking between literati and officials was commemorated in many works of literature. Entirely typical of the genre is the poem "Bie Fan Ciyun" 别方次雲 (Saying goodbye to Fang Ciyun) by the Song dynasty poet Lin Guangchao 林光朝 (1111–78, *jinshi* 1163). This much-anthologized work commemorates the special melancholy associated with the Gusu station, a place where friends parted not knowing when they would meet again:

Gusu Tower stands above Gusu station,
Together we speak of the bamboo braziers in use at Nanshan.
We met on the shores of Lake [Tai] and here we must also part,

---

111. Hargett, *On the Road in Twelfth Century China*, p. 100.

112. The discovery of the ancient inscription that earned the Xu Gate a new lease of life has an interesting parallel in the history of another of the gates to the city of Suzhou: the Shemen 蛇門 (Snake Gate). During the occupation of the city by the Japanese, this gate was slated for demolition to allow for the construction of a new bridge. However, when work began in 1942, they promptly discovered an ancient inscribed stele. The Japanese then decided to restore the bridge, leaving it to be torn down by the authorities in the 1950s, and the stele that earned it a stay of execution carted off during the Cultural Revolution to be used for building material. Suzhoushi Canglangqu bianshi xiuzhi lingdao xiaozu ed., *Suzhoushi Canglangqu*, p. 133.

Who knows where we will meet again to talk of Gusu?
姑蘇臺上姑蘇館, 共說南山竹火爐.
湖上相逢又相別, 不知何處說姑蘇?[113]

Although the New Gusu Tower above the Gusu station had no relationship whatsoever with the ancient monument of the same name or to the last king of Wu, a connection was still occasionally made in poetry. Given that the original Gusu Tower was long gone, the new version could function as a source of inspiration, and a focus of poetic endeavor. This kind of sentiment can be seen in the poem "Gusu guan yeyu" 姑蘇館夜雨 (A rainy night at Gusu station) by the Yuan dynasty statesman Wang Yun 王惲 (1227–1304):

Wu was destroyed and Yue became hegemon in this pointless conflict,
The north wind has whipped up the river, just as their hatred still has not calmed.
The whole night I did not sleep, thinking about past events,
Below the Gusu Tower the rain falls until the bright dawn.
吳亡越霸兩蝸爭, 朔吹翻江恨未平.
一夜不眠思往事, 姑蘇臺下雨連明.[114]

To many visitors to the city, the new Gusu Tower was a reminder of the region's glorious past, as well as an opportunity for the more romantically-inclined to muse on the passage of time and the terrible destruction wrought by Yue upon Wu in antiquity.[115] As with so many other sites discussed in this book, the Gusu station and new Gusu Tower had multiple associations for its visitors. What is striking though, in the case of the new Gusu Tower, was that the name was so well established in the literati cultural tradition that this place needed no further link to the ancient kings of Wu to call forth a host of associations with the ancient history of the region.

Conclusion

Unlike the other commemorative sites considered in this book, nothing concrete remains at Numinous Cliff to remind the visitor of

113. Lin Guangchao, *Aixuan ji* 1.15a–15b.

114. Wang Yun, *Qiujian ji* 30.22a.

115. This can also be seen in the famous diary of a Korean visitor to the site in 1488. Meskill, *Ch'oe Pu's Diary*, p. 92.

the glorious history of the kingdom of Wu, and even the location of Gusu Tower has long been lost. As a result, both these sites exist more in the literati imagination than in fact. Though in practice this does not seem to have resulted in any demonstrable diminution in later writings on the subject, compared to sites with more concrete surviving remains, there is nevertheless a noticeable impoverishment of ideas within *huaigu* literature concerning these two sites. Given that, in the circumstances, literati writers were severely constrained as to what they could say about the physical appearance of the site, many sought refuge in highly stereotyped images. It is perhaps for this reason that some of the best writings about Numinous Cliff and Gusu Tower are entirely imaginary reconstructions of the glorious past, such as Li Bai's erotic portrayal of Xi Shi in the poem "Kouhao Wuwang meiren banzui" 口號吳王美人半醉 (Addressing the king of Wu's half-drunk beautiful companion):

> The wind stirs the water lilies filling the palace with their perfume,
> On top of Gusu Tower, the king of Wu holds court.
> Xi Shi dances drunkenly, charming and weak from exertion,
> Smiling she reclines against a white jade couch in front of the eastern window.
> 風動荷花水殿香, 姑蘇臺上見吳王.
> 西施醉舞嬌無力, 笑倚東窗白玉床.[116]

In spite of the much more tenuous connection between Numinous Cliff and King Fuchai of Wu (compared with Tiger Hill and King Helü), there are nevertheless a number of strong points of similarity between the two sites. In part this impression is natural, given that these sites have a similar history, for they were both originally Wu royal gardens, given to the Buddhist church during the Age of Disunion. Likewise, both have since remained in the possession of the church; wealthy foundations, famous now for their magnificent Southern Song brick pagodas. The presence of monastic foundations at both these sites was no doubt crucial for protecting them, and the monks played a very important part in encouraging and informing

---

116. Qu Tuiyuan and Zhu Jincheng eds., *Li Bai ji jiaozhu*, p. 1485.

tourism to these sites.[117] From the Song dynasty onwards, both sites are portrayed as possessing a special natural beauty, worth visiting for that alone. Both have also been the focus of much literati activity, which has been well preserved in the many gazetteers and anthologies produced about these sites. However, there are also some significant points of difference. One is that in the presentation of Numinous Cliff Mountain in imperial era gazetteers, only three aspects of the site are commonly discussed: its historical significance, its natural beauties, and the state of the Chan Buddhist monastery there. This stands in stark contrast with the portrayal of Tiger Hill, which was a favorite site for burials, as well as being accorded an important role in literati activity through the erection of commemorative shrines that remembered many famous local scholars and officials who served in the region.

The portrayal of King Fuchai of Wu in ancient Chinese texts consistently plays with images of sight and blindness. Wu Zixu clearly sees the dangers threatening the king and demands with his dying breath that his eyes be gouged from his head and hung above the gate in the city wall that he might "see" the triumphal entry of the Yue army with King Goujian at its head; but King Fuchai remains blind to all risks and indeed binds his eyes before committing suicide that he might not have to "see" the accusing innocent victims of his

---

117. In the mid-Ming period, the local painter and poet Tang Yin wrote a poem entitled "Deng Lingyan" 登靈巖 (Climbing Numinous Cliff) in which a monk figures as a tourist guide as well as marking a contrast between the glamorous royal past and the religious present of the site: "The mountain ghosts hurry towards the overgrown Buddhist hall,/ The old monk points and speaks of the king of Wu./ The silver vase has transmogrified leaving behind the palace well,/ Persimmon leaves drift in to choke the [Echoing] Steps Corridor" 山鬼踉蹌佛殿荒, 老僧指點説吳王. 銀瓶化去餘宮井, 柿葉飛來滿屧廊. Tang Yin, *Tang Bohu quanji*, p. 103. The silver vase or water jar mentioned in the third line is a complex allusion, which may perhaps refer to the Du Fu poem "Tongping" 銅瓶 (Bronze vase) which describes just such a vessel, found abandoned in a dried-up palace well after the war. Yao Zhaoao, *Du shi xiangzhu*, p. 624. Equally, this line may allude to the poem "Jingdi yin yinping" 井底引銀瓶 (Drawing a Silver Vase from the Bottom of a Well) by Bai Juyi, which compares the vessel to an abandoned wife. Gu Xuejie, *Bai Juyi ji*, p. 85. The reference to the silver vase could then allude to the destruction of the palace after warfare, the pain of separation, and the abandonment of a beautiful woman.

terrible mistakes. Something of the same idea is found in much imperial era literati writings about King Fuchai of Wu, as he is consistently portrayed as being oblivious of any danger. In his literary incarnation, King Fuchai is described building beautiful palaces, boating with his ladies, playing music with the lovely Xi Shi, and enjoying lavish banquets. Though the troubles that threatened the kingdom of Wu, and that engulfed King Fuchai in the end are often not explicitly mentioned, they nevertheless hang like a threatening cloud in the background. It is the presence of this growing menace that gives literary works about King Fuchai their power, for the character of the last king of Wu then appears like that of a man sleepwalking along a narrow ledge. When he wakes, he falls.

AFTERWORD

Wu in the Modern World

By the end of the Eastern Han dynasty, the highly stereotyped representations of the three most famous members of the Wu royal house were well established within Chinese traditional culture. Prince Jizha of Wu was the perfect Confucian gentleman, King Helü was a violent and bellicose monarch, while Fuchai was an incompetent, luxury-loving, and easily deluded king. How much truth is there in any of these depictions? It is hard to say. Contemporary bronze inscriptions attest to at least some portions of their traditional biographies. But did Prince Jizha go on numerous embassies to the Central States, displaying his erudition and knowledge of Zhou mores at every step? Did King Helü murder every relative he could get his hands on to secure his accession to the throne? Was King Fuchai captivated by the beauty of Xi Shi to the point where he fatally neglected the government of his kingdom? These are questions that the source texts simply do not allow us to answer with any confidence. Furthermore, in spite of the excavation of a number of inscribed bronzes made for members of the Wu royal house, these artworks throw virtually no light on the history of the kingdom. Quite the contrary, through their numerous references to otherwise unknown kings and princes, they make it clear that there is an enormous amount that we do *not* know about the history of Wu—things that at this remove of time it is quite possible that we will never know. Archaeology has in many ways served to make these people more mysterious, not less.

There is sufficient evidence found in ancient texts to provide a slightly more nuanced picture than the stereotypical representation of the royal house of Wu within traditional Chinese culture, but not much more. Given their contemporary political importance at the end of the Spring and Autumn period, both the kingdoms of Wu and Yue are woefully underrepresented in ancient texts: according to calculations by Su Tie 蘇鐵, the history of the kingdom of Yue occupies less than 1 percent of the *Zuozhuan*, while that of Wu represents less than 2 percent.[1] To make matters worse, the vast majority of extant sources for the history of these southern kingdoms was written within the context of Central States culture, which was unsympathetic to the civilization of Wu and Yue and possibly ignorant of even their most basic customs and tenets. Even in the case of Warring States era texts, written in the centuries immediately following the collapse of the kingdom of Wu, there is every reason to be concerned that the writers did not fully understand the culture of the place that they were recording. The only major source of local traditions—the *Yuejue shu*—was not compiled until the Eastern Han dynasty, some five hundred years after Wu was conquered. There is also every reason to be concerned that some of these early Chinese texts, including the *Zuozhuan*, contain fictionalized accounts of the deeds of the Wu kings (and indeed many other historical individuals) but given the paucity of the sources, we have no choice but to work with what there is. There is simply not enough evidence available from other sources to be able to write the history of Wu: the accounts found in ancient Chinese texts, flawed as they are, provide the framework by which we understand events in this ancient southern kingdom.

Part 1 of this book has been an account of a cultural construction—the kingdom of Wu as represented by Chinese authors who may have lived not too long after the kingdom of Wu collapsed but who were nevertheless divorced in either time or place (or both) from the people that they describe. The later imperial era scholars and poets whose work has been the focus of the second part of this book would have relied almost entirely on the accounts found in ancient texts for their information about the ancient kingdom of Wu. Some imperial-era individuals may have had access to local traditions about Wu and Yue, but if so this forms an extremely minor aspect of the massive body of literature produced in response to the events that took place in southern Jiangsu province at the end of the Spring and Autumn period. It is clear that in instances where the historical record directly contradicts popular legend, it is the traditions found within popular

1. Su Tie, "Wu Yue wenhua de tancha," p. 374.

culture that are the most important for literati writings produced by the scholarly elite. How else to explain the enormous number of poems and other works on the subject of Xi Shi? Her legendary love affair with King Fuchai was an extremely late addition to the history of the conflict between the kingdoms of Wu and Yue, and yet this story has proved one of the most famous aspects of King Goujian's campaign to bring down his enemy. The stories found in ancient Chinese texts that fed into popular representations of the kings and princes of Wu were cited as the inspiration for countless works of literature, forming a mutually reinforcing circle in which there was little room for other voices. Any tales that contradicted the mainstream tradition were neglected except by the most erudite. For the purposes of understanding the later commemoration of the kings and princes of Wu, the facts of their biographies are less important than the legends concerning their lives and deaths, the popular traditions that inspired generations of visitors to travel to sites connected with their memory.

⋆ ⋆ ⋆

The city of Suzhou in many ways has been the real focus of this book. Given that so much has already been said about the history of this city during the imperial era, it is now time to consider what happened there during the course of the last century. In recent years, Suzhou has been the subject of much research about Chinese traditional urban planning and design. In such works, two images are often given in close juxtaposition. One is the *Pingjiang tu* 平江圖 (Map of Pingjiang [Suzhou]) of 1229, the earliest known to-scale city map ever produced. The other is an aerial photograph of the city, taken in 1945 by the US Fourteenth Air Force as part of a program to map the whole of China.[2] This clichéd pairing suggests that the city of Suzhou has been unaffected by the passage of time and that this ancient metropolis retained its unique characteristics well into the twentieth century. More historically informed works on the city's history mention the destruction of the city center during the early Ming dynasty, but even there the implicit suggestion remains

2. See for example Carroll, *Between Heaven and Modernity*, pp. 12–13.

that Suzhou is an ancient metropolis that has been preserved largely intact to modern times. In fact, Suzhou has been subject to repeated large-scale destruction on numerous occasions. The conquest of Wu by Yue in 473 BCE, the temporary abandonment of the site from 591–c. 626, the devastation caused by the Wang Ying 王郢 (d. 877) rebellion of 875–877, the sack of the city by the Jurchen in 1130, the Ming conquest of 1367, and the Taiping rebellion in 1860 were all instances of enormous damage.[3] Fire, flood, neglect, old age, and changing fashions have also removed many structures (including some once seen as definitive of life in Suzhou) from the city's landscape.[4] The buildings and ancient structures of the city also suffered considerable damage from warfare and social upheavals during the twentieth century. The modernization programs undertaken during the Republican era (1912–1949) that resulted in the early losses of canals and city walls, the Japanese bombing of 1937, the Great Leap Forward, and the Cultural Revolution were obviously occasions of enormous destruction to the fabric of the city. However, some other government policies, such as the campaign to deconsecrate religious buildings during the 1950s and road-widening programs that cut highways through the heart of the old city have also had a considerable effect on social structures and the quality of life within the confines of the old city.

---

3. Of these sackings of the city, by far the least well-documented is that by Wang Ying during the Tang dynasty. However, the appendix to the *Wudi ji* suggests that this gazetteer was originally compiled to record the state of the city prior to its destruction. This would make the *Wudi ji* a work of nostalgic literature comparable to the *Luoyang Qielanji* 洛陽伽藍記 (A record of Buddhist temples in Luoyang) by Yang Xuanzhi 楊衒之 and the 東京夢華錄 (A dream of splendors past in the eastern capital) by Meng Yuanlao 孟元老 *Dongjing menghua lu*. The first of these texts describes the beauties of Luoyang, with particular reference to its many Buddhist temples, prior to the fall of the Northern Wei dynasty. This book has been translated into English twice: Jenner, *Memories of Lo-yang*; Wang, *A Record of Buddhist Monasteries in Lo-yang*. The second book describes the pleasures of living in Bianliang 卞梁 (now Kaifeng) prior to the fall of the Northern Song dynasty, with emphasis on the sensory pleasures available to men of wealth. A translation of this text is given in West, "Recollections of the Northern Song Capital."

4. This is not a new development. The wooden bridges of Suzhou, with their painted red railings, were once regarded as a defining feature of the city. Since the Song dynasty however, all Suzhou's bridges have been made of stone. Yuan Yixin, *Suzhou gucheng*, p. 14.

City Walls and Gates

The arrangement of city walls and gates in Suzhou has apparently remained virtually unchanged for much of the city's history. The biggest change until the twentieth century was the razing of the walls of the citadel during the Ming dynasty by order of the Hongwu Emperor in 1374. Not only was the city center permanently affected by the removal of the citadel, but the emperor also ordered the execution of many major Suzhou literati figures. By the Ming dynasty any ancient remains within the walls of the citadel had long gone; indeed this area of the city had been devastated a few years previously, in the conflagration that followed the fall of Suzhou to the forces of the future Hongwu emperor in 1367.[5]

One of the great challenges Suzhou faced during the twentieth century was how to develop new uses for old buildings, and how to find appropriate ways to utilize spaces whose traditional usage had become obsolete. A particular challenge was posed by part of the area formerly enclosed within the citadel. During the Qing dynasty, this area had been used as a barracks and parade ground, with the western part functioning as the city execution ground. At the beginning of the Republican era, city authorities were thus faced with a difficult decision. Although the land formerly occupied by the barracks and parade ground could easily be developed for mixed housing and commercial use, the former execution ground was a much more controversial site. This situation was resolved in 1920, when this space was converted into a public park: the Suzhou Gongyuan 蘇州公園.[6]

The few surviving sections of the city walls of Suzhou still preserve their Yuan dynasty appearance—this is in spite of various official repair programs, in particular the significant reconstruction work in the late 1360s and in 1662 to repair damage from the Ming and Qing conquests, respectively. The Yuan walls were built by order of the government in 1351–1352, after significant destruction sustained at the time of the Mongol conquest. This work took five months to

5. Xu, *The Chinese City in Space and Time*, pp. 144–8, gives a detailed account of the destruction that took place at this time.

6. Pan Junming, *Zicheng*, pp. 7–8.

complete, and resulted in the creation of forty-five *li* of new or restored city wall.[7] The best-preserved sections of the city wall, with stone facing, are to be found around the Pan Gate in the south of the city, but some sections of the core survive along the western side of the city. The walls along the northern and eastern sides of the ancient city have been completely razed.[8]

According to the "Ji Wudi" chapter of the *Yuejue shu*, the main city wall was originally pierced by eight gates.[9] During the imperial period, some of these gates were bricked up, and several new gates were made on occasions when it was deemed necessary to ease traffic in a particular direction. Each gate to the old city of Suzhou was noted for its special character. The Changmen (which no longer survives), near the main commercial district of the city and one of the original eight gates into Suzhou, was traditionally by far the busiest since traffic to and from the Grand Canal passed through this gate.[10] The Xumen, another of the original eight gates, is still extant and in good condition. In 1938, during the Japanese occupation of the city, a second gate was built to one side to ease traffic in and out of the city center. This gate, the Xin Xumen 新胥門 (New Xu gate) was demolished in 1958. In 1969 a new road bridge was built utilizing the space created by both the removal of the Xin Xumen and the demolition of a further section of the city wall. Originally known as the Hongqi qiao 紅旗橋 (Red flag bridge), it has subsequently been renamed Gusu qiao 姑蘇橋 (Gusu bridge), using one of the most ancient names for the city of Suzhou.[11]

The only gate at Suzhou that receives significant numbers of tourists is the Panmen, now located at the heart of the Panmen Scenic Area (Panmen jingqu 盤門景區) in the southwest of the city. The last long stretch of city wall to have survived to the present day is located

---

7. The reconstruction and restoration of the city walls of Suzhou is described in detail in Xu, *The Chinese City in Space and Time*, pp. 98–115.

8. The most detailed study of the walls of Suzhou prior to their destruction was carried out by Major Ishiwari Hiezō 石原平藏, as a hobby, during his time in China 1939–41. Wallacker et al. eds., *Chinese Walled Cities*, pp. 175–77.

9. *Yuejue shu*, pp. 11–12 ("Wudi ji").

10. Shan, *Suzhou yaowang Gusu tai*, pp. 24–28.

11. Suzhoushi Canglangqu bianshi xiuzhi lingdao xiaozu ed., *Suzhoushi Canglangqu zhi*, pp. 57–58.

around the Panmen, which preserves much of its original Yuan dynasty appearance. This has been assisted by the work to recreate the Yuan-style building that traditionally topped this gate, which was destroyed during battle just before the Japanese captured the city in 1937. This building was reconstructed in 1986 based on late Qing and Republican era photographs, at the same time as the whole area was established as a scenic spot listed under provincial level protection.[12] The area around the Panmen was the last area of the city to have been built up. This part of Suzhou was devastated when Ming forces entered the city, and seems to have remained uninhabited for many years. An unsuccessful attempt was made in 1872 to move people into this area of the city: as a result, this part of Suzhou remained generally uninhabited until the 1970s. The poem "Xuyong Gusu zhuzhi ci" 續咏姑蘇竹枝詞 (A further poem commemorating the bamboos of Gusu) by the Qing dynasty poet Yuan Jinglan 袁景瀾 records the desolate appearance of the Panmen during the late imperial era:

> A single weeping willow overhangs the painted building,
> Houses were once crowded around the Pan Gate.
> Since this place was plundered by troops at the end of the Yuan,
> People's homes have been deserted, the cold river running past.
> 一樹垂楊一畫樓, 盤門煙户本來稠.
> 自從元末遭兵却, 寥落居民冷水流.[13]

The only major building in the vicinity of the Panmen is the Ruiguangsi 瑞光寺 (Auspicious light temple). Only the pagoda, built in 1086, survived the Taiping assault on the city in 1860. The Shemen, another of the original eight gates and located in the southeast, was initially slated for demolition by the Japanese authorities in 1942, to allow for the construction of a new bridge. However, when demolition began, workmen found an ancient stone stele inscribed with the name of the gate, at which point the Japanese authorities decided to restore the gate and city wall at this location, making an opening for traffic to the bridge to one side. The gate was pulled down after the founding of the Peoples' Republic of China (PRC), and the stone

---

12. Wu Naifu, "Suzhou gu Panmen yu Wu Zixu," p. 6.
13. Quoted in Wang Jiaju, *Suzhou jiumeng*, p. 6.

stele that had earlier earned it a stay of execution was carted off for use as building material during the Great Leap Forward.[14]

The process of taking down most of the city wall and demolishing the majority of Suzhou's gates began during the Republican era, continued through the Japanese occupation of the city, and was completed by the PRC government. The three gates on the eastern side of Suzhou have all been completely destroyed. Thus, the Jiangmen was pulled down in 1934. The Fengmen 葑門 (Brassica gate), not one of the original eight gates, was built in the Song dynasty to ease traffic leaving the city to the southeast. This gate was pulled down in 1934, and the city wall around it was razed in 1953.[15] The Loumen 婁門 (Lou-constellation gate), through which the Japanese army entered the city on November 19, 1937, signalling the start of a three-day massacre, was torn down in 1948.[16] Of the two gates in the northern city wall, the date of the demolition of the Qimen does not appear to be recorded anywhere. The Wumen (renamed the Pingmen 平門 or Peace Gate in imperial times) was demolished in the 1920s to be replaced with a double-arched gateway, to ease traffic in and out of the old city.[17] During the 1960s this gateway, together with the entire city wall on the northern side of the city, was demolished. There is still a building near the original site of this gate that is known as the Pingmen and is a replica of a traditional gatehouse, but it stands in the middle of a park and the "watergate" is not connected to the canal network inside the city.

Roads and Canals

As with many other cities in the Jiangnan region, Suzhou was designed to be accessible both by road and by water. Traditionally, many canals had roads running along each side (*erlu jia yihe* 二路夾一河), allowing road and waterborne transport to make its way to

---

14. Suzhoushi Canglangqu bianshi xiuzhi lingdao xiaozu ed., *Suzhoushi Canglangqu zhi*, p. 133.

15. Wang Jiaju, *Suzhou jiumeng*, pp. 8–9.

16. Lu Wenfu, *Lao Suzhou*, p. 29.

17. A 1920s photograph of the Pingmen can be seen in Lu Wenfu, *Lao Suzhou*, p. 35.

every corner of the city. However, during the 1920s and 1930s, the motor car came to increasingly dominate the thinking of urban planners and they began a program to increase the road network inside the city walls.[18] During the Republican era, many kilometers of canals lying within the city walls were filled in to allow easier access for cars. A further canal elimination program, undertaken in 1958, saw the loss of many traditional "two roads sandwiching a canal" landscapes, including Daru jie 大儒街 (whose name commemorates the famous Ming dynasty scholar Wang Jingchen [1513–94]), and Niujia xiang 牛家巷, which was named after a Zhuangyuan scholar.[19] At the same time, some pre-existing roads were widened, making certain roads up to six lanes wide. Road-widening programs of this kind created the highways that now bisect the city, such as Renmin lu 人民路 (running north to south) and Jingde lu 景德路 (running east to west). Renmin lu, known before 1951 as Wolong lu 臥龍路, had always been a major thoroughfare, but the road-widening program still resulted in losses of what may be termed traditional street furniture.[20] The southern end of Renminlu was the site of a large commemorative arch, recording the achievements of Qian Qi 錢棨 (?–1799): a Qing dynasty scholar who gained first place in the provincial, national, and imperial examinations, and who lived in the neighborhood.[21] Although Suzhou produced many fine scholars during the Qing dynasty, Qian Qi was unique in his achievements. The removal of this arch, as with the loss of many other similar monuments, broke the connection between the city of Suzhou and its distinguished past

18. The Zhonghua quanguo daolu jianshe xiehui 中國全國道路建設協會 (All China road construction society), founded in 1921, seems to have exercised a particularly baleful influence. Stapleton, *Civilizing Chengdu*, pp. 231–33. By the mid-1920s the society boasted 80,000 members, who saw it as their duty to widen China's city streets with a view to enabling motor car traffic.

19. Yuan Yixin, *Suzhou gucheng*, p. 44.

20. During the Qing dynasty, this road was known as Hulonglu 護龍路 (Protecting the dragon road) since both the Kangxi and Qianlong emperors were greeted here on their southern progresses by the officials of Suzhou. Yu Mengren, *Lao Suzhou*, p. 35.

21. This achievement deeply impressed the Qianlong emperor, who wrote a poem about him entitled "Qian Sanyuan" 錢三元 (Three firsts Qian). Pan Rongsheng ed., *Ming Qing jinshi lu*, p. 975.

as a major educational and cultural center.[22] Likewise, the creation of Jingde lu from four much smaller alleyways required significant demolition, including the destruction of the old entrance gate to the temple of the City God.[23]

The creation of major highways bisecting Suzhou has largely served to compartmentalize the city. This was only exacerbated by the construction of Ganjiang lu 干將路 in the early 1990s. The construction of Ganjiang lu, which runs east to west through the heart of the old city, was a major prestige project for the city government. Today, this eight-lane highway serves to cut the ancient city in half. The project was touted as a fusion between modern practicalities of urban living and traditional Suzhou style, because a narrow canal runs down the middle of the road, and is indeed occasionally used by boatmen. However, the construction of this highway involved the demolition of eight thousand homes and the relocation of more than two hundred businesses.

Comparatively little is known of the early history of the waterways inside the city walls. The "Ji Wudi" chapter of the *Yuejue shu* records only one such waterway: running from the Pingmen to the Shemen (roughly north to south).[24] However, it is likely that even at the date of the "Ji Wudi," there were a great many more waterways inside the city than just the one mentioned, otherwise the water gates also recorded in this text would have been unnecessary. Over time, the canal network inside the city walls varied enormously in length, depending on the historical era and the state of upkeep of these waterways. If left unmaintained, these canals quickly filled up with debris and silt.

In 1797, a detailed map of the waterways of Suzhou was produced: the *Sujun chenghe sanheng sizhi tu* 蘇郡城河三横四直圖 (Map of the three horizontal and four vertical canals inside the city walls of Su[zhou] Commandery). This map commemorated a major restoration of these waterways, undertaken by order of the Governor of Jiangsu Province, Fei Chun 費淳 (1739–1811). This map, carved in

22. Wang Jiaju, *Suzhou jiumeng*, p. 38.

23. The original outer archway at the temple to the City God can be seen in a number of old photographs. Yu Mengren, *Lao Suzhou*, p. 42.

24. *Yuejue shu*, p. 10 ("Ji Wudi").

stone by Liu Zheng 劉徵 and now found in the grounds of the City God temple in Suzhou, was produced to commemorate the dredging of the city's canals.[25] From 1745–94, the canals had not been maintained, which resulted in considerable degradation to the waterways of the city. After the dredging, there were 570 kilometers of canals inside the city walls, a figure which was reduced to approximately 400 kilometers during the Republican era, as the canals were filled in to become roads. Between 1945 and 1985, the canal network was further reduced to around 350 kilometers.[26] The loss of waterways and their replacement with roads has significantly altered the character of the old city.

Houses and Gardens

The preservation of houses and gardens in Suzhou during the twentieth century was governed by a number of conflicting considerations. A fundamental difficulty for anyone administering Suzhou is that the center of the city is a finite area. The old city covers 14.2 square kilometers. Even after most of the city wall had been razed to the ground and the ancient gates dismantled, the moat was preserved: so it has proved impossible to integrate the suburban areas with the city center. Although there are many important historical sites, famous gardens, and great temples located in the suburbs of Suzhou, there remains a significant difference between *chengnei* 城内 (inside the walls) and *chengwai* 城外 (outside the walls). This distinction has expressed itself in many ways, from the battles between different groups of Red Guards in 1967 to the strictness with which planning regulations are applied, particularly over issues like the height of buildings.[27]

---

25. Suzhoushi difangzhi bianzuan weiyuanhui biangongshi et al. eds., *Suzhou gucheng dituji*, pp. 18–19.

26. Shi Jianhua et al., *Suzhou gucheng de baohu yu gengxin*, p. 3.

27. Jiangsusheng difangzhi xuehui ed., *Jiangsu changgu*, p. 388. The Red Guards in Suzhou were divided into *chengnei* and *chengwai* groups. In the worst single day of fighting between these two factions, 23 August 1967, they burnt 25 shops and 326 houses in the area around Changmen. 115 people were injured and 461 people were made homeless. Between August 1967 and February 1968, the worst part of the Cultural Revolution in Suzhou, more than 100 Red Guards were killed, as well as several thousand civilians killed or injured.

Suzhou began the twentieth century with the area within the city walls dominated by two types of architecture. The first is *minju* 民居 (vernacular architecture), much of which dated to the late Qing era and the post-Taiping reconstruction of the city. In 1949, according to official statistics, 40 percent of the buildings within the city walls dated to the Qing dynasty or earlier. By the time a survey of the city's architectural heritage was carried out in March 1983, this proportion had fallen to approximately 10 percent. The survey carried out in 1992 recorded no great change in the amount of Ming and Qing dynasty architecture to be found within the city walls.[28] There appears to have been no subsequent survey, but it is clear that significant destruction of Suzhou's architectural heritage occurred during the 1990s, and that the *minju* were particularly vulnerable to demolition.

Surviving examples of Ming and Qing dynasty domestic architecture were significantly adversely affected by the demand for housing within the old city, which during the course of the twentieth century resulted in the demolition of much old housing and the building of Western-style tower blocks. This kind of development was accompanied by a rise in the population density of the old city from 399 persons per square kilometer in 1949 to 681 in the year 2000. During the Maoist era, traditional domestic architecture also fell victim to the demand to make the city appear suitably proletarian. Prior to 1949, the ancient city of Suzhou was the site of only a small quantity of light industry. The vast majority of buildings found within the city walls constituted domestic housing. According to official statistics, in 1957 the old city contained 80 percent housing and 8.5 percent industrial buildings. In 1983, with official encouragement, industry accounted for 30.3 percent of the land within the old city of Suzhou.[29] The rise in population density and the industrial development within the old city has had an extremely detrimental effect on the quality of life for residents of Suzhou. However, since the 1990s

---

28. Interestingly there seems to have been a slight rise in the amount of Ming and Qing era architecture in Suzhou between 1983 and 1992, from 31.2 to 32.03 km^2. The figures for the 1983 survey are found in Suzhoushi fangchan guanliju, ed., *Suzhou gu minju*, p. 37; while the results of the 1992 survey are given in Shi Jianhua et al., *Suzhou gucheng de baohu yu gengxin*, p. 5.

29. Ibid., p. 52.

this situation has been indirectly addressed by the rise of property prices within the old city, which has gradually priced factories out of the city center.

Aside from ordinary domestic buildings, Suzhou has long been famous for its mansions and literati gardens. During the Ming and Qing dynasties, when this was the richest city in the empire, hundreds of merchants and officials built great mansions for themselves and laid out fine gardens. These houses, lacking any connection with imperial glory (royal and imperial sites having been, paradoxically, generally extremely well protected by the Communist government), suffered particularly during the years following the founding of the People's Republic. In 1953–54, seven gardens and mansions were ordered to be restored and were subsequently placed under the protection of the city authorities. (All of these are now World Heritage Sites.) With the exception of these places, not much interest was displayed in preservation and maintenance. As a result, of the more than three hundred mansions and gardens recorded at the end of the Qing dynasty, only seventy-two survive to the present day and that includes sites that have suffered significant damage.[30]

Gardens that were designated for protection shortly after the founding of the PRC nevertheless suffered damage during the 1950s and 1960s. The Great Leap Forward saw trees being chopped down for firewood to feed the new small scale, neighborhood industrial furnaces. Likewise, the campaign of 1965 to do away with flowers resulted in considerable damage; and if nothing else, neglect killed many plants and trees during this time. This campaign then segued into the beginning of the Cultural Revolution, when so much of Suzhou's cultural and artistic heritage was destroyed.[31] Programs to restore these damaged sites began in 1974, and these efforts were rewarded with

30. During the Ming dynasty, 271 gardens and mansions were built in Suzhou, with a further 130 being created during the Qing dynasty. Cao Lindi, *Gusu yuanlin yu Zhongguo wenhua*, p. 12. These figures for the survivors, derived from Shi Jianhua et al., *Suzhou gucheng de baohu yu gengxin*, p. 5, are based on the 1982 survey of the city's architecture.

31. See for example the account of the damage done to Suzhou's only surviving Song dynasty style garden, the Canglang ting 滄浪亭 or Blue Wave Pavilion, given in Zhou Suning, *Canglang ting*, p. 94.

the World Heritage Site status that has now been accorded to nine gardens inside and outside the city center. Although the focus of this chapter is on the fabric of the city, historical artifacts also suffered truly terrible destruction during this time. In 1937, between the twentieth of February and the second of March, an exhibition was held at the Suzhou Museum of some six thousand items related to the history of the city, most of which were in private ownership. In the year 2000, an attempt was made to trace the objects recorded in the exhibition catalog. Less than 1 percent had survived the turmoil of the intervening years.[32]

Temples

Prior to the anti-religious campaigns of the 1950s, the old city of Suzhou was home to a vast array of different religious buildings. In addition to the enormously important Confucian Temple and its attached academy, there were numerous Daoist and Buddhist monasteries and temples. There were also family shrines and temples dedicated to various deities from Chinese popular religion. Although many temples were secularized during the 1950s, a surprising number of religious buildings have survived in relatively good repair, including those dedicated to the City God, the enormous Daoist Xuanmiaoguan 玄妙觀 (Temple of mystery) at the heart of Suzhou's commercial district, and a number of Buddhist foundations. However, many of these religious buildings had their interiors wrecked during the Cultural Revolution.[33] During the 1950s, a couple of temples in and around Suzhou seem to have been designated for preservation. These foundations kept items of religious significance for other less fortunate institutions. The temples that fulfilled this function were the Beitasi 北塔寺 (North Pagoda Temple), Xiyuansi 西園寺 (Western Garden Temple), and Hanshansi 寒山寺 (Cold Mountain

32. Xu Gangyi, *Lao Suzhou*, vol. 1, p. 122.

33. The devastating damage caused by the Red Guards at the Xuanmiaoguan in central Suzhou is illustrated in contemporary photographs. Ibid., vol. 2, p. 297. This temple has now been completely restored, and is the centerpiece of Suzhou's commercial district. Religious worship has returned to this site; in particular the side temple to the Caishen 財神 (God of wealth) is extremely active.

Temple).[34] The wholesale removal of religious objects from their original homes has resulted in some curious anomalies. Prior to 1958, there was a single Tibetan Buddhist temple inside the old city, the Longchi Gu'an 龍池古庵 (Ancient monastery of the dragon's pool), which was the proud possessor of a Tibetan bronze statue of the Buddha. It is not known when this temple was founded, but it was certainly extant prior to the Taiping era. In the early 1950s, the monks in this temple did a deal with a nearby factory, the Guangrong 光榮 scarf factory. As a result, the monks were able to continue living in the monastery, but the whole place was given a suitably proletarian appearance by allowing the factory to use the main hall as a parking lot. (This kind of deal was not unique. The Zhiyuansi 祇園寺, a temple founded in the seventh century, made a similar but less advantageous arrangement with a textile company. In that instance, machines were moved into the temple and worked by the monks.) However, this did not save the monastery; and in 1958 it was deconsecrated to allow the buildings to be used for housing. The Tibetan bronze statue of the Buddha was taken to the Xiyuansi, where it remains to this day. This temple has no connection with Tibetan Buddhism, but to date there has been no plan to restore the statue to a more sympathetic environment.[35]

In recent years a number of temples and shrines have been converted to new uses. For example, following restoration, the Confucian Temple became the Stele Museum, and the Ming dynasty family shrine dedicated to Wang Ao now houses the Suzhou Embroidery Museum. There are also a number of instances in which religious buildings have been reconsecrated. This is the case with the Temple

---

34. The Beisita, originally known as the Tongxuansi 通玄寺, is the oldest Buddhist temple in Suzhou, founded on the site of the home of the mother of Sun Quan, the first emperor of the Three Kingdoms-era state of Wu. The history of this temple is given in Xu Boming, *Wu wenhua gaiguan*, p. 23.

35. Suzhoushi Canglangqu bianshi xiuzhi lingdao xiaozu ed., *Suzhoushi Canglangqu*, p. 217. A similar story can be told of the Longqingsi 隆慶寺, founded during the Ming dynasty. In 1950, this temple was taken over by a school, and the valuable sculptures and religious texts formerly held here were moved to the Hanshan temple for safekeeping. Among the objects moved was an inscription written for this temple by the Qianlong emperor. This inscription has since been kept by the Hanshan temple, though it was never intended for this institution.

to the City God, and also with the Dinghuisi 定慧寺 at No. 35 Dinghuisi nong 定慧寺弄. This temple was constructed in the Tang dynasty, between 860 and 873; and during the Qing dynasty it was the largest Buddhist temple within the old city. Between 1950 and 1954 the temple was used as an umbrella factory. In 1954 the factory was relocated, and the temple taken over by the Suzhou Plastics Research Institute. Finally, in 1986 the institute itself was relocated and the temple was returned to religious use.[36]

Suzhou has faced many challenges in the twentieth century, which have in turn had a major impact on the architectural and cultural history of this ancient city. It would, however, be incorrect to assert that the destruction of buildings during warfare and political upheavals, the filling-in of canals in order to turn them into roads, or the conversion of temples and shrines to other uses caused greater changes to the city than those that took place in the past: it is simply that what has happened in the course of the twentieth century has generally been better recorded. From the fate of Suzhou, it is now time to consider what has happened in modern times to sites specifically associated with the royal family of Wu.

The Tomb and Temple of Prince Jizha of Wu

Throughout the imperial era, the cult of Prince Jizha of Wu was of only minor and local interest, though it proved to be remarkably enduring. In spite of the fact that only a small number of temples and shrines were ever dedicated to the prince's memory, they managed to survive for nearly two thousand years. However, at present there appears to be only one temple dedicated to the worship of the prince within the borders of Jiangsu province, a small modern foundation at Jiulizhen 九里鎮 in Danyang county. The main hall of this temple features a large statue of the prince, looking most benevolent and dressed in a Qing-style dragon robe, clasping a staff of office. Although this is a modern temple, worship of Prince Jizha at Jiulizhen is thought to be of considerable antiquity. This temple still has its own version of the Ten-Character Stele, which stands by the entrance. In

36. Ibid., p. 71; and Shi Jianhua et al., *Suzhou gucheng de baohu yu gengxin*, p. 91.

addition to the main ten-character text written in seal-script, it bears two further late imperial inscriptions. On the left side there is a dated Ming dynasty inscription: "In Guiwei year of the reign of the Jiajing Emperor of the Ming dynasty on the twenty-third day of the fourth lunar month (May 9, 1523), Duan Jin and Zhao Ao of Wujin County, [illegible two-character name] of Danyang County, and Wang Hui of Wuxi County respectfully viewed [this monument]." 明嘉靖癸未四月廿三日, 武進段金, 趙翺, 丹陽□□, 無錫王輝敬觀.[37]

These men have proved impossible to identify. This suggests strongly that, although they must have been members of the local regional elite during the Ming dynasty (or they would not have been able to afford this visit, or to commemorate it in such a way), they were not part of the provincial or national elite, and they never held office. On the right side of the stele, there is a further undated inscription: "The Inspector of Yanling and Official in Attendance on the Emperor, Zhang Congying, oversaw this." 延陵巡檢供奉官張從應監制.[38]

In 1937, at the time of the Japanese invasion, the temple at the site of Prince Jizha's tomb was completely destroyed, together with the Ten-Character Stele. The foundations of the temple have survived to the present day within the grounds of the Shen'gang Middle School, indicating that it originally covered an area of 2,964 square meters. Excavations carried out in 1984 revealed various Republican era stone accoutrements of the temple, and further excavations in 1990 resulted in the discovery of stone incense burners and a marker for the tomb. These items have all been placed around the tomb site, which is subject to a local-level protection unit.[39] At present there seem to be no plans to proceed any further with the restoration of the site. Given the number of poems written during the imperial period that bewailed the lack of visitors at a time when the tomb and its attendant stele were part of a rich and flourishing temple complex,

---

37. The text of this inscription and of the next is given in Jiangsu wenwu zonglu bianji weiyuanhui ed., *Jiangsu wenwu zonglu*, p. 174. Other sources that also mention this inscription do not indicate the two missing characters of the name following the identifying Danyang county.

38. Zhang Kai, *Changzhou fu zhi xuji*, p. 213.

39. Guojia wenwu ju ed., *Zhongguo wenwu ditu ji*, p. 326.

it is ironic to visit this site today when it is indeed neglected and overgrown. The destruction of the Ten-Character Stele, re-cut and re-carved many times over the course of the centuries, and studied by Ouyang Xiu and other scholars and epigraphers, means that it now only survives through rubbings and as transcriptions in books. The loss of the temple—which was once repaired by Bai Ang in accordance with his vow, and which later became the recipient of calligraphic inscriptions from the Kangxi and Qianlong Emperors during their southern tours—means that it has joined the Gusu Tower as part of the heritage of the kingdom of Wu that can only be visited in the imagination.

Tiger Hill

Any visitor to Tiger Hill who is acquainted with Ming or Qing dynasty accounts of the place will realize the enormous debt owed by the modern tourist authorities to the original promoters of this site as a center for literati culture in the late imperial era. Although many of the sites in and around Tiger Hill are of course much more ancient than the attempts to publicize them, from the Song dynasty onwards they were categorized and systematized into lists of "things that one ought to see"; and by the Ming and Qing dynasties they were heavily promoted by gazetteers and guidebook writers as places that no tourist worth his salt could afford to miss. Only the most devoted tourist will visit every surviving site from the *Baicheng yanshui* list, but even the most bored visitor, herded along with his tour group, will be invited to view Kankan's Spring, the Sword-Testing Rock, the Nodding-Head Rocks, the Tomb of Zhenniang, Thousand-Man Rock, Sword Pond, and the Song dynasty Tiger Hill Pagoda, which is now virtually the only reminder of the Buddhist temple that once stood here. For the historically-minded tourist, visiting Sword Pond is particularly interesting. The sheer cliff faces on either side of the water-filled cleft are covered in inscriptions. The waters that cover the site of what is supposed to be the tomb of King Helü are a deep jade-green, making it impossible to see more than a few inches below the surface. There is a thin iron railing that is supposed to prevent people from falling in, but in fact many tourists climb over it and paddle out into the pond for a photo opportunity. At the broad base of the cleft, Sword Pond is clearly extremely shallow. This suggests that the man who drowned here in the reign of Qing Daoguang was very unlucky, for he must have fallen in such a way as to make it impossible for him to climb out safely.

The historical and cultural importance of Tiger Hill are much stressed by the local tourist authorities, not least since its April 2010 listing as one of Jiangsu province's handful of "5A" attractions (the highest level), as rated by the China National Tourism Administration; and numerous guidebooks incorporating lists of key sites and quoting famous works of literature have been produced for sale to Chinese tourists. Reproductions of paintings by Ming and Qing artists of visits to the site are also popular; looking at these pictures it is sometimes possible to think that the only things that have changed are the clothes worn by tourists. The stress on the timeless quality of Tiger Hill obscures its often violent history and the serious interventions that have taken place in the landscape here. Are these buildings really located on the same site as those that previously bore the same name? Do they look anything like the buildings that were here in the Ming or Qing dynasties, let alone the Song? If the evidence of other studies of famous sites in the Suzhou region—such as that of the Song dynasty garden, the Canglang ting—is anything to go by, the answer to these questions is no.[40] Tiger Hill is dominated by the Southern Song dynasty pagoda that is now the only surviving remnant of the Yunyuan Temple, originally founded when Wang Xun and Wang Min gave their homes to the Buddhist church during the Age of Disunion. It is an iconic image, featured in virtually every publication about Suzhou. But what can be seen now is simply the brick core of the ancient pagoda. Unlike other pagodas of a similar age (such as the Ruiguang Pagoda at the Panmen Scenic Area or that attached to the Numinous Cliff Monastery) the one at Tiger Hill has not been restored since it was severely damaged at the time of the Taiping Rebellion. Seeing only the naked core of the structure, divorced from any context, means that modern visitors have a

40. Zhou Suning, *Suzhou yuanlin yu mingren*, pp. 14–17.

completely different experience of the one remaining religious building at Tiger Hill, and understand the pagoda in a very different way from earlier tourists.

Numinous Cliff

Numinous Cliff remains to the present day a flourishing Buddhist temple and the vast majority of its modern visitors are pilgrims. This creates an interesting paradox, whereby Numinous Cliff (which was one of the sites with the most tenuous links to the ancient kingdom of Wu) is today the only one to preserve a strong connection with its traditional identity, whereby the experience of tourists is the closest to that of imperial era visitors. Imperial era accounts like that found in the *Baicheng yanshui* stress the religious significance of many of the sites found in and around the mountain; the modern visitor can see the majority of these sites under the guidance of a monk, just as would have been the case at the start of the Qing dynasty when this text was written. Pilgrims arriving at the temple are periodically confronted with the evidence of previous distinguished visitors; the *Yudao* or Imperial Way constructed for the Kangxi Emperor's visit is still in use today, and the supposed site of the Qin Tower (though no building is at present found there) is marked by two inscriptions in the calligraphy of Wang Ao. Old photographs show that the Southern Song pagoda here was reduced to a truly terrible state during the course of the twentieth century, and that its brick core was exposed to the elements in the same way as the pagoda at Tiger Hill still is. However, as befits what is clearly a wealthy and successful religious foundation, the pagoda has recently been fully restored.

In his book *Inscribed Landscapes: Travel Writing from Imperial China*, Richard Strassberg stresses again and again the importance of the link between nature, history, and literature in the making of famous landscapes. Through works of literature, later visitors found themselves reintroduced to the scene before their eyes; through calligraphic inscriptions on rocks or other associated monuments literati travelers were reminded of famous earlier individuals who also went to the trouble to visit this spot, and they enjoyed the sensation of being part of a distinguished procession. Though some visitors might complain about the over-inscription of a landscape, this criticism was generally directed at either poor quality calligraphy, which ruined the artistic impression of a site (perhaps also detracting from other works in the vicinity), or at vulgar works of literature, which did not do justice to the importance and beauty of the place. Similar criticisms were of course directed at other visitors, who through raucous conversation, drunkenness, or boisterous singing were easily capable of offending the refined sensibilities of a literati traveler. (However, it must be admitted that the presence of vulgar tourists was at least an impermanent evil; the ignorance and indifference of peasants was hardly more pleasing.) Though it might have unexpected and indeed unwanted side-effects, as Richard Strassberg notes, writing about and writing on a landscape played an important cultural function: "It was one way a place became significant and was mapped onto an itinerary for other travelers. By applying the patterns of the classical language, writers symbolically claimed unknown or marginal places, transforming their 'otherness' and bringing them into the Chinese world order."[41]

In the case of *huaigu* writings, particularly those dealing with visits to sites associated with the ancient kingdom of Wu, they describe what may be termed "classic" inscribed landscapes. Though the lands of Wu were incorporated into the empire at the time of the unification of China, this region was inhabited in antiquity by non-Chinese peoples, and their history provides a glamorous and exotic addition to traditional Chinese culture. The tombs of Prince Jizha and King Helü, and the site of King Fuchai's palace at Numinous Cliff: all these scenes were adorned by the calligraphy, carved in stone, of generations of literati visitors, thereby recording their presence at these storied sites. Above and beyond that, the way that later visitors interpreted these places was predicated upon the survival of both ancient texts and a massive body of imperial era poetry and prose. Indeed, awareness of the historical and cultural legacy of these landscapes continues to condition the responses of visitors right up to the present day.

Though understanding these sites as an inscribed landscape may perhaps be helpful for envisaging the mental framework that allowed imperial era travelers to enjoy and interpret what they saw, given the

---

41. Strassberg, *Inscribed Landscapes*, p. 6.

prevalence of *huaigu* literature in the cultural legacy of these places, I would prefer to term these *illusionary landscapes*. By this I mean that the poets and writers (whose works created the inscribed landscapes of southern Jiangsu province) understood that what they were seeing was not the same scene that witnessed the famous historical events that had brought them there in the first place; and they understood that the earlier visitors whose footsteps they were following might well have seen something completely different. In *huaigu* writings, the author speaks of a personal visit to a storied place. The writer makes reference to the famous events that once happened there and to the illustrious people who once walked these lands; to experience a connection with them is either the objective of the visit or the possibility raised by an unexpected encounter with a historical site. And yet in *huaigu* literature, the writer is in the end forced to acknowledge that any sense of connection or understanding is an illusion. The great events of the past have left only ruins in their wake and the famous men and women are long dead.

The longevity of the trees and rocks of the natural landscape encourages people to imagine that they are eternal and unchanging. Much *huaigu* literature plays upon the illusion that initially sustains the visitor: that he or she is seeing exactly the same scenes as once greeted the eyes of a famous historical individual. Though perhaps an effort of the imagination is required to resurrect buildings from the ruins and to re-people them, that is not particularly difficult, because the visitor can call upon a host of helpful texts for assistance. Similarly, the visitor may call to mind a wide array of later writings that helped to confirm the historical significance of this spot and create its cultural legacy. In this way, the traveler can "remember" the past with the help of all that he has read. And yet *huaigu* writings require the visitor, in the end, to confront the fundamental impossibility of the endeavor. Has this landscape really been unchanged in all that time? Ploughed up, built over, ruined, destroyed by fire or flood, planted with trees, deforested, quarried for stone, adorned with pavilions and stele inscriptions—over time even the hardest of rocks grows old and crumbles. The landscape may seem to be the same and yet it has already changed forever.

Works Cited

Abbreviations

AM	*Asia Major*
AO	*Acta Orientalia*
Chunqiu	*Chunqiu Zuozhuan zhu* 春秋左傳注
CLEAR	*Chinese Literature: Essays, Articles, and Reviews*
DNWH	*Dongnan wenhua* 東南文化
EC	*Early China*
Gongyang zhuan	*Chunqiu Gongyang zhuan* 春秋公羊傳
HJAS	*Harvard Journal of Asiatic Studies*
JAOS	*Journal of the American Oriental Society*
JAS	*Journal of Asian Studies*
JESHO	*Journal of the Economic and Social History of the Orient*
KG	*Kaogu* 考古
OE	*Oriens Extremus*
SPP	*Sino-Platonic Papers*
TP	*T'oung Pao*
WW	*Wenwu* 文物
Zuozhuan	*Chunqiu Zuozhuan zhu* 春秋左傳注

Baihutong shuzheng 白虎通疏證. Annotated by Chen Li 陳立. Beijing: Zhonghua shuju, 1994.

Beijingshi wenwuzu 北京文物組. "Haidianqu faxian Chunqiu shidai tongqi" 海淀區發現春秋時代銅器. *WW* 1958, no. 5: 72.

Berkowitz, Alan. "Patterns of Reclusion in Early and Early Medieval China: A Study of the Formulation of the Practice of Reclusion in China and its Portrayal." Ph.D. diss., University of Washington, 1989.

Blakeley, Barry. "Functional Disparities in the Socio-Political Traditions of Spring and Autumn Period China." *JESHO* 20, no. 2 (1977): 208–43; 20, no. 3 (1977): 307–43; 22, no. 1 (1979): 81–118.

Brook, Timothy. *The Confusions of Pleasure: Commerce and Culture in Ming China.* Berkeley: University of California Press, 1998.

Campany, Robert. *Making Transcendents: Ascetics and Social Memory in Early Medieval China*. Honolulu: University of Hawaii Press, 2009.

Cao Jinyan 曹錦炎. "Beishan tongqi xinkao" 北山銅器新考. In Cao Jinyan, comp. *Wu Yue lishi yu kaogu luncong*, pp. 153–61.

———. "Chengqiao xinchu tongqi kaoshi ji xiangguan wenti" 程橋新出銅器考釋及相關問題. In Cao Jinyan, comp. *Wu Yue lishi yu kaogu luncong*, pp. 168–78.

———. "Peier goudiao mingwen ba" 配兒句鑃銘文跋. In Cao Jinyan, comp. *Wu Yue lishi yu kaogu luncong*, pp. 27–32.

———, comp. *Wu Yue lishi yu kaogu luncong* 吳越歷史與考古論叢. Beijing: Wenwu chubanshe, 2007.

———. "Wuwang Shoumeng zhi zi jianming kaoshi" 吳王壽夢之子劍銘考釋. In Cao Jinyan, comp. *Wu Yue lishi yu kaogu luncong*, pp. 14–26.

Cao Lindi 曹林娣. *Gusu yuanlin yu Zhongguo wenhua* 姑蘇園林與中國文化. Taipei: Sanmin shuju, 1993.

Carroll, Peter J. *Between Heaven and Modernity: Reconstructing Suzhou, 1895–1937*. Stanford: Stanford University Press, 2006.

Cedzich, Angelika. "Corpse Deliverance, Substitute Bodies, Name Change, and Feigned Death: Aspects of Metamorphosis and Immortality in Early Medieval China." *Journal of Chinese Religion* 29 (2001): 1–68.

Chaves, Jonathan. *The Columbia Book of Later Chinese Poetry; Yüan, Ming, and Ch'ing Dynasties, 1279–1911*. New York: Columbia University Press, 1986.

Chen Houyao 陳厚耀. *Chunqiu Zhanguo yici* 春秋戰國異辭. Siku quanshu edition.

Chen Huixing 陳慧星. "Wu Yue chunqiu de moulüe sixiang" 吳越春秋的謀略思想. In Gao Xiechu, ed. *Wu wenhua ziyuan yanjiu yu fazhan*, pp. 63–75.

Chen Jian 陳鑒. *Huqiu chajing zhubu* 虎丘茶經注補. In Wang Jiaju, ed. *Suzhou wenxian congchao chubian*, pp. 1037–39.

Chen Mengjia 陳夢家. "Xi Zhou tongqi duandai: Yi Hou Ze gui" 西周銅器斷代宜侯夨簋. *Kaogu xuebao* 考古學報 1956, no. 1: 65–114.

Chen Pan 陳槃. *Chunqiu dashibiao lieguo juexing ji cunmiebiao zhuanyi* 春秋大事表列國爵姓及存滅表譔異. Taipei: Zhongyang yanjiuyuan lishi yuyan yanjiusuo, 1969.

Chen Peifen 陳佩芬. *Shanghai bowuguan zang qingtong jing* 上海博物館藏青銅鏡. Shanghai: Shanghai shuju chubanshe, 1987.

———. *Xia Shang Zhou qingtongqi yanjiu: Shanghai bowuguan zangpin* 夏商周青銅器研究: 上海博物館藏品. Shanghai: Shanghai guji chubanshe, 2004.

Chen Yan'en 陳延恩 and Li Zhaoluo 李兆洛. *Jiangyin xian zhi* 江陰縣志. Taipei: Chengwen chubanshe, [1833] 1983.

Chen Zhiliang 陳志良. "Qingji tamu bian" 慶忌塔墓辯. In Wu Yue, ed. *Wu Yue wenhua luncong*, shidi yanjiuhui, pp. 161–71.

Chen Zhongxiu 陳鍾琇. *Tangdai heshi yanjiu* 唐代和詩研究. Taipei: Shouwei zixun, 2008.

Cheng Gongshuo 程公說. *Chunqiu fenji* 春秋分記. Siku quanshu edition.

Chou, Ju-hsi. *Circles of Reflection: The Carter Collection of Chinese Bronze Mirrors*. Cleveland: Cleveland Museum of Art, 2000.

Chunqiu Gongyang zhuan zhushu 春秋公羊傳注疏. Annotated by He Xiu 何休 and Xu Yan 徐彥. Shanghai: Shanghai guji chubanshe, 1990.

Chunqiu Guliang zhuan buzhu 春秋穀梁傳補注. Annotated by Zhong Wenzheng 鍾文烝. Beijing: Zhonghua shuju, 1996.

Chunqiu Zuozhuan zhu 春秋左傳注. Annotated by Yang Bojun 楊伯峻. Beijing: Zhonghua shuju, 1981.

Clunas, Craig. *Fruitful Sites: Garden Culture in Ming Dynasty China*. London: Reaktion Books, 1996.

Cohen, Paul A. *Speaking to History: The Story of King Goujian in Twentieth-Century China*. Berkeley: University of California Press, 2009.
Cui Zifang 崔子方. *Cuishi Chunqiu jingjie* 崔氏春秋經解. Siku quanshu edition.

Dantuxian xianzhi bianzuan weiyuanhui 丹徒縣縣志編纂委員會, ed. *Dantu xianzhi* 丹徒縣志. Suzhou: Jiangsu kexue jishu chubanshe, 1993.
Dai Yannian 戴延年. *Wuyu* 吳語. In Wang Jiaju, ed. *Suzhou wenxian congchao chubian*, pp. 247–253.
Đao Duy Anh. *Yuenan gudai shi* 越南古代史. Translated by Liu Tongwen 劉統文. Beijing: Shangwu yinshuguan, 1976.
Daoshi 道世 (Han Xuanyun 韓玄惲). *Fayuan zhulin* 法苑珠林. Shanghai: Shanghai guji chubanshe, 1991.
Dardess, John. *Blood and History in China: The Donglin Faction and Its Repression, 1620–1627*. Honolulu: University of Hawaii Press, 2002.
Deng Guangming 鄧廣銘. *Han Shizhong nianpu* 韓世忠年譜. Beijing: Sanlian shuju, 2007.
DeWoskin, Kenneth. *A Song for One or Two: Music and the Concept of Art in Early China*. Ann Arbor: University of Michigan Press, 1982.
Di Hao 翟灝. *Hushan bianlan* 湖山便覽. Shanghai: Shanghai guji chubanshe, 1998.
Di Junlian 翟均廉. *Haitang lu* 海塘錄. Siku quanshu edition.
Dong Chuping 董楚平. *Wu Yue Xu Shu jinwen jishi* 吳越徐舒金文集釋. Hangzhou: Zhejiang guji chubanshe, 1992.
——— and Jin Yongping 金永平. *Wu Yue wenhua zhi* 吳越文化志. Shanghai: Shanghai renmin chubanshe, 1998.
Dong Shouqi 董壽琪. *Huqiu* 虎丘. Suzhou: Guwuxuan chubanshe, 2001.
Du Yu 杜預. *Chunqiu jingzhuan jijie* 春秋經傳集解. Shanghai: Shanghai guji chubanshe, 1997.
Du Zhao 杜詔. *Shandong tongzhi* 山東通志. Siku quanshu edition.
Durrant, Stephen W. *The Cloudy Mirror: Tension and Conflict in the Writings of Sima Qian*. Albany: State University of New York Press, 1995.

Eno, Robert. “The Background of the Kong Family of Lu and the Origins of Ruism.” *EC* 28 (2003): 1–42.
Erya zhushu 爾雅注疏. Annotated by Li Xueqin 李學勤. Taipei: Taiwan guji chubanshe, 2001.

Fan Chengda 范成大. *Fan Shihu ji* 范石湖集. Shanghai: Zhonghua shuju, 1962.
———. *Wujun zhi* 吳郡志. Nanjing: Jiangsu guji chubanshe, 1999.
Fangyan 方言. Compiled by Yang Xiong 楊雄. Congshu jicheng edition.
Fayan yishu 法言義疏. Annotated by Wang Rongbao 汪榮寶. Beijing: Zhonghua shuju, 1987.
Fei Junqing 費君清, ed. *Zhongguo chuantong wenhua yu Yue wenhua yanjiu* 中國傳統文化與越文化研究. Beijing: Renmin chubanshe, 2004.
Feng Menglong 馮夢龍. *Xin lieguo zhi* 新列國志. Shanghai: Shanghai guji chubanshe, 1994.
Feng Puren 馮普仁. *Wu Yue wenhua* 吳越文化. Beijing: Wenwu chubanshe, 2007.

Feng Yingliu 馮應榴, Huang Renke 黄任軻, and Zhu Huaichun 朱懷春. *Su Shi shiji hezhu* 蘇軾詩集合注. Shanghai: Shanghai guji chubanshe, 2001.
Feuchtwang, Stephan. *The Imperial Metaphor: Popular Religion in China*. London: Routledge, 1992.
Fu Zhenzhao 傅振照. "Shilun Yuezu de tonghua yu Yue wenhua de ronghe" 試論越族的同化與越文化的融合. In Fei Junqing, ed. *Zhongguo chuantong wenhua yu Yue wenhua yanjiu*, pp. 415–24.

Gao Deji 高德基. *Pingjiang jishi* 平江記事. In Wang Jiaju, ed. *Suzhou wenxian congchao chubian*, pp. 141–54.
Gao Jin 高晉 et al. *Nanxun shengdian* 南巡盛典. Taipei: Wenhai chubanshe, 1970.
Gao Mingqian 高名乾 et al. eds. *Zhiwu gu Hanming tukao* 植物古漢名圖考. Zhengzhou: Daxiang chubanshe, 2006.
Gao Shiqi 高士奇. *Zuozhuan jishi benmo* 左傳紀事本末. Beijing: Zhonghua shuju, 1979.
Gao Xiechu 高燮初, ed. *Wu wenhua ziyuan yanjiu yu fazhan* 吳文化資源研究與發展. Vol. 2; Suzhou: Suzhou daxue chubanshe, 1995.
Gaoshi zhuan 高士傳. Compiled by Huangfu Mi 皇甫謐. Congshu jicheng edition.
Gong Mingzhi 龔明之. *Zhongwu jiwen* 中吳紀聞. In Wang Jiaju, ed. *Suzhou wenxian congchao chubian*, pp. 3–120.
Goldin, Paul R. *After Confucius: Studies in Early Chinese Philosophy*. Honolulu: University of Hawaii Press, 2005.
Goossaert, Vincent. *The Taoists of Peking, 1800–1949: A Social History of Urban Clerics*. Cambridge Mass.: Harvard University Press, 2007.
Gu Derong 顧德融 and Zhu Shunlong 朱順龍. *Chunqiu shi* 春秋史. Shanghai: Shiji chubanshe, 2001.
Gu Jiegang 顧頡剛. *Shilin zazhi: chupian.* 史林雜誌: 初篇. Beijing: Zhonghua shuju, 1963.
———. *Suzhou shizhi biji* 蘇州史志筆記. Suzhou: Jiangsu guji chubanshe, 1987.
Gu Lu 顧祿. *Tongqiao yizhao lu* 桐橋倚棹錄. Shanghai: Shanghai guji chubanshe, 1980.
Gu Xuejie 顧學頡. *Bai Juyi ji* 白居易集. Beijing: Zhonghua shuju, 1988.
Gu Yilu 顧詒錄. *Huqiushan zhi* 虎邱山志. Taipei: Wenhai chubanshe, [1767] 1971.
Gu Zhentao 顧震濤. *Wumen biaoyin* 吳門表隱. Nanjing: Jiangsu guji chubanshe, 1999.
Guanzi jiaozhu 管子校注. Annotated by Li Xiangfeng 李翔鳳. Beijing: Zhonghua shuju, 2004.
Guo Moruo 郭沫若. "Ze gui ming kaoshi" 夨簋銘考釋. In *Guo Moruo quanji* 郭沫若全集, edited by Guo Moruo zhuzuo bianji chuban weiyuanhui 郭沫若著作編輯出版委員會. Vol. 6; pp. 100–109. Beijing: Kexue chubanshe, 2002.
Guojia wenwu ju 國家文物局, ed. *Zhongguo wenwu ditu ji: Jiangsu fence (xia)* 中國文物地圖集: 江蘇分冊 (下). Beijing: Zhongguo ditu chubanshe, 2008.
Guoyu 國語. Annotated by Shanghai shifan daxue guji zhenglizu 上海師範大學古籍整理組. Shanghai: Shanghai guji chubanshe, 1978.

Han Feizi jishi 韓非子集釋. Annotated by Chen Qiyou 陳奇猷. Beijing: Zhonghua shuju, 1958.

Hansen, Valerie. *Changing Gods in Medieval China, 1127–1276.* Princeton: Princeton University Press, 1990.

Hanshi waizhuan jishi 韓詩外傳集釋. Annotated by Xu Weiyu 許維遹. Beijing: Zhonghua shuju, 1980.

Hanshu 漢書. Compiled by Ban Gu 班固. Beijing: Zhonghua shuju, 1962.

Hargett, James. *On the Road in Twelfth Century China: The Travel Diaries of Fan Chengda: 1126–1193.* Stuttgart: Franz Steiner Verlag, 1989.

———. "Song Dynasty Local Gazetteers and Their Place in the History of *Difangzhi* Writing." *HJAS* 56.2 (1996): 405–42.

Hayashi Minao 林巳奈夫. *Chūgoku In-Shū jidai no buki* 中國殷周時代の武器. Kyoto: Kyoto daigaku jimmin bungaku kenkyūsho, 1975.

———. *Kandai no kamigami* 漢代の神神. Kyoto: Nozokawa, 1989.

He Guangyuan 何光遠. *Jianjie lu* 鑒誡錄. Congshu jicheng edition.

He Linyi 何琳儀. "Chengqiao sanhao mu panyi mingwen xinkao" 程橋三號墓盤匜銘文新考. *DNWH* 2001, no. 3: 78–81.

He Tangkun 何堂坤. *Zhongguo gudai tongjing de jishu yanjiu* 中國古代銅鏡的技術研究. Beijing: Cijincheng chubanshe, 1999.

He Xilin 賀西林. *Gumu danqing: Handai mushi bihua de faxian yu yanjiu* 古墓丹青: 漢代墓室壁畫的發現與研究. Xi'an: Shaanxi renmin meishu chubanshe, 2001.

He Yunzhong 何允中. "Wu-Yue shi xu" 吳越史序. National Central Library, Taipei, microfilm 2124 [1627].

Henry, Eric. "The Motif of Recognition in Early China." *HJAS* 47.1 (1987): 5–30.

Hou Hanshu 後漢書. Compiled by Fan Ye 范曄. Beijing: Zhonghua shuju, 1965.

Hu, Philip. *Visible Traces: Rare Books and Special Collections from the National Library of China*. New York: Queens Borough Public Library, 2000.

Hu Zi 胡仔. *Tiaoxi yuyin conghua* 苕溪漁隱叢話. Taipei: Shijie shuju, 1976.

Huainanzi jishi 淮南子集釋. Annotated by He Ning 何寧. Beijing: Zhonghua shuju, 1998.

Huang Shengzhang 黄盛璋. "Tongqi mingwen Yi, Yu, Ze de diwang ji qi yu Wuguo de guanxi" 銅器銘文宜虞夨的地望及其與吳國的關係. *KG* 1983, no. 3: 295–305.

Huang Xian 黄獻. *Wugang qinpu* 梧岡琴譜. In Zha Fuxi, ed. *Qinqu jicheng*, Vol. 1; pp. 373–441.

Huang Yuji 黄虞稷. *Qianqingtang shumu* 千頃堂書目. Siku quanshu edition.

Hulsewé, A.F.P. *Remnants of Ch'in Law: An Annotated Translation of the Ch'in Legal and Administrative Rules of the 3rd century B.C.*, Discovered in Yün-meng prefecture, Hu-pei province in 1975. Leiden: E.J. Brill, 1985.

———. *Remnants of Han Law.* Leiden: E.J. Brill, 1955.

Hunter, John. *Land into Landscape.* London: George Goodwin, 1985.

Jenner, W.J.F. *Memories of Lo-yang: Yang Hsüan-chih and the Lost Capital (493–534).* Oxford: Oxford University Press, 1981.

Jensen, Lionel M. "Wise Man of the Wilds: Fatherlessness, Fertility, and the Mythic Exemplar Kongzi." *EC* 20 (1995): 407–37.

Jiang Hui 蔣暉. *Jinfen renjian: Mingshi Suzhou* 金粉人間: 明式蘇州. Shenyang: Liaoning renmin chubanshe, 2007.

Jiangnan tongzhi 江南通志. Siku quanshu edition.

Jiangsu wenwu zonglu bianji weiyuanhui 江蘇文物綜錄編輯委員會, ed. *Jiangsu wenwu zonglu* 江蘇文物綜錄. Nanjing: Nanjing bowuyuan, 1988.

Jiangsusheng difangzhi xuehui 江蘇省地方志學會, ed. *Jiangsu zhanggu* 江蘇掌故. Wujin: Jiangsu guji chubanshe, 1997.

Jiao Hong 焦竑. *Zhejiang tongzhi* 浙江通志. Siku quanshu edition.

Jin Dejian 金德建. *Sima Qian suojian shu kao* 司馬遷所見書考. Shanghai: Shanghai guji chubanshe, 1963.

Jin Hua 晉華. "Shanxi Yushe chutu yijian Wuwang Gufa jian" 山西榆社出土一件吳王貼發劍. *WW* 1990, no. 2: 77–79.

Jin Youli 金友理. *Taihu beikao* 太湖備考. Nanjing: Jiangsu guji chubanshe, 1998.

Jinlouzi jiaozhu 金樓子校注. Annotated by Xu Deping 徐德平. Taipei: Jiaxinshuini gongsi, 1969.

Jinshu 晉書. Compiled by Fang Xuanling 房玄齡. Beijing: Zhonghua shuju, 1974.

Johnson, David. "Epic and History in Early China: The Matter of Wu Tzu-hsü." *JAS* 40.2 (1981): 255–71.

Kangxi Emperor 康熙皇帝. *Shengzu Renhuangdi yuzhi wenji* 聖祖仁皇帝御製文集. Siku quanshu edition.

———. *Yuxuan guwen yuanjian* 御選古文淵鑒. Siku quanshu edition.

Karlgren, Bernhard. *Early Chinese Mirror Inscriptions*. Stockholm: Bulletin of the Museum of Far Eastern Antiquities, 1934.

Katz, Paul R. *Images of the Immortal: The Cult of Lü Dongbin at the Palace of Eternal Joy*. Honolulu: University of Hawaii Press, 1999.

Kiang Chao-yuan. *Le Voyage dans la Chine Ancienne, considéré principalement sous son aspect magique et religieux*. Translated by Fan Jen. Shanghai: Commision Mixte des Oeuvres Franco-Chinoises, 1937.

Knechtges, David. *Wen xuan or Selections of Refined Literature, Volume One: Rhapsodies on Metropolises and Capitals*. Princeton: Princeton University Press, 1982.

———. *Wen xuan or Selections of Refined Literature: Volume Three, Rhapsodies on Natural Phenomena, Birds and Animals, Aspirations and Feelings, Sorrowful Laments, Literature, Music, and Passions*. Princeton: Princeton University Press, 1996.

Kong Xiangxing 孔祥星 and Liu Yiman 劉一曼. *Zhongguo gudai tongjing* 中國古代銅鏡. Beijing: Wenwu chubanshe, 1984.

———. *Zhongguo tongjing tudian* 中國銅鏡圖典. Beijing: Wenwu chubanshe, 1994.

Kuhn, Dieter. "Decoding Tombs of the Song Elite." In *Burial in Song China*, edited by Dieter Kuhn, pp. 11–159. Heidelberg: Edition Forum, 1994.

Lanciotti, Lionello. "Sword Casting and Related Legends in China." *East and West* 6.2 (1955): 106–14.

Laozi Daodejing zhu 老子道德經注. Annotated by Wang Bi 王弼. Beijing: Zhonghua shuju, 1998.

Li Ao 李翱. *Lainan lu* 來南錄. Taipei: Xinxing shuju, 1960.

Li, Chu-tsing. "Tang Yin." In *Dictionary of Ming Biography*, edited by L. Carrington Goodrich, pp. 1256–59. New York: Columbia University Press, 1976.

Li E 厲鶚, ed. *Songshi jishi* 宋詩紀事. Taipei: Zhonghua shuju, 1971.

Li Fang 李昉 et al. *Taiping yulan* 太平御覽. Taipei: Xinxing shuju, 1959.

——— ed. *Wenyuan yinghua* 文苑英華. Siku quanshu edition.

Li Jiaqiu 李嘉球. "Sun Wu yu Gusu" 孫武與姑蘇. In *Wu wenhua yu Suzhou* 吳文化與蘇州, edited by Shi Qi 石琪. Shanghai: Tongji daxue chubanshe, 1992, pp. 371–81.

Li Jifu 李吉甫. *Yuanhe junxian tuzhi* 元和郡縣圖志. Congshu jicheng edition.

Li Mingwan 李銘皖 and Feng Guifen 馮桂芬. *Suzhou fu zhi* 蘇州府志. Taipei: Chengwen chubanshe, [1881] 1970.

Li Xueqin 李學勤. "Fan Li sixiang yu boshu *Huangdi shu*" 范蠡思想與帛書黃帝書. *Zhejiang xuekan* 浙江學刊 1990, no. 1: 97–99, 90.

———. "Yi Hou Ze gui de ren yu di" 宜侯夨簋的人與地. In Suzhoushi chuantong wenhua yanjiuhui, *Chuantong wenhua yanjiu*, pp. 87–89.

——— and Wang Linchang 汪林昌. "Yue wenhua zai Zhongguo wenmingshi zhong de diwei yiji dui Dongya lishi wenhua de yingxiang" 越文化在中國文明史中的地位以及對東亞歷史文化的影響. In Fei Junqing, ed. *Zhongguo chuantong wenhua yu Yue wenhua yanjiu*, pp. 1–10.

Li Yujie 李玉洁. *Chuguo shi* 楚國史. Kaifeng: Henan daxue chubanshe, 2002.

Li Yuqing 李裕慶. *Jiangsu mingcheng lu* 江蘇名城錄. Beijing: Beijing lüyou chubanshe, 1987.

Li Zongtong 李宗侗. "Chunqiu shidai shehui de biandong" 春秋時代社會的變動. *Guoli Taiwan daxue wenshizhe xuebao.* 國立台灣大學文史哲學報 22 (1973): 263–303.

Liang Baiquan 梁白泉. *Wu Yue wenhua* 吳越文化. Shanghai: Shanghai yuandong chubanshe, 1997.

Liang Yusheng 梁玉繩. *Shiji zhiyi* 史記志疑. Beijing: Zhonghua shuju, 1981.

Liangshu 梁書. Compiled by Yao Silian 姚思廉. Beijing: Zhonghua shuju, 1973.

Liji zhengyi 禮記正義. Annotated by Kong Yingda 孔穎達. Shanghai: Shanghai guji chubanshe, 1990.

Lin Guangchao 林光朝. *Aixuan ji* 艾軒集. Siku quanshu edition.

Lin Huadong 林華東 and Liang Zhiming 梁志明. "Yuewang Yunchang lingmu kao" 越王允常陵墓考. *Zhejiang xuekan* 浙江學刊 1999, no. 1: 151–53.

Lin Tianwei 林天蔚. *Fangzhixue yu difangshi yanjiu* 方志學與地方史研究. Taipei: Nantian shuju, 1995.

Lin Tinggang 林庭棡 and Zhou Guang 周廣. *Jiangxi tongzhi* 江西通志. Siku quanshu edition.

Liu, Cary Y., Michael Nylan, and Anthony Barbieri-Low et al. *Recarving China's Past: Art, Archaeology, and Architecture of the "Wu Family Shrines."* New Haven: Yale University Press, 2005.

Liu Dianjue 劉殿爵 et al. *Yuejue shu zhuzi suoyin* 越絕書逐字索引. Hong Kong: Shangwu yinshuguan, 1993.

Liu Dunyuan 劉敦愿. *Meishu kaogu yu gudai wenming* 美術考古與古代文明. Taipei: Yunchen wenhua chubanshe, 1994.

Liu Guangsheng 劉廣生 and Tang Haozheng 唐鶴徵. *Chongxiu Changzhou fu zhi* 重修常州府志. National Palace Museum Library, microfilm 3366 [1618].

Liu Jianguo 劉建國. *Xinyi Yuejue shu* 新譯越絶書. Taipei: Sanmin chubanshe, 1997.

Liu Lexian 劉樂賢. *Mawangdui tianwenshu kaoshi* 馬王堆天文書考釋. Guangzhou: Zhongshan daxue chubanshe, 2004.

Liu Xing 劉興. "Wu Zangsun zhong mingkao" 吳臧孫鐘銘考. *DNWH* 1990, no. 4: 107–8.

Liu, Yongping. *Origins of Chinese Law: Penal and Administrative Law in Its Early Development*. Oxford: Oxford University Press, 1998.

Liu Zehua 劉澤華 and Wang Liansheng 王連升. "Xian Qin shidai de jianyi lilun yu junzhu zhanzhi zhuyi" 縣秦時代的諫議理論與君主專制主義. *Nankai xuebao* 南開學報 1982, no. 1: 58–66.

Liu Zhenghao 劉正浩. "Taishigong Zuoshi *Chunqiu* yishu" 太史公左氏春秋義述. *Taiwan shengli shifan daxue guowen yanjiusuo jikan* 台灣省立師範大學國文研究所集刊 6 (1962): 259–425.

Loewe, Michael. "The Han View of Comets." *EC* 9/10 (1983–1985): 1–31.

Lu Guangwei 陸廣微. *Wudi ji* 吳地記. Nanjing: Jiangsu guji chubanshe, 1999.

Lu Kanru 陸侃如. " Wuyue wuri" 五月五日. *Guoxue yuebao huikan: Chuci hao* 國學月報會刊: 楚辭號 1 (1928): 61–63.

Lu Sicheng 盧思誠 and Li Nianyi 李念詒. *Jiangling xian zhi* 江陵縣志. Taipei: Chengwen chubanshe, [1878] 1983.

Lu Wenfu 陸文夫. *Lao Suzhou* 老蘇州. Nanjing: Jiangsu meishu chubanshe, 2000.

Lu Xiong 盧熊. *Suzhou fu zhi* 蘇州府志. Taipei: Chengwen chubanshe, [1379] 1983.

Lu Xuanjing 陸璇卿. *Huqiushan xiaozhi* 虎邱山小志. Suzhou: Yichou chubanshe, 1925.

Lu Xuemei 陸雪梅 and Qian Gonglin 錢公麟. "Chunqiu shidai Wudacheng weizhi zaikao: Lingyan gucheng yu Suzhou cheng" 春秋時代吳大城位置再考: 靈巖古城與蘇州城. *DNWH* 2006, no. 5: 15–24.

Lunheng zhushi 論衡注釋. Annotated by Beijing daxue lishixi *Lunheng* zhushi xiaozu 北京大學歷史系論衡注釋小組. Beijing: Zhonghua shuju, 1979.

Lunyu yizhu 論語譯注. Annotated by Yang Bojun 楊伯峻. Beijing: Zhonghua shuju, 1980.

Lüshi chunqiu xin jiaoshi 吕氏春秋新校釋. Annotated by Chen Qiyou 陳奇猷. Shanghai: Shanghai guji chubanshe, 2002.

Luo Wobai 羅我白 and Shi Hong 史洪. *Changzhou shihua* 常州史話. Nanjing: Jiangsu renmin chubanshe, 1984.

Luo Yunhuan 羅運環. *Zongheng baihe: Chuguo lishi gaishuo* 縱橫捭闔: 楚國歷史概說. Wuhan: Hubei jiaoyu chubanshe, 2001.

Mai Yinghao 麥英豪 and Wang Wenjian 王文建. *Lingnan zhi guang: Nanyue wangmu kaogu* 岭南之光: 南越王墓考古. Hangzhou: Zhejiang wenyi chubanshe, 2002.

Mair, Victor. *Popular Narratives from Tun-huang*. Cambridge: Cambridge University Press, 1983.

Marmé, Michael. *Suzhou: Where the goods of all the provinces converge*. Stanford: Stanford University Press, 2005.

Mattos, Gilbert L. "Eastern Zhou Bronze Inscriptions." In *New Sources of Early Chinese History: An Introduction to the Reading of Inscriptions and Manuscripts*, edited by Edward L. Shaughnessy, pp. 85–123. Berkeley: Society for the Study of Early China, 1997,

Mawangdui Hanmu boshu zhengli xiaozu 馬王堆漢墓帛書整理小組, ed. *Mawangdui Hanmu boshu* 馬王堆漢墓帛書. Vol. 3; Beijing: Wenwu chubanshe, 1983.

McMullen, David. "The Real Judge Dee: Ti Jen-chieh and the T'ang Restoration of 705." *AM* 6.1 (1993): 1–81.

McNair, Amy. *Donors of Longmen: Faith, Politics, and Patronage in Medieval Chinese Buddhist Sculpture.* Honolulu: University of Hawaii Press, 2007.

———. *The Upright Brush: Yan Zhenqing's Calligraphy and Song Literati Politics*. Honolulu: University of Hawaii Press, 1998.

Meng Yuanlao 孟元老. *Dongjing menghua lu* 東京夢華錄. Shenyang: Chunfeng wenyi chubanshe, 1992.

Meskill, John. *Ch'oe Pu's Diary: A Record of Drifting Across the Sea*. Tucson: University of Arizona Press, 1965.

Meyer-Fong, Tobie. *Building Culture in Early Qing Yangzhou*. Stanford: Stanford University Press, 2003.

Miller, Tracy. *The Divine Nature of Power: Chinese Ritual Architecture at the Sacred Site of Jinci*. Cambridge: Harvard University Press, 2007.

Milburn, Olivia. "Image, Identity, and Cherishing Antiquity: Wang Ao and Mid-Ming Suzhou," *Ming Studies* 60 (2009): 95–114.

———. "Kingship and Inheritance in the State of Wu: Fraternal Succession in Spring and Autumn Period China (771–475 BC)." *TP* 90 (2005): 195–214.

———. *The Glory of Yue: An Annotated Translation of the Yuejue shu*. Leiden: E.J. Brill, 2010.

———. "The Towers of Yue." *AO* 71 (2010): 159–86.

———. "The Weapons of Kings: A New Perspective on Southern Sword Legends." *JAOS* 128.3 (2008): 423–38.

Mozi xiangu 墨子閒詁. Annotated by Sun Yirang 孫詒讓. Beijing: Zhonghua shuju, 2001.

Murray, Julia. "Varied Views of the Sage: Illustrated Narratives of the Life of Confucius." In Thomas Wilson, ed. *On Sacred Grounds*, pp. 222–64.

Nanjing bowuguan 南京博物館, Jiangsusheng kaogu yanjiusuo 江蘇省考古研究所, and Wuxishi Xishanqu wenwu guanli weiyuanhui 無錫市錫山區文物管理委員會. *Hongshan Yuemu fajue baogao* 鴻山越墓發掘報告. Beijing: Wenwu chubanshe, 2007.

Ning Yunpeng 寧雲鵬, Lu Shenglong 盧勝龍, Shen Shiyi 沈世奕, and Miu Tong 繆彤. *Suzhou fu zhi* 蘇州府志. National Palace Museum Rare Books Collection, 1692.

Niu Ruolin 牛若麟. *Wuxian zhi* 吳縣志. Harvard-Yenching 1642 edition.

Ouyang Feiyun 歐陽飛雲, "Duanwu wuri kao" 端午惡日考. *Yijing* 易經 32 (1937): 28–31.

Ouyang Xiu 歐陽修. *Jigu lu* 集古錄. In *Ouyang Yongshu quanji* 歐陽永叔全集, edited by Zhu Gaiyang 朱荄陽. Shanghai: Dadong shuju, 1936.
Ouyang Xun 歐陽詢. *Yiwen leiju* 藝文類聚. Shanghai: Shanghai guji chubanshe, 2007.
Owen, Stephen. *Remembrances: The Experience of the Past in Classical Chinese Literature*. Cambridge, Mass.: Harvard University Press, 1986.

Pan Junming 潘君明. *Zicheng: Xiangmo jisuiyue* 子城巷陌記歲月. Nanjing: Dongnan daxue, 2004.
Pan Rongsheng 潘榮勝, ed. *Ming Qing jinshi lu* 明清進士錄. Beijing: Zhonghua shuju, 2006.
Peng Dayi 彭大翼. *Shantang sikao* 山堂肆考. Siku quanshu edition.
Peters, Heather. "Tattooed Faces and Stilt Houses: Who Where the Ancient Yue?" *SPP* 17 (1990): 1–28.
Pines, Yuri. "Beasts or Humans: Pre-imperial origins of the "Sino-barbarian" dichotomy." In *Mongols, Turks, and Others: Eurasian Nomads and the Sedentary World*, edited by Reuven Amitai and Michael Biran, pp. 59–102. Leiden: E.J. Brill, 2005.

Qian Gonglin 錢公麟. "Guanyu Wuxian Lingyanshan Chunqiu yuqi jiaozang xingzhi de zai renshi" 關於吳縣靈巖山春秋玉器窖藏性質的再認識. *DNWH* 1999, no. 2:13–17.
Qian Gu 錢穀, ed. *Wudu wencui xuji* 吳都文粹續集. Siku quanshu edition.
Qian Mu 錢穆. "Lun Chunqiu shidai ren de daode jingshen 論春秋時代人的道德精神." *Xinya xuebao* 新亞學報 2.2 (1957): 35–77.
Qian Peiming 錢培名. *Yuejue shu zhaji* 越絕書札記. Shanghai: Shangwu yinshuguan, 1956.
Qian Shuoyou 潛説友. *Xianchun Linan zhi* 咸淳臨安志. Siku quanshu edition.
Qian Zhonglian 錢仲聯. *Han Changli shixinian jishi* 韓昌黎詩繫年集釋. Shanghai: Shanghai guji chubanshe, 1984.
———. *Suzhou mingsheng shici xuan* 蘇州名勝詩詞選. Suzhou: Suzhou wenlian chubanshe, 1985.
Qin Shizhi 秦士芝. "Yutaixian Wangzhuang chutu Chunqiu Wuguo tongyi" 盱眙縣王莊出土春秋吳國銅匜. *WW* 1988, no. 9: 96.
Qu Tuiyuan 瞿蜕園 and Zhu Jincheng 朱金城, eds. *Li Bai ji jiaozhu* 李白集校注. Shanghai: Shanghai guji chubanshe, 2007.
Quan Tang shi 全唐詩. Beijing: Zhonghua shuju, 1960.
Quan Tang wen 全唐文. Beijing: Zhonghua shuju, 1983.

Rao Hengjiu 饒恒久. "*Guoyu* 'Yueyu xia' zuoshi xianyi" 國語越語下作時獻疑. *Shaoxing wenli xueyuan xuebao* 紹興文理學院學報 30.5 (2010): 1–4.
———. "Wu Jin Huangchi zhengmeng shishi kaobian: Jian lun *Guoyu* 'Wuyu' de shixue jiazhi" 吳晉黄池爭盟史實考辨: 兼論國語吳語的史學价值. *Shehui kexue zhanxian* 社會科學戰綫 2001, no. 3: 123–28.
Reed, Carrie. "Early Chinese Tattoo." *SPP* 103 (2000): 1–52.
Ren Fang 任昉. *Shuyi ji* 述異記. Siku quanshu edition.

Ren Xianghong 任相宏 and Zhang Qingfa 張慶法. "Wuwang Zhufan zhi zi Tong jian ji xiangguan wenti tantao" 吳王諸樊之子通劍及相關問題探討. *Zhongguo lishi wenwu* 中國歷史文物 (2004): 15–23.

Rong Geng 容庚. *Shang Zhou yiqi tongkao* 商周彝器通考. Shanghai: Shanghai renmin chubanshe, 2008.

Rudolph, Richard. "The *Shih Chi* Biography of Wu Tzu-hsü." *OE* 9 (1962): 105–20.

Rosen, Sidney. "Changing Conceptions of the Hegemon in Pre-Chin China." In *Ancient China: Studies in Early Civilization*, edited by David Roy and Tsuen-hsuin Tsien, pp. 99–114. Hong Kong: Chinese University Press, 1976.

Ruan Yuan 阮元. *Jiguchai zhongding yiqi kuanshi* 積古齋鍾鼎彝器款識. Siku quanshu edition.

Schaberg, David. *A Patterned Past: Form and Thought in Early Chinese Historiography*. Cambridge Mass.: Harvard University Asia Center, 2001.

Schoppa, R. Keith. *Song Full of Tears: Nine Centuries of Chinese Life at Xiang Lake*. Boulder: Westview Press, 2002.

Schwitzgebel, Marc. "Han Peng fu: Quellenstudie, Edition und Übersetzung." *Asiatische Studien* 64.4 (2010): 817–55.

Sha Menghai 沙孟海. "Peier goudiao kaoshi" 配兒鉤鑃考釋. *KG* 1983, no. 4: 340–42.

Shan Gu 山谷. *Suzhou yaowang Gusu tai* 蘇州遙望姑蘇臺. Shanghai: Shanghai guji chubanshe, 2001.

Shang Zhitan 商志𩡝. "Wuguo ducheng de bianqian ji Helü jiandu Suzhou de yuanyou" 吳國賭城的變遷及闔閭建都蘇州的緣由. In *Wu wenhua yanjiu lunwen ji* 吳文化研究論文集, edited by Jiangsusheng Wu wenhua yanjiuhui 江蘇省吳文化研究會, pp. 1–13. Guangzhou: Zhongshan daxue chubanshe, 1988.

Shanghai bowuguan 上海博物館. *Shanghai bowuguan zang qingtongqi* 上海博物館藏青銅器. Shanghai: Renmin chubanshe, 1964.

Shanghai bowuguan 上海博物館. *Shanghai bowuguan zang qingtongqi fuce* 上海博物館藏青銅器附册. Shanghai: Renmin chubanshe, 1964.

Shanhaijing jiaozhu 山海經校注. Annotated by Yuan Ke 袁珂. Chengdu: Ba-Shu shushe, 1996.

Shek, Richard. "Sectarian Eschatology and Violence." In *Violence in China*, edited by Jonathan N. Lipman and Stevan Harrell, pp. 87–114. Albany: State University of New York Press, 1990.

Shi Jianhua 史建華, Sheng Chengmao 盛承懋, Zhou Yun 周雲 and Zhang Liansheng 張連生. *Suzhou gucheng de baohu yu gengxin* 蘇州古城的保護與更新. Nanjing: Dongnan daxue chubanshe, 2003.

Shi Nengzhi 史能之. *Xianchun Piling zhi* 咸淳毗陵志. Taipei: Chengwen chubanshe, [1268][1820] 1983.

Shi Quan 石泉. *Gudai Jing-Chu dili xintan* 古代荊楚地理新探. Wuchang: Wuhan daxue chubanshe, 1988.

Shi Yongyun 施涌雲. "Jiangning Taowu chutu tongge mingwen shishi" 江寧陶吳出土銅戈銘文試釋. In *Kaogu lunwen xuan* 考古論文選, edited by Aomen daxue lishixi 澳門大學歷史系, Aomen daxue lishi yanjiusuo 澳門大學歷史研究所, and

Aomen daxue renlei bowuguan 澳門大學人類博物館, pp. 102–14. Aomen: Aomen daxue chubanshe, 1980.

Shiji 史記. Compiled by Sima Qian 司馬遷. Beijing: Zhonghua shuju, 1959.

Shirakawa Shizuka 白川靜. *Kimbun tsushaku* 金文通釋. Tokyo: Hakutsuru bijutsukan shi, 1974.

Shizi 尸子. Annotated by Wang Jipei 王繼培. Congshu jicheng edition.

Shuowen jiezi zhu 説文解字注. Annotated by Duan Yucai 段玉裁. Shanghai: Shanghai guji chubanshe, 1981.

Shuoyuan jiaozheng 說苑校證. Annotated by Xiang Zonglu 向宗魯. Beijing: Zhonghua shuju, 1987.

So, Jenny F. *Eastern Zhou Ritual Bronzes from the Arthur M. Sackler Collections*. New York: Arthur M. Sackler Foundation, 1995.

Song Jian 宋建. "Wu wenhua huihuang de qingtongqi" 吳文化輝煌的青銅器. In *Wudi wenhua yiwan nian* 吳地文化一萬年, edited by Pan Lixing 潘力行 and Zou Zhiyi 鄒志一, pp. 57–69. Beijing: Zhonghua shuju, 1994.

Stapleton, Kirstin. *Civilizing Chengdu: Chinese Urban Reform, 1895–1937*. Cambridge Mass.: Harvard University Asia Center, 2000.

Sterckx, Roel. "Food and Philosophy in Early China." In *Of Tripod and Palate: Food, Politics, and Religion in Traditional China*, edited by Roel Sterckx, pp. 34–61. New York: Palgrave Macmillan, 2005.

Strassberg, Richard. *Inscribed Landscapes: Travel writing from Imperial China*. Berkeley: University of California Press, 1994.

Su Qiong 蘇泂. *Lengranzhai shiji* 冷然齋詩集. Siku quanshu edition.

Su Tie 蘇鐵. "Wu Yue wenhua de tancha" 吳越文化的探查. In Wu Yue shidi yanjiuhui, ed. *Wu Yue wenhua luncong*, pp. 372–83.

Su Wenlian 蘇文連. *Suzhou shici* 蘇州詩詞. Shanghai: Shanghai guji chubanshe, 1985.

Sun Junxi 孫均錫. *Tao Yuanming ji jiaozhu* 陶淵明集校注. Zhengzhou: Zhongzhou guji chubanshe, 1986.

Sun Yiyuan 孫一元. *Taibai shanren man'gao* 太白山人漫藁. Shanghai: Shanghai guji chubanshe, 1993.

Suzhou bowuguan 蘇州博物館, Qian Gonglin 錢公麟, Zhu Weifeng 朱偉峰, and Chen Ruijin 陳瑞近. *Zhenshan Dongzhou mudi: Wu Chu guizu mudi de fajue yu yanjiu* 眞山東周墓地: 吳楚貴族墓地的發掘與研究. Beijing: Wenwu chubanshe, 1999.

Suzhoushi Canglangqu bianshi xiuzhi lingdao xiaozu 蘇州市滄浪區編史修志領導小組, ed. *Suzhoushi Canglangqu: Wenwu guji juan* 蘇州市滄浪區文物古跡卷. Suzhou: No publisher, 1988.

Suzhoushi chuantong wenhua yanjiuhui 蘇州市傳統文化研究會, ed. *Chuantong wenhua yanjiu* 傳統文化研究. Vol 2; Suzhou: Guwuxuan chubanshe, 1993.

Suzhoushi difangzhi bianzuan weiyuanhui bangongshi 蘇州市地方志編纂委員會辦公室, Suzhou bowuguan 蘇州博物館, Suzhou beike bowuguan 蘇州碑刻博物館, and Guwuxuan chubanshe 古吳軒出版社, eds. *Suzhou gucheng dituji* 蘇州古城地圖集. Suzhou: Guwuxuan chubanshe, 2004.

Suzhoushi fangchan guanliju 蘇州市房產管理局, ed. *Suzhou gu minju* 蘇州古民居. Shanghai: Tongji daxue chubanshe, 2004.

Suzhoushi Huqiushan fengjingqu guanlichu 蘇州市虎丘山風景區管理處. *Wuzhong diyi mingsheng-Huqiu* 吳中第一名勝-虎丘. Beijing: Changcheng chubanshe, 2000.

Tang Yin 唐寅. *Tang Bohu quanji* 唐伯虎全集. Hangzhou: Zhongguo meishu xueyuan chubanshe, 2001.

Tao Zongyi 陶宗儀. *Shuofu* 説郛. Siku quanshu edition.

Thompson, Lydia. "Confucian Paragon or Popular Deity? Legendary Heroes in a Late Eastern Han Tomb." *AM* 12.2 (1999): 1–38.

Tong Shuye 童書業. *Chunqiu shi* 春秋史. Ji'nan: Shandong daxue chubanshe, 1987.

Tschepe, Albert. *Histoire du Royaume de Ou*. Changhai: Librarie de la Mission Catholique, 1896.

Twitchett, Denis. "Hsüan-tsung. Reign 712–56." In *The Cambridge History of China, Vol. 3, Sui and T'ang China 589–906, Part 1*, edited by Denis Twitchett and John K. Fairbank, pp. 333–463. Cambridge: Cambridge University Press, 1979.

Umehara Sueji 梅原末治. *Shōkō kokyō shūei* 紹興古鏡聚英. Kyoto: Kuwana bunseido, 1939.

Vansina, Jan. *Oral Tradition as History*. Madison: University of Wisconsin Press, 1985.

von Falkenhausen, Lothar. *Chinese Society in the Age of Confucius. 1000–250 BC: The Archaeological Evidence*. Los Angeles: Cotsen Institute of Archaeology, University of California, 2007.

———. *Suspended Music: Chime-Bells in the Culture of Bronze Age China*. Berkeley: University of California Press, 1993.

Wagner, Donald. *Iron and Steel in Ancient China*. Leiden: E.J. Brill, 1993.

Waley, Arthur. *Ballads and Stories from Tunhuang*. London: George Allen and Unwin, 1960.

Wallacker, Benjamin E., Ronald G. Knapp, Arthur J. Val Alstyne, and Richard J. Smith, eds. *Chinese Walled Cities: A Collection of Maps from Shina Jōkaku no Gaiyō*. Hong Kong: Chinese University of Hong Kong, 1979.

Wang Ao 王鏊 et al. *Gusu zhi* 姑蘇志. Shanghai: Shanghai shuju, 1990.

Wang Bin 王賓. *Huqiushan zhi* 虎丘山志. National Central Library, Taipei, microfilm 3896, [1486].

Wang, C. H. *From Ritual to Allegory: Seven Essays in Early Chinese Poetry*. Hong Kong: Chinese University Press, 1988.

Wang Duanshu 王端淑. *Mingyuan shiwei chubian* 名媛詩緯初編. Harvard-Yenching 1667 edition.

Wang E 王鍔. *Liji chengshu kao* 禮記成書考. Beijing: Zhonghua shuju, 2007.

Wang, Eugene Yuejin. "Mirror, Death and Rhetoric: Reading Later Han Chinese Bronze Artifacts." *The Art Bulletin* 76.3 (1994): 511–34.

Wang Guowei 王國維. *Yin-Zhou zhidu lun* 殷周制度論. Shanghai: Zhongguo tushu gongsi, 1917.

Wang Jia 王嘉. *Shiyi ji* 拾遺記. Siku quanshu edition.

Wang Jiaju 王稼句. *Suzhou jiumeng: 1949 nian qian de yinxiang he jiyi* 蘇州舊夢1949年前的印象和記憶. Suzhou: Suzhou daxue chubanshe, 2001.

———, ed. *Suzhou wenxian congchao chubian* 蘇州文獻叢鈔初編. Suzhou: Guwuxian chubanshe, 2005.

Wang Jian 王謇. *Song Pingjiang chengfang kao* 宋平江城坊考. Nanjing: Jiangsu guji chubanshe, 1999.

Wang Jianwen 王健文. *Zhanguo zhuzi de gu shengwang chuanshuo ji qi sixiangshi yiyi* 戰國諸子的古聖王傳説及其思想史意義. Taipei: Guoli Taiwan daxue chubanshe, 1987.

Wang Jiehua 王結華, Mao Ying 毛穎, and Liu Liwen 劉麗文 eds. *Gu Yue yizhen yanjiu* 古越遺珍研究. Beijing: Kexue chubanshe, 2010.

Wang, Liping. "Paradise for Sale: Urban Space and Tourism in the Social Transformation of Hangzhou, 1589–1937." Ph.D. diss., University of California San Diego, 1997.

Wang Shilun 王士倫. *Zhejiang chutu tongjing* 浙江出土銅鏡. Beijing: Wenwu chubanshe, 1987.

Wang Suijin 王遂今. *Wu Yue wenhua shihua* 吳越文化史話. Hangzhou: Zhejiang daxue chubanshe, 2005.

Wang Wenqing 王文清. "Zailun Wu Yue tongzu" 再論吳越同族. In *Jiangsu shi lunkao* 江蘇史論考, edited by Jiangsusheng shelian lishi xuehui 江蘇省社聯歷史學會 and Jiangsusheng shehui kexueyuan lishi yanjiusuo 江蘇省社會科學院歷史研究所, pp. 1–18. Wuxi: Jiangsu guji chubanshe, 1989.

Wang Xiqi 王錫祺. *Xiaofanghu zhaiyu dicong chaoxuan* 小方壺齋輿地叢鈔選. In Wang Jiaju, ed. *Suzhou wenxian congchao chubian*, pp. 905–1012.

Wang Yi 王毅. *Yuanlin yu Zhongguo wenhua* 園林與中國文化. Shanghai: Shanghai renmin chubanshe, 1990.

Wang, Yi-t'ung. *A Record of Buddhist Monasteries in Lo-yang*. Princeton: Princeton University Press, 1983.

Wang Yun 王惲. *Qiujian ji* 秋澗集. Siku quanshu edition.

Wang Zhongmin 王重民, Wang Qingshu 王慶菽, Xiang Da 向達, Zhou Yiliang 周一良, Qi Gong 啓功, and Zeng Yigong 曾毅公. *Dunhuang bianwen ji* 敦煌變文集. Beijing: Renmin wenxue chubanshe, 1957.

Wang Zhongshu 王仲殊. "Qingyang wei Wujun jing gongkao: Zai lun Dong Han, Sanguo, Xi Jin shiqi Wujun suochan de tongjin" 青羊爲吳郡鏡工考再論東漢三國西晉時期吳郡所產的銅鏡. *KG* 1986, no. 7: 639–46.

———. "Wuxian, Shanyin he Wuchang: Cong mingwen kan Sangou shidai Wu de tongjing chandi" 吳縣,山陰和武昌:從銘文看三國時代吳的銅鏡產地. *KG* 1985, no. 11: 1026.

Wang Zusu 王祖肅, Yang Yilun 楊宜侖, Yu Mingqiu 虞鳴球, and Dong Chao 董朝. *Wujin xian zhi* 武進縣志. Jiangsu: Zhonghua shuju, 1992.

Watson, James L. "Standardizing the Gods: The Promotion of T'ien Hou, 'Empress of Heaven' Along the South China Coast, 960–1960." In *Popular Culture in Late Imperial China*, edited by David Johnson, Andrew Nathan, and Evelyn Rawski, pp. 292–324. Berkeley: University of California Press, 1985.

Wei Juxian 衛聚賢. "Taibo zhi feng zai Xiwu" 太伯之封在西吳. In Wu Yue shidi yanjiuhui, ed. *Wu Yue wenhua luncong*, pp. 14–45.

———. "Wu Yue minzu" 吳越民族. In Wu Yue shidi yanjiuhui, ed. *Wu Yue wenhua luncong*, pp. 310–56.

Wei Zhonghua 魏仲華 and Xu Bingruo 徐冰若. *Shaoxing* 紹興. Beijing: Zhongguo jianzhu gongye chubanshe, 1986.

Wen Yiduo 聞一多. "Yuhanwang hu ba" 禺邗王壺跋. In *Wen Yiduo quanji: Gudian xinyi* 聞一多全集:古典新義, pp. 609–10. Shanghai: Kaiming shudian, 1949.

Wen Zhengming 文徵明. *Wen Zhengming ji* 文徵明集. Shanghai: Shanghai guji chubanshe, 1987.

Wenxuan zhushi 文選注釋. Annotated by Li Shan 李善 et al. Taipei: Zhengzhong shuju, 1971.

West, Stephen H. "Recollections of the Northern Song Capital." In *Hawai'i Reader in Traditional Chinese Culture*, edited by Victor Mair, Nancy S. Steinhardt, and Paul R. Goldin, pp. 405–22. Honolulu: University of Hawai'i Press, 2005.

Wilson, Thomas A., ed. *On Sacred Grounds: Culture, Society, Politics, and the Formation of the Cult of Confucius*. Cambridge: Harvard University Press, 2002.

———. "Ritualizing Confucius/Kongzi: The Family and State Cults of the Sage of Culture in Imperial China." In Thomas Wilson, ed. *On Sacred Grounds*, pp. 43–87.

Wu Enpei 吳恩培. *Gouwu wenhua de xianzai chanshi* 勾吳文化的現在闡釋. Nanjing: Dongnan daxue chubanshe, 2002.

Wu, Hung. "Art and Architecture of the Warring States Period." In *The Cambridge History of Ancient China: From the Origins of Civilization to 221 BC* edited by Michael Loewe and Edward L. Shaughnessy, pp. 651–744. Cambridge: Cambridge University Press, 1999.

———. *The Wu Liang Shrine: The Ideology of Early Chinese Pictorial Art*. Stanford: Stanford University Press, 1989.

Wu Naifu 吳奈夫. "Suzhou gu Panmen yu Wu Zixu" 蘇州古盤門與伍子胥. In *Suzhou gu Panmen* 蘇州古盤門, edited by Xu Wentao 徐文濤, pp. 1–18. Shanghai: Shanghai wenhua chubanshe, 1998.

Wu Qiming 吳企明. *Suzhou shiyong* 蘇州詩咏. Suzhou: Suzhou daxue chubanshe, 1999.

Wu Qu 吳趨. *Gusu yeshi* 姑蘇野史. Nanjing: Jiangsu wenyi chubanshe, 1990.

Wu wenhua yanjiu cujinhui 吳文化研究促進會, ed. *Gouwu shi ji* 勾吳史集. Nanjing: Jiangsu guji chubanshe, 1999.

Wu wenhua yanjiuhui choubeizu 吳文化研究會籌備組, ed. *Wu wenhua ziliao xuanji* 吳文化資料選輯. Vol. 3; Suzhou: Jiangsu guoying xinmin chubanshe, 1982.

Wu Yue chunqiu jijiao huikao 吳越春秋輯校匯考. Annotated by Zhou Shengchun 周生春. Shanghai: Shanghai guji chubanshe, 1997.

Wu Yue shidi yanjiuhui 吳越史地研究會, ed. *Wu Yue wenhua luncong* 吳越文化論叢. Shanghai: Shanghai wenyi chubanshe, [1937] 1990.

Wu Yuming 吳聿明. "Bola ge kao" 伯剌戈考. In *Wu wenhua yanjiu lunwenji* 吳文化研究論文集, edited by Jiangsusheng Wu wenhua yanjiuhui 江蘇省吳文化研究會, pp. 144–46. Guangdong: Zhongshan daxue chubanshe, 1988.

Xiao Fan 蕭璠. "Qin Han shiqi Zhongguo dui nanfang de jingying" 秦漢時期中國對南方的經營. *Shiyuan* 史原 4 (1973): 17–53.

Xiao Luan 蕭鸞. *Xingzhuang taiyin buyi* 杏莊太音補遺. In Zha Fuxi, ed. *Qinqu jicheng*, Vol. 3, pp. 297–407.

Xiao Menglong 蕭夢龍. "Dui Wuguo lishi wenhua de xin tansuo" 對吳國歷史文化的新探索. In *Jiangsu shi lunkao* 江蘇史論考, edited by Jiangsusheng shelian lishi xuehui 江蘇省社聯歷史學會 and Jiangsusheng shehui kexueyuan lishi yanjiusuo 江蘇省社會科學院歷史研究所, pp. 22–27. Wuxi: Jiangsu guji chubanshe, 1989.

Xie Chen 謝忱. *Gouwu shi xinkao* 勾吳史新考. Beijing: Zhongguo wenlian chubanshe, 2000.

Xie Xiaosi 謝孝思. *Suzhou yuanlin pinshang lu* 蘇州園林品賞錄. Shanghai: Wenyi chubanshe, 1998.

Xinxu xiangzhu 新序詳注. Annotated by Zhao Zhongyi 趙仲邑. Beijing: Zhonghua shuju, 1997.

Xinyu jiaozhu 新語校注. Annotated by Wang Liqi 王利器. Beijing: Zhonghua shuju, 1986.

Xu Bohong 徐伯鴻. "Chengqiao sanhao Chunqiu mu chutu pan yi fu mingwen shizheng" 程橋三號春秋墓出土盤匜簠銘文釋證. *DNWH* 1991, no. 1: 153–59.

Xu Boming 許伯明. *Wu wenhua gaiguan* 吳文化概觀. Nanjing: Nanjing shifan daxue chubanshe, 1997.

Xu Gangyi 徐剛毅. *Lao Suzhou* 老蘇州. Suzhou: Jiangsu guji chubanshe, 2001.

Xu Jianchun 徐建春. *Zhejiang tongshi: Xian Qin juan* 浙江通史: 先秦卷. Hangzhou: Zhejiang renmin chubanshe, 2005.

Xu Song 徐崧 and Zhang Dachun 張大純. *Baicheng yanshui* 百城烟水. Nanjing: Jiangsu guji chubanshe, 1999.

Xu Weiyu 許維遹. *Han Shi waizhuan jishi* 韓詩外傳集釋. Beijing: Zhonghua shuju, 1980.

Xu Xiqi 徐錫祺. *Xi Zhou (Gonghe) zhi Xi Han lipu* 西周 (共和) 之西漢歷譜. Beijing: Beijing kexue jishu chubanshe, 1997.

Xu, Yinong. *The Chinese City in Space and Time: The Development of Urban Form in Suzhou*. Honolulu: University of Hawai'i Press, 2000.

Xu Zhongshu 徐中舒. *Yin-Zhou jinwen jilu* 殷周金文集錄. Chengdu: Sichuan renmin chubanshe, 1984.

Xunzi jijie 荀子集解. Annotated by Wang Xianqian 王先謙. Beijing: Zhonghua shuju, 2008.

Yan Zhitui 顏之推. *Huanyuan ji* 還冤記. In *Jiu xiaoshuo* 舊小說, edited by Wu Zengqi 吳曾棋. Shanghai: Shangwu yinshuguan, 1965.

Yang Jialuo 楊家駱. *Yuan Zhonglang quanji* 袁中郎全集. Taipei: Shijie shuju, 1990.

Yang Shanqun 楊善群. *Yuewang Goujian xinzhuan* 越王勾踐新傳. Shanghai: Shanghai renmin chubanshe, 1988.

Yang Shuda 楊樹達. *Jiweiju jinwen shuo* 積微居金文說. Beijing: Kexue chubanshe, 1959.

Yang Xuanzhi 楊衒之. *Luoyang qielan ji* 洛陽伽藍記. Beijing: Zhonghua shuju, 1991.

Yang Xunji 楊循吉 et al. eds. *Wuzhong xiaozhi congkan* 吳中小志叢刊. Yangzhou: Guangling shushe, 2004.

Yang Zhenghong 楊正宏 and Xiao Menglong 肖夢龍. *Zhenjiang chutu Wuguo qingtongqi* 鎮江出土吳國青銅器. Beijing: Wenwu chubanshe, 2008.

Yantie lun 鹽鐵論. Annotated by Wang Liqi 王利器. Beijing: Zhonghua shuju, 1996.

Yao Kuan 姚寬. *Xixi zongyu* 西溪叢語. [No place of publication]: Renhe geshi kanben, 1897.

Yao Nai 姚鼐. *Xibaoxuan quanji* 惜抱軒全集. Sibu beiyao edition.

Yao Qinde 姚勤德 and Gong Jinyuan 龔金元. *Wuguo wangshi yuqi* 吳國王室玉器. Shanghai: Renmin yishu chubanshe, 1996.

Yao Zhaoao 姚兆鰲. *Du shi xiangzhu* 杜詩詳註. Beijing: Zhonghua shuju, 2007.

Ye Wenxian 葉文憲. *Wuguo lishi yu Wu wenhua tanmi* 吳國歷史與吳文化探秘. Beijing: Wenwu chubanshe, 2007.

Yin Weiren 殷偉仁. "Gouwu, Gouhua yuwen zhi guo" 勾吳勾畫魚紋之國. In Suzhoushi chuantong wenhua yanjiuhui, ed. *Chuantong wenhua yanjiu*, pp. 123–30.

Yin Zhiqiang 殷志强 and Ding Bangdiao 丁邦釣. *Dongzhou Wu Chu yuqi* 東周吳楚玉器. Taipei: Yishu tushu chubanshe, 1993.

Yongle dadian 永樂大典. *Suzhou fu zhi* 蘇州府志. Taipei: Chengwen chubanshe, [1409] 1983.

Yoshimoto Michimasa 吉本道雅. "Dan Kyū kō" 檀弓考. *Kodai bunka* 古代文化 44.2 (1992): 38–46.

———. "Shunjū Shinha kō 春秋晉霸考." *Shirin* 史林 76.3 (1993): 69–107.

Yu Huai 余懷. *San Wu youlan zhi* 三吳游覽志. In Wang Jiaju, ed. *Suzhou wenxian congchao chubian*, pp. 847–75.

Yu Jidong 俞紀東. *Yuejue shu quanyi* 越絶書全譯. Guiyang: Guizhou renmin chubanshe, 1996.

Yu Mengren 余孟仁. *Lao Suzhou: bainian jiuying* 老蘇州百年舊影. Nanjing: Jiangsu renmin chubanshe, 1999.

Yu Xianyao 俞顯堯, "Guankui Fan Li de sixiang mailuo" 管窺范蠡的思想脉絡. In *Fan Li yanjiu wenji* 范蠡研究文集, edited by Fu Zhiting 傅志亭, pp. 40–45. Beijing: Xiyuan chubanshe, 1998.

Yuan Yixin 袁以新. *Suzhou gucheng: Pingjiang lishi jiequ* 蘇州古城: 平江歷史街區. Shanghai: Shanghai sanlian shudian, 2004.

Yuejue shu 越絶書. Compiled by Yuan Kang 袁康 and Wu Ping 吳平. Shanghai: Shanghai guji chubanshe, 1985.

Yue Junjie 岳俊傑, Cai Hangang 蔡涵剛, and Gao Zhigang 高志罡. *Suzhou wenhua* 蘇州文化. Shanghai: Renmin chubanshe, 1993.

Yue Shi 樂史. *Taiping huanyu ji* 太平寰宇記. Siku quanshu edition.

Zeitlin, Judith. "Disappearing Verses: Writing on Walls and Anxieties of Loss." In *Writing and Materiality in China: Essays in Honor of Patrick Hanan*, edited by Judith Zeitlin, Lydia Liu, and Ellen Widmer, pp. 73–132. Cambridge, Mass.: Harvard University Press, 2003.

Zha Fuxi 查阜西, ed. *Qinqu jicheng* 琴曲集成. Vol. 1-; Beijing: Zhonghua shuju, 1981-.

Zhang Chenghua 張橙華. "Gan Jiang he Ou Ye shi gangtie shidai kaichuangzhe de daibiao" 干將和歐冶是鋼鐵時代開創者的代表. In Gao Xiechu, ed. *Wu wenhua ziyuan yanjiu yu fazhan*, pp. 260–71.

Zhang Dachun 張大純. "Gusu caifeng leiji" 姑蘇采風類記. In *Xiaofanghu zhai yudi congchao xuan* 小方壺齋輿地叢鈔選, Vol. 8, edited by Wang Xiqi 王錫祺, 5:38a–95a. Hangzhou: Hangzhou guji shudian, 1985.

Zhang Defu 張德夫, Jiang Yingke 江盈科, Huangfu Fang 皇甫汸, and Zhang Fengyi 張鳳翼. *Changzhou xian zhi* 長洲縣志. Beijing: Zhonghua shuju chubanshe, [1598] 1992.

Zhang Gun 張衮. *Jiangyin xian zhi* 江陰縣志. Shanghai: Shanghai guji chubanshe, 1963.

Zhang He 張荷. *Wu Yue wenhua* 吳越文化. Shenyang: Liaoning jiaoyu chubanshe, 1991.

Zhang Honglin 張宏林. "Yi shi wei jian de Wu Zixu huaxiang jing" 以史爲鑒的伍子胥畫像鏡." *Shoucangjia* 收藏家 2011, no. 3: 49–54.

Zhang Huijian 張慧劍. *Ming Qing Jiangsu wenren nianbiao* 明清江蘇文人年表. Beijing: Renmin wenxue chubanshe, 2008.

Zhang Ji 張籍. *Zhang Siye ji* 張司業集. Siku quanshu edition.

Zhang Jun 張君. "*Guoyu* chengbian xinzheng" 國語成編新証. *Hubei daxue xuebao* 湖北大學學報 1991, no. 2: 77–82.

Zhang Kai 張愷. *Changzhou fu zhi xuji* 常州府志續集. Taipei: Chengwen chubanshe, [1513] 1983.

Zhang Shangjin 張尚金, Mao Wenhui 毛文輝, Wu Zhiguang 吳之光, Yang Ti 楊堤, and Mao Xueqin 毛學勤. *Wujin xian zhi* 武進縣志. Shanghai: Shanghai renmin chubanshe, 1988.

Zhang Weixiang 張惟驤. *Piling mingren yinianlu* 毗陵名人疑年錄. In *Piling sanzhong* 毗陵三種, edited by Yang Jialuo 楊家駱. Taipei: Dingwen shuju, 1978.

Zhang Yachu 張亞初. "Wushi xinzheng" 吳史新證. In Wu wenhua yanjiuhui choubeizu, ed. *Wu wenhua ziliao xuanji*, pp. 29–35.

Zhang Yiliu 張一留. *Suzhou Lingyanshan zhi* 蘇州靈巖山志. Suzhou: Lingyanshan si, [1947] 1994.

Zhang Yiren 張以仁. *Guoyu Zuozhuan lunji* 國語左傳論集. Taipei: Dongsheng chubanshe, 1980.

Zhang Zilin 張紫琳. *Honglan yicheng* 紅蘭逸乘. In Wang Jiaju, ed. *Suzhou wenxian congchao chubian*, pp. 255–314.

Zhang Zongxiang 張宗祥. *Yuejue shu jiaozhu* 越絶書校注. Shanghai: Shangwu yinshuguan, 1956.

Zhanguo ce jijiao huikao 戰國策集校彙考. Annotated by Zhu Zugeng 諸祖耿. Yangzhou: Jiangsu guji chubanshe, 1985.

Zhejiangsheng wenwu kaogu yanjiusuo 浙江省文物考古研究所 and Shaoxingxian wenwu baohu guanlisuo 紹興縣文物保護管理所. "Zhejiang Shaoxing Yinshan damu fajue jianbao" 浙江紹興印山大墓發掘簡報. *WW* 1999, no. 11: 4–16.

Zheng Huchen 鄭虎臣. *Wudu wencui* 吳都文粹. National Central Library, Taipei, microfilm 14409.

Zheng Liangshu 鄭良樹. *Zhujian boshu lunwen ji* 竹簡帛書論文集. Beijing: Zhonghua shuju, 1982.

Zhengxie Suzhoushi Huqiuqu weiyuanhui 政協蘇州市虎丘山委員會, ed. *Shihu shang Fangshan* 石湖上方山. Suzhou: Shuzhou daxue chubanshe, 2000.

Zhong Xing 鍾惺. *Mingyuan shigui* 名媛詩歸. Harvard-Yenching late Ming edition.

Zhonggong Jiangsusheng weiyanjiushi 中共江蘇省委研究室, ed. *Jiangsu wenwu* 江蘇文物. Nanjing: Jiangsu guji chubanshe, 1987.

Zhou Bida 周必大. *Wujun zhushan lu* 吳郡諸山錄. In Wang Jiaju, ed. *Suzhou wenxian congchao chubian*, pp. 809–23.

Zhou Bokan 周伯戡. "Chunqiu huimeng yu bazhu zhengzhi de jichu" 春秋會盟與霸主政治的基覆. *Shiyuan* 史原 6 (1975): 19–62.

Zhou Chenghe 周振鶴 and You Rujie 游汝傑. "Gu Yueyu diming chutan" 古越語地名初談. In Wu wenhua yanjiuhui choubeizu, ed. *Wu wenhua ziliao xuanji*, pp. 61–63.

Zhou Hongdu 周鴻度. *Lingyanshan* 靈巖山. Suzhou: Guwuxuan chubanshe, 1998.

Zhou Shengchun 周生春. "*Yuejue shu* chengshu niandai ji zhuozhe xintan" 越絶書成書年代及作者新探. In *Zhonghua wenshi luncong* 中華文史論叢, Vol. 47, edited by Qian Bocheng 錢伯成, pp. 121–39. Shanghai: Shanghai guji chubanshe, 1991.

Zhou Suning 周蘇寧. *Canglang Ting* 滄浪亭. Suzhou: Guwuxuan chubanshe, 1998.

———. *Suzhou yuanlin yu mingren* 蘇州園林與名人. Beijing: Lüyou tiyu chubanshe, 1997.

Zhou Yinbin 周寅賓. *Li Dongyang ji* 李東陽集. Vol. 3. Changsha: Yuelu chubanshe, 1985.

Zhou Yuebao 周越寶 and Luo Haidi 羅海迪. *Shaoxing wenwu* 紹興文物. Beijing: Zhonghua shuju, 2004.

Zhou Zumo 周祖謨. "Li Yangbing zhuanshu kao" 李陽冰篆書考. In *Wenxue ji* 文學集, pp. 801–42. Beijing: Zhonghua shuju, 1966.

Zhu Changwen 朱長文. *Wujun tujing xuji* 吳郡圖經續記. Nanjing: Jiangsu guji chubanshe, 1999.

Zhu Yu 朱昱. *Chongxiu Piling zhi* 重修毗陵志. Taipei: Chengwen chubanshe, [1484] 1983.

Zhuangzi jishi 莊子集釋. Annotated by Guo Qingfan 郭慶藩. Beijing: Zhonghua shuju, 1961.

Zhushu jinian 竹書紀年. Annotated by Hong Yixuan 洪頤煊. Sibu congkan edition.

Zou Houben 鄒厚本, Wu Jianmin 吳建民, and Gu Jianxiang 谷建祥. *Jiangsu kaogu wushinian* 江蘇考古五十年. Nanjing: Nanjing chubanshe, 2000.

Zou Zhifang 鄒志方. "Zhedong Tang shi zhi lu (Shaoxing duan) wenhua yichan de baohu yu lüyou kaifa" 浙東唐詩之路(紹興段)文化遺產的保護與旅游開發. In Fei Junqing, ed. *Zhongguo chuantong wenhua yu Yue wenhua yanjiu*, pp. 266–76.

Zuffery, Nicholas. *To the Origins of Confucianism: The Ru in pre-Qin Times and during the Early Han Dynasty*. Bern: Peter Lang, 2003.

Index

Harvard-Yenching Institute Monograph Series
(titles now in print)

24. *Population, Disease, and Land in Early Japan, 645–900*, by William Wayne Farris
25. *Shikitei Sanba and the Comic Tradition in Edo Fiction*, by Robert W. Leutner
26. *Washing Silk: The Life and Selected Poetry of Wei Chuang (834?–910)*, by Robin D. S. Yates
28. *Tang Transformation Texts: A Study of the Buddhist Contribution to the Rise of Vernacular Fiction and Drama in China*, by Victor H. Mair
30. *Readings in Chinese Literary Thought*, by Stephen Owen
31. *Remembering Paradise: Nativism and Nostalgia in Eighteenth-Century Japan*, by Peter Nosco
33. *Escape from the Wasteland: Romanticism and Realism in the Fiction of Mishima Yukio and Oe Kenzaburo*, by Susan Jolliffe Napier
34. *Inside a Service Trade: Studies in Contemporary Chinese Prose*, by Rudolf G. Wagner
35. *The Willow in Autumn: Ryutei Tanehiko, 1783–1842*, by Andrew Lawrence Markus
36. *The Confucian Transformation of Korea: A Study of Society and Ideology*, by Martina Deuchler
37. *The Korean Singer of Tales*, by Marshall R. Pihl
38. *Praying for Power: Buddhism and the Formation of Gentry Society in Late-Ming China*, by Timothy Brook
39. *Word, Image, and Deed in the Life of Su Shi*, by Ronald C. Egan
40. *The Chinese Virago: A Literary Theme*, by Yenna Wu
41. *Studies in the Comic Spirit in Modern Japanese Fiction*, by Joel R. Cohn
42. *Wind Against the Mountain: The Crisis of Politics and Culture in Thirteenth-Century China*, by Richard L. Davis
43. *Powerful Relations: Kinship, Status, and the State in Sung China (960–1279)*, by Beverly Bossler
44. *Limited Views: Essays on Ideas and Letters*, by Qian Zhongshu; selected and translated by Ronald Egan
45. *Sugar and Society in China: Peasants, Technology, and the World Market*, by Sucheta Mazumdar
49. *Precious Volumes: An Introduction to Chinese Sectarian Scriptures from the Sixteenth and Seventeenth Centuries*, by Daniel L. Overmyer
50. *Poetry and Painting in Song China: The Subtle Art of Dissent*, by Alfreda Murck
51. *Evil and/or/as the Good: Omnicentrism, Intersubjectivity, and Value Paradox in Tiantai Buddhist Thought*, by Brook Ziporyn
52. *Chinese History: A Manual, Revised and Enlarged Edition,* by Endymion Wilkinson
53. *Articulated Ladies: Gender and the Male Community in Early Chinese Texts*, by Paul Rouzer
54. *Politics and Prayer: Shrines to Local Former Worthies in Sung China*, by Ellen Neskar
55. *Allegories of Desire: Esoteric Literary Commentaries of Medieval Japan*, by Susan Blakeley Klein

56. *Printing for Profit: The Commercial Publishers of Jianyang, Fujian (11th-17th Centuries)*, by Lucille Chia
57. *To Become a God: Cosmology, Sacrifice, and Self-Divinization in Early China*, by Michael J. Puett
58. *Writing and Materiality in China: Essays in Honor of Patrick Hanan*, edited by Judith T. Zeitlin and Lydia H. Liu
59. *Rulin waishi and Cultural Transformation in Late Imperial China*, by Shang Wei
60. *Words Well Put: Visions of Poetic Competence in the Chinese Tradition*, by Graham Sanders
61. *Householders: The Reizei Family in Japanese History*, by Steven D. Carter
62. *The Divine Nature of Power: Chinese Ritual Architecture at the Sacred Site of Jinci*, by Tracy Miller
63. *Beacon Fire and Shooting Star: The Literary Culture of the Liang (502–557)*, by Xiaofei Tian
64. *Lost Soul: "Confucianism" in Contemporary Chinese Academic Discourse*, by John Makeham
65. *The Sage Learning of Liu Zhi: Islamic Thought in Confucian Terms*, by Sachiko Murata, William C. Chittick, and Tu Weiming
66. *Through a Forest of Chancellors: Fugitive Histories in Liu Yuan's* Lingyan ge*, an Illustrated Book from Seventeenth-Century Suzhou*, by Anne Burkus-Chasson
67. *Empire of Texts in Motion: Chinese, Korean, and Taiwanese Transculturations of Japanese Literature*, by Karen Laura Thornber
68. *Empire's Twilight: Northeast Asia Under the Mongols*, by David M. Robinson
69. *Ancestors, Virgins, and Friars: Christianity as a Local Religion in Late Imperial China*, by Eugenio Menegon
70. *Manifest in Words, Written on Paper: Producing and Circulating Poetry in Tang Dynasty China*, by Christopher M. B. Nugent
71. *The Poetics of Sovereignty: On Emperor Taizong of the Tang Dynasty*, by Jack W. Chen
72. *Ancestral Memory in Early China*, by K. E. Brashier
73. *'Dividing the Realm in Order to Govern': The Spatial Organization of the Song State,* by Ruth Mostern
74. *The Dynamics of Masters Literature: Early Chinese Thought from Confucius to Han Feizi*, by Wiebke Denecke
75. *Songs of Contentment and Transgression: Discharged Officials and Literati Communities in Sixteenth-Century North China*, by Tian Yuan Tan
76. *Ten Thousand Scrolls: Reading and Writing in the Poetics of Huang Tingjian and the Late Northern Song*, by Yugen Wang
77. *A Northern Alternative: Xue Xuan (1389-1464) and the Hedong School*, by Khee Heong Koh
78. *Visionary Journeys: Travel Writings from Early Medieval and Nineteenth-Century China*, by Xiaofei Tian
79. *Making Personas: Transnational Film Stardom in Modern Japan*, by Hideaki Fujiki

80. *Strange Eventful Histories: Identity, Performance, and Xu Wei's* Four Cries of a Gibbon, by Shiamin Kwa
81. *Critics and Commentators: The* Book of Poems *as Classic and Literature*, by Bruce Rusk
82. *Home and the World: Editing the Glorious Ming in Woodblock-Printed Books of the Sixteenth and Seventeenth Centuries*, by Yuming He
83. *Courtesans, Concubines, and the Cult of Female Fidelity*, by Beverly Bossler
84. *Chinese History: A New Manual*, by Endymion Wilkinson
85. *A Comprehensive Manchu-English Dictionary*, by Jerry Norman
86. *Drifting among Rivers and Lakes: Southern Song Dynasty Poetry and the Problem of Literary History*, by Michael Fuller
87. *Martial Spectacles of the Ming Court*, by David M. Robinson
88. *Modern Archaics: Continuity and Innovation in the Chinese Lyric Tradition, 1900-1937*, by Shengqing Wu
89. *Cherishing Antiquity: The Cultural Construction of an Ancient Chinese Kingdom*, by Olivia Milburn